Messages 3

Messages 3

The Washington Post Media Companion

The Washington Post Writers Group

Edited by Thomas Beel

Allyn and Bacon

Boston • London • Toronto • Sydney • Tokyo • Singapore

Editor in Chief, Humanities: Joseph Opiela
Editorial Assistant: Susannah Davidson
Marketing Manager: Karon Bowers
Production Administrator: Marjorie Payne
Cover Administrator: Linda Knowles
Cover Designer: Jennifer Burns
Manufacturing Buyer: Aloka Rathnam

ISBN: 0-205-17390-X

Printed in the United States of America
10 9 8 7 6 5 4 3 2 1   00 99 98 97 96 95

Preface to Messages 3

This is an exciting time to study the mass media. They are undergoing greater change now than at any time since Johannes Gutenberg ushered in the age of print in 1454.

Virtually every form of mass communication is being restructured by new technology and economic and political forces that didn't even exist a few years ago. And the changes are occurring at warp speed.

Just look at all that's happened since the first edition of *Messages* was published in 1991:

The Internet has become an important new medium of information and advertising. The Library of Congress has gone "on line" with its vast collection, as have many daily newspapers and national magazines. Several of the biggest media companies in the United States are for sale or already have new owners. A major new movie studio has been established. Direct home satellite TV has begun operation. The Disney Company, for perhaps the first time in its history, has suffered a public relations black-eye. The word game Scrabble is censored for politically incorrect language. And governments everywhere have stepped up efforts to control what their citizens can see and hear.

Some media institutions are thriving in the turmoil; others may not make it to the millennium. To a large extent, survival will depend on the ability of the media to anticipate a changing world. Will people still want to read printed newspapers and magazines in the next century? Will movie theaters and cable television still find an audience?

Keep these questions in mind as you read the articles in *Messages 3: The Washington Post Media Companion.* See if you can spot the trends that will shape the media of the future.

We've assembled 98 articles for this edition, 69 of which are new. Most were published in the Washington Post in 1993 and 1994. One, by former Post publisher Katharine Graham, first appeared in April 1986. Her remarks about the coverage of terrorism are as thoughtful and valid today as when she wrote them.

As with the previous editions, we've tried to make *Messages 3* interesting, relevant, and as exciting as the mass media themselves.

Publisher's Foreword

The book you hold in your hand is unusual in mass communication education. Most compilations of articles on media are on the scholarly side and, while very useful, are somewhat removed from our daily experience of media. They are glances from afar. We set out to publish something closer to the action.

The mass media today have unprecedented impact on our daily lives. We are bombarded by messages of every sort: informative, entertaining, and, most of all, persuasive. We are daily persuaded to buy something, vote for someone, or think a certain way about a company or an institution or a government. In the face of this saturation, it is easy to become desensitized, to stop thinking clearly or critically about the messages we are asked to process. That is a mistake, particularly for the student of communication, who, like all of us, is a user of media, but who one day may also be one of its creators.

But if the media are the source of so many messages, they also provide the vehicles for understanding them. In this book, you will find 98 articles on the media from the pages of *The Washington Post,* itself one of the most prominent voices of one of the oldest, most prominent mass media. Individually these pieces range from straightforward news stories on media industries and issues, to profiles of media creators, to thoughtful overviews of trends in media today. And that is exactly their value—their focus on the media today. Together, these articles are a cross-sectional look at the mass media and their place in our society over the last few years. They are not scholarly. They are day-to-day dispatches from the front lines.

In organization, *Messages 3: The Washington Post Media Companion* closely parallels the structure of the usual beginning course in mass communication. It is intended to be used as a supplement to a regular textbook, or to an instructor's notes, both of which will provide depth, rigor, and a grounding in history and research. It is our hope that what *Messages 3* will provide is good writing from one of the great newspapers of the day. Enjoy.

Preface to the First Edition

John Campbell launched the first successful American newspaper—the *Boston News-Letter*—in 1704. For fifteen years he enjoyed a monopoly in the colonies. Then, James Franklin, the more celebrated Benjamin's older brother, began publishing the *New-England Courant* and became America's first "media critic." Campbell's newspaper, he said in the first issue of the *Courant,* suffered from an excess of "dullness." Campbell responded with a denial and demanded chapter and verse. Franklin had the last word:

"[The critic] need not tell you where you're flat and dull; Your Works declare, 'tis in your skull."

In the subsequent history of the American media, criticism has had uneven traditions. Newspapers criticized one another vigorously and frequently in the 19th century. The *New York Courier and Inquirer* announced in 1836 that "we are compelled, for the first time, to soil our columns with an allusion to a beggarly outcast [James Gordon Bennett] who daily sends forth a dirty sheet in this city under the title of *The Herald.* Bennett could hold his own in that company. He said of Horace Greeley's *Tribune:* "The *Tribune* establishment, from top to bottom has been recently converted into a socialistic phalanx . . . that has produced on public affairs and the public mind a more deleterious, anti-Christian, and infidel effect . . . than all the publications that have hitherto appeared from the time of Voltaire."

This critical tradition—or polemic, as the case may be—is a relic of the past insofar as newspapers are concerned. The ownership of the American press is now concentrated in a relative handful of large communications conglomerates. Local monopolies have arisen in virtually all of our cities. So there are few competitors left to criticize. Self-criticism is a rarity and, where it exists, is rarely aggressive. Some of the slack has been taken up by the "alternative press," by both local and national magazines, and by various authors and academicians. But the audience for these forms of criticism is limited and, so far as we can tell, so is the impact.

The critical tradition has never existed within the broadcasting industry and has not taken hold despite the ever-growing competitiveness within the broadcasting marketplace. The evening news programs have very sizable local and national audiences that undoubtedly would be receptive to press criticism, for example, or to criticism of local and network news practices. A thorough investigation of the techniques of "60 Minutes" by its competitor, "20-20," would be made into fascinating television. But broadcasters, out of a sense of vulnerability or for other commercial reasons, do not nurture programming of that nature.

So the burden of broadcasting criticism falls primarily on newspapers and magazines. That is true with respect to literature, films, the recording industry, and other expressions of the popular culture. Much of what is done along these lines may not qualify as true "criticism," which is often defined as systematic analysis within a framework of certain aesthetic and philosophical principles and standards; academic work, in a word. The book, film, or record review, by way of contrast, is designed, essentially, to introduce an audience to a new work or production. In that sense its critical value may be of less significance than its commercial value as a form of publicity.

In any case, it is newspaper and magazine writers who produce the reviews, the criticism, and the commentary on our popular culture and its various media of communication and art. As you will find in these essays, writers approach these critical tasks not only from abstract aesthetic positions but from political, sociological, ethical, and historical perspectives as well. They promote some value systems and seek to discredit others; they can be preachy on subjects such as ethics, social justice, highbrows, and lowbrows. They may disagree on definitions of obscenity and pornography and the political implications involved.

But in demographic terms, the essayists represented in this volume have much in common in addition to a common employer, *The Washington Post*. We are, without exception and by government definition, members of the upper middle class. Racially, we are overwhelmingly (but not entirely) white. Few of us have had special training or instruction in the arts and crafts of "criticism." We tend to come out of universities and colleges with degrees in the liberal arts, with interest in politics and popular culture, with general experience as newspaper reporters, and with present assignments that are to one degree or another the result of happenstance rather than design. There is, thus, an accidental and amateurish quality to much of what we do. But it is a quality that can lend freshness, authenticity, and variety to the work.

Editors at *The Post* have for many years encouraged the development of popular and relevant forms of criticism and created in various sections—Style, Book World, and Outlook, among others—forums in which it all fits and from which most of these pieces were taken.

> Richard Harwood
> Ombudsman
> *The Washington Post*

Contents

Mass Media Essentials   1

Internet Creates a Computer Culture

JOHN BURGESS

I t may be the world's most eclectic community: scientists and comic book fans, hunters and gun-control activists, prudes and pornographers, kindergartners and septuagenarians, computer hackers and their trackers, rock-and-rollers and classical musicians, Serbs and Croats.

It is perhaps 15 million strong and growing fast—Bill Clinton and Al Gore joined this month.

Members almost never meet face to face. Scattered all over the world, they are bound together by a computer communications system known as the Internet. Ham radio operators use the airwaves; this new global tribe uses satellites, fiber-optic cables and desktop computers to trade a rich and varied flood of information. Much of it is brief "electronic mail" messages typed on computer keyboards. But increasingly the network is shuttling video footage, photos, government studies, novels, dissertations, music, sounds—information of all kinds in the digital form that computers understand.

"The size of the planet is no boundary to communications," writes Jeff Ashurst, a resident of Britain responding by E-mail to a Washingtonian's electronic query.

Along the way, the Internet has evolved into a remarkable culture of remote intimacy, in which people convey love and contempt, excitement and boredom without ever laying eyes on each other.

They rail at each other in electronic "forums" on subjects that run from genetic research to European elections. They jump to the aid of fellow network navigators who have a real problem, such as how to combat disease in Africa, or just need to know something—a good hotel to stay at in the Thai city of Chiangmai, for instance.

Occasionally, they meet in the flesh and marry.

Laszlo and Andrea Kiss, for instance. They "met" on an Internet forum devoted to their home country, Hungary. From Japan, where he was conducting physics research, he transmitted to the forum a satirical essay on feminism; she, reading it from Purdue University, where she was working on a doctorate, responded with comments of her own.

As Internet users often do, they then began exchanging electronic mail privately. Soon they discovered that they shared a deeply religious bent. They began courting—sometimes 10 messages a day flew across the Pacific.

After exchanging photographs and $3,000 worth of phone calls, they decided to get married. "Everybody told me that we were mad," Laszlo recalled. "Without the Internet, it would not have happened." They now live in Sweden with their 5-month-old son and remain on "the net."

Today the network is open to anyone who has a personal computer with a modem and communications software, a phone line and an account with a computer services company that is linked to the Internet.

In the Washington area, these firms include PSI Inc. of Herndon, Digital Express Group Inc. of Greenbelt and UUNET Technologies Inc. of Falls Church. For the most basic type of connection, charges start at about $10 a month.

To begin a session, the home user commands his or her computer to use the phone line to link up to a "host" computer at the services company. Messages typed on the home screen are sent over the phone line to the host, which in turn puts them on the network; incoming information is displayed on the user's screen.

It is the closest thing yet to a functioning "information highway," the digital conduit that theorists predict will one day allow any human anywhere to trade information effortlessly with any other.

"The Internet may well be setting the model for the entire future of telecommunications," said Anthony Rutkowski, who heads the Reston-based Internet Society.

Along the way it is demonstrating both the benefits and dubious by-products that such a creation would bring. Laboratories, schools and companies give testimonials on how its instant communication has spurred learning and productivity. Yet at the same time, the network is getting clogged with mind-rot: lame humor, endless stream-of-consciousness musings and some of the hardest-core smut imaginable.

The Internet was born in 1969 as a Pentagon experiment aimed at helping researchers trade information by computer. It continues to draw about $30 million in federal subsidies annually from the National Science Foundation, but most of its money comes from states, universities and many individual users.

Traffic on the network has doubled in the past year. But as Stephen Wolff of the National Science Foundation notes: "There is no supreme deity in charge."

Rather, the Internet is a confederation of about 12,000 small networks of linked computers, most of them at universities, government agencies and companies. Just as the postal systems of countries agree to trade letters, these member networks agree to exchange the modern equivalent, electronic packets of digital information.

The Internet does not have its own private set of communications wires. Instead, it uses whatever is available. An ordinary phone line is likely to carry data out of the home. The links between the 12,000 small networks are typically big-bore circuits leased from a telecommunications company—the data might travel over fiber-optic strands or satellites.

The network is growing fast in part because it has banished the great demon of computer technology—incompatible standards that make one machine unable to talk to another. Users address and transmit their material by precise rules, or standards.

In its simplest form, the "net" is electronic mail. A person types a message onto a computer screen, including the recipient's private electronic mail "address."

The message flows over telephone or data lines to hub computers, which sort it using the address and send it on its way. It normally arrives in seconds. The addressee reads it on a computer screen and can reply in the same way.

Since early this month, network users have been able to send their thoughts to President Clinton and Vice President Gore this way—though White House staffers, not the two leaders themselves, scan the messages.

The Internet also provides thousands of "bulletin boards," electronic meeting places for people who share an interest. There are boards on computer programming, superhero comic books, DNA research, Iranian society and David Letterman.

As with cork boards, people post messages for anyone to read. With a few strokes on the keyboard, other Internet users order their machines to link up to the bulletin board and transfer the messages posted there to their own screens for reading.

With billions of bits of information flying back and forth, a vibrant electronic culture has sprung up. Friendships, feuds and collaborations form over the net. Network users may spend hours at their screens, checking bulletin boards, firing off E-mail. To add nuance to messages, people often use "smiley" symbols. Many a stern statement on the Internet is followed by this symbol: ;-)

It is a semicolon, a hyphen and a parenthesis. Viewed with the head turned to the side, it resembles a winking face. It means "just kidding."

Many messages contain purposeful information. Others are from people just having fun.

Said Brett Berlin, an Alexandria technology consultant, "a lot of the traffic is people experimenting with communicating in new ways." It is much like ham radio operators chatting with someone who lives in a distant country they've never before reached.

"I have made many friends on nearly every continent," wrote Russell Noble, an Internet user in Wollongong, Australia. "Next year I am planning a trip to the U.S.A. and many of the people I have mailed with are going to let me stay in their homes."

But many Internet transactions are between person and machine. More and more, companies, government agencies and universities are putting their computerized data banks on line. That allows the network users to reach across the world and browse through what they find, then transfer it to their own machines.

Libraries have put card catalogues on-line. Elsewhere, you can find the full texts of "Hamlet" and H. G. Wells's *The War of the Worlds*.

State Department travel advisories are available, as are the academic schedules of George Washington University and the surrender documents that ended World War II. Available too are countless computer programs—the network may well be the world's biggest distributor of software.

It seems that almost every day a new use is invented. One computer offers a song lyrics database: Type in a line from your home computer and the distant machine will search through its files and list all the songs it knows that contains those words.

Much information on the Internet is "in the public domain," that is, not owned by anyone or protected by copyright. That helps lower costs, as people generally are paying not for the information itself, just for transport.

Each year, the transport becomes cheaper because of advances in digital technology. The network further reduces costs because, unlike the long-distance phone system, it does not establish a private two-way circuit between points.

Rather, a message feels its way across the network on a one-way basis, slowing down during periods of congestion, but seeking out the fastest, lowest-cost route.

In some cases, said Duncan Briggs of InterCon Systems Corp., a Herndon company that makes Internet software, "The message gets busted up and may go by several routes. It gets reassembled at the other end." The answer is likely to come back by yet another route.

Data transmission is so cheap that people give no thought to whether the computer they're linking up with is across the street or around the globe. Either way, the cost to them is the same.

Thus it is that Internet messages from Singapore to Malaysia, which are separated by just a mile of water, go first to the United States, then back to Malaysia.

Typical of the traditional user is Scott Ramsay, a Washington-area computer programmer. If he's stumped late at night over a software problem, he posts a cry for help on one of the world's hundreds of programming bulletin boards.

"I come back and someone will have an answer," Ramsay said. It may be from Taiwan, from England, from the United States. To him that's not important—the answer is.

The Centers for Disease Control in Atlanta use the Internet to stay in touch with outside researchers and to distribute findings. "Every worker at the CDC, except janitors, has a computer and electronic mail," David Ross of the CDC told a recent conference. "We couldn't live without it. It lets us work."

But the net has more than a few users after-hours. They flock to bulletin boards to argue over the motivations of soap opera characters, advise each other on shopping for a sailboat and exchange tips on antique firearms. Political junkies dissect Ross Perot's latest speech (the text will have been posted there), rock-and-rollers compare notes—Nikko Suhonen, an Internet user in Finland, relies on it to stoke his passion for the Beatles.

Serbs all over the world feud with Croats all over the world, by way of a Yugoslavia bulletin board. Other members of the two groups use the net to try to join hands—peace activists in two cities in Serbia and Croatia use the Internet to stay in touch.

Popular boards quickly become cluttered—people who tap into one after a week's absence may find 200 new messages to wade through. If a board gets too busy, people often get disgusted and split off to start new ones. This is a prime complaint about the Internet—too much information. Some people get hundreds of pieces of E-mail a day, far too many to read and respond to.

As software technology advances and the data "pipes" become bigger, the Internet is going "multimedia," carrying pictures, video and sound. All are reduced to the ones and zeroes of "digital" computer language for the ride.

City Hall in Wellington, New Zealand, has a computer that, among other things, stores children's artwork in digital form for the world to see. Responding to a distant typed command, it sends a stream of code that represents a picture. Using special software, which may well have been obtained from another Internet computer, the recipient can turn it into a full-color picture.

From Arlington, Internet devotee and author Carl Malamud has set up "Internet Talk Radio." It is an hour-and-a-half a week of professionally produced talk shows on technical subjects. It flows over the network to about 30 countries, decoded into sound by the computers it reaches. Others groups are using the network to send video signals.

Because of the inherent anonymity the Internet can accord, the network has generated a vast sexual subculture as well. One bulletin board specializes in bondage, another contains reviews of bestiality videos. Still others provide a place where amateur writers post their efforts at hard-core adult fiction. And pictures scanned from adult magazines are increasingly there for the asking.

Not surprisingly, the network has given birth to new forms of harassment. One woman recently found that a man was sending her unsolicited erotic pictures over the network.

Given developments like this, the community is struggling to craft rules of use. It starts with common courtesy. Many network users try to get people to avoid the invective that physical separation seems to encourage whenever there's even a small disagreement. And to resist posting a message on a bulletin board that has nothing to do with the subject at hand. Anyone who does is likely to be "flamed," Internet-speak for being the target of venomous E-mail.

At issue too is the illegal circulation over the network of copyrighted material. Users aren't supposed to do it. Sometimes network operators back up their rules with technology: a campus computer that provides students a copyrighted on-line dictionary, for instance, may be programmed to slam the door to anyone trying to get access from off-campus.

But most Internet users turn thumbs down to any effort to control content. From its earliest days, the net has been a place where no idea or expression is too extreme, too daring to be denied exposure.

The University of Michigan is taking what has become a standard approach. It doesn't censor. But it is rewriting its campus code of conduct to ask that students at least be considerate: If a student has been using a library computer to look at potentially offensive material, it should be cleared off the screen so the next person won't see it inadvertently.

Brad Reese, computer director at George Washington University, said, "We have to face such issues as, can the parents of a 17-year-old student sue the university for creating a network over which pornography is available? . . . At the same time, could another student sue us for not making it available, for violating his right to information?"

For now, probably the main thing slowing the growth is that for the technologically uninitiated the network remains a less than welcoming place.

"I think the Internet is cool," said Mark McCahill, a University of Minnesota software engineer who has done pioneering work in designing the Internet. "My mom and dad aren't so sure."

Much of the information found there is highly specialized—one bulletin board is for discussion of the field of geophysical fluid dynamics. And getting at the general interest material can be a challenge. The user must type a bewildering slew of arcane commands on the screen to "navigate."

Publishing guidebooks to the Internet has become a cottage industry of sorts, but the fact of the matter is that no one has a full list of what's out there, just as no one knows all the restaurants to be found along all the roads of the United States.

"I always have this feeling that there's more out there—if I just knew how to get to it," said David Whip, an Internet user in Baltimore.

Software engineers are working to simplify the search. Along the net they are placing computers that act as directories, so that if you're looking for information on French cooking you can find which computer contains it rather than searching thousands individually.

Companies are creating software to make the job of navigation easier—InterCon, for instance, makes a program that lets a user explore with the basic commands of the Macintosh computer.

But for now, the typical Internet user often is someone who enjoys the hunt as much as the catch, the type of person who bores friends with stories of tapping into a computer in Israel at 11:45 the night before. Or in Brazil, or South Africa, or Mexico.

Viacom's Bid Wins Paramount

PAUL FARHI

T he corporate takeover battle went on for months. Refusing to yield, Sumner M. Redstone increased his bid once, twice, three times, ultimately wearing down a group of younger rivals to cinch the multibillion-dollar deal.

The year was 1987, and Redstone was after a cable TV company called Viacom Inc. Wall Street should have learned then that Sumner Redstone is a man not easily denied.

Yesterday, after five wearisome months, Redstone emerged victorious again. Withstanding the challenge of rival QVC Inc., Redstone's Viacom completed its $10.1 billion deal to buy Paramount Communications Inc. His bid, modified four times in five months from the original $8.4 billion, was enough to top QVC's equally tenacious Barry Diller in a down-to-the-wire contest for Paramount's shares.

Redstone, 70, now stands as the richest and perhaps most commanding figure in the global entertainment and culture business. After engineering a plan to merge Viacom with video retailer Blockbuster Entertainment Corp. last month, Redstone would own 62 percent of a three-headed entertainment colossus.

"There are so many possibilities," said an enthusiastic Redstone yesterday, describing himself as "exhausted but exhilarated" by the months of boardroom combat.

"The idea now is not to have three different companies but one. One company—all together." His voice rising, he added: "We're going to build a global super powerhouse!"

The Paramount-Blockbuster-Viacom combination claims a piece of virtually every part of the entertainment business: cable and broadcast TV networks, movie and TV production, radio and TV stations, movie theaters, book publishing, home-video retailing, amusement parks, sports teams.

It brings together dozens of household names. Viacom owns cable TV networks MTV, Showtime and Nickelodeon; Paramount operates a major movie studio, TV programming ("Star Trek"), Madison Square Garden, New York's Rangers and Knicks, and publisher Simon & Schuster. And Blockbuster, besides video-rental stores, controls Spelling Entertainment ("Beverly Hills 90210," "Total Recall").

Redstone said he foresees taking some of these pieces and putting them together differently.

For starters, he sees Paramount making movies for the Nickelodeon children's channel; Paramount making a movie out of the MTV characters Beavis and Butthead; and Paramount-Viacom-Blockbuster capitalizing on all of their trademarks with a chain of retail stores, following the lead of Disney and Warner Bros.

There will not be, however, a Paramount movie about the takeover, he vowed yesterday.

Redstone acknowledged that the three companies (he hasn't figured out what to call them) will face formidable challenges trying to find their collective way on the emerging "information highway."

The two mergers will create $10.4 billion in debt, saddling the company with interest costs that will suppress profits for years to come. What's more, the companies' managements will have to be integrated without the dissension and fallout that has plagued other mega-mergers. And Wall Street is still questioning whether the Blockbuster deal will be approved by shareholders.

Yet unlike any other mega-deal in memory, Redstone will be left with greater control over his dominion than any other member of the entertainment barony, be it Rupert Murdoch, Ted Turner or cable titan John C. Malone. Total value of Redstone's 62 percent stake: at least $5.5 billion.

Born Sumner Murray Rothstein to working-class parents in Boston, Redstone clambered to his present peak through a combination of hustle, foresight and bare-knuckled toughness.

Despite a right hand that was badly scarred by a 1979 hotel fire, Redstone plays a ferocious game of tennis by gripping the racket with a special leather strap.

After graduating from Harvard in 2-1/2 years, Redstone joined an elite military intelligence unit that helped crack Japan's naval codes during World War II. Thereafter, he earned a Harvard Law degree and spent six years in Washington in the Justice Department and in private practice.

Ultimately, he once told an interviewer, he abandoned the legal business because "litigation is generally offensive to me. All that happens is dissipation of intellectual and financial resources."

That is at best disingenuous, since Redstone has used the courts to build his business.

Taking over his family's small chain of drive-in theaters in the 1950s, Redstone personally litigated a case that forced the movie studios to release first-run movies to drive-ins as well as to indoor theaters (the drive-ins grew into an 800-screen theater and real estate company called National Amusements Inc. that was the source of Redstone's original fortune).

Later, after his purchase of Viacom, Redstone fired off a massive lawsuit against Time Warner Inc., charging that its HBO cable network was unfairly restraining Viacom's rival Showtime service.

The suit eventually was settled out of court, but not before Redstone had deposed virtually every major executive in the cable industry.

Redstone's pursuit of Paramount had a similar take-no-prisoners-feel to those on the other side.

Early in the bidding, Viacom sued one of QVC's allies, Malone, calling him an "evil monopolist," and retained no fewer than six top Washington law firms to work the suit and an attendant lobbying campaign.

Viacom even hired Kroll & Associates, an investigation firm, to dig into its opponents.

"They pulled out every stop," said a top executive close to QVC. "After a while, you had to realize he was going to do anything to win."

Asked yesterday if he sent Redstone a congratulatory message, Diller said pointedly, "That would be wildly hypocritical of me."

Among other irritations, those in the QVC camp were regularly nettled by Redstone's repeated characterization of QVC as "a jewelry merchant."

Said Redstone, "I would be a hypocrite to say I was not upset that [Diller] tried to break up" Viacom's original friendly merger with Paramount in September.

"There were some unhappy moments, and at times it was mean-spirited."

Rupert Murdoch

Global Gatekeeper

EUGENE ROBINSON

C ritics charge that Rupert Murdoch is trying to conquer the world, but aides say his aims are more modest: He'd settle for being its gatekeeper, sitting astride a growing network of electronic "superhighways" and happily collecting tolls.

Two years ago Murdoch's News Corp. was long on debt and short on cash, and it looked to some as if the company might not survive.

But now Murdoch is back with a vengeance, having spent the summer making a rapid-fire series of deals designed to capitalize on what he sees as a technological revolution whose shape is still only hazily defined. In a speech here last month, Murdoch announced that the day of the media baron was over.

"Technology is racing ahead so rapidly," he said, "that the media mogul has been replaced by a bevy of harassed and sometimes confused media executives, trying to guess at what the public wants."

To many ears, that sounded like undue modesty. The peripatetic, 62-year-old Australian-born tycoon, a man of many time zones, has been relatively stationary lately, spending most of his time in Los Angeles running his Fox Inc. movie and television empire and, more recently, trying to work out his repurchase of the New York Post.

Meanwhile, in one big flurry of long-distance dealmaking, he has gone global.

The key transaction came in July, when Murdoch spent $525 million to buy a majority stake in Star TV, a satellite broadcasting system based in Hong Kong that reaches 38 countries, including China and India. At the same time, he began expanding his existing Sky Television satellite network, a Britain-based system now taking aim at the rest of Europe.

The result is that one-third of the world's landmass and two-thirds of its population are within reach of Murdoch's satellite broadcasting companies.

Four years ago, skeptics here doubted that Sky Television would succeed because it required users to buy or rent relatively expensive individual satellite dishes. But the little dishes have sprouted on rooftops and chimneys throughout

Britain, and Murdoch's one-half stake in Sky brought him a profit last year of more than $50 million—a figure that could double in 1993.

Even more important, according to company officials, is the fact that ownership of Star and Sky gives News Corp. the opportunity to define the rules of the road—to set technological standards and distribution protocols that latecomers to the market will have to adopt.

"We believe that the distribution channel, for example a satellite system, becomes more and more important in the future," said August Fischer, chief operating officer for News Corp.

Star TV is only one of Murdoch's recent deals. He also has gone into a venture with a British firm called National Transcommunication to develop a digital satellite system that could deliver far more channels than current hardware can manage. He has thrown in with a German firm to invade the television market in Germany, Switzerland and Austria; and he is launching a Latin American cable television channel to reach from the Rio Grande to Patagonia.

Murdoch has joined with British Telecommunications PLC to try to invent the interactive telecommunications link of the future. He also bought a Massachusetts-based computer network called Delphi that gives him entree into the global Internet network—and that, he hopes, will give him the technology and the reach to publish an electronic newspaper.

Murdoch, once known as a hard-nosed newspaperman with ink in his veins, has become a believer in the proposition that a new era is dawning in telecommunications, and dawning fast.

"Convergence is seeing some of the world's largest industries trying to accept a new age in which few of the old rules seem to apply and traditional distinctions are breaking down," he said in his speech here. "Five of the world's biggest industries—computing, communications, consumer electronics, publishing and entertainment—are converging into one dynamic whole."

He is still a major newspaper tycoon, owning five national newspapers in Britain alone, including the august Times of London—along with magazines around the world such as TV Guide, the book publishers HarperCollins, and a string of newspapers in Australia and places such as Fiji and Papua New Guinea.

But analysts see it as significant that Murdoch recently sold his 50-percent stake in the enormously profitable, Hong Kong-based South China Morning Post.

"I think his heart is still in print media, but I believe the balance of News Corp. will inevitably shift to the television media," said Derek Terrington, an analyst with Kleinwort, Benson Ltd. "I think he does have a very strong idea of where the new technology is going, but translating it into reality is where Rupert Murdoch really comes to the fore—turning it around into profits very quickly."

Murdoch's newspapers devote more coverage to Sky Television's activities and programs than other London newspapers do. At first this was seen as an attempt to give the fledgling satellite network a boost, but lately Sky has been doing well on its own.

Last month, Sky began scrambling some of its popular stations, offering viewers a chance to subscribe and pay for material they previously had been getting free of charge. To sweeten the pot, Sky threw in an assortment of other offerings, mostly U.S. cable channels.

To the surprise of analysts, Sky was swamped with takers, at one point getting more than 100,000 phone calls a day from satellite dish owners who wanted to buy the package. "Sky is going to be an incredible business," said Fischer, predicting that News Corp.'s profits from Sky this year would reach $100 million.

Star TV, the Asian satellite venture, is a more complicated proposition. Company officials said one major question is how any single service could hope to offer relevant programming to both of the world's most populous nations—China and India—at the same time.

Some analysts believe Star's future hinges on the development of low-cost satellite dishes affordable by the mass market. Also, Chinese authorities might not approve of direct satellite broadcasts, and instead could insist on channeling the material through cable networks, over which the government could have more control.

Whenever the hardware issues are ironed out, Murdoch has plenty of freight to send down his new ethereal superhighways. In Fox he has an entertainment factory that churns out movies and television shows. Soon he will begin to produce soap operas in connection with Televisa in Mexico City, one of the biggest and slickest soap opera producers in the world. With his London-based all-news channel, Sky News, he has the foundation for a global news network similar to Cable News Network.

"We still believe that the most important people in all this are editors, producers, directors, journalists, entertainers," Fischer said. "Above all we still believe we are a creative company, a software company."

Education as Business

CHARLES TRUEHEART

C hristopher Whittle belongs to a very small league of late-century media entre-preneurs—Ted Turner and Steven Brill are two remarkable others—who transformed mass communications well before they turned 50.

Whittle's empire began more than two decades ago in a run-down pillow factory on the outskirts of Knoxville with "Knoxville in a Nutshell," the University of Tennessee students' guidebook. That grew into the little media company that could, 13-30 Corp., named for its demographic target ages. Today Whittle Communications is a big company valued at $700 million, with 1,000 employees across the country, and even bigger plans that major corporate investors seem to want a piece of.

Whittle's original business concept was to deliver to magazine advertisers what they couldn't find elsewhere—for instance, the right to appear exclusively in a Whittle magazine. In the mid-'80s, Special Reports doubled the exclusivity by guaranteeing, more or less, that it would be the only reading option in a physician's waiting room.

You've probably seen these bright oversized magazines, designed to accommodate the average patient's wait and attention span; they're now supplemented by pamphlets, "wall media" and video presentations. Health clubs, veterinary clinics, school corridors are also Whittle media venues. Occasionally, Whittle's properties have indulged his fancies; the statewide boaster Tennessee Illustrated, for example, was a symptom of Whittle's professional romance with then-governor Lamar Alexander, [former] U.S. secretary of education, and with the idea of running for governor himself.

Over the years Whittle Communications has been outstanding at incubating business concepts and successful at launching them into an uncharted marketplace—"We grew by inventing new things," says its longest-serving executive, Laura Eshbaugh—but not so good at managing its own businesses, at apportioning time and resources, at follow-through.

The proliferation of product carried invisible baggage that cramped Whittle's flexibility and growth, too. "We had a culture here for years that essentially put equal weight on all ideas," Whittle says. "If you came in with an interesting concept that had a business potential of $3 million and the next person had an interesting concept worth $100 million, we gave those equal attention."

Five years ago, according to a seasoned officer of the company, Whittle Communications "was a nice little $120 million media company composed of $10 million print vehicles." But in the late 1980s, Channel One's exponentially greater financial promise dazzled everyone, from Whittle down, to the possibilities of becoming a technology-oriented company, and eventually a billion-dollar one.

Thus the return to Whittle's side of management guru Nick Glover, who told employees in the company newsletter, Fred, about the latest reorganization of the company by drawing airplanes with different numbers of propellers. The restructuring, the second in two years, also meant tough decisions: The older, more marginal print properties have shrunk in number, size and ambition. Breaking into tears before his assembled corps in Knoxville, Whittle in May declared he had to let 100 people go—a big jolt in the paternalistic, sky's-the-limit atmosphere he cultivates.

Inside the company, all eyeballs have swiveled to the big properties Whittle is now incubating: Edison, Channel One, the Special Report Network, and the new Medical News Network, which will do for doctors' private offices what Channel One does for classrooms: provide physicians with a constant daylong current of infomercial product.

Disbelief in Whittle's ability to pull the whole thing off, Edison especially, is only natural. But Whittle's partners serve as bona fides to their confidence in him. Time Warner owns 37 percent, the Dutch electronics giant Philips, 25, Britain's Associated Newspaper Holdings, 24, Whittle himself, 8, and a few score executives, limited partners, the rest.

The schools project alone will require a $2.5 billion additional investment, at least. "We're going to have to raise a lot of money for Edison," Whittle says, "and though I don't have all that figured out yet intuitively, I think Whittle Communications is going to be the farm to pledge. . . . It's the collateral."

All the more reason to wonder, as many do: Whittle knows how to dream and how to sell and how to start things, but does he know how to level off, concentrate and run things profitably? And by any minimum long-term standard, is there any evidence that Whittle properties have staying power?

The scope of Edison sharpens both questions. But Whittle himself is seductively blithe. "I don't have a P-and-L [a projected profit-and-loss statement] on Edison," he declares. "We've never done one."

Are his partners just as serene?

"Remember," he says, "they have driven over many cliffs with me." He smiles. "What I mean by that is, they've suspended judgment before." He laughs. "They're very trusting in general, and we are very intuitive. You'd be surprised . . .

"We believe," he says matter-of-factly, not really meaning to deliver an aphorism. "And we proceed."

The FCC's Wheel of Fortune

MIKE MILLS

A re you down about your job, feeling entrepreneurial, hoping to get in on The Next Big Thing?

Then you may want to take part in the upcoming auction of radio licenses for "personal communications services," or PCS. Federal analysts say this next generation of lightweight pocket telephones and paging devices could generate a $50 billion industry within a decade.

To encourage small businesses to bid, especially ones owned by minorities or women, the Federal Communications Commission is giving them special breaks. But if you fit that bill, you'll still have to bring a lot of money.

It will take a down payment of roughly $100,000 to get into the room to vie for most of the licenses available in the Washington area, judging from rules adopted by the FCC yesterday.

Then there's the bid itself: The cost of the one license available to the entire Washington area is expected to easily top $50 million. Then the winner will have to spend another $100 million to develop the wireless telephone system, not to mention the cost of buying new equipment for businesses such as Amtrak that now use the frequencies in question.

Licenses for smaller markets, such as those in Cumberland, Md., or Winchester, Va., could cost in the millions to buy and develop, according to rough estimates. And the market there for pocket phones is less than guaranteed.

"The reality is, it's not going to be easy to succeed at PCS," said Jerry Lucas, president of Telestrategies Inc., a McLean-based consulting company.

Numbers like these make James Winston, executive director of the National Association of Black Owned Businesses and a prospective bidder, pessimistic. "I'm not sure there is going to be a significant number of minority businesses involved in PCS," he said. "I think the opportunities are very limited for people who are currently not business owners."

But FCC Chairman Reed Hundt disagrees. "I really do believe this is the single most important opportunity that's been fairly made available to women and minorities in our country's history," he said yesterday. He compared the difficulty of financing a small PCS venture with that of opening a restaurant or a car dealership in a big city.

Hundt predicts that a special block of licenses set aside for businesses with annual revenue under $125 million would spawn firms owned by minorities and women that one day will serve 12 million customers and earn $12 billion in revenue.

It remains unclear who will eventually bid to operate the Washington-area systems. But one license has been reserved free of charge for American Personal Communications Inc., which the FCC designated as a "pioneer" to develop the technology. The company is owned by a partnership that is 70 percent owned by The Washington Post.

The FCC predicts the auctions will open today's cellular telephone market to competition, creating 100,000 new jobs and a $50 billion business within the next 10 years. Consumers, in return, will get lower prices for the highly advanced pocket telephones.

Under the FCC plan, two of six licenses in each market would be barred to big companies. Some small businesses and all firms owned by women, blacks and other minorities also get bidding "credits" when vying for these licenses. For example, bids by a firm owned by a woman or minority that also has annual revenue below $40 million would be marked up by 25 percent.

Just as valuable in aiding these firms would be deferred payments on the bids that they win. Small businesses owned by women or minorities would have to pay only interest on the value of their licenses for five years, before being required to begin paying off principal.

Those groups also would have to comply with strict ownership rules intended to keep big businesses from using minorities or women as "fronts" for their companies.

FCC officials said that entrepreneurs should not think the coming PCS auctions will begin a repeat of its much-criticized cellular telephone licensing process, in which speculators made billions of dollars by winning licenses through lotteries and then selling them in the private market.

Auction rules impose penalties on companies that do not build their wireless networks within set periods of time after receiving the license. Fines would be imposed on those who get into the business for "unjust enrichment," meaning the trafficking of licenses with no intention of actually offering PCS services.

"Investors will have to have some staying power to take advantage of this opportunity," said FCC Commissioner James Quello.

Corporate America's Sporting Chance

MARK POTTS and BILL BRUBAKER

There was a time when most professional sports teams were owned by rich sportsmen and the occasional beer baron.

These days, however, team owners are more likely to be giant media or entertainment conglomerates, or the titans that run them. The list includes the publisher of the Chicago Tribune, cable TV mogul Ted Turner, movie-maker Paramount Communications Inc. and the head of the Nintendo video game empire.

Two of the glitziest names yet joined the ownership ranks earlier this month. The National Hockey League awarded expansion franchises to Walt Disney Co. and the chief executive of video giant Blockbuster Entertainment Co., H. Wayne Huizenga—who also owns a baseball team and part of the Miami Dolphins.

The entry of Disney and Huizenga are further evidence of how the worlds of sports and show business are converging in the owners' boxes of pro teams. An increasing number of entertainment and media titans are purchasing pro franchises, lured by the potential ties between sports, broadcasting, marketing and merchandising. Just imagine being able to buy Mickey Mouse souvenirs at hockey games, or NHL team jerseys at Disneyland.

That kind of involvement is part of a trend that is bringing more corporations, with their deep pockets, to sports ownership at a time when the prices of many teams are rising to the $100 million mark and beyond—out of the reach even of many of the nation's richest individuals.

"I think many of us—myself included—are dinosaurs," said Bruce McNall, the Los Angeles financier who owns the NHL's Los Angeles Kings and, as chairman of the league's board of governors, helped broker the Disney and Huizenga deals. "I mean, in the next 10, 20 years, private ownership of sports franchises is going to be less and less a possibility."

Some in professional sports are concerned that the trend may tilt the competitive balance among franchises toward rich corporate owners able to afford marquee players and to market their teams on cable television superstations or through unique merchandising relationships. Indeed, that worry is strong enough that the National Football League has a ban on corporate ownership of teams.

But the NFL is reevaluating the prohibition, and many experts say corporate ownership, especially by media and entertainment interests, is the wave of the future in professional sports.

"I think it's a logical marriage, if there's going to be one between corporate ownership and professional sports, to have companies like Disney or Blockbuster in there as owners, because they are in the entertainment business," said Steve Matt, a sports franchise expert at Arthur Andersen & Co. in Dallas.

Some analysts say media and entertainment companies gain an advantage that escapes other deep-pocketed corporate sports team owners: The combination of sports and either broadcast or merchandising interests can add a cushion of profit in an otherwise risky business in which some teams barely break even or even lose money.

"To own a stand-alone team is like owning racehorses. You're taking a gamble on it," said David Londoner, an entertainment industry analyst at Wertheim Schroder & Co. in New York.

The new Disney-owned hockey team in Anaheim, Calif., which is to begin play either next year or the year after, offers a number of potential tie-ins. Among them: sports programming for the independent television station that Disney owns in Los Angeles, new lines of hockey-related merchandise for Disney's theme parks and stores, and new outlets for Disney's existing products.

"There are cross-marketing possibilities for merchandise and the characters, which they are past masters at," said Margo Vignola, who follows Disney for the brokerage firm Salomon Brothers Inc. "So there are a lot of ways they could feed back—they're complementary, so to speak."

Vignola and other Wall Street analysts say buying the NHL expansion franchise also is an important strategic and political move for Disney in Anaheim. By providing an anchor tenant for a planned city-owned arena, the company is said to hope that Anaheim officials will look more favorably on a projected $3 billion addition to Disneyland, for which the company has been seeking city approval.

The advantages are not as obvious for Huizenga's new NHL team in Miami—Blockbuster's 2,000-plus stores don't need the hockey connection to sell sports videotapes. But experts say Disney and Huizenga also bring big-time credibility and marketing and merchandising expertise not only to their teams, but also to the entire league.

"They're fabulous companies," said Gary Bettman, the NHL's newly appointed commissioner, "and the prospects of being able to do business with two of the great marketing companies in the world is incredibly exciting."

"What we'll see here, I think, with Blockbuster and Disney is enormous help and input . . . in the merchandising and marketing areas, possibly television," McNall said. "The bottom line is that companies of that caliber can help put their people and their thinking processes, their innovations, their creativity to work for the National Hockey League."

Not every union between sports and media or entertainment companies is successful. Washington-based Communications Satellite Corp., the owner of basketball's Denver Nuggets, has scaled back dramatically from the grandiose plans for creating a collection of sports teams and cable television networks that it envisioned when it purchased the team three years ago. Comsat officials now say that running a team is difficult enough by itself without worrying about how it fits into a grander scheme—although they don't rule out future expansion of their interests.

In spite of Comsat's experience, several other media and entertainment corporations have enjoyed considerable success by adding sports teams to their empires.

Turner, for instance, has built a powerful Atlanta-based sports and communications mix by broadcasting games played by his Atlanta Braves baseball team and Atlanta Hawks basketball team on his WTBS superstation. Chicago-based Tribune Co. offers its Chicago Cubs' baseball games on superstation WGN. Both superstations promote other programming during their sports broadcasts, providing another form of cross-pollination.

Paramount, the New York-based movie and entertainment company, has an even more vertically organized sports-media arrangement. Not only does it own the Knicks and Rangers and the cable television network that broadcasts many of their games, it also owns Madison Square Garden, the arena in which the teams play their home games.

Another prominent entertainment-sports connection, the purchase last summer of the Seattle Mariners by a group backed by Nintendo Ltd. chief Hiroshi Yamauchi, has yet to exploit the ties between sports and video games such as Super Mario Brothers—although jokes about the "Seattle Marios" already abound.

While some analysts say that the number of media and entertainment companies that truly could turn sports team ownership into significant profits with their other businesses is limited, others predict that more sports-entertainment ventures are ahead.

Media conglomerate Time-Warner Inc. and Japan's Sony Corp., which already has added a movie studio and a record company to its core technology business, are mentioned as possible team buyers. Other experts suggest that companies with strong marketing backgrounds, such as Coca-Cola Co. and Pepsico Inc., also might be interested in buying teams and exploring the merchandising possibilities.

Such moves would be in the tradition of breweries that long have exploited the natural cross-marketing possibilities of beer and baseball, such as Anheuser-Busch Cos., which owns the St. Louis Cardinals, and Canada's John Labatt Ltd., which is principal owner of the Toronto Blue Jays.

Baseball, the NHL and the National Basketball Association have no rules prohibiting corporate ownership of teams. But the NFL's prohibition reflects concerns by the league that it could lose control over its owners if corporations were allowed to buy teams.

"One of the enduring virtues of this league has been the fact that families and individuals could operate the teams and operate them successfully," said Jay Moyer, the NFL's vice president and general counsel. "If corporate ownership connotes some kind of mass infusion of outside money, then that's not a healthy development."

Moyer said NFL officials also are concerned that if a diversified corporation owned a team, some of its non-football holdings could reflect badly on the league's image. "What if [casino company] Bally bought a whole bunch of shares" in a company that owned a team, Moyer asked. "Now you've got a gambling organization owning shares in your team. So the business conflicts are almost as numerous as the mind can create them."

Nonetheless, some sports business experts predict that the NFL eventually will have to repeal its prohibition to keep the pool of potential owners robust and keep franchise values rising. That, in time, could attract a new generation of media and entertainment companies to team ownership.

"I understand why in the past there's been reluctance on the part of the leagues to allow corporate ownership, but . . . I don't think they have any alternative," Arthur Andersen's Matt said. "As the value of these franchises continues to escalate, the potential universe of individuals or groups of individuals [to be team owners] keeps shrinking. . . . I think you're going to see a lot more of this in the future."

Books and Publishing   2

Simon & Schuster Boss Fired

PAULA SPAN

T he rumor flashing through the publishing industry this afternoon was so startling that several top executives assumed it must be a joke. But it was true: After
33 years at Simon & Schuster, and 15 as its CEO, Richard Snyder had suddenly been
fired.

Snyder, known as both a brutal boss and a brilliant publisher, had built Simon
& Schuster into the powerhouse it is today. The firm had revenues of less than $40
million when he took the corporate helm in 1979 and has diversified into a multi-
tentacled $2 billion-a-year business. And it has been having a good year, industry
sources say, with numerous hardcover and paperback bestsellers.

Jonathan Newcomb, Simon & Schuster's president and chief operating officer
since January 1991, will take Snyder's place. Though he has been responsible for
day-to-day publishing operations, Newcomb is largely an unknown quantity to the
editors and agents who were burning up the phone lines today.

"It was boom—out of the blue," said literary agent Morton Janklow, a friend
and longtime associate of Snyder's. "I haven't spoken to one person in the business
who knows what this is about, who even has an acceptable theory."

Actually a number of theories were circulating. Simon & Schuster is a division
of Paramount Communications, which was acquired by the entertainment conglomerate Viacom in March after a bruising takeover duel. It was Viacom's CEO, Frank
Biondi, who walked into Snyder's office about noon today, Snyder told associates,
and fired him.

There has been speculation that Viacom might sell the publishing house to
reduce its debt, and that the presence of Snyder, 61, would have proved an impedi-

ment. But Viacom's press release announcing the transition made a point of pooh-poohing the sales rumors.

The other, more prosaic, theory postulated a personality clash between the acquirers and the acquired. "It was a difference in styles and philosophy," a source familiar with the decision said. "It was not a single event. . . . Dick just has a different style and philosophy about running a big business."

In the aftermath, publishing insiders recalled a New York Times story about the takeover battle in which Viacom Chairman Sumner Redstone was asked whether he knew the high-profile Snyder. Redstone's hesitation and his eventual lukewarm response—"I think I've met him"—was widely noted in the gossipy book business. "Snyder had sort of fallen below their threshold," an executive at another publishing house recalled today. "It made people think that Simon & Schuster was a very big deal to New York but didn't register very much with the acquirers."

Viacom will pay the four remaining years of Snyder's contract. It offered him a consultancy, which he declined; he has told associates he wants to be free to seek other opportunities in publishing. Friends have hypothesized that, should Viacom spin off S&S, Snyder would try to raise the money to buy it.

Redstone himself, in the bland Viacom press release announcing Snyder's dismissal and Newcomb's succession, called Snyder "a major contributor" to S&S and notes that he "leaves the company well positioned for the future." Snyder was not talking to the press today, except perhaps to Bob Woodward of The Washington Post, an S&S author. "I got a sense of someone going through life reassessment," Woodward said.

Snyder is not a widely beloved figure. In 1984, Fortune named him one of "the country's toughest bosses," jokingly comparing him to the Ayatollah Khomeini. (Snyder had more hostages.) One publishing executive today recalled the many people Snyder himself had fired, using a room that came to be known around S&S as "the executive departure lounge." But even those who dislike him credit him with smarts, vision and a phenomenal track record. S&S had been a modest trade publisher, sold by its founders to Gulf & Western for $11 million in 1975. Snyder led the company as it acquired Prentice Hall, moved into electronic and business publishing, and added audio and CD-ROM units. He had recently completed the absorption of Macmillan and Scribner's, which S&S purchased in 1993.

"He professionalized what was sort of a loopy business," Janklow said. "It was a business run by professorial types. He wanted it to be profitable. . . . He ran a creative enterprise with real discipline."

"In the minds of most people in publishing, he's been synonymous with Simon & Schuster as long as anyone can remember," said another industry insider.

Newcomb, on the other hand, is not well known. "No one thinks of him as a publishing person; they think of him as a finance guy," said the insider. It is telling that neither Janklow (whose S&S-published clients include David McCullough, Jackie Collins and Garry Wills) nor his equally high-powered partner, Lynn Nesbit, has had any dealings with the new CEO.

Rumors that S&S Consumer Group President Jack Romanos would move up to serve as Newcomb's second-in-command were branded as just that—rumors—by Viacom.

"I don't have the traditional editorial pedigree," Newcomb, 48, acknowledged in a brief phone interview this evening. He spent 14 years at McGraw-Hill, becoming president of its Financial and Economic Information Unit, before joining Simon & Schuster in 1988. His educational background—bachelor's in economics from Dartmouth, master's in finance from Columbia—is also a fiscal one.

But Newcomb said, "Publishing is a large and complex industry today. . . . There's a different skills set needed to run a $2 billion business."

Bit by Bit, an On-Line Collection

ELIZABETH CORCORAN

In the windowless preservation laboratory in the Library of Congress, a man clad in a smock carefully opens a Gutenberg bible from the 15th century to show off its graceful print to two dozen special visitors.

Few people ever see this piece of the library's holdings. Even fewer have listened to any of the thousands of wax cylinder recordings of early American songs in the library's collection or traced changes on the American frontier by studying the original maps it stores.

The library, with the help of other institutions nationwide, hopes to use electronic technology to change all that. On Thursday it plans to unveil a multimillion-dollar National Digital Library project. According to the plan, by the year 2000 images of 5 million rare American artifacts will exist in electronically transportable bits and bytes.

Some people may see these items by transferring them over phone lines to their home computers. Others may buy multimedia compact discs for their computers, based on the library's material but produced by commercial companies. Or one day, people might be able to tune in to see such material on interactive television.

But don't expect to be able to peruse the latest Anne Rice novel via your personal computer. The library will start by digitizing maps, photographs, recordings and other pieces of American lore, almost all of which are in the public domain—in other words, materials that can be used freely because they no longer are covered by copyright restrictions.

No one knows if large numbers of people want to tap into historical collections via personal computers. Yet putting libraries on-line has become one of the mantras of Vice President Gore and other advocates of the information highway.

"We have a responsibility to share more information with more people," Librarian of Congress James H. Billington said. Eventually, Billington hopes that the library's full collection will be available electronically.

The library wants to build "a kind of electronic version of what Andrew Carnegie did a century ago," he said, when the famous industrialist helped create the U.S. public library system.

Yet building a digital library will be far harder than laying down bricks and mortar. None of the old paper-bound rules work in cyberspace. Protecting authors' rights is a daunting task when entire files can be copied with a few keystrokes. Systems for searching through trillions of bits of information are in their infancy.

One challenge is familiar, though: finding the money to pay for the project.

The Library of Congress said it plans to work with other institutions around the country to create a digitized collection of 5 million items. The National Science Foundation recently awarded $24 million in grants to six university-industry teams to work on digital library technologies. The National Gallery of Art and the Getty Art History Information Program also are taking their first, tentative steps toward putting canvasses and sculptures on-line.

Still, it is the Library of Congress—housing more than 105 million items, 35 million of which are books—that will need to ignite public enthusiasm to help fund such work. Although the library has secured more than $10 million in private donations for the project, estimated to cost at least $20 million, it will need much more financing to go beyond the experimental stage.

To get started, the library has been meeting with officials from high-tech companies and other libraries. For instance, the visitors who recently enjoyed a peek at some of the library's treasures included representatives from Microsoft Corp., Walt Disney Co. and AT&T Corp.'s Bell Laboratories.

The library has some experience with on-line services. An electronic version of its card catalogue is available on the Internet network. It also has put on-line images and text from several recent exhibits. But those are small programs compared with what Billington hopes to do.

The starting point for the digital library will be items from the nation's past, particularly the Civil War. Over the last five years, the library has made digital versions of about 210,000 artifacts, such as Civil War era photos by Mathew Brady and hundreds of African American political pamphlets published after the war, and audio recordings of President Warren G. Harding.

"The library's goal is to make the material widely available for free," said Laura Campbell, director of distribution at the library.

So far the library has created computer-readable compact discs to store these images. Bell Atlantic Corp. is showing some of the material to New Jersey school-children via telephone lines. A cable TV operator in Denver is doing the same on its network.

The library also plans to put the materials on the Internet so that anyone with modem gear and digital fluency can view the images.

As the library expands its digital collection to include millions of items, it plans to serve up only "plain vanilla" digital versions, Billington said.

The library might digitize a Brady photograph and attach a brief caption, which people would view on computer screens. But a private company such as Microsoft or Disney might weave it into a more elaborate and expensive work on the Civil War in general.

By starting with historical items, the library postpones dealing with the most vexing issue in the digital domain: How to make materials widely available electronically and yet also protect the rights of artists and publishers.

The "fair use" provisions in existing law are complex, but show some tolerance for copying: A grade-school teacher can duplicate a few pages of a book for a class, or one person can copy an article for one friend.

However, the difference between fair use and misuse is cause for much debate. Once a picture or manuscript exists on an electronic network, it can be copied precisely and sent to thousands of people with only a few keystrokes. Publishers and artists worry that if electronic copying becomes widespread, payments and royalties for their works could dry up.

About a year ago the Clinton administration created a task force on intellectual property, headed by Patents and Trademarks Commissioner Bruce A. Lehman, to try to tailor copyright law to the digital world. According to Lehman, the group is likely to recommend only a few amendments when it finishes drafting its proposals in early 1995.

The basic conclusion: "You have the same rights when you sell your materials on an electronic network as when you put them on a bookstand," he said. Other legal experts suggest that the administration is playing down just how hard it will be to amend copyright law.

Lehman said that authors and publishers will continue to rely on the courts to enforce their copyrights, as they do today.

"There will always be some leakage from the information highway, just like someone will now photocopy an article," he said. But that won't permit organizations to freely reprint or distribute the works of others, he said.

Yet because of the ease of digital reproduction, Lehman does not foresee that digital libraries will put copyrighted works within easy reach on-line, the way they do books on a library shelf. Copyrighted digital materials are likely to be available only to subscribers—libraries, for example—who pay royalty fees, he said.

People who want the material might have to go to their local library and use a computer there that would not allow them to copy or redistribute the work, Lehman said.

Although people might freely explore public-domain materials via their own personal computers, copyrighted works would come at a price.

Who ultimately would pay that bill remains unclear—it could be the local library, the taxpayer or the individuals reading the materials. Whatever proposals finally are made are likely to evoke criticism in a country where library use has traditionally been free.

Dozens of technical challenges must also be met before digital libraries open for business. Creating useful electronic catalogues of material that might be scattered across dozens of libraries is tricky.

"Browsing isn't very helpful over trillions and quintillions of pieces of information," said Robert E. Kahn, president of the nonprofit Corporation for National Research Initiatives in Reston.

Putting materials into digital shape also is difficult. Kahn's group is building an experimental system that might enable the library to receive new materials sent for copyright registration in a digital format.

Existing materials offer a different challenge. Cornell University, for instance, is steadily building a digital collection of works on mathematics and New York state history by taking apart books and running individual pages through a sophisticated black-and-white scanner that, like a fax machine, makes an electronic image. But the Library of Congress wants to digitize multicolored materials and keep the original intact in the process, a far more costly and time-consuming approach.

Whatever the method is used, a digital library will never replace books, Billington said. But he hopes it will add substance to the emerging digital sphere.

D.C. Comics

JOE BROWN

U h-oh! Unstoppable mutant man-monster Doomsday is breaking down a rei-
nforced door. Maybe he's just trying to be the first to grab a copy of the comic
book series he stars in.

Released late last year, the eight-part "Death of Superman" series was the hottest story in 60 years of comic book history, and the hype had hundreds of comics
fans lining up around the block at such comics emporiums as Another World
in Georgetown, Cosmic Comix in Adams-Morgan, the 24-year-old Barbarian
Bookshop in Wheaton and more than two dozen other comics specialty shops in the
area.

Imagine a world without Superman: The Comicazie comics shop in Jersey City,
N.J., went so far as to have a memorial service for the Man of Steel in December,
and hundreds lined up to view the closed casket, right next door to Santa's sled.

No wonder Superfans impatiently queued up again in April, when D.C. Comics
brought the big guy back to life.

Or did it? There are now four crime-fighters claiming to be the true Superman . . .

Like Superman, in his alter ego as Clark Kent, the neighborhood comic book
shop masquerades as mild-mannered business establishment. It's not much to look
at on the outside, but initiates know that the humble comics shop is a portal to a
glittering cave, a noisy, magical alternative universe full of DEATH-DEFYING,
ACTION-PACKED, PULSE-POUNDING adventures, across time, space and
OTHER DIMENSIONS!!! and populated by the likes of The Uncanny X-Men,
Wolverine, The Mighty Thor, Superman, Amazing Spider-Man, Uncle Scrooge
McDuck, Iron Man, Incredible Hulk (and the Incredible She-Hulk), Silver Surfer,
New Teen Titans . . .

"If it weren't for comic book stores, all these great characters would probably
be dead," says Ron Goulart, who just published "The Comic Book Readers Companion" ($15, HarperCollins), an informal paperback encyclopedia covering the
whole 60 years of what we know now as a comic book, from Action Comics to
Zorro, from the birth of comics (1934's Famous Funnies) to Ninja Turtles and the
death of Superman.

"I used to buy comics at the neighborhood drugstore—you just don't see them
at the drugstore or newsstand the way you did," says Goulart. "That all-American

kid custom almost disappeared because of the malling of America. Now there are several thousand comics shops in America."

Goulart, 60, frequents two or three comics shops in the Connecticut/New York area and drops upwards of $20 per visit. "We have a chain here called the Dream Factory that is going to branch out all over the country. I'm in there once or twice a week like when I was a kid. . . . Sometimes when I go in there, I feel a little bit silly—everybody else seems to be about 14. But sometimes I'll walk in, and it's all gray-haired guys and older women. It's like having an acceptable addiction, and a place where you can have it catered to."

"I like a comics store that's very personable," says Darren Metzger, a 21-year-old developmental psychology/government double-major at Georgetown University. And self-admitted comics collector. Metzger's a regular at Another World.

"Another World is kind of a nook in the wall," he says. "You wouldn't even know it was there if you weren't looking for it. But whenever I go, it's always been packed with people. I guess it's kind of like Cheers—you walk in and they know you by sight, so by the time I walk from the door to the counter, they've pulled my subscription comics out of the file and it's on the counter waiting for me. The customers in there will discuss issues you've read and don't like, or argue over minutiae and arcana."

A comics store, in Metzger's opinion, is definitely a neighborhood asset.

"Of course, there are all these new mail-order catalogues you can order comics through," he says. "But it's sort of like a soap opera or serial—every week you want your weekly dose. If you order by the first of the month, then you have to wait four to six weeks for your comics to arrive, and you're guaranteed them. But it's a long time to wait. It's like a narcotic event. You want your comics."

"There are four guys who work here, and none of us read comics," says Another World assistant manager Stewart Miller, noting that the store relies on its customers to recommend comics or dissuade purchases.

"They'll ask what issue did such and such happen—we'll say, 'Ask this guy over here.' "

"When you hire people who read comics a lot, that's what they do," says manager Scot Steeno, explaining the unusual store policy. "We're geared more toward the mainstream of comic people. We don't carry a lot of the underground books; it's more the main superheroes."

There are about 270 regular subscribers at Another World, which also stocks trading cards, T-shirts, models, humor books, adaptations of current cartoons and series like "Ren & Stimpy" and "Star Trek," and comics-preserving paraphernalia like Pro-Skins polypropylene comics bags, cardboard backers, dividers and binders. The subscribers come in weekly to pick up their favorite comics, reserved for them by the staff. Customers range in age from 6 to 60, Steeno says, and though it's still a male-dominated hobby, more and more girls and women are getting interested.

"I've seen nothing but steady growth in comics," Steeno says. "The superheroes and the artists and the writers have all recently reestablished themselves, after a lull in the industry." This August, comics followers will line up again to learn which, if any, of the four Supermen is the real deal, and to watch as Batman, who broke his back this year, hands over his cape and cowl to a successor.

"And they're trying to appeal to more audiences than strictly fantasy," Steeno says. "A lot of the books that are coming out today are dealing with real-life problems. Spouse abuse, drugs, that kind of thing. A recent Batman book had a story called 'Seduction of the Gun,' which mentioned going to Virginia from Washington, D.C., and buying guns and bringing them back into the city. That was a very popular book."

Superman books dominated the Top 10 comic books ordered by retailers in April: Adventures of Superman; Action Comics (Superman) #687; Superman #78; Adventures of Superman #501; Superman: The Man of Steel #22; Turok: Dinosaur Hunter #1; Deathblow #1; Spawn #12; Bloodstrike #1; Adventures of Superman #500.

But some comics fans aren't buying it.

"I'm just ignoring this whole Superman hype," says Corey Hunter, 21, who stopped into Adams-Morgan's Cosmic Comix on a break from his job at Bally's Fitness Center. It's his third visit of the week.

"Some people are going to buy into it, because it's something that happened. But then lots of people understand they're just trying to get over on us. Marvel's notorious for that: They'll do something, then change it back in, like, months. So I just kind of ignore the whole thing. When they decide to throw it back on track, then I'll pick it up and start reading again."

A comics reader for 14 years, Hunter is a devotee of The Uncanny X-Men.

"The quality stays consistent and it doesn't insult my intelligence," Hunter says. "And I've been reading it so long that I understand the characters. I understand what they will do or won't do, no matter what the writer writes. They're an outlaw group, multicultural and international, which means there's something everybody can probably relate to."

The X-Men, the flagship comic of Marvel, are celebrating their 30th anniversary this summer with a 64-page Uncanny X-Men (#304) with a wraparound cover, plus a hologram of Magneto, Master of Magnetism, plus a glossy 48-page anniversary magazine. X-Men are currently the most popular comic characters—an estimated 4.3. million kids aged 2 to 17 tune in to the half-hour cartoon series on Fox each week, making it the No. 1 Saturday morning program. And the nine monthly titles generate sales of 50 million comics a year, almost a third of Marvel's annual 180 million copies sold. Not to mention the toys, clothing, home videos, games and trading cards . . .

Just imagine if you were a comics character, like Batman—or even Batman's agent! Three movies, a prime-time animated series, Saturday morning cartoons, an old TV series in reruns, five regular comic books, graphic novels, crossovers, cameos and merchandising deals . . .

"Most of my friends read comic books," says Hunter, who has about 5,000 comic books at home. "We'll sit down and have fierce comic book discussions.

You'll say, 'He'd never do that, and he did this' and so on, and 'He's stronger than him and he has these powers, so he'd beat him,' and so on. All but my last girlfriend read comic books—they just kind of got it by osmosis.

"I just moved here from Michigan, but I've met some people here who read comics. It's like 'Oh, you read comic books?' and all of a sudden you have a friend."

Long stigmatized as "kid's stuff," the once-lowly comic book is a big business now: The monthly trade tabloid Comic Buyers Guide notes that if you were to buy every major comic that came out in a month, you would have spent $1,300.

Also, according to Comic Books Guide, the last week of April was the biggest shipping week for comic books in the history of the direct-sales market.

Comic book conventions attract thousands of devotees, from the casually curious to the free-spending fanatic, and the continuing craze for comics is evidenced in the pervasive popularity of comics-based movies: Superman, Batman, Army of Darkness, um, Brenda Starr. . . . Brandon Lee recently lost his life on the set of a film version of a neo-comic called "The Crow." On the production slate are live-action films based on Blondie, Plastic Man, Richie Rich, Sgt. Rock, The Fantastic Four and Spider-Man.

And opening in August is Robert Townsend's $20-million "The Meteor Man," starring Townsend, Marla Biggs, Luther Vandross and young R&B group Another Bad Creation, in a story about a timid Washington schoolteacher who obtains magical powers after he's hit in the chest by a melting meteor, which dissolves into his skin. (His mom designs his costume.)

In Japan, comic books are epidemic, as the bulky comics called manga are mass-marketed to attract readers from the tiniest tot to the most harried businessman. But in America, many still sniff at comics as a juvenile habit to be outgrown and forgotten.

"Most people think a comics store equals kids," says Mauricio Lloreda, the soft-spoken 25-year-old owner of Cosmic Comix, an alternate universe hidden in the basement of an Adams-Morgan townhouse. "And it's not so anymore. Ninety percent of my customers are adults, so I carry the underground stuff. Adults will read the normal mainstream comics, but they like a little bit of uniqueness. People just can't seem to associate comics with being mature—they still think comics are childish."

"Mature" comics don't necessarily mean naughty cartoons, though there are plenty of those. Adult-themed comics are represented by such recent offerings as True Crime Comics special issue #1 on "The Death of George Reeves," the actor who played Superman ("Was it suicide—or murder?!! It can finally be told . . ."). The same company recently put out a 32-page two-in-one comic, "The Amy Fisher Story/The Joey Buttafuoco Story." ("Presented exactly as it really occurred, using the actual words of the characters themselves—finally, see what REALLY happened! With full color Amy pinup!")

Lloreda said he was drawn to the comics biz because he's been a fan since childhood.

"My favorites were all in Spanish, because I'm Colombian," Lloreda says. "I still have a few of them here. They're called Caliban, about this guy who had mind powers, a hypnotic type thing. Then I went to the mainstream comics, like Captain America, the Avengers, when we moved to England. Now I just basically read the mature comics, in terms of the stories. Like D.C.'s Vertigo line, where it doesn't necessarily deal with superheroes in capes."

"I thought this would be an easy business to start," Lloreda says. "Comics don't go bad—it's not like a restaurant. And you can get people hooked on comics and they'll keep coming back. You don't have to call them up every week to get them back in here. If the story's good, they'll keep coming back."

It's now nearly 3:30, and Lloreda says "the kids" are due in soon after the school bus drops them off.

"I think they're supposed to go straight from school to home," says Lloreda, looking at his watch. "They have to do their homework before anything, but they sneak in here for five minutes before going home."

Sure enough, at 3:30 on the dot, four neighborhood kids come trooping in the door at Cosmic Comix. Dropping their backpacks at the cash register near the front door, Julio, 8, William, 6, Antoine, 9, and Joshua, 7, make beelines for their favorite books, shouting all the way. "Wow, Batman!" "James Brown!" "Dick Tracy!"

"I like Conan," says Julio, once he's caught his breath long enough to browse through a single book. "We're here to look, and next time we have money we'll just buy the one that we want."

"I like Wolverine," says William, 6. "I like when he fights."

"I like to come here and look so I can save money to buy a comic book about Iron Man," says Joshua.

"These are for my baby, I'm not into them," says a considerably calmer Jennifer Bingham, who's popped in from her Adams-Morgan shopping to buy a pair of Wolverine and Iron Man comics.

"When Joaquin-Ismael says his prayers at night, he asks for Wolverine, Iron Man and Venom and all that stuff. He gets on his knees and says, 'God, please give me all that Wolverine stuff. . . .' He knows to ask God, that's all I care about, so I try to make his wishes come true. I put them under his pillow so he thinks God brought them."

Bingham says she grew up reading comic books, "Superman, Batman, Richie Rich, Archie . . ." and has to read the Wolverines to her 6-year old son. "He can read BOOM! and BAM! and the noise sounds, but that's about it. I think they're pretty violent, but he doesn't get scared. I'm not really into these guys, but he's a boy, so I'll read them."

"Reading comics was something your parents didn't want you to do," says Metzger. "I'm never timid to say that I collect comics. But a lot of my friends will kind of sheepishly grin and say, 'I used to collect.' I have to admit, I have to keep it together when I walk in there with girlfriends. When I get in there I'm like a kid in a toy store. My eyes go wide, I stare, I look at the back issues that hang above the counter to see what's gone up in value, then I talk to the guys to see what's new. I can spend anywhere from half an hour to 45 minutes if I just let myself, but I always have to be conscious if I'm with someone to be businesslike, buy what I want and leave. When I get home, [I can] sit down and read.

"It's pretty much my only vice," Metzger says. "On average I probably pick up about five or six comics a week. I collect some of the Amazing Spider-Man titles, Batman and Detective, I collect Wolverine, Ghostrider, Uncanny X-Men. It's pretty broad. Something that I've liked recently is some of the titles Image has come out with, like Spawn, Wildcats and some of the Valiant titles."

Metzger says he's primarily a purist, a comics reader. "But I do collect, too, so when I go in, I'll often pick up two copies of a comic, speculating. I was told when I first started reading comics, everyone wants to know does this comic have value, will I be able to sell this comic in a few years and make money. And this older comic collector said to me, 'If you can't read the comic and you don't enjoy the comic, then you're not getting anything out of it. So don't bother.'

"I treat my comic books with such care," Metzger says. "I bag them and back them [with cardboard] and keep them in a proper box. When I pick them up at the store, I make sure there's no creases or anything, and when I bring them home, I open them very carefully.

"Once you start collecting it becomes very personal. I've not sold any of my comics. I tell myself one day I will. But parting with one is like parting with a child. Or my childhood."

In a way, comic books are suffering a sort of a lost innocence, a plague of self-consciousness.

Remember when your best-beloved comics were well-worn from being stuffed in back pockets, stashed under pillows and between mattresses, and hidden behind textbooks during class?

Now comics are stored in expensive, chemically inert containers to preserve collectibility and value. Comics used to be considered unique if they had a cover; now they come with flashy scratch 'n' sniff, die-cut, holographic covers. Comics used to be a cheap source of escapist entertainment. Now comics are thought of as issue-oriented educational supplements, and as a source of financial investment.

Even kids consider collectibility when buying comics. At Cosmic Comix, Jafar Malek, 11, has a copy of Wizard—the hot price guide for young comic collectors (each issue usually comes with a quiz and several trading cards)—stuffed in his catcher's glove.

"You can see how much your comic book is worth," Malek says. "We trade them at school. We usually trade according to who's your favorite hero, but sometimes according to how much they're worth."

Comics historian Goulart says: "I've seen fathers with their 10-year-old children at comic shops saying, 'OK, buy three of those, and we'll keep two, and you can read this one.' Over the past few years, the idea has gotten abroad that these things are better than the stock market. I don't think that's going to prove to be true in all cases, because if a million people buy copies of the 'Death of Superman' issues, it'll be a long time till another million people want to come along and buy them.

"When I was a child, you went in and bought a comic because you liked Superman or Batman or Captain Marvel, or, like in my case, you admired a certain artist—'Oh boy! A new Bill Evert, or a new Basil Wolverton, I gotta get this!' "

Goulart's dad built shelves for his son's Amazing Colossal Comics Collection—at his mom's behest. "I held on to most of them till 25 years ago," says Goulart, who sold them and reaped several thousand dollars. "My God, now I could retire on them."

In addition to authoring five tomes on comic book history, Goulart writes a Marvel comic called "William Shatner's Tek World" and is finishing a short story in trading card form. "You have to collect all 95 cards to complete the whole story," he says. Goulart, who bought the first issue of "Batman" on the newsstand, and remembers paying a dime for the debut of "Captain America," says he still occasionally marvels that he can make a living from his interest in comic books. "I guess all this is really just to prove to my father that all those dimes he gave me as a kid weren't wasted," says Goulart, who sounds a lot closer to twentysomething than his 60 years.

"Hey, I never grew up," he says. "There's some kind of dust in comic books that keeps you eternally young."

Riding the Wind

Scarlett Revisited

SARAH BOOTH CONROY

A lexandra Ripley, in a Southern rite of passage into womanhood, first read "Gone With the Wind" when she was 12 years old. What difference did it make to her life? "I wanted to be Melanie Wilkes because she was perfect." Alas, "at 13 I discovered I'd never be perfect."

More than four decades later, the epic of gentle men, gracious ladies and feudal plantations has swept away Ripley's old life as surely as the Civil War did Scarlett's. For Ripley dared take up Margaret Mitchell's fallen pen, and write the sequel the Atlanta author never would. For this, she has been reviled, vilified and greatly enriched.

Today, 900,000 copies of "Scarlett: The Sequel to Margaret Mitchell's 'Gone With the Wind' " will finally be available to the hundreds of thousands who signed up at bookstores across the country, requested it from two book clubs and ordered it in 18 languages in 40 countries.

Some have called the book with the long-winded title a sacrilege to the sacred Southern Testament. And that's before learning that, for half of the book, Ripley shipped Scarlett from Georgia to Ireland.

The Mitchell heirs, who instigated the sequel before their copyright on the 1936 book runs out in 2011, have been denounced as snake oil salesmen. The author has been declared a robber who dares dig up Margaret Mitchell's characters from their moldering graves. Already, the heirs, the author and their agents have split (though not equally) a $4.9 million advance.

Publisher Warner Books and author Ripley are said to have fought an uncivil war over the first draft. Thanks to a four-month strike by the author in indignation over editorial criticism, the book took longer to write than the War Between the States took to fight.

A week or so ago, Ripley came to Washington to hunt for antique silver in Georgetown, to have her picture taken before the white columns of Robert E. Lee's Arlington House, and, through a heavy smoke screen of low-tax Virginia cigarettes, to talk. The antebellum mansion looks very like everyone's Tara, the plantation of

Mitchell's fantasy. Ripley doesn't look as though she belongs there. She's tall, trim, very New York publishing, with red hair and trendy haircut, brilliantly colored ensemble and purple shoes.

It was only 10 years ago that "Charleston," Ripley's first book about poor but plucky Southern belle-ringers, attracted attention to the author. After that she wrote two more gardenia-scented books, "On Leaving Charleston" and "New Orleans Legacy." Those books, plus the fact that Ripley, 57, is a white-glove-carrying, born-in-the-moss-land Southerner prompted her literary agents, who also represented the Mitchell heirs, to negotiate a contract for her to write the "sequel" of the century.

"Scarlett was such a nice change after writing about all those 17-year-old virgins," said Ripley.

Psyching Out Scarlett

Scarlett O'Hara Hamilton Kennedy Butler is 28 years old when Ripley's novel begins. Ripley had to think about how to resolve Scarlett's temper and temperament, Rhett's disdain, Ashley's chastity, Atlanta's carpetbaggers, Charleston gentility— and how to persuade her heroine to skip the country so as to put distance between Mitchell-land and Ripleyland.

"I'd always felt comfortable with Rhett and not just because he is a Charlestonian," she said. "His dialogue is the way I think—even if I'm not skilled enough to talk like that. He has a lovely sense of self-mockery. Though he's more of a realist than we are, he is romantic—and kind as I would like to be."

Ripley found "Scarlett took some getting used to."

Early in the writing she told a friend Scarlett was giving her trouble. "She's the kind of person I would least like to have lunch with." The friend said, "Well, you don't have to have lunch with her—or even like her—you have to learn to love her." Ripley came to agree. "It meant rereading 'Gone With the Wind' once more, trying in my head to recognize and feel the pressure that made her do the things she did. There are moments when she has pangs of conscience—one nice quiet moment when she thinks, "I wish I had been nicer to Frank" [Scarlett's second husband].

"Indeed, I did learn to love her. And I found she's fun to write because of her energy and impetuosity. She lends herself to great plot development because she acts first and thinks later—if at all. Mind you, I still wouldn't want to have lunch with Scarlett."

Of all the characters, Ripley most identifies with Ashley, the Southern-beau ideal, faithful to his wife, his honor, his state. A warrior against his will. "I often feel as Ashley did that the world has changed and left me behind. I get angry when people call him a wimp," she said. "He was holding on to a noble ideal. He had great psychic strength. But he is so out of joint with the times we live in." Beginning today, Ripley will need all her wit—and all her Southern command of socially acceptable excuses—to explain 490 pages of her 823-page sequel. In them, Scarlett's Irish O'Hara relatives conspire to ship her from Savannah to Ireland with guns for insurrections hidden in her gowns. In her Irish adventures, she buys the O'Hara land, a legendary fiefdom of patrons and peasants, as a place to rear the daughter Rhett does not know she has borne him.

"I tried to write the first section as close as I could come to Margaret Mitchell's style," Ripley said. (She tends to call the author of the original book by both names, a Southern habit.) Indeed, a true Southerner had best read the first section with a box of tissues to hand. Ripley has said she read "GWTW" through at least six times and even copied by hand several hundred pages "to get the feel of her prose in my fingers."

"But the last half is more my book" and her own characters: a conspiratorial cleric, a Gaelic witch, a London lord—and a bookish nanny whom Scarlett sends to the United States in the hopes she'll marry Ashley.

The idea for Scarlett to go to Ireland came, Ripley said, when "I was desperate. I had a contract to write the book. I read the history of the period. And it was the dullest time in the history of the United States. The Panic was the important thing going on. I read six books about economics. My husband brought home a university economics professor to explain the Panic to me. The more I listened, the more I didn't understand. Nothing else was going on. So I moved on to Europe—unrest in the Balkans. I thought I'd grow cotton in Yugoslavia."

Nothing struck or even nudged her fancy. Then she came across a reference in a history book to "peasants in Ireland, burning barns and cutting cows' throats. . . ."

"I felt like God had given me a gift-wrapped package. So I started going through 'GWTW.' And I kept seeing Scarlett's Irish half referred to. Rhett kept bringing it up. So I read lots of books about Ireland of the period. And my husband and I went over for five weeks."

Daughter of the South

Ripley is to the manner—if not the manor—born. "My parents were Old Charleston, but not Great Old Charleston," she said. Her father was an insurance man—he started "by collecting a dime a week" from the insured.

Even so, Ripley likes her hometown. "Charleston is so nice, it didn't matter officially who was rich or poor. Those who were rich did their damnedest not to look it, because that meant you didn't lose your money in the Civil War—you were on the wrong side."

Ripley's aunt, the designated family historian, documented the Confederate veteran ancestor, Archibald, who made Ripley eligible for a United Daughters of the Confederacy scholarship to Vassar College.

When she came home after her freshman year, Ripley related, her mother said she was sorry, they couldn't afford to send her back to Vassar and give her a debutante party too. "She thought I would say, 'Oh, that's all right, I'll take the party.' " Not so. She graduated with a major in Russian, then worked as a publisher's publicity director and as an airline clerk.

Ripley married a small record company owner in 1958 and divorced him in 1963 after having two daughters. She was married again 11 years ago to a University of Virginia professor.

She wrote her first book as a student at Vassar. It was about how everybody would love each other if they could communicate. "And then I read a book review saying all first novels were about people communicating," she said. "I tore my book up."

Ripley wrote her second in 1972, "Who's That Lady in the President's Bed." "Dirty title, clean book, about a woman president," she said. "After that, I wrote a couple novels no one wanted to publish. They're in the attic. I could sell them now," she chortled.

When her novels didn't sell, Ripley moved from New York to Virginia, where rents and cigarettes were cheaper. "A carton was $2.50 then, $12.50 now." While she was working for minimum wage in a B. Dalton bookstore, she went to New York and had a drink with her former editor. The editor said she was looking for a big Southern historical novel. Ripley said, "Do you know where I'm from?" The editor asked, "How soon can you get me an outline?" Ripley retorted, "How soon can you get me a check?" "Within 24 hours."

Ripley promptly spent the advance, wrote "Charleston," borrowed $500 from a bank to pay her rent until the final payment on publication day in 1981. And she dedicated the book to the bank official who had lent her the money.

The Reconstruction

Ripley, who like Mitchell learned her trade listening to relatives tell stories about ancestors "gathered to Abraham's bosom," admitted that "I do talk in a rich, verbose way."

To cut the cream, she writes with a pen, not a computer, "because that way my hand gets tired before I write too fulsomely." Puns, author's asides, funny remarks—she edits them out of her manuscripts as she writes. She's not as sparing in speech. Her most famous current line: "Margaret Mitchell is a better writer than I, but she's dead."

After Ripley agreed to write the book, the estate paid her $25,000 for the outline. She also gets 15 percent of the $4.9 million advance, the sales, the doll babies, the movie rights and whatever else the hype produces. In the immortal words of Scarlett she need "never be hungry again."

Ripley got along with the Mitchell nephews well. "They approved the outline. They were gentlemen, I am a lady. We had no disagreements."

Before they've even read the book, critics and skeptics have worn out their quips; they've applied to the sequel Rhett Butler's famous dismissal of Scarlett, "My dear, I don't give a damn." (The movie added the "frankly.") Macmillan Publishing Co., publisher of "Gone With the Wind," is sending out postcards saying, "Accept No Substitute," over a reproduction of the original book's cover. Gossip has thrived like kudzu in Georgia about the publisher's rejection of the first draft, and the decision to bring in editor Jeanne Bernkopf.

Ripley says she won the war. She speaks with derision of the publisher's critique of her first draft. To hear her tell it, she had to fend off a corps of editors bent on the reconstruction of her book.

"They wanted me to send Scarlett and Rhett out to California! They said that 'Gone With the Wind' was irrelevant to the sequel! And while they didn't come out and say it needed more sex, when they got to the sex scene on the beach, they wrote 'At last! At last! This is what we need!' Their critique was screamingly funny. At the time it wasn't screamingly funny. It was so dead wrong, I was livid. By extension they were prepared to trash 'Gone With the Wind.' I said, 'This isn't editing, it's insulting and ignorant attacks on the manuscript.' "

"I was murderously angry."

She went on strike for four months. "My husband kept me from slashing my wrists." She told her agent she would not speak to "those people." And she demanded "they bring me an editor who loves 'Gone With the Wind.' "

Her agency, William Morris, offered up Jeanne Bernkopf. The freelance editor has worked on such bestsellers as Kitty Kelley's biographies of Frank Sinatra and Nancy Reagan, as well as "Whirlwind" by James Clavell.

Bernkopf said she was chosen by agreement of the agents, the Mitchell estate and Warner because the book "needed a lot of editorial time." She explained her role this way: "I'm a book doctor—it's midwifery, being there, deep collaboration."

For about a year, the two worked the sequel over. Bernkopf said she gave solutions and ideas, but "it's the author's book."

Warner officials would rather not think about the first draft, today or tomorrow, and politely laugh at a Publishers Weekly report that said a Warner editor criticized the first version as "too Southern."

"I don't think anyone told her that 'GWTW' was irrelevant," Warner publisher Nansy Neiman said. "I think the PW story was a case of other people looking for mischief. Alexandra was chosen for her very Southernness." Neiman said she always had faith in the book and the author's ability. "She worked like hell. It took a little longer than we'd hoped." (The publishing date was pushed back by more than a year by the controversy.)

"I got the book I wanted," Ripley said. "Warner sends me flowers a lot. No one wants to risk my having a fit."

And now more than five years since she began, she's off on the month-long book tour. Before the tour started, Warner sent Ripley 5,000 book plates to autograph. In New York, 25 boxes were delivered to her hotel room to sign for the Southeastern Booksellers Association convention.

Sunday night Ripley received a standing ovation from the association in Atlanta after she "ranted and raved about publishers and how they don't care about writers. After all, at this stage, what could Warner say? 'We don't want to publish your book?' "

Mitchell's Ghost

Those who carry away copies of "Scarlett" from their bookstores will doubtless spend the night finding out if Rhett and Scarlett live happily ever after. But for Ripley, the question is: Will she?

"It's scary," she said. Considering all those Yankee dollars you'd think Ripley would be as happy as one of her fictional debutantes at a St. Cecilia's ball in Charleston. And mostly she is.

But she is haunted by the specter of Margaret Mitchell. What's really worrying her is that "Margaret Mitchell never had any fun" with all her money and all her fame. "It was the greatest success of all time, and all she got was a mink coat," Ripley said.

For one thing, Ripley remembers that Mitchell was beset by her fans. The picture she draws seems to suggest that they tore Mitchell's life into as many pieces as The War did Scarlett's. Ripley has become frightened of anyone knowing the location of her home, a 1740 restored tavern outside Charlottesville.

Even so, Ripley thinks that the end of Scarlett's story hasn't been written nor does she intend to. "I left the story so that Scarlett's about 35. I think I did something very clever."

That's plenty of time for her to win and lose Ashley, Rhett and any number of husbands several times before she settles down to be the Widow Whoever. But then, somebody else can think of that tomorrow.

It Was a Good Hear

GAIL FORMAN

L iving in "double time," call it. I get twice as much out of my day as I did before
I discovered the pleasures of listening to books recorded on tape—and I feel a
lot happier and calmer, too. It is no exaggeration to say that discovering audio books
has changed my life.

Before I started listening three years ago, I felt frustrated about how few books
I had time to read. I'd fume as I sat stuck in my car during rush hour. I'd rage as I
wasted precious moments doing dishes or laundry. As an English teacher with an
abiding love for literature, I often felt as I imagine a drug addict does without a
"fix." I craved what kept me going but just couldn't get enough. The days were too
short and I had too much work to do to find the time to sit down and read a novel
"just for fun."

When I did read for relaxation, the piles of newspapers, magazines and journals
took precedence over novels, plays or poetry. I felt keenly the truth of Wordsworth's
immortal words, "The world is too much with us; late and soon, / Getting and
spending, we lay waste our powers."

Nostalgic memories of my youth kept popping up, a time when I thought
nothing of whiling away a Sunday afternoon deep in Madame Bovary or Middle-
march, when I would stay up late into the night reading the Magic Mountain, when
a leisurely bath meant an opportunity to loll in the tub with the Karamazov brothers.
For years, though, my Sundays have been devoted to correcting student essays,
while the only reading I do late at night is preparation for the next day's classes. And
it's pretty hard to read a book during a quick shower.

When a friend suggested that I try renting taped books, I demurred. I like to
read books, not hear stories. I don't approve of "painless learning." I like classics, I
don't read "trash" and I abhor condensed anything. Nor am I good at taking in
information aurally, I protested. I don't think I could pay attention. Besides, it
wouldn't be as satisfying as reading, I objected.

But out of desperation, I decided to give it a try. I called Books on Tape, a
California outfit with an inventory of more than 2,000 unabridged recorded books,
a mixture of classics and contemporary, fiction and nonfiction. I ordered *Out of
Africa,* one of the masterpieces I had always wanted to read but never got around to
starting although it has been sitting on my shelf for years. Since this was pre-Meryl

Streep/Robert Redford, I hadn't been able to substitute seeing the movie for reading the book.

Springing for first class postage, I received my "book" in two days. A compact box of nine 1 1/2-hour tapes arrived, pre addressed and post paid for the return trip. When I was finished, all I needed to do was seal the box and drop it in the nearest mailbox.

With trepidation and curiosity, I turned on the first tape. "I had a farm in Africa at the foot of the Ngong hills," the mellifluous voice of reader Wanda McCaddon began, and my life has not been the same since. Now I'm never without a taped book, and I live what I call the "expanded day" aspect of life.

With my Walkman on my belt and my earphones plugged in, I listen as I race around doing housework—washing laundry, preparing salads, cleaning up the dinner table, even vacuuming no longer seem onerous chores. Whereas I always used to be in a snit when I performed these necessary but unrewarding jobs—and pity the person who got in my way while I did them—now I almost look forward to them as an excuse to continue hearing an especially interesting section of a taped book.

I listen in my car and don't mind the commute to work. I purchased a tiny tabletop speaker to be able to listen to my Walkman without earphones, too. I listen while I ride my exercise cycle and find the tapes actually an incentive to do so. I haven't figured out a way to listen while I use my hair dryer, but I do listen as I apply my makeup and no longer wish it could be tattooed on my face to save time.

Though I would never just sit down to listen to a book, not when I could be reading, listening, it turns out, can be as pleasurable as reading—different but with its own rewards. As it would be if I were reading a great novel, another world is available to me through a recorded book, with the difference that I do not have to suspend daily tasks to get to it. No matter how fragmented my day, no matter how many conflicts, I know that when I get in my car to drive home, I can turn on the book and there is continuity. Chaotic thoughts give way to calmness, and I'm glad for the escape.

At other times, in contrast, the sound of silence is important, so when I find my mind drifting, I know that I need to pay attention to what's going on in my own head. That's when I turn off the machine and give reign to my own thoughts.

To people who worry about the "dangers" of having a tape going while driving or doing other risky tasks, I reply that it's no different from listening to the news on the radio. I hear the book but I also pay attention to the road, and when something requires my full awareness, I unconsciously tune out the audio. The nice part is the ease with which I can rewind the tape if I've lost the thread, though I find that if it's a good book I've chosen, I'm a better listener than I expected to be.

Thanks to recorded books, I have experienced a new relationship with the human voice, and I love the sound of the different readers' accents and intonations. Mostly the people who read unabridged books are professionals, though not usually famous actors and not the authors themselves. Sometimes I practice imitating their sounds or trying out different ways of emphasizing certain passages, for every reading is an interpretation.

And I feel an unmatched intimacy with a book whose words enter my head through my earphones. After all, language is primarily sound, and when a well-written book is read aloud, each word counts, as it should. If the reader is fine, the language of the work—poetry or prose—shines. An example is Dem Cheng's Life and Death in Shanghai, which I heard a few weeks ago. This harrowing tale of one victim's heroism during the Cultural Revolution in China, a best-seller, is beautifully described by the author's tough but lyrical prose. The reading by Penelope Dellaporta perfectly corresponds to my imagined idea of the way Cheng, now a Washington resident, must sound in Chinese.

Since 1985 I have heard more than 70 books on tape. Some are old friends I'd never gotten around to rereading—all of Jane Austen's novels, for example, also Jane Eyre, Hard Times, Jude the Obscure and Cry, the Beloved Country. Others are new works that had passed me by when they first came out. That's how I discovered the genius of John Gardner—and went through October Light, The Sunlight Dialogues, Grendel and others—and Larry McMurtry, especially Lonesome Dove. Because I sometimes exchange tapes with friends to keep the cost down (rented tapes average around $15, about the price of a new hardcover novel), I've enjoyed books I never would have ordered on my own: The Manticore, The Left Hand of Darkness. Biographies such as Nabokov's Speak Memory and history books have taken on new interest to me, as have travel accounts such as From Heaven Lake.

Now I am a books on tape evangelist. I go around preaching the importance of making the most of our time on earth. I search out my subjects with keen insight because the type of person who likes to listen to audio books is hard to define. According to the president of the Maryland-based Recorded Books company, Henry Trentman, "the common denominator is an active mind—manic people who like to keep their minds occupied." So if you see me waxing eloquent at a party, it's a safe bet that I'm extolling the virtues of audio books. And I modestly admit that I've made my share of converts.

Last year when I visited my sister in Chicago, I told her about my passion and tried to persuade her to try it, but she put up all the same arguments against it that I had mustered before I converted. I could see by the expression on her face that she thought I had fallen over the edge, and I could also see that she had no intention of taking my good advice despite my repeated efforts to bring her into the fold.

A month later my sister called to say she had just finished her first taped book. "You have given me the best gift I have ever received," she said. "You've shown me how to make my day seem longer, how to enjoy the literature I love but haven't had time for and, most of all, how to calm myself when I am angry. Now I don't yell at my family when I'm doing mindless tasks, and I hardly mind doing the dishes. My rage level is much lower. Thank you."

Washingtonian Flo Gibson, reader extraordinaire who started her own company (Audio Book Contractors) a few years ago—after many years as a reader for other commercial companies and for the Library of Congress "Talking Books" program—considers audio books perfect for times "when hands and eyes are occupied but the mind isn't." They give book lovers a marvelous opportunity to reread classics, catch up on more recent titles and discover new authors.

Magazines   3

The Cold World of Hot Magazines

HOWARD KURTZ

In the weeks before he took over as editor of New York magazine, Kurt Andersen began making a list of the hottest writers around—those who could turn out the "big blockbuster pieces" and "agenda-setting essays" and "breathtaking pieces of criticism" he wanted.

Unfortunately for many of New York's staffers, their names were not on the list.

Kay Larson, the magazine's art critic for 14 years, got a brief fax from Andersen, telling her she was out. Rhoda Koenig, the book critic for 17 years, was also fired by fax. Within a few weeks of taking charge in February, Andersen had dismissed or eased out many of the journalists hired by his predecessor, Edward Kosner.

"If Kurt had treated me like a human being and just taken me to lunch and poured me a stiff drink, I would've said, 'Okay, that's the way it goes,' " Larson says. Instead, he was "abrupt and hostile. . . . It's in Kurt's interest to try to terrorize New York magazine to the maximum extent possible so all of Ed's people will leave."

Andersen's flurry of moves is part of a musical-chairs minuet that has transfixed the gossipy magazine community here, with each move endlessly dissected over power lunches at 44 or the Royalton. Everyone understands that the genteel days of lifetime loyalty to a single publication are gone, replaced by a sizzling free-agent market in which each player looks to cut the best deal. Big-name editors change places every few seasons, casting off veteran staffers as if they were political appointees from a defeated administration.

For two years now, the action has been a blur: Andersen, who used to run Spy, jumps from Time to New York. Kosner leaves New York for Esquire. Tina Brown, a glittering success at Vanity Fair, takes over the New Yorker. Graydon Carter, Andersen's old partner at Spy, hops from the New York Observer to Vanity Fair.

In the '90s magazine world, the editor is the star, the draw, the outsize personality who can turn a lukewarm publication into the proverbial hot book. And the editor does this by amassing a stable of well-known writers, working the social circuit and marketing the hell out of the product.

"It is your canvas, with all these people painting bits of the canvas," Andersen says.

He doesn't deny that he botched things by faxing employees their dismissals and leaking the news to the New York Times. "It's horrible to fire people, and it's made more horrible when it doesn't happen smoothly and quietly," says Andersen, a foot-high pile of resumes littering the floor of his Second Avenue office. "I hope I've learned how to do it better." But, he says, "people should expect that they might not necessarily stay when a new editor comes in."

Andersen has given pink slips to media columnist Edwin Diamond, advertising columnist Bernice Kanner and financial writer Christopher Byron, among others. At the same time, he has hired Jacob Weisberg of the New Republic as political columnist, Jon Katz of Rolling Stone as media columnist, Michael Hirschorn of Esquire as executive editor, Sarah Jewler of the Village Voice as managing editor, Tad Friend of Esquire as a feature writer, Mark Stevens of the New Republic as art critic and Walter Kirn, late of Elle and Mirabella, as book critic.

Andersen has also ticked off his predecessor by disparaging the magazine he inherited. After he told interviewers that New York magazine seemed to be put out by "slightly clueless outsiders" and badly needed a redesign, Kosner sent Andersen a tart note asking him to stop misrepresenting the magazine's record.

New editors at other magazines have taken a more gradual approach to change. "There's a natural inclination to say I want to fire everyone and bring in my own team," says Carter, sitting beneath a huge reproduction of Jodie Foster's face on a Vanity Fair cover. "I sort of go counter to that. . . . I wanted to keep the assets here and bring in new assets."

Carter has attracted some big names—the Wall Street Journal's Bryan Burrough, Newsweek sportswriter Frank Deford, the Nation's Christopher Hitchens—while replacing 40 percent of Vanity Fair's staff over two years. "It's a pretty big magazine," Carter says. "You don't want to muck around with it too much."

Kosner, a former editor of Newsweek, has his own group of loyalists. "In a tough advertising environment, part of the editor's appeal is they can bring talent with them," he says.

When he left New York, Kosner took along feature writer Julie Baumgold (no surprise there—she's his wife), political writer John Taylor, gossip columnist Jeannette Walls, Chris Byron and fashion writer Michael Gross. Kosner has imported tabloid veteran Pete Hamill, Rolling Stone celebrity writer Bill Zehme and ex-Spy man Jamie Malanowski.

Tina Brown is also steeped in this tradition. When she moved to the New Yorker in the summer of 1992, Brown brought some of her A-list writers—Marie Brenner, Peter Boyer, James Wolcott—and her publicist, Maurie Perl. She raided the New Republic for Executive Editor Hendrik Hertzberg and Washington correspondent Sidney Blumenthal, and hired David Remnick from The Washington Post and James Stewart from the Wall Street Journal. Fifteen people, including such stalwarts as Elizabeth Drew, were cut loose, underscoring the downside of the new mobility.

"It's tough on older people to live with that degree of insecurity," Jake Weisberg says. "It's making magazine journalism more of a young person's game."

This revolving-door journalism is very different from the more stable environment of newspapers, where most jobs are protected by union rules. When Joe Lelyveld succeeds Max Frankel as editor of the New York Times this summer, for example, no one will lose his job. But then, the Times isn't marketed as a collection of "hot" writers, while magazines splash their authors' names on the cover as if they were as important as the celebrities and trends they chronicle.

The Editor as Avatar

Ed Kosner comes right to the point: "The world being what it is, I have to blow you off for Charlie Rose."

Kosner is canceling lunch with a reporter, and the reason is self-evident: He's not about to pass up a chance to tout his new magazine on Rose's TV show.

"The marketplace is so crowded and the competition is so fierce—not only among magazines but between magazines and newspapers, magazines and television, magazines and MTV—that you have to be able to embody the sensibility of the magazine," Kosner says. "You're part of the promotion."

Most editors relish this high-profile role. Esquire sends Kosner's picture and bio to reporters along with his first issue. Carter's publicist leaks Vanity Fair's juiciest celebrity tidbits to selected newspapers just before publication. Andersen uses an outside PR firm. Television ads tout "the new New Yorker, edited by Tina Brown," and advance copies are hand-delivered to movers and shakers each Sunday.

It was Brown who took the concept of writer-as-star to new heights at Vanity Fair, luring top journalists with unheard-of fees (as much as $20,000 an article) and running their pictures in the magazine. But the biggest star was Brown herself, who wrote a monthly "Editor's Letter" (adorned with a little sketch of her), regularly graced the gossip columns and was profiled by "60 Minutes."

Brown says she initially promoted herself "because the magazine was failing so desperately. There wasn't anything to do except trot the editor out."

These days, she says, "I don't do nearly as much promotion as you might imagine. I've never been on 'Charlie Rose,' but all my writers have. I try to push the writers out there because I want attention for the articles. We can't deny this helps sell magazines."

Lavish entertaining has become a way of life for editors trying to make their mark. At Academy Awards time, Brown and Carter (whose magazines are both owned by Si Newhouse) found themselves throwing dueling Hollywood parties. Brown's soirée was to promote a special issue on the movies.

"It spoke volumes to big potential advertisers in L.A. that a magazine that does not have celebrity covers could draw guests of the caliber of Streisand, Barry Diller and Whoopi Goldberg," Brown says. "It made a statement that the magazine is modern and in the action."

Carter's glitzy gathering (which warrants a 19-picture spread in the June issue) came a week later. "We had Lee Iacocca, Prince, Nancy Reagan, Tom Cruise, James Carville and Mary Matalin all at the same party," he says. "That's a Vanity Fair party. It's an ineffable thing, but it shows that this magazine is different from everything else. . . . It's a glamorous magazine."

(Some of the glamour may have been missing. A Vanity Fair staffer told the Observer that Carter's people were "not exactly happy" that Roseanne Arnold, Demi Moore and Jack Nicholson didn't show: "We may think twice before we give them another cover.")

Carter, who also threw a Beltway bash after last month's White House Correspondents' Dinner, says he has no desire to be a celebrity editor. "It works well for Tina," he says. "It may work better for a woman than a man because they can be more glamorously clever. I'm not going to dye my hair blond and put on pumps and run around the office."

While Carter, in his Spy incarnation, delighted in ridiculing Donald Trump, he showed up at the Trump-Marla Maples wedding. (What a coincidence: The couple soon made the cover of Vanity Fair, while Andersen put Maples on New York's cover.)

"Getting good tables at restaurants is fun," Andersen says. "Some fraction of the job is party-hosting, gala-attending, midtown-public-figure kind of thing." But, he says, "there's a danger and temptation of that becoming the end rather than the means."

As for the writers on this magazine merry-go-round, many of them are happy to peddle their services to the highest bidder. Weisberg, for one, says a regular New York column is a "better showcase" than occasional articles in the New Republic.

Jon Katz had a different reason for leaving Rolling Stone. "I've been sort of waiting for Andersen to get a magazine," he says. "He was the big lure. If he left next week, I'd certainly be interested in where he was going."

John Taylor says his friendship with Kosner was paramount. "The writer's loyalty is to the editor because you have no relationship with this remote corporate shell that controls the finances of the magazine," he says. "You develop a relationship with an editor who likes you, and you tend to follow him the way book writers follow editors who jump from house to house."

Fueling the Buzz Machine

As the dust settles, each magazine is undergoing an identity transplant. Andersen's New York is running more new age fare (holistic healing, a "Miracle Cure" finger-waving therapy). Kosner's Esquire has added more service features (everything you wanted to know about sexual performance, hair and golf). Brown's New Yorker serves up more sex (Heidi Fleiss, sex in cinema, priests who like young boys) and stories pegged to breaking news (Whitewater, Oliver North, Bob Packwood).

"Vanity Fair was about the things that interested me that month," Brown says. But she says she was able to slip in serious articles while using a "Kevin Costner cover" as "reader seduction and bait. At the New Yorker, my challenge is to run 45,000 words by Mark Danner on El Salvador and make it sell."

Making it sell, of course, is the bottom line. But the advertising community, like the stock market, moves in strange and mysterious ways, embracing a publication one year and cooling on it the next.

The Madison Avenue buzz about Vanity Fair has not been good (one writer fired by Carter has dubbed it "Vanishing Flair"). While circulation (now 1.2 million) is up marginally, ad pages dropped nearly 20 percent last year. The conventional wisdom is that Carter has let Brown's winning formula go stale.

"This magazine was absolutely hers in the '80s, but it's a different time now and the magazine has had to make the transition to the '90s," Carter says. While courting tastemakers and advertisers is important, he says, this media elite should not be confused with the real world. "When Spy was at its hottest, we lost more money than at any other period," he says.

Carter says he has run more Washington stories, sports features and "staggeringly thorough" profiles of Yasser Arafat and Fidel Castro. Still, the Vanity Fair issue in which Castro was interviewed had Donald and Marla and Baby Tiffany on the cover.

Brown has boosted the New Yorker's advertising by 10 percent and circulation from 628,000 to 809,000, and the magazine is livelier and more topical than in the past. The paradox is that it is losing millions of dollars, although Brown predicts it will turn a profit in the next few years.

"We think we might even get there by the end of next year, although I may regret saying that," she says. "It was losing an enormous amount of money when I took over. I can't make a miracle."

Circulation has been flat at Esquire (737,000) and at New York (434,000), but Kosner has the greater rescue mission. Esquire's ad pages dropped by more than 10 percent last year, and the magazine seemed to lose its identity under former editor Terry McDonell. Kosner is quick to note that his first issue, with Tom Cruise on the cover, sold particularly well at the newsstands.

All of which underscores the need for an editor who knows how to generate good buzz. But Tina Brown, the acknowledged master of the art, says the notion of self-promotion is oversold.

"Buzz is about the content of the magazine," she says. "No amount of promotion can get you a writer on TV unless the piece is hot. Editors who think they can add a good public relations department and everything will change are kidding themselves."

Here at the New New Yorker

CHARLES TRUEHEART

Anyone wondering what Tina Brown means to inflict upon The New Yorker will not have to wait long for answers. The first issue bearing her stamp, dated Oct. 5, appears Monday. The cover illustration, the new editor says, will convey "impishness." The table of contents henceforth "will tell you what the stories are about"—and she laughs that anyone would find this revolutionary. There will be bylines at the tops of many stories, rather than signatures at the end. Look for a new back-page humor feature. Splashes of color. Subheads. Fewer lines to the page. New use of old New Yorker "decorative friezes" atop columns. But no type on the cover. Not yet.

For any other magazine, such tinkering would fall squarely into the realm of so-what and who-cares. But at The New Yorker, it is the beginning of a revolution— "Tinafication" is one word being used—that will push the 67-year-old magazine into a new sensibility and, its owner fervently hopes, a new prosperity.

"The New Yorker has skipped a generation of readers," those her age and younger, declares the 38-year-old Briton, who turned Vanity Fair into the golden egg-layer of the Conde Nast magazine empire. "We don't read The New Yorker the way our parents did."

Still sitting amid packing boxes in spare temporary offices, Brown is matter-of-fact about her distaste—and, one can infer, the distaste of owner S. I. Newhouse— for what The New Yorker still clings to, even after five years of editor Robert Gottlieb's leavening influences.

"Statuesque" and "daunting" are two of the words she uses in an interview to describe the magazine she inherits this week.

Brown is not chary of saying what many readers (and many advertisers) have come to believe: that the articles are too long. She speaks of adding "rhythm" and "mix" to the magazine, but she says more concretely that while two- and three- and five- and even eight-thousand-word articles will find a home in her New Yorker, 20,000-word stories will not. To say nothing of 60,000-word three-parters, such as the one by New Yorker legend John McPhee that concludes in Gottlieb's final issue (Sept. 28).

This is a credo of revolutionary intent, for the New Yorker tradition is founded on, among other things, very long articles. Those that dwelled on arcana helped turn a once-revered form—the novella of nonfiction, in one New Yorker writer's phrase—into a caricature of ponderousness and prolixity.

She wants the magazine to be "reader-friendly," she says. "I hate the word," but she uses it anyway. Worthiness is not enough; worthiness just sits in stacks, unread.

From the day of her appointment, however, Brown has insisted that she does not plan to remake The New Yorker in the image of Vanity Fair, another Newhouse property.

"People assume that if you've done one thing you'll do it again. When I was handed Vanity Fair, it was a glossy Conde Nast magazine. . . . If I'd been handed the [London] Times Literary Supplement—I could have done that too, if you know what I mean. I've got five or six magazines in my head, and they're not all the same." The New Yorker, she says, "is very much a reader's magazine. That's its currency. . . . I think it's very important to preserve that reading-room atmosphere."

Such ambiguous comforts aside, the mere announcement of Brown's impending arrival has bewitched the advertising community. Proving the power of suggestion—and of Brown's reputation as the creator of the "hot book" of the 1980s, Vanity Fair—Madison Avenue has fattened her first issue with 85 pages of ads, more than twice the number The New Yorker has been accustomed to lately.

A very happy publisher, Steven Florio, says he and his people are busy reassuring advertisers that The New Yorker will still be The New Yorker. But surely they must be reassuring them of just the opposite. Well, he says, some of both.

Tinafication has been swift inside the magazine's West 43rd Street offices—and in some old-guard quarters, traumatic. Within days of her appointment in June, Brown's PR apparatus was announcing the acquisition of new writers and editors, many of them members of Brown's Vanity Fair entourage. (All three of the magazine's previous editors were loath to make any such announcements, let alone speak to reporters.)

Brown brought along her managing editor, Pamela Maffei McCarthy, and two of her senior editors, Kim Heron and Virginia Cannon. Reportedly she has given six-figure contracts—seldom known at The New Yorker—to such Vanity Fair scribes as James Wolcott, Peter Boyer, Stephen Schiff and Marie Brenner. John Lahr will become theater critic, displacing Gottlieb-hire Mimi Kramer. Other critics are talking as if their days are numbered.

One Gottlieb-era writer who's been asked to stay on says even "freaked-out" colleagues are reserving judgment, perhaps because they have no plausible alternatives. "People feel she's got something special—the Tina juju—so they want to stick around. Just out of curiosity." Another New Yorker writer says he feels like a dinosaur and is beginning to think about a life outside The New Yorker.

One of the first to feel an ax blade was Elizabeth Drew, The New Yorker's longtime Washington correspondent, who will become an occasional contributor after the November elections. Her successor is another of Brown's Vanity Fair contributors, Sidney Blumenthal, who will head a list of Washington contributors.

Brown's determination to better cover Powertown is clear in her choice of a new executive editor, Hendrik Hertzberg. The former Jimmy Carter speechwriter and editor of the New Republic will be focusing his attention on—and frequently writing—The New Yorker's "Notes and Comment," or editorial, pages.

Just as striking, but as yet not on board, was her choice to edit the magazine's signature "Talk of the Town" section. He's another Briton, Alexander Chancellor, formerly editor of Britain's Spectator and the Independent newspaper's Sunday magazine.

When he arrives in a month, Brown said, Chancellor will put so-called "Talk" items—brief pieces of reportage, soon to be much briefer—"through his type-writer." Brown offered Chancellor's current Independent column of ruminations, musings and asides—signed "The Weasel"—as an approximation of what the new New Yorker's voice might sound like. "Very sharp and at the same time very friendly," she calls it.

Brown says she and Chancellor have been debating what to do about the editorial "we" that has long been the voice of "Talk of the Town"—what Hertzberg, a onetime Talk writer himself, calls "the baffled naif."

Brown declares: "We don't want to be 'we' anymore . . . We don't really like 'we.' " She replays some emblematic dialogue with Chancellor. He asks: "If I'm 'I,' who am I? Am I Eustace Tilley?" Brown giggles. "Noooo, you are not Eustace Tilley." Poor Tilley is the monocled mascot of The New Yorker.

So—Brown is asked—will "friends" still "write"?

"No, friends will not write," she replies. The "A friend writes . . ." rubric, which allows a Talk piece to employ the more natural first person, is both unnecessary and "arch," Brown says. "John Updike will write when it's our friend from Massachusetts."

Gottlieb, who went to The New Yorker after a long career as head of Alfred A. Knopf, still another Newhouse property, has gone quietly, without apparent acrimony. The cover of his last issue is a bit of Gottliebian whimsy: Cinderella fleeing at midnight toward her pumpkin. He has announced no professional plans.

Choreographer Paul Taylor threw his friend Gottlieb a going-away party last Friday, reportedly a bittersweet affair for the staff in attendance. Yet Gottlieb's appointment in 1987, following the clumsily harsh dismissal of William Shawn, had been greeted with all bitter and no sweet—notably a petition to Newhouse signed by 143 New Yorker staffers demanding that the decision be rescinded.

Gottlieb, in time, proved himself a champion of The New Yorker's many virtues, and certainly of its writers and editors. In retrospect, those who admire him see him as a natural successor to Shawn and founder Harold Ross, and no longer regard him as the kitsch-prone bomb-thrower they had once imagined.

In Hertzberg's opinion, "the staff wants a lot more change now than it did five years ago." And Gottlieb, in this view, has made it easier for Tina to be Tina. "He demystified The New Yorker," says Hertzberg. "He changed it from a church into a magazine again."

Others, who wish Gottlieb had done more to change the magazine, believe he became a captive of the institution. If anyone will test the hypothesis that The New Yorker is bigger and stronger than its editor, it is Tina Brown, for whom the expression "tough as nails" could have been coined.

Those who have worked with her over the years—after stipulating her brilliance—describe her as managing by intimidation more than collegiality, and by frenzy more than process: driving her subordinates crazy with questions and worries and changes of mind, adopting favorite writers with a passion and dropping them just as quickly.

"She's happy to treat you like a star," according to one New Yorker writer, "but she doesn't want to treat you like an artist." The distinction between the perceived sensibilities of the old and the new New Yorkers could not be more aptly made.

But to hear Brown tell it, the incumbent writers at the magazine are responding with alacrity to her wishes—for instance, her desire to publish more and shorter pieces. "These are people who have three strings to their bow, and they're only using one string. They can write shorter, and they want to."

The move from Vanity Fair to The New Yorker, Brown says, has "liberated" her, and not just from the boredom that had beset her after eight years.

She claims to feel liberated from Vanity Fair's driving emphasis on the visual, and even the artistic staples of The New Yorker have opened new doors of perception to her. She is sticking with the hoary New Yorker tradition of cover illustrations that bear no relation to any of the magazine's contents; in part, she says, that's because of the talent she is beginning to find. "I thought it was a dead art, and I was completely wrong about that."

Photographs will begin to take their place on the inside pages of the magazine—often as full pages—but not, she says, on the cover. "Every time you put a photograph on the cover it doesn't look like The New Yorker."

Cover lines advertising the contents of the issue are also a wait-and-see proposition. It is technologically possible to use cover type on just the copies intended for newsstand sales, and Brown and Florio would like to be selling 100,000 a week on the newsstand—five times the current number. It's that minority of impulse readers (as distinct from paid subscribers, who now number around 600,000) that matters to advertisers.

Brown also wants to quell rumors that she intends to spend her way to success by hiring the best talent at any cost, a habit that helped her make her mark at Vanity Fair. "I've walked away from several arrangements [with writers] because I can't compete with Vanity Fair. Which is kind of funny—this monster I created."

She goes on: "The fact is that the choice to work at The New Yorker isn't just based on money. And—you're going to get the best editing you can get anywhere."

The Time It Is A-Changin' Magazines

WILLIAM CASEY

Newsmags

I was excited to hear that Time magazine was available on-line to personal computer users. Most excellent. Visions of a multimedia Time rose up, complete with sound bites, video insets and all the rest.

Wow.

Quick as a wink, I dialed up America Online from my home computer. Once I was connected, powerful-looking colorful icons populated my screen.

America Online is considered state of the art when it comes to on-line services, so I was viewing the best, or close to it. Additional attractive icons appeared: bulletin boards, letters to the editor, access to past issues as well as a list of current articles, all available with a click on my mouse. I called up a story.

Disappointment. I know Time, Time is a good friend of mine, and this is no Time.

Each article I requested was, after the wait necessary for the phone line to capture it, displayed as a collection of gray lines. Duller than dull. Deader than a Latin textbook. I wasn't being provided with a Time story at all: I was looking at text from a Time story. For me, it was unsatisfying.

This America Online adventure and a couple of other incidents have made me aware of the vast—and largely unacknowledged—disparity between traditional print media and their new electronic forms. In most ways they're separate products, largely unequal, and do not seek to serve the same audiences.

Many of us think of technology's advance as a one-way street: onward and upward, better and better. Stereo systems improved upon their monaural predecessors in all ways; incompatibilities aside, 5 1/4-inch floppies offered us nothing that 3 1/2-inch high-density diskettes don't provide.

In fact, though, the blessings of new advances are often mixed. We pay a price in some dimension for gains made in another. The view that instantly available on-line magazines represent a great leap forward puzzles me.

Here are some of the advantages I detect in the hard copy issue of Time on my desk:

- It's portable. It fits in my briefcase or folds into a pocket.
- It's readable (if there's enough light). No laptop, desktop, PowerBook, modem, batteries or anything is else needed for proper operation.

- It's disposable. When I'm finished, it's gone or I can pass it on.
- It has it all. Text, photos, graphics, everything. At its best, it's exciting.

The has-it-all category means the most to me. Who doesn't take for granted the richness, the texture, the overall wholeness that speaks to us when we read through printed material?

That wholeness is built into the newspapers and the magazines we read daily: photos, charts, headlines and text, advertising too. The artful and appealing arrangement of components, while part of the background, is nevertheless critical to the reading experience.

The total product reflects hundreds of decisions about page design and other display issues made with the idea of presenting coherence, not just the words of a story, to the reader.

On-line magazines claim their own advantages:

- They are available sooner than printed media. Time is available through America Online by 4 p.m. Sunday; it comes in the mail on Monday or Tuesday. But no one expects the latest ball scores, stock prices or other up-to-the-minute information from magazines, anyway, so why is this significant?
- They let you send electronic mail to editors. This class of benefits includes other interactive doodads such as bulletin boards, chat groups and the like. It's handy to be able to send a piece of electronic mail to query the author of an article.
- Archival access. I can get at text from previous issues via America Online. This might qualify as another marginal plus, especially if I'm writing a term paper or another magazine or newspaper article.
- Promise of a greatly improved product in the future.

Even with their fancy-looking, icon-based front ends, the new on-line services remain rooted in a tradition of electronic library technology, where ability to access electronic archives has been available for more than a decade. But the needs of the electronic researcher are not the needs of someone who wants to flip through magazines.

We are nowhere near where we want to be in terms of on-line access, use and benefit when it comes to publications. At the moment, these limitations are mostly technical, not human: We can't move large amounts of high-resolution graphic material across phone lines and into computers as quickly as we'd like. In the meantime, what we can move isn't exciting compared with the real thing.

We know change in all media—print, audio, video—is coming and coming fast. One periodical that both symbolizes and embodies those advances in media is Wired, the monthly magazine published in San Francisco that describes itself as "a new magazine for the digital generation."

Visually, Wired is a feast for the eyes, with lavish use of color and unusual graphic design. November's issue includes articles about a new media topics, including satellite-based telephones, computer music, on-line education and an appealing piece entitled "The Luckiest Nerds in the World."

Wired, too, is available through American Online, but in the end is given the same dismal treatment as Time: at the level of the individual article, it's just another dreadful screen full of text.

Right now, the most appealing feature of these two magazines at American Online is the button in the lower right of the display screens. Click on the button, and you can sign up for a subscription to the real magazines.

At the moment, that's my choice. — FUNNY —

The Aging of Mad

A Backward Look at the Zany Magazine that Rotted Boomers' Brains

CHARLES TRUEHEART

The instructor is patiently explaining underground comics to a score of young people not yet born when the '60s' twisted pixies plied their terrorist mischief. He tries to explain this piece of ancient history as slides of R. Crumb caricatures and Ramparts posters and San Francisco Oracle psychedelia flash past the faces in the darkened room. And he finishes the spiel by paying tribute to the common ancestor of countercultural satire, Mad magazine.

This last is by way of introducing the instructor's guest for the evening, Maria Reidelbach. As author of "Completely Mad," just out from Little, Brown and already selling out its 30,000 printing, she is the magazine's court historian; she is, too, Alfred E. Neuman's Boswell, a sub-specialty. To this audience of young design students at the School of Visual Arts in Chelsea, she might as well be lecturing on Thomas Nast or William Hogarth. Still, she tries to explain.

"It was a lifeline," Reidelbach says. "Kids couldn't get this stuff anywhere else. Mostly the stuff you could get was 'Archie' or 'Donna Reed.' No one else admitted that kids thought bad things, loved life on the edge."

Perfectly true. Mad was born at the outset of the baby boom and, just as parents feared, rotted a generation's mind. To look at the floppy-footed, slump-shouldered, goggle-eyed antiheroes of Don Martin and Mort Druckert is it any wonder that giggly drugs were such a hit or that '60s' persons ended up looking so . . . unusual? To recall Mad's smart-aleck skepticism, the reflexive suspicion of authority figures and the lampooning of TV and Madison Avenue, is it any wonder segregation, the Vietnam War and conventional middle-class life were so massively resisted?

Having given voice to a generation's contrariness, however, Mad fell away. People got older, Mad seemed sillier, National Lampoon came along and frittered itself away, and then Spy had its ruthless day. But Mad? Kids read Mad. And unlike in the old days, their parents don't mind. Mad is pretty tame. Which may explain why circulation has fallen from 2.4 million two decades ago to 800,000 today, not that 800,000 is anything to sneeze at. On the other hand, you're not likely to run into anyone of a certain age who didn't, once upon a time, turn to Mad for guidance in the art of healthy laughter.

One piece of evidence that Mad is history, paradoxical but unmistakable, is the appearance of Reidelbach's illustrated book (design by Alexander Isley). An authorized effort of which Mad has a financial piece, "Completely Mad" draws for the first time on the magazine's voluminous archives. and displays Mad memorabilia lavishly (reprinting every cover since 1952, for instance). The book's effect on the onetime Maddict is akin to that on Proust as he tasted his, er, Madeleine. It brings back the whole Mad Zeitgeist, with its furshlugginers and potrzebies and axolotls and yecchs, and its regular vehicles for wit ("Spy vs. Spy," "The Lighter Side of . . . ," the song parodies, the primers, the fold-ins), and its random boldfacing of words, the antic tone and droll sympathy have sharpened one's lifetime appreciation for all manner of sharks, bores, idiots and poltroons.

The adult world, especially the world represented in television, was a china shop of hypocrisy, and Mad, its snorting bull. The vanities of the age, and capitalism's seamy underbelly, were sent up in a selection of "dummy status symbols"—fake fins to attach to the car, a fake dormer for the roof, a fake air conditioner in the window. Mad proposed a new divorce-survival merit badge for Boy Scouts. Wondered what it would be like if Chinese people visited an American restaurant (customers to waiter: "What is in 'ham and eggs'?"). Labeled a jar of Tang "Old!" Chose Ringo Starr to illustrate the virtues of Blecch shampoo. Designed a pain reliever ad whose cutaway of a human torso showed, in place of organs, metal pipes and industrial machinery.

As Reidelbach talks about Mad, clicking her slides of these images and captions, the room full of students is otherwise silent. No giggles are muffled.

A slide of "Howdy Dooit"—Mad's savage riff on the '50s kiddie show—appears on the screen.

"Does anybody in this room know who Howdy Doody is?" Reidelbach asks.

Two hands haltingly go up.

Undeterred, Reidelbach goes on. She flashes the originals and reads them the lyrics of Mad's "East Side Story."

"When you're a Red you're a Red all the way from your first party purge to your last power play."

And, as sung by John Kennedy, Adlai Stevenson and Co., "Tonight, tonight, Nikita lost tonight . . ."

The instructor, Reidelbach's host, can't help himself. He's giggling. Alone.

"No, Sir; This Is Fantasy"

The November 1953 issue of Ladies' Home Journal published an alarming report from an influential psychiatrist, Frederic Wertham, detailing the insidious effects of reading comic books. According to "Seduction of the Innocent," horror and crime comics especially caused children to kill and maim themselves and others. Yeow, arghh, thunk, blam, glurg and currack were dangerous words. Batman and Robin were lovers, and Wonder Woman was a lesbian role model!

Funny. But not really so quaint if you listen to the frightened pulse of the heartland today, or recognize the folly of would-be censors on Capitol Hill. In 1953 William M. Gaines certainly did. The publisher of Tales of the Crypt, Weird Fantasy and a year-old satirical comic book called Mad ("Humor in a Jugular Vein"), was called before the Senate Subcommittee to Investigate Juvenile Delinquency and had this to say about the whole crazy business:

"It would be as difficult to explain the harmless thrill of a horror story to a Dr. Wertham as it would be to explain the sublimity of love to a frigid old maid," Gaines said. "The truth is that delinquency is the product of the real environment in which the child lives and not of the fiction he reads."

Gaines was asked about depictions of homes with vampires.

"Do you know of anyplace where there is any such thing?"

"As vampires?" said Gaines.

"Yes."

"No, sir; this is fantasy."

A better answer would have been "certainly."

But Gaines had answers of that kind too. At one point Sen. Estes Kefauver held up an issue of Crime SuspenStories.

"This seems to be a man with a bloody ax holding a woman's head up which has been severed from her body. Do you think that is in good taste?"

"Yes, sir, I do, for the cover of a horror comic. A cover in bad taste, for example, might be defined as holding the head a little higher so that the neck could be seen dripping blood from it and moving the body over a little further so that the neck of the body could be seen to be bloody. . . ."

Gaines's dry humor aside, and thanks to the Werthamesque hysteria, new codes of conduct would be imposed on comic books. Gaines, who then drew the bulk of his income from horror and action titles, would have to withdraw from the field. Luckily for everyone, he rescued Mad by turning it from a pulp comic into a glossy magazine, thus exempting it from the Pecksniffs and, forever since, any definition of sanity or restraint.

The Pecksniffs were, as usual, partly right. Reidelbach confirms that Mad, especially in small communities, "was the only semi-sanctioned place where kids could read about sex, divorce, alcoholism, drugs, corruption, other religions and lifestyles, then considered over the heads of and therefore off-limits to healthy children."

Mad also, early and often, preached against cigarette smoking and bigotry, and who's to say the message didn't come through?

"Nice Old Boys"

Reidelbach is a fixture around the Mad offices on—where else?—Madison Avenue. She breezes into these squalid linoleumed rooms the morning after her lecture, drawing greetings from the unkempt middle-aged men who create and put out the magazine.

"They're old boys but they're nice old boys," she says, and she means it. One rampart Mad never mounted, or even stuck its tongue out at, was sexism, either behind the scenes or in its pages. Mad, says Reidelbach with generosity, "is an interesting look into the male psyche."

In a corner office, being tended to by the assistant to the publisher, his third wife, Anne, is William M. Gaines. He is 69 now and, he says, glancing down at his desk, "I plan to die here."

It's an unusual crypt, but very much his own. The place is closed off to natural light, crowded with boxes and old furniture. Zeppelins hang from the ceiling. Pieces of Gaines's King Kong collection are perched or wedged here and there. That moronic Alfred E. Neuman is everywhere. Other kitsch abounds, mingled with containers of microwave popcorn, Christmas paper, plastic wrap.

Behind a nameplate announcing "Chairman of the Board, Exxon Corporation," presides the massive Gaines. His long white hair is held back with plastic combs, just as all the profiles say. He looks like Santa Claus dressed by Goodwill Industries. Like so many great editors, Reidelbach reports, he is both tyrant and teddy bear, and sui generis (or, as Mad might say, soo-ee generous).

Virtually alone in the magazine business, Mad has never taken advertising, run a direct-mail campaign to draw subscribers, or done any market research. Gaines insists on paying artists by the page for their work and retaining the copyright, which makes him a scrooge and an oddball in the modern freelance hustle. His obsession with control lost him his earliest talent, Harvey Kurtzman, who went on to draw "Little Annie Fanny" in Playboy. Gaines takes his staff on exotic all-expenses-paid cruises as a family bonus (and took Reidelbach along this year too).

That circulation has declined dramatically since the 1970s doesn't seem to bother him. "What—me worry?" as brother Neuman invariably says.

So who are Mad's readers today?

"We really don't know and we really like it that way," says Gaines, rocking in his swivel chair, proud.

Even though—little-known fact—the magazine is now owned by Time Warner (it came with Warner in the merger), you get the impression that, however little the corporate chieftains know about what they're doing elsewhere, they know enough not to touch Mad with a barge pole.

"My technique is to be such a maniac that they're afraid to deal with me," Gaines says. He chuckles bigly.

"We publish for ourselves. Fortunately what we like the readers like," Gaines goes on. "We don't want to start pandering. If we find we've only got young readers we don't want to know it. We'll have to start running more juvenile material."

But the old editor is torn. He clearly knows, and a few minutes earlier had said, that Mad's readers are younger. "We used to have the college kids, but now I think they read Playboy and Penthouse," he says. "But then they come back to us."

It would be pretty to think so. Reidelbach doesn't seem to.

"Kids are more sophisticated, more cynical about the system" than Mad's original boomer-generation readers. "Not much has meaning to them anymore. So there's not a whole lot left to tear down."

Alfred E. Neuman—He's Older than Mad

Maria Reidelbach's previous book was "Miniature Golf," chronicling the game as folk art. "I'm interested in how people amuse themselves, what tickles people, what transports them," she says.

Reidelbach is a 35-year-old Army brat who makes a living in and from New York's art world. She's an art historian and archivist—she's organized exhibits on Victorian underwear, editorial cartoons and furniture designed by architects—and earns her bread and butter as a private registrar for artists, collectors and art estates. She cares about "eccentrics and visionaries," she says, and "outsider art."

Evidently. The Mad project began six years ago when Reidelbach was in Lookout Mountain, Ga., the birthplace of miniature golf. She was going through some moldy newspaper clippings when she saw in the background of a grainy photo a ghostly image, a ghastly face. "The hair went up on the back of my neck." she says. It was Alfred E. Neuman.

Only it wasn't. This was a turn-of-the-century newspaper, and not even Bill Gaines had been born, let alone the face that launched a thousand quips. As her research into the Mad archive deepened, Reidelbach found dozens of examples of pre-Mad imps with freckles and ovoid faces and missing front teeth. Proto-Neumans were cast in plaster for garden statuary, touted village dentists, yummed at Cherry Sparkle, served as a Democratic Everyman on FDR's campaign postcards, did mascot duty for Bob Adamcik's cafe near Schulenberg, Tex. Even the slogan "What—me worry?"—a phrase used most recently by political strategist Geoff Garin to describe President Bush's attitude toward the economy—was part of the lad's mythic baggage when he was given a permanent home on the cover of Mad.

Alfred E. Neuman is, wouldn't you know it, an archetype. "The trickster's role is in opening up chaos, and with the chaos comes creativity," says Reidelbach.

She admits that this inane persona is "ubiquitous to the point of banality." He is easily detestable yet strangely likable. "Alfred E. Neuman is somebody who's mentally impaired, which is very politically incorrect," she says. "He's a whipping boy, a kid brother." A poll found that "most Mad readers don't admit to liking Alfred E. Neuman," but, she says brightly, "He pinches Madonna's butt. Who among us has not wanted to do that?"

Virtually Unreal!

MARTHA SHERRILL

R. U. Sirius sat like a lump, but he was staring, eyes boring with the intensity of a laser, a pulsar, a supernova. He seemed very smart. It was as though his mental powers were so exceptionally strong, they had burned off the ends of his hair. Wisps of wisps dangled past his armpits. It was matted too—Sirius isn't interested in the biological world—just below where his hair stuck to the back of his head. He wore black, totally, including a T-shirt with a portrait of Satan silk-screened on it and high-top Converse sneakers that seemed a tad long in the toe.

Queen Mu, by contrast, was vapor, air, loose electricity. She was all giggles. Her smile was half the size of her head. When the photographer asked her to close her mouth, she said, "I can't!" She seemed an unlikely "domineditrix" of a cyber-punk magazine. A light breeze caught her long flower-print skirt, and blew it around her white tights and white shoes. Alice in Wonderland! She kept riffling through papers and folders and books, piled next to the open window in a wobbling heap, a haystack, an every-which-way jumble.

"Why don't we pay attention to the interview?" Sirius asked her.

"I was looking for something," Mu said.

"Allison," he said—calling her by her real name, "sit down."

High in those dark green hills of Berkeley, far above the university, you will find the headquarters of Mondo 2000. It is situated pleasantly, in Queen Mu's large redwood house with tangled vines and tile roof, designed at the turn of the century by the legendary Bay Area architect Bernard Maybeck. There are potted plants inside, alive and dead. There are pieces of mission furniture, mostly inherited by Mu. There are brass oddments, dark wicker, dark rugs. A Franciscan monk's portrait was hanging above a fireplace. Aside from some Macintosh computers, stuck on old dusty tables here and there, the place seems a pre-Raphaelite backdrop.

"Yes," Mu giggled. "Our techno-gothic citadel."

It was Mu who came up with the idea to call the magazine Mondo. It was Sirius who came up with the 2000. "The name has all the right resonances," said Mu. Indeed. Gloriously colorful and glossy and ironic and original—unusual in so many ways—it's also slightly unfathomable. For one thing, Mondo 2000 likes to pretend we live about 10 years in the future.

We're not new age, they say, but new edge. We are not a magazine, but a mutazine. "It's not about lifestyle" said Mu, "but mindstyle."

"Implicit in that word *mindstyle*," said Sirius, "is what I was saying before—a large portion of our existence now is in data and in media and in stuff that has less to do with our bodies and physical location than it has to do with cyberspace, all mediated space, all technological space."

Computer hackers make up a chunk of the Mondo 2000 readership (50,000 copies of the current issue were printed). The other chunk must be people who share Sirius's taste in music, who enjoy reading science fiction novels by William Gibson, contemplating fractals, ordering smart drugs from international purveyors or learning about odd things like how to plug up their left nostrils for 90 minutes at a stretch in order to stimulate the right side of their brains. The mix is masterful. The mix is unique. The mix is Mu and Sirius.

The creators embody a certain Bay Area sensibility, the land of new old ideas, still new mostly because they never really get off the ground. Conversation tended to include bits of Carlos Castaneda, Buckminster Fuller, Timothy Leary, Sappho, "Star Trek" and the Warren Report. Mu wandered again and again into talk of sex. Sirius kept up a dialogue about rock-and-roll music, about "downloading my mind into dataspace." He spoke with great hope about "the post-biological future." He skipped his politics around the room too.

"We are soft-core decadent commercial anarchists," he explained. Mondo staff members (called *Mondoids*) stood around for a group portrait. There was Marcy Walpert, 22, whose official title is "Ministress of Information." There was Andrew Hulkrans, 25, or "The Tall Editor." There was Jas. Morgan, 30, the music editor, who joked that while under the influence of smart drugs he can not only hear each note being played during a concert, "but each sound between the notes and the shape of the instrument."

Happily for computer types, Mondo 2000 romanticizes them into valiant cyberpunks, daring electronic-age outlaws. "I think we are making a mythos for people to step into, and fulfill," said Sirius. 'But the creative technological person is out here." Unlike straight technology magazines like Byte or PC World or PC Computing, it offers hackers cultural solace and the promise of a sex life—unless they already happen to have one. There are countless articles about recreational applications for "virtual reality," although it is important to call this computer technology "VR" now, in the same way that it's important to say "AI" instead of "artificial intelligence."

And VR, 10 years from now?

Wearing blackout goggles and a Lycra glove, or perhaps a full-body cybersuit, you might be plugging into your PC and mentally inhabiting space there. You might build yourself a room there. And decorate it. You might entertain good-looking-friends there. You might fall in love. In Mondo 2000, there are many, many, many articles about "dildonics," the term for VR sex.

Cybersolutions are everywhere too, for problems from cancer to pollution. The mood is hopeful. The future is a nice place to wind up. The editors live in California, and that isn't easy to forget. "The East Coast of America is really in Europe at this point," said Sirius. "It's an old country back there. It's a brand new country out here."

There is talk about "surfing" dataspace. There are articles ranging from fringe science to pseudoscience to science fiction. Written in neuro-jargon about transmitters and dendrites and cerebral blood flow, there are updates on smart drugs and how they enhance memory and learning—Deprenyl, used to treat Parkinson's disease; Piracetam, used to treat stroke victims. In "A Modest Proposal," Robert Anton Wilson suggests that laboratory experiments not be performed on animals but on cigarette smokers.

The language can be impossible. There's a certain amount of Silicon Valley speak. "Cyber" is stuck in front of anything—an all-purpose prefix taken from "cybernetics"—to computerize a word. It's not enough to have a life, you have to have a "cyberlife." It's not enough to be a punk, you have to be a "cyberpunk." Another favorite prefix is "neuro," as in a "neuronaut"—someone who travels inside the mind. Other words are given the suffix of "oid"—for that special science fiction feeling—as in "technoid" or "Mondoid." Cyber-catchy cute-isms are everywhere, but you can slog along without knowing about much. Just let it wash over you.

There's even a love poem:

Let's surgically merge our organs;
Our kidneys, our lungs, and our hearts;
Let's read physics journals together
And laugh at the dirty parts.

Let's Bell-connect our bellies
With some quantum-adhesive glue;
Let's do new stuff to each other
That Newton never knew.

It wants to be a quarterly, but with five issues in 2 1/2 years, it's not there yet. The cover girl of the latest Mondo 2000, Winter 1992, is a lovely and massively endowed blonde who turns out to be Fiorella Terenzi, a professor of mathematics and physics at the University of Milan. She is also a music composer who experiments with transforming radiation from celestial objects into sounds. The interview is strictly astrophysics and frequencies, synthesizers and radio waves.

Letters to the editor arrive from around the world, and from all reality states. One regular contributor calls himself Xandor Korzybski, but will not reveal his actual whereabouts to Mu or Sirius because of his own peculiar strain of paranoia. (Example: Horrible genetic experiments are being conducted, he says, by "the Gray Aliens from outer space who also control the Trilateral Commission." Korzybski also says AIDS was created by the CIA and refers to our president as "nuclear-winter Bush.")

A book review of "Three-Fisted Tales of Bob" appeared in the fourth issue. The reviewer was Douglass St. Clair Smith, who is also the editor of "Three-Fisted Tales of Bob."

Have they no journalistic integrity?

"I don't see us as a journalistic magazine," explained Sirius. "We are an art form."

"We don't even want to do reviews," said Mu, "unless they are things we are personally smitten with."

"I think everyone should write their own reviews," Sirius continued.

"I'm also really good at interviewing myself."

And Mu: "I interviewed myself in Issue 4! Nothing like a sympathetic ear!"

Is it true that advertisers get puff pieces written about their products?

"That's something people like to tar you with," said Mu. "The puff pieces are usually just about our friends."

Ersatz Realities

Queen Mu's real name is Allison Kennedy. She wouldn't reveal her age, but she used to be married to a Berkeley professor of Taoism and Buddhism. She doesn't drink coffee, because "it contains a natural antagonist for endorphins," she said. "It also has all the pesticide residues that we've been dumping in Third World countries, and they're coming home to us like karmic chickens coming home to roost. They are lodged in the oil fraction of the coffee bean—right there in the roasted coffee."

She is an "indirect descendant" of Noah Webster and a "direct descendant" of Mary Todd Lincoln, she said. "And I'm carrying Mary's mad genes into the 21st century."

And what about the 21st century?

"I've been thinking about VR," she said, "and what it's going to mean. I think it means that reality as we know it, and our fantasies—or our ersatz realities, these new cyber-realities, or virtual realities—will become so real that they are almost palpable. They satisfy all the cognitive criteria of reality. At that point—and this is the definition of schizophrenia, you know, in the past century, the inability to distinguish between reality and your fantasies—when you reach that point, it's going to signal a very special change in human consciousness. The full implications of that we can't even cognize at this moment."

Is she a hacker?

"No, I'm an anthropologist! I am still a computer illiterate, but perhaps I shouldn't admit that." She giggled wildly. "I am," she said, giggling more, "a total impostor. I couldn't do this without my cyber-amanuensis here."

She pointed at Sirius, who was shrugging.

"I'm not," he said, "that much of a hacker either, actually."

A Lot More Far Out

R.U. Sirius was born Ken Goffman, and he's 39. Queen Mu still calls him "Ken" all the time. He used to be a Yippie. He used to be a singer-songwriter also. He grew up in Binghamton, N.Y., "where IBM is located," he said. "My father was, like, a tax collector or something. My mother worked for the university."

"His father was a rabid Marxist," said Mu.

"Not really," said Sirius, "just a liberal. They believed in taxes. I don't. I was once a lyricist, and I'm doing that again. I'm forming a band called Mondo Vanilli."

Sirius first became interested in having a cyberlife in the late '60s. "I was interested in the revolutionary effects of technology—when people were talking about post-scarcity anarchism, where the machines would do all the work," he said. "That was something the Yippies really looked forward to, because they didn't want to work. We wanted to believe in this cybernetic vision, that the machines would do it for us. And I maintained that vision, somewhere in the back of my head. I never wanted to do trivial, menial labor, and so the only ethical excuse I could have for my own sensibility was to believe that the machines would do it for me. Otherwise, you're leaving it up to other people."

In the '70s, he was "very influenced by the stuff that Timothy Leary wrote while he was in prison," he said. "I'm always attracted to somebody who has everybody— left and right—pissed off at them. Salvador Dali. Andy Warhol. Anybody who most people disapprove of."

Geraldo Rivera?

"Except maybe Geraldo Rivera," he said. "But I was fascinated with where science and technology was leading, so in the early '80s, I married that to psychedelia and brought out a newspaper called High Frontiers. Drugs were very peripheral to all that. If our media and information technologies and digital stuff is really an expression of who we are in a post-biological sense—we are moving out beyond our bodies and downloading ourselves into silicon and into media and information— then that's a lot more far out than popping a pill."

Womblike Technologies

The logo of *Mondo 2000* is the head of a baby—eyes maniacal, ears laughing, mouth lush. A nimbus of electric current.

"We are being infantilized, wrapped in womblike technologies," explained Sirius, who then turned to Mu for help.

"Why the baby?" he asked.

"I chose it," she said.

"It's a great image," he said.

"It came to me in an oracle,' she said.

"There's something about this intelligent looking baby—with those tentacles," said Sirius. "It's the electric baby. That's our kid. It's certainly not the Gerber baby."

"It came to me, spoke to me," said Mu. "It has powerful resonances. We all grew up with the Gerber baby. In the '60s, the successor was the baby in '2001.' And then, finally, as a basic piece of Americana, there's the New Year's baby."

"Who?" asked Sirius.

"The New Year's baby," said Mu.

"The baby who comes in with the new year," someone else said. "The old year is the old man with the crook."

Sirius was silent, as though trying to access his hard drive. And then he said: "Learn something new every interview."

"Powerful subconscious semiotics," said Mu. "It speaks deeply. It's Cyber Baby."

A Digital Pollyanna

As she showed the way to the door—and this was sad, because it's the sort of place you could imagine crashing for a weekend—Queen Mu handed over a cassette tape of music that she happily described as "homo-erotic." She smiled hugely. Her teeth themselves are huge too, so the effect was quite something. Half her head. She said she was looking forward to the future.

"I'm a new age Pollyanna," she said. "A digital Pollyanna."

The future.

What's it going to be like?

"I'm upbeat in the final analysis," said Sirius, smiling too.

What does he look forward to most? "The cure of venereal diseases and the free passage of RU 486 and the orgiastic end of the 20th century," he said.

Mu had something: "And the Dionysiac revival! Techno-paganism!"

"And I'm looking forward to Mondo Vanilli's version of 'I Am the Walrus' becoming a number one hit," said Sirius. "And after that happens, being able to spend, like, an entire year sitting in a hotel room smoking cigarettes and watching cable TV."

Newspapers 4

Post to Launch Computerized
Version of Paper

HOWARD KURTZ and PAUL FARHI

The Washington Post Co. took a step into the electronic future yesterday by announcing that a computerized version of its newspaper will be available in the Washington area next summer.

The service, available to anyone with a personal computer and a phone modem, initially would include all the news and information in the daily newspaper, additional details and documents as well as classified ads, along with music and sound effects. It also would enable subscribers to communicate with Post editors and reporters through electronic mail.

The computer service is the first phase of a more ambitious plan that Post executives say eventually will allow subscribers to order goods and services electronically, search the Post's archives for articles and view videotape clips of news events.

A number of major media companies, such as Times Mirror Co., Cox Enterprises Inc., Dow Jones & Co. and Knight-Ridder Inc., are moving toward electronic delivery of news and advertising to supplement their print publications. These experimental ventures could lead to a time when publishers can deliver news instantly over the so-called information superhighway, conceivably without printing presses, newsprint and delivery trucks, and with reduced labor costs.

"Right now, the superhighway is a dirt road and the tools we are using are like a Model T," said Donald K. Brazeal, a Post editor who was named publisher and editor of Digital Ink Co., the new subsidiary that will develop the computerized newspaper. Nevertheless, he is optimistic about the potential market, noting that an estimated 150,000 area households have the necessary computer equipment to receive the service. Company officials said it will be available around 6 a.m. each day and cost about the same or less than the daily paper, which has a circulation of about 814,000.

Despite widespread industry interest, no one has yet proved that there is a large market for electronic newspapers. Among other things, existing services lack graphics or photographs, are awkward to browse and can't be read for long periods without fatigue. What's more, subscribers can't take their electronic newspaper on a bus or into their back yard without access to a phone connection.

Roger Fidler, who is developing electronic technology for Knight-Ridder, said he believes on-line services will reach only "a narrow niche audience" and "will not be successful in providing alternatives to ink-on-paper newspapers. You have to have a medium that is portable."

Unlike other media companies that are forming partnerships to develop computer news products, The Post is entering the field on its own, although company officials say they have had preliminary discussions with major corporations to distribute the product nationally.

Such an effort someday could raise the national profile of the newspaper, which, unlike the New York Times, Wall Street Journal and USA Today, has limited distribution outside its home market.

The electronic Post prototype, which uses the newspaper's typefaces and graphics, features a colorful facsimile of the front page and other section fronts, with more important stories carrying larger headlines and placed at the top of the screen. Existing services simply list headlines in a box, with no indication of their relative importance.

In addition to replicating the daily paper, Post editors said they plan to provide such specialized information as sports statistics, neighborhood news, entertainment listings, school lunch menus and texts of presidential speeches.

Post executives said that before long the service would include photographs and a 24-hour headline service, with wire service reports and weather, sports and stock market updates. Within two years, they hope to include videotape highlights related to major stories.

The Post Co. has had preliminary talks with local advertisers about tapping into the interactive feature of the service. With it, a subscriber could, for example, open up a restaurant ad to see a menu and a Post review of the food, then make reservations.

Mark Potts, the Post new-media editor who was named director of product development for Digital Ink, said "nobody really knows" how much revenue the venture will produce—no profits are expected for the first two to four years—but that there is "a feeling that if we don't do it, somebody else is going to."

Newspaper publishers are concerned that electronic competitors, including local phone companies, will steal part of their market by offering news and classified advertising.

Post officials said they plan to invest several million dollars in the new venture but declined to be more specific. While some analysts wonder whether newspaper companies might be cutting into their traditional business, others said they are uniquely positioned to deliver information for the time when the average American home is able to receive hundreds of TV channels and other sophisticated electronic services.

Eli Noam, a Columbia University business professor, said brand-name news organizations will play a central role in processing the flood of electronic information. "To the busy reader, it means someone . . . has been checking out the validity and significance of the information," he said.

Post Managing Editor Robert G. Kaiser, an early advocate of the computer service, compared its limitations to the early days of television, saying, "We really want to have services that exploit the power of computers. It's going to be hard for all of us to start thinking in the new ways this will require."

Extra! Extra! Who Cares?

ELEANOR RANDOLPH

I *tem:* The first fax newspaper war began this February in Minnesota. The St. Paul Pioneer Press started sending out a daily news digest called NewsFAX. Across the river in Minneapolis, the Star Tribune started a similar digest called Executive FAX. "We've got to experiment with other ways of delivering information than dropping dead trees on peoples' porches," explains Larry Werner, business editor of the Star-Tribune.

Item: Executives of Hearst newspapers called a meeting in Houston recently to talk about why reasonably intelligent people weren't reading the paper. At one session, an advertising director confessed that she doesn't read the paper she works for and mostly doesn't miss it. "People were stunned; it was a very telling, incredible moment," said Lawrence S. Kramer, executive editor of the San Francisco Examiner.

Item: Virtually every newspaper company has someone assigned to find out where the readers are going. The newspaper industry as a whole has sponsored at least six major groups to study their future and come up with new ideas. New Directions for News, a think-tank at the University of Missouri, has held a series of brainstorming sessions in the last two years that have produced suggestions ranging from a news-digest that wraps around the paper to a newspaper that smells like baked bread.

As more than 600 editors and educators arrive in Washington this week for the American Society of Newspaper Editors convention, one topic that has absorbed many news executives increasingly in recent years is barely on the agenda. The issue: Do newspapers have a future? And if they do, will they be a mass medium that does more than serve a wealthy segment of the public? Will future editors use their time and space to educate? Will they cover the unpopular issues? Will the hometown paper be the community watchdog? Research on who reads newspapers—and who doesn't—is widely referred to now in the journalism trade as "the gloom and doom" numbers. These data show that newspaper circulation has declined since World War II in relation to the number of households that could subscribe. Population is up; newspaper circulation is flat.

"More and more, people don't need newspapers. Intelligent individuals can lead productive lives and be informed and never read a newspaper," laments Robert

Cochnar, editor of the Alameda Newspaper Group in Hayward, Calif. "And it gags me to say that."

For newspapers, many of which have reaped huge profits over the last decade, the death of newspapering is not tomorrow's headlines. Many newspapers have also continued to increase their circulation and enjoyed healthy profits,

"I don't see any point in shutting down now and saying it's too hard. It's still a wonderful way to impart information and to get information," said Benjamin Bradlee, executive editor of The Washington Post. "If we could lick the ink problem, we could do very well," he added, referring to the common complaint by readers that newspapers leave their fingers grimy.

Newspapers still get the biggest slice of the nation's advertising budget, according to data from McCann Erickson, with 26.4 percent going to newspapers, 21.8 to television, 17.9 for advertising mailed directly to the home or business, 6.6 to radio and 5.1 to magazines. The remainder goes to weeklies, yellow pages and other media.

But the news industry as a whole seems to have decided that the warning bell has tolled, and it's time to react before it's too late.

"We aren't dying, but I think we have to change," said Susan Miller, director of editorial development for the Scripps Howard newspaper chain. Miller said she recently told executives that for the year 2000, "we have to stop worrying about whether it will be a fax newspaper or computers. If we get the topics right . . . then we'll survive. If we get the topics wrong, nobody's going to want us in any form."

Daily newspaper circulation has stayed about the same in the last 20 years: 62,108,000 in 1970 and 62,695,000 in 1988. Between 1970 and 1988, the number of daily papers sold grew by less than 1 percent, while the number of Sunday papers sold increased 25 percent. In the same period, the number of adults in the United States grew by 36 percent and the number of households went up by 44 percent, according to the Newspaper Advertising Bureau, which provides data for newspaper advertisers. For many editors, it is the younger non-readers who create the most concern in this industry. As Albert Gollin, vice president of the Newspaper Advertising Bureau, put it recently: "With each generation, the habit of regular readership has weakened." In 1970, surveys showed that 73 percent of the 18-to-24 set read a newspaper on an average weekday. In 1989, that figure was down to 57 percent.

A visit to John F. Kennedy High School in Wheaton gives clues about what is happening to teenagers. When 17-year-old Goret Smith was asked whether she reads a newspaper even occasionally, she shook her head and explained her reason: "It's boring."

Some news executives have suggested that the increase in illiteracy in this country may explain some of the problem facing newspapers. Some estimates suggest that by the end of the decade there will be 90 million adults who either can't read English or read it so poorly they cannot function in our society.

But teenagers interviewed recently can and do read. They simply don't always choose to read newspapers. "I don't really have time," says Delilah Szegedi, age 15, who looks at the paper when it's required for school. "If I read anything it'll be a magazine." Most recently she read Seventeen magazine, she explained, "to find a prom dress."

"I look at the sports pages and glance at the front page," says Craig Simmons, a 17-year-old senior who reads Sports Illustrated and Car & Driver.

The data from newspapers show that these students are not unusual. Young people have not stopped reading entirely, and those whose parents are avid newspaper readers will probably pick up the habit. But fewer are starting out reading even the comics. Newspapers used to take comfort in the thought that young people would get interested once they really grew up—the old cliché that newspapers would go out of business if nobody turned 30. Today, even the 30-year-olds aren't as addicted as they once were.

"I think we have to work at it and have to stop putting out newspapers for 54-year-old editors like myself," said Gregory Fauve, executive editor of the Sacramento Bee. "I remember an old guy told me once, "Keep a foot in both generations and you'll make it in this business." Those editors who don't do that aren't going to succeed."

Fauve said that after news industry research showed young people were falling away from newspapers, the Bee created a new entertainment section called "Ticket" for young people and another called "Scene" for young people with families.

"Ticket" features such items as a list of places where you can eat out for less than $10. The reviewer includes an item on the restaurant with the best video games.

"Scene" analyzes Dr. Seuss or gives advice on how to keep the kids calm when they're visiting relatives: "Their favorite TV shows can help calm them down" one headline suggests.

"This doesn't mean that you diminish the investigative reporting or political reporting," Fauve added. "You have to care about trying to create readers among our young people and be willing to do things that are different. I'm not talking about turning into USA Today . . . or Rupert Murdoch kind of journalism either."

The Syracuse (N.Y.) Herald-Journal has begun pursuing the young even more avidly. Its youth pages include articles and cartoons that address kids as: "Hey, you. Yeah, you." or "You knuckleheads" or even "Yo, buttheads."

"Our thinking right now is that fewer teenagers are reading newspapers, which means when they are 30–35 they won't be reading newspapers and our circulation will simply go down," said Herald-Journal youth editor Larry Richardson. "We decided we would give them things that they wanted to read, not only things we think they should read."

Richardson's youth page and "hj" section have piqued the curiosity of other newspaper editors. The section, which focuses on news about young people, is scheduled to become a regular weekly feature this Thursday. Richardson said that to date he has been asked to send examples of their efforts to over 100 other newspapers. Like other industries in the last decade of the 20th century, newspapers now face customers whose lives have changed drastically. They watch television.

Many of them have computers. They listen to the radio during longer and longer commutes to work.

One of the most important changes for newspapers, however, has been in the lives of young women—the people who most often do the shopping in a household. Decades ago, the mother of two stayed home, had plenty of time to read the newspaper, clipped the ads and went to the store. She was an easy and direct target for advertisers.

"We are fascinated by the decline in readership among women. It is far more pronounced than among men," said Lou Heldman, who is studying the "baby boomers" aged 25 to 46 for the Knight-Ridder newspaper chain. "The number of baby-boomer women now in the workforce is between 70 and 80 percent. Sometime in the '90s it's supposed to reach 80 percent."

In readership surveys, these young people, especially the working parents, almost always talk about the lack of time available to read the newspaper. Other surveys also show these same people want some stories—like movie reviews or trend articles—in depth. The trick will be for editors to figure out how to provide both depth and a quick read.

"People today treat time like a commodity, an investment," pollster Anthony Casale said in the "Survival Guide to the Year 2000" put out by the Associated Press Managing Editors Association. "When they walk away from a newspaper, this means they aren't getting enough return on their investment."

The same survival guide noted that on big breaking stories, more people are beginning to be satisfied with the information they get from television news. In 1982, 30 percent of those surveyed got enough details on a big story from television. In 1987, that figure leapt to 42 percent.

Neil Postman, a professor of communications at New York University, told the managing editors that in the future "we're not going to go to the newspaper to get reports of events. Other media handle that. We go to the newspaper for meaning, for a narrative."

Also, he says, for a sense of community. Already one key newsman agrees. James K. Batten, chief executive officer of Knight-Ridder, Inc., said recently that Knight-Ridder did "the most ambitious readership study in the history of our company" last fall and found that people with a real sense of connection to their community "are almost twice as likely to be regular readers of our newspapers."

Talking about newspapers that are "disconnected" with their communities, Batten described "newsrooms (that) often are over-stocked with journalistic transients . . . Their eyes are on the next and bigger town, the next rung up the ladder . . . There is always the temptation to make their byline files a little more glittering at the expense of people and institutions they will never see again."

"Out of our manic concern about being compromised, we sometimes piously keep the community at arm's length, determined not to be in anybody's pocket," Batten said. "So we come off as distant, unfeeling, better at criticizing than celebrating, better at attacking than healing."

Such talk makes other newsmen and women nervous, especially when it sounds like asking readers what they want for news. For these journalists, newspapers designed by readership polls are on a par with politicians who fabricate their persona and policies on the basis of voter polls.

"I think the notion of giving people what they want in order to have an ever-expanding market of consumers in order to capitalize your profit—well, I don't believe that's the reason the press is protected in the Constitution," said Bill Kovach, curator of the Nieman Foundation at Harvard University. "At some point managers of the press have to remember that there is a responsibility attached to the protection we have. Constantly thinking in commercial terms is ignoring that responsibility."

Kovach said that most people don't have a distinct idea of what news is available to them as choices. And he now believes that the stagnant circulation can be attributed "to the fact that news organizations are trying harder to match each other in catering to the same taste. As a result they're becoming irrelevant . . . The more they devote to entertainment, the easier it is to pass the newspaper up."

With such bleak talk, the question for many newspapers becomes not whether to change, but how. A recent report from the Newspaper Advertising Bureau in New York City noted that newspapers have been around for 200 years and that every product has a beginning, middle and end phase. "The newspaper enjoyed a long, rich life cycle. How long can it continue?"

We Want News, McPaper Discovers

HOWARD KURTZ

U SA Today, the widely imitated McPaper that popularized the tighter-and-brighter approach to daily journalism, has rediscovered the adage that news sells newspapers.

In the last two years, Gannett Co.'s flagship paper has taken on a noticeably harder edge, playing down some of the fluffier pieces that drew so much journalistic ridicule and beefing up its coverage of Congress, the economy and other nuts-and-bolts issues.

In one nine-day period last month, USA Today's front page included three stories on the crime bill, two on the civil rights bill, three on other congressional issues, seven on the economy, five on health care, three on the Soviet Union, three on national politics, three on Haitian refugees and two on transportation—but just one on Michael Jackson. The seven stories on the crime bill included such incremental pieces as "Crime package held hostage in conference."

"It's become a much more substantial newspaper just at the time when all the apes are aping the thing that didn't work," said Bill Kovach, curator of the Nieman Foundation at Harvard University and former editor of the Atlanta Constitution. "This is the greatest announcement possible that the readers want real news." The editors, he said, "are bucking the tide they created."

Tom McNamara, the paper's managing editor for news, calls the shift "very deliberate." He said it reflects in part the 1989 departure of Allen H. Neuharth, the former Gannett chairman who founded the paper, and the more traditional news backgrounds of Editor Peter S. Prichard and Publisher Thomas Curley.

"After all the years of McNuggets and silly and superficial crap, we are now considered in the top four or five papers on the major stories," McNamara said.

He also credits the addition of veteran big-city reporters to an inexperienced staff that was largely drawn from smaller Gannett papers. "To be honest, three years ago we didn't have enough talent to really compete . . . in the big leagues of journalism," he said. "We weren't terribly deep."

USA Today, which styles itself as a newspaper for the television generation, has had a profound impact on the industry since its 1982 debut. Virtually all papers now pay more attention to graphics and design. Many have expanded their sports sections and switched to color presses. Many others have shortened their stories in an attempt to lure busy readers bombarded with dozens of choices for news and entertainment.

USA Today's original, upbeat tone reflected what Neuharth called the "journalism of hope." A now-famous headline in the paper's first edition announced a plane crash with "Miracle: 327 survive, 55 die."

A review of USA Today front pages from January 1984 reveals such stories as "We still believe in American dream," "Our dollar buys more travel abroad," "Hitting slots for therapy," "Card tells if you're under stress," "Slopes set for record ski crowds" and "Enjoy job, live longer, other tips."

Curley said USA Today went "way too far" in trying to distinguish itself from ordinary newspapers. "We were too unique," he said. "There were headlines like 'Men and women are different' and 'We eat more broccoli.' That ate at some of us, and it ate at our credibility."

Curley said the paper has been using its late deadlines—which, to satellite printing plants, can accommodate developments as late as 3:30 a.m. Eastern time—to stay ahead of rivals on such stories as the Persian Gulf War and the abortive Soviet coup.

"This was the year we earned credibility as a newspaper," he said. "At some point, we had to face up to the fact that we were competing with The Washington Post, Philadelphia Inquirer, Boston Globe, New York Times, Los Angeles Times—all of them great newspapers."

Unlike those papers, however, USA Today does little investigative reporting, has limited space in its news section and only one foreign correspondent. It also does not publish on weekends. But the paper excels at blanketing major stories by slicing them into smaller, digestible chunks.

When hostage Terry Anderson was released, USA Today ran seven stories, two graphics and excerpts from Anderson's news conference. It also published seven stories and six shorts on the William Kennedy Smith rape verdict and eight pieces on the Democratic presidential debate. One reason for dividing the big stories into smaller pieces is the paper's insistence that only one article in each section "jump" to an inside page.

"Readers have enough distractions in their lives," Prichard said. "If you make a newspaper hard for them to read, you're putting one more obstacle between you and the customer."

Financial success has proved elusive. USA Today has racked up $800 million in pretax losses over nine years, and after edging closer to profitability, the paper expects to lose $18 million this year.

Circulation has grown steadily and recently increased by 71,000, to 1.9 million. That includes about 350,000 bulk copies sold to hotels and airports. Six in 10 readers are men.

"We like to play sports on the front page when we've got a good sports story because it sells well," Prichard said.

Prichard, whose 17th-floor Rosslyn office has five television sets, says the paper strives to be a daily newsmagazine. He pointed to this month's series on race and sports, which dealt with stereotyping and such questions as why most professional quarterbacks are white and most running backs, black.

No one would suggest that the paper is free of fluff. While giving a reporter a tour of the building, Prichard came upon an artist preparing a computer graphic on "Percentage of Adults Who Say They Sleep Nude." (The answer 26 percent of men, 6 percent of women.)

When Julia Roberts called off her planned marriage to Kiefer Sutherland, USA Today ran a banner headline on the front page. There also have been Page 1 shorts on new crayon colors and "Kids of hippies in the groove." The little "skyboxes" alongside the logo at the top of the page often feature pictures of Vanna White, Jay Leno, Martina Navratilova and other celebrities.

USA Today often has only one or two foreign stories and a column of one-paragraph briefs on world news. Prichard said the paper, which has one reporter in Moscow and is adding a second, is covering more stories abroad but cannot afford a foreign staff.

"We're not going to send a reporter to Yugoslavia," McNamara said, referring to the civil war there. "We're not saying our readers don't care about it, but given our news hole, we're going to have to downplay it."

Many staff members welcome the hard-news emphasis. "The tilt here has been to move slightly from what we think readers want to what we think readers need," said reporter Dennis Cauchon. "We haven't gone as far as the New York Times, putting a Bolivian currency story on the front page. But the Times has moved more toward USA Today and USA Today has moved more toward the Times."

Political reporter Adam Nagourney, hired from the Daily News in New York, said he has been surprised by the paper's appetite for politics. "They gave me 20 inches to do a story on the candidates' economic positions—one of the most boring stories in America, but they pushed me to do that story," he said.

Originally conceived as a second paper for most people, USA Today is the primary source of information for nearly 40 percent of its readers. And hard news seems to be selling. Circulation officials boost the press run by as much as 300,000 during major news events, although Curley said above-the-fold stories about red cars, taxes and celebrities also pump up street sales.

Neuharth called USA Today "a far better news and editorial product than when I left there 2 1/2 years ago. I don't think it has lost what it had in the beginning—a quick, interesting read—but it has added in-depth reporting on a lot of subjects. It has matured."

Could the paper be losing its maverick edge? "We have cut back on the frivolous things," Cauchon said. "Part of the reason is that people here want to be respected. USA Today would love to win a Pulitzer Prize, which to me is one of the basest goals a newspaper can strive for."

The shift at USA Today remains a blip on the journalistic screen at a time when many editors, worried about declining readership, are simplifying, shortening and featurizing the news.

"The interesting thing," Kovach said, "is how quickly the people who mimicked the earlier, dumb version of USA Today will recognize this and return to hard news, not just snippets."

Garry Trudeau's Cartoon Beat

HOWARD KURTZ

Garry Trudeau, investigative cartoonist, is once again tweaking the press. Last fall, Trudeau's "Doonesbury" strip dredged up allegations about a federal drug investigation involving Vice President Quayle. Two dozen papers killed the strips, but the resulting flap forced the little-noticed investigation (which found the charges untrue) into the news.

On Sunday, Trudeau had fictional Washington Post reporter Rick Redfern ask President Bush a question that has been privately debated among journalists but rarely discussed in print: "Mr. President, have you ever had an extramarital affair?" (The fictional George Bush said no.)

This week, Trudeau bestowed four-panel fame on an obscure figure from Supreme Court Justice Clarence Thomas's confirmation hearings. Angela Wright, now an assistant city editor at the Charlotte Observer, had accused Thomas of making sexual comments and pressuring her to date him, but the Senate Judiciary Committee, which took Wright's statement, decided not to call her as a witness.

"Her statement was quietly slipped into the record," Trudeau's fictional congresswoman says. "Few people have ever seen it . . . until now, dear hearts."

Has "Doonesbury" become a vehicle for slipping into the comics pages (or, in some places, the editorial pages) sensitive material that newspapers wouldn't print on the front page? Or a way of pumping up modest stories into scandals?

"It raises the question as to why Garry Trudeau, as opposed to the news department," says Bill Kovach, curator of the Nieman Foundation at Harvard University. "I was astounded that the press didn't pick up on the Quayle material more than it did. Trudeau was raising a legitimate issue." Trudeau, who begins a three-month sabbatical Monday, is squarely in the tradition of editorial cartoonists, from Thomas Nast to Pat Oliphant, who use humor to deflate the official gasbags of their day. But while some comic strips, dating to Walt Kelly's "Pogo," have used veiled political satire, none has explicitly ridiculed presidents, polls and assorted moguls. And certainly no other comic artist spends time poring over transcripts, as Trudeau did in the Angela Wright case.

Many news organizations reported Wright's allegations last fall, but her account was overshadowed by Anita Hill's testimony. Now, however, Trudeau's 1,400 client newspapers are bringing Wright's account to a much wider audience, albeit with some of the anatomical references deleted. (Trudeau even has a White House aide describe the strips as a "low-tech lynching."

Richard Oppel, editor of the Charlotte Observer, which is running the strips, says Trudeau called Wright to notify her and that she had no objection.

"I think Trudeau is a terrific cartoonist who will make my life uncomfortable once or twice a year," Oppel says. "My best reporters do the same thing. He's a serious journalist who happens to use the medium of cartoons."

Lee Salem, editorial director of Universal Press Syndicate, which distributes "Doonesbury," says he has received several requests from editors for backup documentation on the Wright charges.

"This type of offbeat story, that's kind of under the news, has attracted Garry's eye for a while," Salem says. "He generally does all the research himself. . . . We lawyer the material thoroughly."

While Trudeau has always depicted journalists (such as TV ace Roland Burton Hedley) as pompous buffoons, his quill seems to have grown sharper in recent months. Reporters traveling with Bill Clinton's presidential campaign cringed after Trudeau portrayed political scribes as failing in love with Clinton and declaring him ready for Mount Rushmore.

Trudeau also has lampooned the press in his occasional columns for the New York Times. In a column on Oliver Stone's film "JFK," he said parts of the "Establishment Media" seemed "hellbent" on destroying Stone's reputation, including "Tom 'Wild Dog' Wicker," "Forrest Sawyer, a paid front man for ABC's 'Nightline,' " and Washington Post reporter George Lardner Jr., who "has known ties to organized journalism."

The 22-year-old syndicated strip has been controversial from the start. In 1973, many papers (including The Post) refused to run a Watergate strip in which a character declared former attorney general John Mitchell "guilty! guilty! guilty!" In 1985, numerous papers refused to publish a sequence on Frank Sinatra that included a photograph of an associate once charged with a mob murder (Trudeau didn't mention that the man had been acquitted).

In 1987, when Trudeau ripped into then-Arizona Gov. Evan Mecham (showing him patting a black child and saying, "My! What a cute little pickaninny!"), it sparked a front-page story in the Mesa Tribune and a huge reaction in the state. Salt Lake City's Deseret News canceled "Doonesbury" that year after a strip about condom use and safe sex.

The Quayle strips focused on charges that a federal prison inmate, Brett Kimberlin, was placed in solitary confinement at the end of the 1988 presidential campaign to prevent him from talking to reporters about his allegation that he sold marijuana to Quayle in the early 1970s.

Newsday ran the comics with a disclaimer, noting that Quayle had denied the drug allegations and the Drug Enforcement Administration had found them to be baseless. "The closer you get to real journalism, the more you've got to play by journalism's rules," says Editor Anthony Marro. "That was a story that a lot of papers had spent time chasing and decided not to run, period."

Oppel got a call from Trudeau after killing the Quayle strips. "He demanded to hear my reasoning for not running it," Oppel says. "He was pretty passionate about it. He was trying to say, 'Look, buddy, here's the facts, here's the reasoning, what the hell are you doing not running my column?' "

Trudeau later wrote in an opinion piece: "Political cartoons are a kind of reality cocktail—part fact, part fiction, part serious and part frivolous—and they don't always go down smoothly."

The Recording Industry   5

In Hollywood: A Sonic Boom

RICHARD LEIBY

T here aren't many places you'll find Nine Inch Nails, Bob Dylan, Peter Gabriel
and Perry Farrell hanging out together, except maybe on a Mudstock reunion
tour. Or on a movie soundtrack, also featuring, say, Jello Biafra, the Cowboy
Junkies, the ghost of Patsy Cline and . . . oh, what the hell, Snoop Doggy Dogg and
Dr. Dre.

All of those acts are part of the wildly disparate musical lineup on the 27-cut,
hot-selling soundtrack issued for "Natural Born Killers," the latest cinematic
knuckle sandwich from director Oliver Stone. The movie is plenty frightening, and
so is hearing actress Juliette Lewis moaning "Born Bad" and Nine Inch Nails
frontman Trent Reznor howling "Burn."

Those who grew up in an era when a movie soundtrack meant the artistic unity
of "Saturday Night Fever," "The Big Chill" or "Dirty Dancing" probably wonder
why anyone would possibly buy the "Natural Born Killers" soundtrack. If you've
been keeping up with music in the '90s, though, you might be among the 400,000
people who rushed to own this mind-bending compilation, which represents not
only what's new about soundtracks but also how they have changed the music biz.

Today's soundtracks, like yesteryear's, are vehicles for possible hits. But now
they move more units than ever, providing a phenomenal string of sales successes
in the past two years: "The Bodyguard" (11 million), "Sleepless in Seattle" (3 million), "Above the Rim" (2 million), "Reality Bites" (2 million), "Boomerang"
(2 million), "Singles," "The Crow" and "Philadelphia" (1 million each). "The Lion
King," at 6 million sold, is currently the top album in the country, and "Forrest

Gump," a two-CD oldies compilation that's sold 2.5 million copies in a matter of weeks, is No. 2.

Increasingly, soundtracks serve as hype-wagons for movies themselves. A good track can help promote a film before it opens and extend its run at the box office. Video clips from singles released off the soundtrack become mini-trailers—for example, Elton John's "Can You Feel the Love Tonight," which got heavy VH1 play and provided a preview of "The Lion King" animation. Sometimes, as in the case of "Above the Rim" or "Reality Bites," a soundtrack can provide unexpected revenues for a studio that watches its movie sink quickly at the box office.

"There's no doubt that a soundtrack provides exposure," says Budd Carr, executive producer of the "Natural Born Killers" soundtrack, whose songs are beginning to get airplay on radio. "And everyone today needs multiple format exposure."

Carr has worked on finding music for 40 films, beginning with 1984's "The Terminator." "There is more clout in the soundtrack today," he says, "and so much more music to choose from. You can do a low-budget picture these days and find great artists who are dying to get their stuff in the picture."

Just about every movie released has a soundtrack of some sort, whether it's original music composed for the film (officially called scores, these are generally not huge sellers); specially written songs or newly recorded tunes pitched to film directors and soundtrack producers; or oldies that are dusted off to provide period atmosphere. There's even a totally new beast, the soundtrack "inspired by" a movie, which means the music on the CD wasn't really in the picture, but somebody saw a way to possibly make a buck. (Take, please, "Songs From and Inspired by the Motion Picture 'Speed,' " a haphazard collision of a bunch of car- and driving-themed songs.)

Soundtracks merge the best and worst traits of Hollywood: hyper-marketing meets visionary artistry, very often resulting in dubious product. (Did the world really need a "My Girl 2" soundtrack?) CDs are relatively cheap to produce, and the "Soundtrack" bin at the record store is overflowing. The upcoming Sharon Stone–Sylvester Stallone coupling "The Specialist" will spawn an unprecedented three soundtracks: a score, music from the motion picture and an album of remixed dance tracks.

Glen Brunman, senior vice president of Epic Soundtrax, who produced the soundtracks for "Sleepless in Seattle," "Singles," "Philadelphia" and "The Specialist," puts it this way:

When record companies see that some tracks are selling a lot of copies, everyone gets to get into the act. And when movie companies see what a soundtrack can do, they say, "Hey, we can make money! We can enhance the success of the movie!" Inevitably, when something works, you can end up with excess. Yes, there are too many soundtracks being done, but who's to say which one is gonna work and which isn't?

No one could have predicted, for example, that Lisa Loeb's pouty, angular tune "Stay (I Missed You)," tacked onto the end credits of the Gen-X film "Reality Bites," would reach No. 1 this summer. Loeb, who happened to be a neighbor of "Bites" star Ethan Hawke, got on the soundtrack by sheer coincidence; she didn't have a recording deal, but Hawke knew and liked her music.

Another example of serendipity: When Mary Stuart Masterson was preparing for her role in 1993's "Benny & Joon," she repeatedly played "I'm Gonna Be (500 Miles)," a crush-anthem released in 1988 by the Scottish duo the Proclaimers. It ended up as the film's signature song, and became a hit. But U.S. radio wouldn't touch "500 Miles" in 1988, and never would have in 1993 had it not been for callers demanding it after seeing the film.

A good soundtrack is more than an aural souvenir of the movie; it's like a good mix tape lovingly made by a friend with a truly inspired record collection. It exposes you to new music from unexpected sources. This is especially important as commercial radio becomes more genre-bound; unlike radio programmers, soundtracks allow competing tastes to coexist.

"Today's music buyer is interested in finding new things," says "Killers" music producer Budd Carr. "And people certainly have the opportunity to do that through this soundtrack. It wasn't calculated to be commercial. Putting Patsy Cline and the Dogg Pound on the same record is doing something different."

Though opposites in approach, the "Killers" and "Forrest Gump" albums provide a good example of how soundtracks are compiled today. Both demonstrate an overarching artistic vision that began with the movie director but allowed for strong input from musicians. That both products are successful is not only the result of the strength of movies ("Gump" is No. 1 at the box office, "Killers" No. 2); it also speaks to the public appetite for music of all kinds.

Despite relying on oldies beloved by baby boomers—among them classic tracks by Jefferson Airplane, the Doors and the Four Tops—"Gump" is selling surprisingly well among teenagers. "We all sell consumers short—we just think they want what they like and what they live with," says Brunman. "If you expose people to great songs, even if they don't know them, they will respond. That is really the lesson of 'Sleepless in Seattle' and 'Forrest Gump.' "

"Sleepless" was basically a compilation of director Nora Ephron's favorite "make-out music" from when she was growing up in the '50s, Brunman says, yet standards by Jimmy Durante and Nat King Cole struck a chord with listeners of all ages. The music became a vital, if sometimes intrusive, character in the movie.

That's also true of "Gump." The movie features pieces of 58 songs—culled from an estimated 5,000 potential numbers considered by executive music producer Joel Sill, whose soundtrack experience dates to 1969's "Easy Rider." As Forrest moves through 30 years of history, the songs act as literal time markers in the script. Thirty-one selections—all by American artists—ended up on the two soundtrack CDs.

Representatives of bands whose songs were being licensed were shown rough cuts of the movie to ensure that they concurred with the placement. In the case of the Doors, who have five songs in the movie, this was a contract requirement. But more often it was a courtesy to the musicians, as song licensing rights are frequently controlled by music publishers or other third parties.

Sill wasn't able to get rights to at least one song that he wanted: "The Candy Man" by Sammy Davis, Jr. The rights, he said, turned out to be controlled by the Mars Candy Co. So the soundtrack producers subbed in B. J. Thomas's "Raindrops Keep Falling on My Head."

One song was ultimately scrapped from the picture because it had the wrong "tone," says Sill. "In the Nixon resignation sequence, we talked about using Crosby, Stills, Nash & Young's 'Ohio.' But the sentiment is so strong, and using that over Nixon's image just hammers him." Instead, the movie ended up using "Tie a Yellow Ribbon" to score a Nixon sequence.

The "Natural Born Killers" soundtrack also has its share of oldies, but hardly the shopworn fare of Classic Rock stations. Its tone is as primal, fringy and gut-clenching as the motion picture. The movie was essentially scored by Trent Reznor, who took computer equipment and a rough cut on the road and worked on the music for three months while touring. Using a pastiche approach, Reznor interwove movie dialogue, sound effects and splices from about 135 different songs. The pared-down CD was hailed by the Los Angeles Times as "a soundtrack like no other."

The CD includes three punishing NIN tracks and two by dirge-master Leonard Cohen. L7, Patti Smith and Jane's Addiction offer their own special beams of happy sunshine. Another heavy hand in the mix is LA rapper Dr. Dre, who's produced hits for Snoop Doggy Dogg. Dre was invited to an early screening of "Killers" and invited to suggest songs.

"We are getting better opportunities as music supervisors to go to [musical] artists and tell them, 'Here are the characters, here are the scenes, here is what the movie's about,' and let them become part of the creative process," says Carr, who's worked on director Stone's soundtracks since "Salvador" (1986).

"Once Oliver decided there would be no composer for the picture, I listened to 10 CDs a day, from producers, record labels and music publishers," says Carr. Among them were songs pitched by the adventuresome Mute label, which represents British soundscape composer Barry Adamson and New York performance artist Diamanda Galas. Both ended up on the soundtrack CD, giving hope of wider public attention to their obscure work.

In the main, though, the public still savors soundtracks that provide the accessible commercial pap that has always been a big part of the movie-going experience: the inevitable, overblown signature tunes like "Up Where We Belong" or "Wind Beneath My Wings" or "I Will Always Love You." Out in Hollywood, music supervisors are busy coming up with the perfect song for "Love Affair," the remake of "An Affair to Remember," the 1957 weeper that was key to the success of "Sleepless in Seattle."

Vic Damone did the honors in the original, and this time it's likely to be somebody in the schmaltz tradition. What, you were expecting Snoop Doggy Dogg?

Making Music in New Ways

JOHN BURGESS

I n the neighborhood music store a few years from now, you tell the clerk you want the new compact disc by country singer Garth Brooks. No problem, comes the answer, "I'll make one for you."

International Business Machines Corp. and Blockbuster Entertainment Corp. yesterday announced a joint effort to recast the American music store as a CD factory. On getting your order, the clerk would use a computer to dial up a distant database, draw out the music in electronic form and put it onto a blank platter. A color printer would churn out a package and liner notes.

The companies predict that stores would initially use the computer technology to obtain out-of-stock titles. But over time, as the nation develops vast new networks for electronic communications, music stores might close the stock room altogether and rely entirely on computerized delivery.

This approach also might find wide use for movies, video games and computer software, IBM and Blockbuster contend. Music stores, said IBM spokesman Christopher Clough, may be transformed into "entertainment stores."

Industry sources say that IBM and Blockbuster hope to start equipping music stores by a year from now.

But the U.S. recording industry, which must provide the music, remains skeptical. Executives say that the current system works well, and they worry that their own costly factories would be rendered obsolete.

"This is an incredible technology—very, very interesting," said Jay Berman, president of the Recording Industry Association of America. But he said that most record companies don't need a new distribution channel for their mainstream business.

"The music industry is very healthy right now," said Jordan Rost, marketing vice president for Warner Music Group Inc., which has such labels as Atlantic and Elektra. The industry would be "all ears" if IBM and Blockbuster could demonstrate a real benefit, but Rost said his company has yet to hear directly from them.

Music stores have mixed feelings as well. Some worry that the technology ultimately might put them out of business, if it became cheap enough for people to install in their homes.

Matthew Owen, general manager of the record department at the Washington area's Olsson's Books & Records chain, said he would want such a system to get out-of-print classical titles. But for mass market music, he sees little use.

One reason is that Owen doubts that the cover and liner notes, which remain key to consumers' buying decisions, would be as attractive and well printed as they are now.

As conceived, the corner CD factory would be a new stop along the so-called "information highway," a vast network of high-capacity data circuits that companies are building across the country with the encouragement of the Clinton administration.

IBM and Blockbuster contend that delivering music this way offers another example of the social and economic benefits that the highway could provide. It would improve quality of life by making music available faster and in greater quantities, they maintain. "A typical retailer has 7,000 titles," said Clough. "But there are in existence some 100,000 titles. . . . You would be able to essentially tap any of those titles."

Music companies would not have to manufacture, store and transport cases of individual albums around the country. They would not be burdened by unsold albums because demand would match supply precisely, IBM and Blockbuster said.

Under the plan, music companies would have to provide recorded music in the "digitized" language of modern information science to a joint venture company that the two partners have founded, Fairway Technology Associates. Fairway would store the music in a central computer.

A record store, linked to that computer by a high-capacity data circuit, would order up a particular title in response to a customer's request. The "bits" of digital information representing the music would flow to the store, where a machine costing in the tens of thousands of dollars would record them on a compact disc.

In many parts of the world, illegal "pirate" stores use a low-tech version of this approach. People wanting a copyrighted audio tape or video movie go to a shop, place an order and a copy is made for them on the spot. No royalty is paid to the owner of the rights to the movie or music.

Under the IBM-Blockbuster system, however, the record company would receive a royalty. Each time a record store made a copy, a message would flow back to the central computer, giving recording companies a precise count of each copy made.

For computer maker IBM, battling to find new businesses in the face of $5 billion in losses last year, the venture is a foot in the door of what it hopes will be a rapidly expanding field. Blockbuster, a chain of video rental stores, also is looking for ways to stay abreast of new technology. Many experts believe that in years ahead, people will rely more on electronic delivery of movies, rather than stopping by a store for a cassette.

A Blank Future for Cassette Tapes?

PAUL FARHI

I ts first victim was the vinyl record, which disappeared from store shelves in about the time it takes to play the latest Top 40 hit. And now, the compact disc is doing a number on another old standard—the audiocassette tape.

Yes, the cassette—cheap, convenient, formerly ubiquitous—is slowly but surely making its way to the endangered species list thanks to the surging popularity of those shiny little discs with the crystal-clear sound.

With a swiftness that has surprised even people in the recording industry, the CD has shot past the cassette in unit sales and is far outrunning it in dollar volume. Cassette sales peaked five years ago, and have dropped 25 percent since. Tape's inexorable decline—down another 4 percent in the first half of 1994—has prompted some companies to stop releasing recordings on cassette.

"I guess it was bound to happen," said Kevin Stander, owner of Record & Tape Traders, an eight-store chain in the Baltimore area. "CDs sound better, they're more durable, they're better quality." The chain now derives about 75 percent of its sales from CDs, up from about half two years ago, prompting Stander to give some thought to changing his stores' increasingly anachronistic name.

As recently as 1989, prerecorded cassettes outsold CDs by more than 2 to 1, according to the Recording Industry Association of America, a Washington-based group that represents manufacturers. (The vast majority of cassettes are sold with music already on them and are never used by the consumer for recording.) Just three years ago, says the RIAA, the cassette was still hanging on as the most popular form of prerecorded media.

No more. Recording companies shipped nearly twice the number of discs as prerecorded tapes during the first half of 1994. In dollar terms, it isn't close—CDs represent a market nearly three times as large as cassettes, owing to both greater unit sales and relatively higher prices (the average list price of a CD was $11.92 vs. $8.34 for a tape in the first six months of this year).

The rise of the CD, and fall of the tape, offers a window on the larger trend toward digitalization, a shift to the technology of converting sound, images and text into the language understood by computers.

Much of electronic communications—telephone calls, television shows, movies, music—is moving toward digital media, which can store and manipulate information far more efficiently than its precursor, the analog technology used in records and most tapes.

For music buyers, digitalization has meant vastly superior sound quality. CD units use a laser to "read" electronic digits stored on a disc and a microprocessor to translate these numerical codes into sound. The result is sound free of the hiss and noise of conventional records and tapes.

At the same time, falling prices for CD players and discs have spurred an ever-broader market, putting CD players into an estimated 50 percent of all U.S. homes. Sophisticated CD hardware now generally sells for less than $200—down from more than $1,000 a decade ago—and the price differential between discs and tapes has narrowed to about $3.60 from $4.56 two years ago.

What's more, said Jay Berman, chairman of the RIAA, home CD units offer superior convenience to tape players because CD players can be programmed to play as many as seven discs consecutively and to skip to selected recordings.

But people in the recording industry say cassettes won't suffer the same fate as vinyl—at least not as quickly—for two reasons: tapes are portable and enable consumers to make their own recordings.

Although the cassette market is in decline, it still represents an important part of the recording industry's sales, said Pete Jones, president of BMG Distribution, a unit of Bertelsmann AG, which owns the RCA and Arista record labels.

"The question is, is the glass half empty or half full?" Jones said. "It's clear many consumers continue to want cassettes. . . . There's still a huge demand for a portable [format]"—one that can be carried from a car stereo to a personal stereo to a boombox.

Well, give it time. Sales of car CD players and portable units such as Sony Corp.'s Discman personal stereo are booming as prices fall, indicating that many consumers are consigning their old tape players to the closet. Factory sales of portable CD hardware will climb to more than 14 million units this year, three times the level of 1991, according to estimates by the Electronic Industries Association.

Meanwhile, in a further assault on the portable market, two new portable digital formats are being touted, Philips Electronics' Digital Compact Cassette tapes and Sony's Mini-Disc.

Though neither has yet to capture much consumer interest—some say they have canceled each other out—Sony's Paul Smith remains confident. Within five years, predicted Smith, chairman of Sony's music distribution arm, Mini-Disc sales will outstrip conventional tapes.

"The future," he said, "is in digital."

Plan to Challenge MTV Draws Federal Scrutiny

Five Record Firms Hope to Form Music Channel

SHARON WALSH and BRETT D. FROMSON

T he Justice Department's antitrust division—hip to the economics of music videos—has begun an inquiry into the plan of five powerful record companies to form a channel to compete with MTV.

The music divisions of Time Warner Inc., Sony Corp., Thorn EMI, PolyGram Holding NV and Bertelsmann Music Group—which together control about 80 percent of the worldwide trade in recorded music—plan to challenge MTV with their own 24-hour channel by the end of the year.

That project has raised concerns at the Justice Department about whether MTV or other companies could be deprived of videos they need.

Justice has sent each of the companies "a request for information regarding the supply and delivery by any electronic means of music videos," according to a PolyGram spokeswoman.

"We are cooperating," she said. "We're satisfied that the music video channel complies with the law."

One of the issues Justice will be looking at, according to antitrust lawyer Robert A. Skitol, is whether the five companies have agreed to stop supplying programming to MTV.

"Excluding MTV would look like boycott activity," Skitol said. "That would be very dangerous under antitrust laws." MTV has been a highly successful music video channel in the United States for 13 years. But competitors are popping up around the world, and other companies have said they intend to jump into the competition here as well.

For the companies, the immortal words of rapper Snoop Doggy Dogg apply: "Got my mind on my money and my money on my mind."

In the past, MTV had negotiated with each of the record companies separately. But when its parent company, Viacom Inc., launched MTV Europe, it found out that the record companies had set up a "copyright collecting" agency that represented all the major record companies.

"MTV found that it had to pay much higher prices for music videos than it paid in the U.S. where it could bargain with each company on its own," said one industry source. Consequently, MTV has paid tens of millions in additional fees for its European channel.

"MTV had to pay the price," he said. "There is nobody else to buy from."

A record industry lawyer said that MTV sees the record companies' intention to launch another music channel in the United States as partly an attempt to get MTV to pay higher licensing fees, "to put pressure on MTV."

MTV has suggested to Justice that the combination of the record companies in Europe is a barrier to MTV's doing business overseas, and that Justice should look into the new combination in the United States as well, sources said.

The investigation by Justice is likely to slow the record companies' plans to compete with MTV. "The last thing they need is a Justice Department hurdle," said one source familiar with the plan.

The Long Rush to Judgment

RICHARD HARRINGTON

Torn from the headlines:

A *Billboard* editorial titled "Control the Dim-Wits" criticizes sexually explicit records by black artists and urges the music industry to control itself lest someone else do it . . .

Radio stations announce that they will no longer air records considered offensive . . .

A "Wash Out the Air Committee" assembles a list of objectionable records it wants banned from the air and threatens to file complaints with the FCC if they are played . . .

Record distributors say they will stop carrying suggestive albums and have in fact already started screening records . . .

A major New York radio station sends a warning to record labels urging them to cut "blue material" and criticizes the industry for supporting "filth passing under the guise of pop lyrics" . . .

Gangsta rap under attack in 1994?

Actually, no. The target was rhythm and blues, and the year was 1954. The outcry 40 years ago was against R&B's "poor quality and obscene content," what one critic dubbed "pornophony" (later, "stereopornophony"). Targeted songs included such double-entendre classics as Hank Ballard and the Midnighters' "Work With Me Annie," the Dominoes' "Sixty Minute Man," the Drifters' "Honey Love," Roy Brown's "Good Rockin' Tonight" and Bullmoose Jackson's "Big Ten Inch" and "I Want a Bow-Legged Woman."

Almost everything reported about R&B in the mid-'50s provokes a sense of deja ecrit.

That's true even of the mandatory ratings system proposed at last week's hearing on "negative rap music" before the House consumer protection subcommittee and likely to surface again at next week's Senate hearing on "gangsta rap," called by Rep. Cardiss Collins (D-Ill.) and Sen. Herb Kohl (D-Wis.). Collins will hold further hearings in March and April on the effects of gangsta rap lyrics as judged by African American psychiatrists, educators, ministers and cultural historians.

Fifteen years before the Parents Music Resource Center and the National PTA made a similar suggestion in 1985—and subsequently backed off when the record industry came up with its voluntary parental guidance sticker—one major broadcaster, Gordon McLendon, suggested ratings for each (presumably objectionable) song: D for drugs, S for sex, L for language, G for general, with sub-categories for records that were acceptable (A), marginal (M) and unacceptable (X). The broadcaster also recommended a committee of (hopefully former) prostitutes and junkies to screen suggestive lyrics for teen slang that seemed to change every week.

This was two years after the Motion Picture Association of America's ratings system was instituted, but a similar system for the music industry has never moved beyond the frustration stage—such as when Jesse Jackson proposed "ethics review boards" in major radio markets.

As for the other headlines, here are other corollaries and connections:

Last December, Billboard ran another editorial, this one titled "Culture, Violence and the Cult of the Unrepentant Rogue," declaring that "no form of popular music is important enough to justify or excuse racism, sexual bigotry and the endorsement of sociopathic violence" and decrying "racial and sexual hatred, the legitimization of criminal culture and the cynical promotion of brutality as a path to self-aggrandizement."

Focusing on gangsta rap, Billboard remained opposed to government censorship but applauded a turning away from "the propagation of the hatefully self-destructive material currently threatening to overshadow the more meaningful segments of the marketplace. . . . To claim any moral authority or enlightened common interest for the profit-minded act of pandering to racism and other social evils is obscene. It is an insult to, and a corruption of, the public trust accorded the artistic community."

New York's Inner City Broadcasting announced last Thanksgiving that its stations would not air songs that were "derogatory, profane or misogynistic" or that promoted violence. KACE in Los Angeles has made a point of regularly taking a similar editorial position on the air, and other radio stations are currently making a big deal out of their "non-playlists." Again, it's *deja écout*: Forty years ago, WABB of Mobile, Ala., trumpeted "About Music You Won't Hear on WABB," and a Memphis station ran spots announcing that "WDIA, your goodwill station, in the interest of good citizenship, for the protection of morals and our American way of life, does not consider this record [name given] fit for broadcast on WDIA. We are sure all you listeners will agree with us."

After a number of controversial releases—from 2 Live Crew to Ice-T—many major labels have in the past two years dropped acts, edited releases and instituted lyric review boards. But controversial acts and releases still find a home with independent labels—just as R&B acts had 40 years earlier when the majors were mostly lily-pop.

And while a disconcerting number of today's rappers seem to be spending time in court on criminal charges, the courtroom in 1954 was a CBS show, "Juke Box Jury," in which host Peter Potter judged the music guilty, saying "all rhythm and blues records are dirty and as bad for kids as dope." Forty years later, Rep. Collins holds the position that "the record industry is out of control, and if it has to be regulated, so be it."

Much of this historical information can be found in a new book, "Anti-Rock: The Opposition to Rock'n'Roll" by Linda Martin and Kerry Segrave. The book is a virtual catalogue of every complaint, movement and attack on rock from the '50s through the '80s, not just in the United States but around the world. The attacks on R&B were but a small part of the cultural wars, and events in the '90s suggest that Martin and Segrave may have to start working on Volume 2.

Exercising the Right to Censor the Censors

To Superfirms, Borders Are Just a Nuisance

RICHARD HARRINGTON

"A wave of vulgar, filthy and suggestive music has inundated the land . . . with its obscene posturings, its lewd gestures. Our children, our young men and women, are continually exposed . . . to the monotonous attrition of this vulgarizing music. It is artistically and morally depressing and should be suppressed by press and pulpit."

The American Spectator on N.W.A.? No, the Musical Courier on ragtime, back in 1899, toward the end of a decade-long war declared on ragtime by press, pulpit and "women organized to be of service to some worthy cause," as Russell Sanjek notes in "American Popular Music and Its Business: The First 400 Years."

Yes, we're now closing in on a full century of attacks on popular music styles. Usually, the styles originate in African American culture, and are decried for their moral, intellectual and physical threat, and dismissed for their musical inferiority. The names change—blues, rhythm and blues, rock-and-roll, rap—but the approach remains the same: Equate vernacular music with the debauching of children and the debasement of traditional values.

Since 1984, the focus has been on explicit lyrics, and as recently as a year ago there were bills in more than two dozen states to require labeling of albums with explicit lyrics, to prevent minors from purchasing such albums, or threatening fines and jail terms for retailers and manufacturers handling such albums. Most of those bills were tabled, defeated or withdrawn after the Recording Industry Association of America introduced a voluntary but uniform label warning consumers (and parents) that certain albums did in fact contain explicit lyrics.

However, Louisiana became the first state to approve a mandatory labeling bill, only to have it vetoed on constitutional grounds by Gov. Buddy Roemer. Recently, a new bill requiring a government warning on songs sold to adults, prohibiting children from buying certain records (even with parental permission) and penalizing store owners for selling certain albums to minors (stickered or unstickered) passed the Louisiana House and a Senate committee. It must be voted on by tomorrow, Louisiana's constitutionally set adjournment date. Should the bill pass, music industry observers believe Gov. Roemer will simply veto it again, on the same grounds he did last year.

Such action at the highest level of state government may provide relief for the music industry, but author Dave Marsh suggests grass-roots activism is even more important. In fact, he's written a 128-page guide called "50 Ways to Fight Censorship" (Thunder Mouth Press). Marsh does not focus solely on censorship issues in music, of course, insisting that in light of attacks on Salman Rushdie, Bret Easton Ellis, Robert Mapplethorpe, 2 Live Crew, movies and NEA grants, "There is no way to separate the censorship of one form of expression from that of any other. The indivisibility among different kinds of censorship is a hard lesson to learn. . . . No matter how vile you may find what that other guy has to say, there is always a better way to disarm the message than by silencing it."

"If I have a vision, it's of a rainbow coalition of anti-censorship people—but that's tough," Marsh admits. It's possible, though. Witness the Media Coalition that has come together to oppose the Pornography Victims Compensation Act of 1991 (S. 983), which would allow victims of sex crimes to sue retailers if they allege the criminal was influenced by a sound or video recording the dealer sold or rented. It has brought together 18 groups, including the American Civil Liberties Union, the Motion Picture Association of America, the RIAA, the American Booksellers Association, the American Association of Journalists and the Video Software Dealers Association, to oppose a bill the Media Coalition says embodies "an unconstitutional theory of incitement."

Censorship, Marsh points out, "isn't about intentions—it's about consequences. Whether they're presented as 'consumer information' or 'child protection' or 'public safety,' regulations and activities that deny the right to speak are forms of censorship, no matter what name their sponsors give them."

Marsh, author of two best-selling biographies about Bruce Springsteen and editor of Rock and Roll Confidential, suggests that the United States is full of freelance censors and that the most effective countermeasures are likely to be rooted in adapting some of their tactics. In fact Marsh says his book was inspired not by Paul Simon's "50 Ways to Leave Your Lover" or the flood of environmental tip-sheets, but "from pro-censorship handbooks on how their people should act." "50 Ways to Fight Censorship" is subtitled "& Important Facts to Know About the Censors," and it gleefully identifies the fundamentalists, right-wingers, government officials and business leaders who are the adversaries in this battle (such as Focus on the Family, American Family Association, Parents Music Resource Center, Truth About Rock Ministries and the National Coalition on Television Violence).

Marsh suggests his troops get to know these groups, study their literature, and then expose them to public scrutiny—such as investigating the tax-exempt status of pro-censorship lobbying groups.

The book also lists anti-censorship resources and organizations. It urges people to put pressure on lawmakers and retailers; patronize those that carry controversial material; write movie moguls and tell them to eliminate the MPAA Ratings Code;

boycott products made and marketed by companies that feed the censors; and speak out ("the single most important thing you can do").

And, naturally, fight record labeling. Marsh finds it disturbing that many new bands—"say those younger than Fishbone"—cannot imagine being unlabeled. "In five years you've had this massive erasure of freedom and people don't even remember that this was a controversy, or they think the controversy was over laws, not pseudo-voluntarism."

The pressure, Marsh suggests, comes from the system's arbitrariness: The challenge is not at the higher levels—most superstars can contractually keep warning labels off their product—but "down in the ranks with people who have relatively less control over their product. What you find is that not only is there the imposition of labels, but that sometimes the reason that there's not a label is because a song was modified or was taken off a record by whatever star-chamber proceeding exists at the record company."

The ultimate argument against censorship, Marsh adds, is that "from a moral point of view, it won't work. What works is dialogue, education. More speech works; less speech fails."

To that end, Marsh would like to see the Senate hold another hearing on lyrics, "to show how the music has been slandered and all this stuff isn't true and the government's involvement. If they refuse, we'll hold hearings ourselves in Los Angeles, a Bertrand Russell-type Vietnam war crimes trial."

Speaking of trials, Marsh also is concerned about the end result of 2 Live Crew's conviction on obscenity charges in Florida. If the group's appeal reaches the new, conservative Supreme Court, there's already speculation that the majority will hold that "community standards by themselves are indeed sufficient grounds for going after certain works," Marsh says.

Being an advocate of free speech has not turned Marsh into a defender of 2 Live Crew—he finds much of the group's canon reprehensible—just of their right to rap freely. Racism, according to Marsh, is a familiar component in censorship, particularly on the musical side of things. He points to 1911 and an Irving Berlin song, "Everybody's Doing It Now," written soon after his first hit, "Alexander's Ragtime Band."

"It" was inspired by the vigorous, sexually charged dances popular in the African American community, dances with names like turkey-trot, monkey, lame duck, humpback rag, bunny hug, come-to-me-tommy, dances where partners actually pressed their loins together on the dance floor in full view of the public (long before the tango and lambada!).

The ever practical Berlin chose the generic "it" to avoid identification with a particular dance that might quickly go out of style, but the mere suggestive connotations of "it" drove the authorities crazy. Newspapers ran editorials asking "Where Is Your Daughter This Afternoon?" and the New York Commission on Amusements and Vacation Resources for Working Girls found evidence that "reckless and uncontrolled dances" could create "an opportunity for license and debauch."

"The Catholic Church, the big censorship group at the time, and the city grand jury came right straight after Berlin; he was corrupting the morals of women," Marsh explained. "You see (this pattern) all the time and it's when it hits the white audience that it becomes a controversy. . . . If it's black enough, you get into trouble."

The Groove Robbers' Judgment

RICHARD HARRINGTON

In a case that could send a cold chill through the rap industry, a New York judge last week ordered Biz Markie's "Need a Haircut" album taken off the market after finding that the rapper had "sampled" (used a portion of) Gilbert O'Sullivan's 1977 ballad "Alone Again (Naturally)" without O'Sullivan's permission. The sample appears on "Alone Again," one of 13 cuts on the four-month-old album released on the Cold Chillin' label.

U.S. District Judge Kevin Thomas Duffy ordered "I Need a Haircut" pulled from shelves by last Friday. The judge had referred the case for possible criminal prosecution for copyright infringement but late yesterday a spokesman for Warner Bros. Records, which distributes Cold Chillin', reported that the two sides had settled out of court and the case would be dismissed with prejudice tomorrow.

Lawyers say this is the first sampling case actually to go to court; hundreds of other complaints have been settled out of court. "It's dirt simple," said O'Sullivan's attorney, Jody Pope. "You can't use somebody else's property without their consent. That's why the judge didn't make reference to a single legal authority except the Seventh Commandment." Biz Markie and his lawyers probably had an indication of ill tidings when Judge Duffy led off his decision with the admonition 'Thou shalt not steal.'

According to Pope, sampling "is a euphemism in the music industry for what anyone else would call pickpocketing." The methodology has often been to sample, then negotiate. As a result of last week's decision, Pope added, "the effect will be that people will be careful to obtain consent and clearance before they make use of someone else's property—isn't that the way it should be?"

Monica Lynch, president of Tommy Boy Records, says the decision "will send a very direct message to artists themselves that they have a responsibility to clear samples. It won't discourage people from sampling or even make the rates go up, but it will make labels, artists and producers a lot more cautious about making sure their t's are crossed and their i's are dotted before they put music out in the marketplace."

Sampling has been a major legal issue since deft deejays starting "borrowing" from older records in the '70s, using identifiable bits without permission in much the way collage artists use printed art. Rap's first hit, Sugarhill Gang's "Rapper's

103

Delight" (1979), rode the instrumental track from Chic's "Good Times," and recording technology (particularly the digital sampler) has allowed numerous artists to build new songs on portions of older recordings, both hits and obscurities.

Some call it groove robbing, with the digital sampler little more than a high-tech copying machine that makes it possible to appropriate someone else's creative effort. Rappers, deejays and producers defend it as fair use (with compensation as called for) and critics claim it makes possible the "deconstruction" and "recontextualization" of past popular music. Judge Duffy said the only issue was "who owns the copyright . . . and the master recording."

The U.S. Copyright Act forbids unauthorized appropriation of popular music, but allows non-compensated use of material if that use is minimal, noncompetitive and not harmful or detrimental to the original work. Often samples are built on a bass line or simple hook. For instance, two recent hits, P. M. Dawn's "Set Adrift on Memory Bliss" and Naughty by Nature's "Down With O.P.P.," are built, respectively, on hooks from Spandau Ballet's "Trust" and the Jackson 5's "ABC"—both negotiated before release.

Robert W. Cinque, Markie's attorney, noted that if "Alone Again" is removed from "I Need a Haircut" or if the song is remastered, the album could be re-released. "There's only one song that this decision affects." Cinque said a request to use a sample from the song was first made in July to O'Sullivan's brother, who appeared to be the copyright owner. "Negotiations began and lasted until mid-October and ended when the O'Sullivans learned the album had been released and they said they wanted to terminate negotiations."

According to expert testimony during the trial, as many as 50 percent of all rap albums are released without finalized sampling clearances, an argument that Duffy apparently didn't buy, saying that the apparent prevalence of theft was "not an impressive argument as social policy or law."

"Certainly had [the O'Sullivans] told us in July when we sent them the tape that there was no way they'd ever grant a license for this, we would not have used it," says Cinque. "We weren't told that and we got involved in a tough negotiation. The other side made it clear it wasn't going to come to us cheaply."

Biz Markie took the first eight bars of "Alone Again (Naturally)"—about 20 seconds—and looped them continually as the musical foundation of the song. Pope said that O'Sullivan, "a retiring fellow," was particularly displeased with what Biz Markie had done because he had regained rights to the songs when a British judge had ruled that O'Sullivan's former manager had breached trust and ordered him to give the publishing and master recording copyrights back to O'Sullivan. Pope notes that the artist has not allowed that particular song to be used in a humorous context, and will allow it to be used only in its complete, original form.

Because sampling has become such a staple of rap recordings—a single album may have several dozen samples—most labels now demand that artists and producers deliver songs to them with everything cleared. Payments—or settlements—can be recouped from royalties accruing to the musician's royalty account.

In the past, most disputes have been settled for cash or a share of the proceeds. Among the better known cases: Flo & Eddie's suit against De la Soul for $1.7 million for sampling 12 seconds of the 1969 single "You Showed Me" on "Transmitting Live From Mars."

The problem, some rappers have suggested, is that artists often ask ridiculous prices for permission to sample their works. Fees can range from $500 to $50,000, and some albums have been delayed, and tracks removed, when clearances proved either too expensive or were simply not negotiable. Sometimes rappers have gambled that a sample would not be recognized, or that no suits would be filed (and generally they aren't—unless an album or single is successful). Last week's ruling is likely to blunt any "wait and see" attitudes.

Overall it's been a bad month for Biz Markie: Earlier, MTV, BET and Video Jukebox all refused to show his new video for another song from the "Haircut" album, one that he says "is drawing attention to something that is a natural part of everyone's daily life." It's called "Toilet Stool Rap." The video was rejected not for the visuals, which include scenes of the porky rapper on the commode, but because of its lyrics. Perhaps if Biz Markie had changed one line to "waiting for my vowels to move," it could have passed . . . for poetry.

The Jukebox

A Century of Spinning Dreams

RICHARD HARRINGTON

It's been a long century for the jukebox.

Of course, the juke as we know it today is really only in its mid-fifties, approaching retirement age, but its prototype was introduced Nov. 23, 1889, at the Palais Royale in San Francisco, and today marks the beginning of the industry's centennial celebration. That primitive machine was actually a coin-operated phonograph with no speakers, four individual listening tubes—and a coin slot for each tube. Even then, the underlying principle was as much money as music.

Forty-five years later, they started building the classics, the kind where you slip your nickel into the dream machine and wait for the magic to happen. The nickel would drop down the slot—usually you could hear it join its brethren—and then came the sudden illumination of translucent plastic panels, sometimes creamy as unsunned skin, just as often rainbow-hued. There might be revolving color panels or oil-filled tubes, psychedelic before psychedelics.

You'd stand at the machine, not necessarily conscious of its soft shoulders and gentle curves, the subtle seduction of its finely crafted wood cabinets. Would look at the card titles—or flip through one of those little carousel remotes if you were sitting at a table in the malt shop—and press the buttons that matched your mood. You could peer through the glass window and listen for the whir of the motor as the chrome-plated mechanism searched out your selection, moving up and down or sideways, looking for connection. Then it would stop and the tray would swing out, the chosen disc flipping into position.

Then, the music.

During the golden age of the jukebox—roughly 1935 to 1950 for the manufacturers, another decade for the consumer—this scene was played out in front of 700,000 machines scattered across the United States in restaurants, bars, bowling alleys, soda shops, any place people tended to gather. Of course, if there was a jukebox, they would gather a little harder, often jitterbugging or whatnot to favorite songs of the moment—there to dance and make romance, as Chuck Berry would say.

The jukeboxes from this era are highly treasured now. They evoke a bygone era of innocence, which may be why baby boomers are willing to spend big bucks for them (into the low five figures for a 1946 Wurlitzer 1015, the Classic of Classics, and the most popular jukebox ever made). Having one in the basement—in working order, of course—creates an ambience in which people can conjure up their past. Some hip executives have even converted old Wall-O-Matic models into grand Rolodexes.

In the Swing Era of the '40s and even more in the early days of rhythm and blues and rock 'n' roll in the '50s, the jukebox was a symbol of independence—musically, socially, esthetically. You didn't hear a lot of classical music on the jukes; the emphasis was on American music rooted in American communities. Little wonder that during World War II, jukeboxes were often shipped to the troops overseas to give them a little taste of home. Rally round the juke, boys.

After the war, with America feeling its oats, there was a sudden national compulsion to make everything bigger and better. This was particularly true in the auto industry, and pretty soon the big five of the jukebox world—Wurlitzer, Mills, Seeberg, Rock-Ola and AMI—were mimicking Detroit's option consciousness. They offered 100 or 200 selections where, there had only been dozens before, and moved away from gracious curves, dark wood and colored plastics to angular shapes, metallic trim and a harsh fluorescent glare that reflected the more aggressive sound of postwar music.

Even in the late 1890s, when the sound was terrible, coin-operated phonographs were a familiar sight; there were "phonograph parlours," forerunners of today's video arcades, with dozens of machines, each with a linen towel to clean the earphone. Of course, back then, not only were phonograph players and records rare, they were so expensive most people couldn't afford to buy them. But they could afford to rent them, one play at a time. An industry was born.

Unfortunately, no effective selection system was developed until the 1900s. And even when the format moved from clumsy cylinders to the more convenient and longer-lasting 78 disc, the early models suffered from amplification problems, rendering them ineffective in public places. They competed with mechanical instruments (pianos in particular), and it wasn't until the mid-'20s, with the arrival of the Simplex multiselection mechanism and AMI's first electrically amplified phonograph, that people could gather to hear, and dance to, decently amplified music.

Then came the Depression, when even a nickel's worth of entertainment was a serious commitment. But with the repeal of Prohibition in 1933 and the return of alcohol and good times, people looking for cheap entertainment could turn to radio (which replaced the phonograph as the dominant musical medium) and to the jukes. Some places would rent a jukebox for the weekend instead of hiring a band, and the primal relationships that still fuel the industry—operators and locations splitting the money, hot music being hyped—were reestablished.

The '30s also marked the emergence of the legendary manufacturers. Henry Ford-like characters came forth, foremost among them Homer Capehart, designer of 1928's Orchestrope, the first automatic machine able to play both sides of its 28 selections (it also spun off those remote control wall boxes). Unfortunately, the Orchestrope didn't work particularly well and it wasn't until after the Depression that the industry took hold.

Over the next 15 years, classic model after classic model was shipped out: Wurlitzer's Model 950 and its famous 1015; Rock-Ola's Rhythm King and Monarch; Seeberg's Gem, Crown, Casino Royal and Symphanola (in 1938, the first light-up jukebox); AMI's Streamliner, Singing Tower and Model A, a huge, garish machine dubbed "Mother of Plastic." Seeberg even had its Play-Boy, a juke that was wheeled around from table to table, much like a dessert wagon.

During World War II, and with jukeboxes hardly a vital commodity, the manufacturers converted to defense work. Since most of the world's shellac came from Japanese-controlled Southeast Asia, there was an immediate record shortage; new releases were few and far between. There was also a two-year musicians' union ban on recording, fueled partly by the popularity of jukeboxes and their ability to put musicians out of work (the head of the union referred to jukes as "Public Scab No. 10").

After the war, renewed competition between the various companies was marked by industrial espionage and one-upmanship. New models came out every other year, and when Seeberg brought out its M100A Selectomatic, for example—offering 100 selections where the norm has been half that—it vaulted to the top of the pack. Suddenly, anything with less than 100 choices seemed archaic.

The next advance was the introduction of the 45, and in 1950, Seeberg once again led the way. Seeberg sensed that the smaller, lighter format was perfectly suited to the jukes, and could in fact expand the capacity to as many as 200 records per juke; its M110B was the first jukebox built strictly to accommodate 45s.

It took some of the other manufacturers two or three years to make the same commitment and, just as today's consumer has to choose among album, cassette and CD, early '50s jukebox owners had to choose among machines that played 78s, 45s and even LP's. Also in the 1950s, the cost of a single play went from a nickel to a dime (it helped that the cost of a phone call went up at the same time). The last juke to accept nickels was built in 1951.

By this time, the classic art-decoish designs were a thing of the past. Instead, you could see the influence of Detroit in models like Rock-Ola's Rocket, Comet and Fireball, some of which mimicked the grills and the tailfins of the autos du jour. Jukeboxes became symbols of the developing youth culture. In almost any youth-oriented film of the time, a jukebox figures somewhere in the action.

Then, without warning, times changed.

By the early '60s, the music industry focus had shifted to albums. A mass suburban migration meant there just weren't as many venues receptive to jukeboxes. Now it was car radios—and later, cassette players—that gave young folks their music. The '50s suddenly seemed hopelessly passé. Television took hold. Fast-food restaurants sprouted up, undermining the casual culture of diners, drugstores and malt shops. Restaurants shifted to Muzak, radio or tapes. Bars stuck televisions in the corner, often unplugging the jukebox. In the '80s came video games, stealing all the quarters.

Over these years, jukebox designs became more subdued and functional than grand and artistic; the jukes were consoles now, no longer dream machines. They are no longer the center of attention, but mechanical employees, often at bars and bowling alleys, working for tips.

Still, there are a lot of them out there (225,000 according to the Amusement and Music Operators Association, which estimates that 48 million songs are played each week, and that 78 million people hear them). Wurlitzer's last model came out in the early '70s—the 1050 was a nostalgic (but technically updated) version of the classic 1015, but it didn't take hold.

Seeberg went bankrupt, then went back into business in 1983 and now manu-factures only the LaserMusic CD jukebox, the one with a thousand-plus selections, three for a dollar. You can play a whole album on the LaserMusic machine, which doesn't take coins: only dollar bills. AMI/Rowe manufactures a jukebox that plays both singles and CDs and there are several models of videojukeboxes, though they seem only marginally more popular than the Mills Panorama models that failed in the '40s.

Rock-Ola's recent Nostalgia jukebox—with a bubble top, plastic panel, fancy grillwork and light shows based on a Wurlitzer design—didn't really catch on. But Wurlitzer's German division has started manufacturing the Wurlitzer One More Time—a faithful recreation of the 1015, with modern electrical components—and it has done well.

The new machines cost between $3,000 and $9,000; for quite a few dollars more, you can get the real thing at a place like Rockville's Home Amusement Company, which has hundreds of old jukes on its premises. A 1015 in top condition goes for as much as $12,000, though most models are priced considerably lower. Most of the refurbished classic models have changed their mechanisms from 78s to 45s, but for diehards, the Rhino label in California has started pressing 78s featuring the classic tunes you'd want on a jukebox. With the 45 format in serious decline these days, Rhino may have even more work in the 1990s.

What does the next century hold? Certainly not 1,200 options like the Laser-Music machine. Still, the jukebox will stick around as long as people keep feeding it. It won't occupy quite the same place in American culture it did from 1935 to 1960, but it will undoubtedly remain a resonant pop artifact—a machine that mirrors dreams and makes money in the bargain.

The Movies   6

The Cats That Chased the Mouse

KIM MASTERS and LISA LEFF

Remember the sound the dinosaur feet made in "Jurassic Park"? Booom! Booom! Booom!

That's the noise Walt Disney Co. Chairman Michael Eisner must have heard yesterday morning as the news caromed through Hollywood: Jeffrey Katzenberg, whom Eisner had but recently axed as chairman of the Disney studios, was starting a new studio.

With Steven Spielberg.

Boom!

And music mogul David Geffen.

Boom!

Sounds like a dream team or, if you're Michael Eisner, perhaps a nightmare combination—though Eisner said yesterday that he thinks the news about the new company is "fabulous."

This is the latest of several tremors to rock the industry in recent weeks—and will likely not be the last. High-level management changes at major studios have started a game of musical chairs and the players are still circling.

The new company creates further instability. Industry insiders said yesterday that the triumvirate is already questing to buy something—such as an existing studio. Veteran studio executives say such a purchase would accelerate the building of the Spielberg-Geffen-Katzenberg empire, which otherwise would take years.

The birth of a new studio is a rare event, and this one is unprecedented in bringing together three of the most powerful men in Hollywood. "Success for me would be creating a company that would outlive us all," Spielberg said.

Spielberg is arguably the most powerful individual in the movie business, particularly since his career resurgence with "Jurassic Park" and "Schindler's List."

Geffen is a preeminent music-industry executive who has demonstrated his skill in building successful record companies (current acts include Guns N'Roses and Aerosmith). He also produced such films as "Beetlejuice" and the upcoming "Interview with the Vampire." And Katzenberg is on anyone's short list as one of the most talented studio executives in the business. While Katzenberg's record on live-action films has been spotty, he has been closely associated with Disney's wildly successful animated hits such as "Aladdin" and "The Lion King."

There are many unknowns about the new studio, which does not yet have a name or offices. At an exuberant news conference at a Beverly Hills hotel, Geffen said the three began talking about the idea after Katzenberg left Disney and signed the contract establishing their partnership only two days ago.

The partners said they will act as equals in every aspect of entertainment, from film and television production to animation, music and interactive video. Despite Katzenberg's well-established reputation for cheapness while he ran Disney, the partners said they have no preconceived limit on the types or costs of their productions.

Spielberg said his partners share his belief that the new company should give "great freedom to filmmakers" and be a magnet for young directors and writers. Katzenberg said the trio has not yet approached any stars or production companies, but he envisions it as "a home for talent." One longtime Katzenberg associate was quick to note that such an approach would be a repudiation of everything Katzenberg stood for at Disney, where he sometimes tinkered with the minutest details of moviemaking.

Katzenberg said the studio will be launched after Jan. 1 and entirely funded, owned and directed by its three wealthy partners—Spielberg and Geffen are each estimated to be worth as much as $1 billion. "Our own capital is substantial enough to get this venture up and running for some time," he said, adding that the trio wants to retain total financial and creative control.

Katzenberg said the studio also would have an easy time soliciting outside financial backing. Already the fledgling company has been offered billions of dollars from investors seeking a piece of the action, he said.

However, the chairman of another entertainment company said if the trio tries to buy an established studio, they will need outside investors who will likely demand more control than the principals seem willing to cede. That executive said he believes the partners announced the new company to generate excitement as they troll for a deep-pocketed backer.

"I think they're basically going to wait for the phone to ring," concurred a senior executive at another studio.

Spielberg said his production company, Amblin Entertainment, will eventually leave Universal Pictures, its home of 12 years, and become part of the new studio. He will honor previous commitments to Universal, including making a sequel to "Jurassic Park."

But the new company has the blessing of top executives at MCA, the parent of Universal, who also waived a restriction that would have precluded Geffen from competing with MCA in the music business. MCA acquired Geffen's record company in 1990.

Some sources close to the new company suggested it will form some kind of alliance with MCA—possibly even attempting to purchase the studio outright from its owner, Matsushita Corp. While launching such a multi-billion-dollar offer would be difficult, it would immediately give the triumvirate a diversified entertainment company that includes theme parks.

Sid Sheinberg, president and chief operating officer of MCA, said yesterday he wishes Spielberg the best and added: "I am confident that one way or the other, we will continue to work together."

Katzenberg had presided over Disney's film, television and video units for 10 successful years, taking the division from a struggling $244-million-a-year operation to a $3.7 billion behemoth. When Katzenberg bucked for a promotion to the No. 2 man at Disney—expanding his turf to include theme parks—Eisner balked.

Everyone in the entertainment community wondered where Katzenberg would land. And with his noted role in bringing about the dazzling resurgence of Disney's animation division, would he compete with Disney in the cartoon business? Now the answer is clear.

Spielberg has long had an interest in animation and collaborated with Disney on "Who Framed Roger Rabbit."

Asked about the potential competition with his old employer, Katzenberg noted that Eisner had already called to congratulate him.

"I think they'll do well," Eisner said. "And competition never has worried me."

The Man at the Top of "Schindler's List"

TOM SHALES

S teven Spielberg squirms so much in his chair that one half-expects him to bolt out the door with an "Excuse me, I've got another movie to make," or maybe "I've got to put another $200 million in the bank." He is the most successful filmmaker in history, after all.

But this particular chair is in a special place, a conference room in the basement of the U.S. Holocaust Memorial Museum, where Spielberg is to be guest of honor at a luncheon. And when the great director is asked about his new film, "Schindler's List," a wrenching and thrilling story about Jews and Nazis, he sits still, quite still, and his eyes cease their darting.

And he concedes that people had a right to be skeptical when they heard that the man who made "E.T." and "Jaws" was going to make a film about the Holocaust.

"I've always been the victim of my own success," Spielberg, 45, says matter-of-factly. "I have so many years of sort of the Good Housekeeping Seal of Approval stamped on my forehead. I sort of wear that the way the Jews wore the star, you know, and I'm proud of it; the Jews were proud to wear the star as well.

"But it's been detrimental in many ways—simply getting taken seriously, or getting people to imagine that I might be able to tell a story that didn't fall prey to the tricks of the trade and the tools of the trade that I've been able to use to make for myself a career.

"When people first heard I was tackling the subject, even friends of mine were skeptical: 'Why do you want to make this movie?' 'Why don't you leave this to somebody who's made a lot of serious movies before and will be taken seriously?' 'Could your name be a detriment to it?' "

There was even official objection to Spielberg from the World Jewish Council, though more over the fact that he intended to shoot scenes at Auschwitz than that he was making a film. "I understood," he says. "I protested it for a while because they had not objected when a number of other films, including 'War and Remembrance,' were filmed there. I felt really used when that happened."

A judicious compromise allowed Spielberg to film outside the gates and still get authentic shots.

Spielberg says a few fellow directors—"I won't tell you who they are"—came to him and urged him to let them make the film so it would get more respect. Were they laughing at him behind his back or right there in front of him? It doesn't matter. They won't be laughing now.

The film, based on a novel by Thomas Keneally, is the story of Oskar Schindler, a cunning war profiteer who persuaded Nazi officials to let him use Jews as cheap labor in his factory, but who eventually and heroically saved more than 1,100 from the death camps. Somewhere along the way, Schindler's conscience conquered his greed. The film shows his transformation as gradual; there is no defining moment in which he makes the switch.

But "Schindler's List" may be a defining moment for Spielberg, a turning point in which he ascends to a higher plateau of filmmaking and takes the audience with him.

"The old Steven Spielberg would have loved a cathartic change to heighten the drama" in "Schindler's List," Spielberg says. "That would have been something in my repertory about five years ago, that I would have searched for, and found, the Rosetta stone, the Rosebud of the story, and made a big deal out of it."

What does he mean by "the old Steven Spielberg"?

"I just mean in my old days, and I'll probably go back to my old days soon. I would have had much more drama if I had made this picture when I first bought the book in '82. I would have looked for the drama instead of the reporting of the facts. I would have been looking more for the histrionics."

In other words, if the old Steven Spielberg had made the film, he might have proven all those skeptics correct.

"I think something told me I shouldn't make the picture when I bought the book. I still had so many stories of a positive nature I wanted to tell, movies that were life-affirming, and I didn't have this in me 11 years ago."

Making the film did not heighten Spielberg's Jewish consciousness, he says, because it had already been heightened by the births of his two children. "I was brought up Orthodox, even bar mitzvahed that way, but as my family moved away from back East, from New Jersey and Cincinnati, and we moved to Phoenix, Arizona, we became less than Orthodox. We became actually all the way over to non-kosher Reform. And then I fell out of it for a number of years, from like 1965 to 1985. I wasn't really a practicing Jew—until the birth of my first child.

"Having my children reawakened all my Judaism, which is why I made the movie. The movie is the result of what I went through as a person. I think I'm prouder now of being a Jew than I ever was in my history. And my parents are probably prouder of me because of it. Especially my mother."

Yes, one can have all the money in the world—and Spielberg could end up making $200 million from "Jurassic Park" alone—but it is still of paramount importance to make your mother proud of you. Spielberg doesn't look young anymore, much of his hair having gone gray, his eyes deeper and more lined behind his glasses, but he is still the kid who's crazy about movies, a kid who has now grown up to make a movie that is likely to reach people in a profoundly emotional way.

If some despaired that Spielberg was making the film, others knew his name on the project virtually guaranteed it would get made. "Universal wouldn't say no to you," he is told, "if you said you wanted to film the telephone book."

"This was the telephone book, as far as Hollywood was concerned, for a long, long time," Spielberg says. He credits Universal chief Sid Scheinberg with encouraging him to make the film, indeed with sending him the book in the first place. "But there were other people at other studios saying, 'Look, the Holocaust is not even uncommercial, it's anti-commercial,' and, 'Why are we going to such extremes to spend money when it would be better spent on a museum or charitable contributions?'"

"And that was just the kind of response that I think encouraged me to make the movie."

Was it an act of saying, in effect, "I'll show them"?

"No. Not in that sense. But 'I'll show the Nazis'; I felt a lot of that in my heart. I didn't want to prove anything to anybody except just to the memory of the Holocaust and the fact that it is an event where people continue to look the other way."

He has an unprintable adjective to describe the atmosphere on the set. The film was shot in and around Krakow, Poland. "No humor, somber every day, everybody, thank God, taking it very seriously," he recalls. "Every film company has natural comics in the crew, and the few we had never cracked a joke. I've never been on a movie where the mood was as heavy behind the scenes as it was in front of the cameras."

Yes, in Poland they know about "E.T." And about Steven Spielberg. "They have all seen 'E.T.,' and they all wanted my autograph." But what they did not seem to know about was the era being re-created in the film.

"I felt a kind of ignorance about the Holocaust from rank-and-file Poles. It's not taught in schools, not gossiped about. There was no curiosity about it. The curiosity was that we were bringing money to a bad economy. There was great curiosity about 'How can we be involved?'"

He was moved, however, by some of the reactions of those who were hired to work on the film. "I received so many apologies from Germans playing Nazis," Spielberg says. "I don't know any of them who didn't at one point in the filming come over to apologize to me for what happened: 'I'm sorry for what my father did, I'm sorry for what my grandfather did.'

" 'I'm sorry' was said so many times by young Germans playing Nazis in this movie. They even said it on tapes made for the casting. It was incredible the atonement that was going on just in the casting of this movie in Germany."

On the other hand: "We had hostility. Fights broke out. They were mainly from visiting German businessmen of World War II age, in their seventies, who came into the hotel and picked fights with some of my Jewish Israeli actors, just over their being Jews. We had several incidents where there were fistfights in the hotel."

Having made arguably the most moving film of the year is one thing, but Spielberg had already made the most successful film of the year. "To me, 'Jurassic Park' was like the sequel I never made to 'Jaws,' " he says. "To me, it was the Land Shark from 'Saturday Night Live,' and it was fun. All I really wanted to make was the modern-day Godzilla movie."

Will he leave the sequels of "Jurassic Park" to other directors? "Yes." He does not want to direct any of them? "No." We're assuming there will be at least one, a very safe assumption to make.

Although Spielberg has had phenomenal success in films, he still hasn't been able to make much of a splash on television. His "Amazing Stories" bombed big on NBC in the mid-'80s. He was a partner in the long-awaited, short-lived CBS cartoon show "Family Dog" this year. And now "seaQuest DSV," the oddly capitalized underwater series his company is producing for NBC, is sinking fast.

"The show has disappointed me," Spielberg flatly admits. "But the potential of the show and some of the scripts I'm now reading are wonderful. We just hope the audience will continue to give it a chance because some of the scripts coming up are terrific."

His own tastes in television viewing don't include much network fare, except for "Seinfeld" on NBC and "Cops" on Fox ("a strange combination," he concedes). Most of what he watches is on public TV or cable.

"I love 'Mystery Science Theater 3000' " on Comedy Central, Spielberg says. "I watch it with my kids. I watch everything produced on 'NOVA,' everything on the Discovery Channel. Our sets are tuned to A&E, Bravo and the Discovery Channel, and CNN.

"I don't even know why I'm in the television business. I don't watch network television, so why am I even in the business? I guess I still feel a debt because I started in the business. TV gave me my break." In 1969, when Spielberg was 21, Rod Serling hired him to direct one segment of the pilot episode of "Night Gallery." It starred Joan Crawford, who reportedly tried to get Spielberg thrown off the show because of his youth.

Serling believed in him. Seems to have seen a spark of talent there.

Not all of Spielberg's TV ventures have tanked. "I'm very proud of the animation. We do 'Animaniacs' and 'Tiny Toon Adventures' on the daytime," Spielberg says. These are syndicated cartoons that are indeed big hits with kids. "But I've never done anything really show-worthy at night, and I just feel like I'm going to stick with it until something good comes out of my company, and then I'll quit."

Apparently the Old Steven Spielberg and the New Steven Spielberg will coexist; the latter has not banished the former. But Spielberg says he does see himself making more personal films. He says he would like to try filming a story by his sister Ann about how they resolved their own "intense sibling rivalry" when they both reached 40.

Spielberg is asked how he would react to a comment like this: Here is a man with such a gift for filmmaking and storytelling, and he wastes it on a piece of crap like "Hook" (except the interviewer didn't have the nerve to use the word crap). He doesn't seem to resent that at all.

"I would think that was a brilliant criticism," he says. "I would subscribe to that theory, in a way. I see so many movies that I wish I had made that are serious adult films. . . . When I really began to admit to myself that I could have made a movie like 'Silence of the Lambs,' I asked myself the next question, which was, 'Why haven't I, and what's keeping me from it?'

"And I keep thinking that what keeps me from it is this sort of urge to entertain, urge to fill theaters, urge to get people clapping and laughing when I want them to, when I expect them to, when I plan for it. And when it pays off, I feel great. And I've had a lot of that in my life, and it's almost like prefabricated housing. I got to the point where I was just doing prefabricated housing."

Got to that point when? "Before I made 'Hook,' I got to that point. I swear I got to that point before I made 'Hook'! It's not like I made 'Hook,' read the reviews and said, 'Oh, I get it now.' I knew what I was doing before I got into 'Hook.' "

The Oscar thing is a delicate issue. No, he has never won for Best Director, but neither did Alfred Hitchcock. "Hitchcock never won, but Hitchcock never complained. So, I'd like to be like Hitchcock," Spielberg says with something that might pass for a grin, albeit a pained one. But he'd like to win the Oscar, right? "Well, who wouldn't? But I'm certainly not in the business of chasing one. If it finds me someday, even in an honorary way, that's fine. If it never finds me—it wasn't bad for Hitchcock, I don't think it would be bad for me."

Guests mill outside the conference room, pressing in to see the famous director, waiting for him to join them for lunch. Scheinberg is there, MCA chief Lew Wasserman, tall and white-haired and impeccably tanned, is there, and many of the actors from "Schindler's List" are there too. Spielberg may or may not get his Oscar for directing the picture, but the film seems so deeply heartfelt and so important that all the usual movie hype about Oscars and reviews and box office grosses tends only to insult it.

Besides, Steven, you've already won the biggest prize of all: Your mother is proud of you. And she's not the only one.

Squaring Off over a Hollywood Empire

KIM MASTERS

The combatants in the tug-of-war over the future of MCA Inc. confronted each other yesterday, as officials of Japan's giant Matsushita Electric Industrial Co. traveled to San Francisco to meet with the two hard-bitten Hollywood executives who run MCA.

Pressing for greater control over the studio were MCA Chairman Lew Wasserman and its president, Sidney Sheinberg. At 81, Wasserman is often described as the last of Hollywood's great patriarchs, and he and Sheinberg are the longest-reigning management team in the studio business.

Representing the Japanese side were top executives of Matsushita, the huge and conservatively managed electronics company that acquired MCA in 1990 for $6.6 billion.

The Japanese-American culture clash over the future direction of the studio has been the talk of Hollywood for the past week, and has added to the sense that many of the biggest entertainment assets—from television networks to movie studios—are up for grabs. This interest in acquiring entertainment properties, in turn, is being driven by the demand for programming that can be carried on the "information superhighway" of the future.

Although the Matsushita-MCA deal was initially touted in 1990 as an ideal marriage, Wasserman and Sheinberg are said to have grown increasingly frustrated over what they perceive as Matsushita's passivity during a time when other big communications companies—such as Viacom Inc. and Time Warner Inc.—are growing through strategic alliances.

MCA had hoped to buy Virgin Records in 1991 and, more recently, the company reportedly explored acquiring a stake in NBC. In both cases, the Japanese owners were not interested in making the deals, according to MCA executives.

"The Japanese don't want to do anything," complained a source close to MCA. "The company [MCA] is very profitable. Why change?" But the MCA executives feel they have to get bigger to survive, that source continued. "In the entertainment business, if you're not growing, you're going to be beaten by other competitors who are bigger than you."

The stakes in this Hollywood power play rose sharply a week ago when Steven Spielberg and music mogul David Geffen announced that they were teaming up with

Jeffrey Katzenberg, former chairman of the Walt Disney Co. studios, to launch a new entertainment company.

Both Spielberg and Geffen have close ties to MCA. Spielberg has made most of his movies at MCA's studio, Universal, and the company enjoyed a billion-dollar windfall from last summer's hit, "Jurassic Park." MCA also earned prestige and profit from his Oscar-winning film, "Schindler's List."

Geffen has ties with MCA, too: He sold his record company to the company for $550 million in 1990 and he has a contract there that reportedly expires next year. Groups that record on his label include Aerosmith and Guns 'N Roses.

The members of this Dream Team, as it was dubbed in Hollywood, have signaled their desire to be allied with MCA—but only if Wasserman and Sheinberg remain at the company. The nature of that prospective alliance is undefined—as is everything else about the new studio. At least, the new studio could release its movies through Universal until it builds its own distribution arm.

But the Spielberg-Geffen-Katzenberg group could acquire an empire overnight if Matsushita would agree to sell them a stake of 51 percent or more in MCA. But buying out the Japanese would be very costly, even for these princes of Hollywood: Analysts calculate that MCA is now worth at least $8 billion and perhaps far more.

Initially, the president of Matsushita, Yoichi Morishita, expressed surprise that Wasserman and Sheinberg were airing their unhappiness publicly.

Although Matsushita executives in Japan initially signaled that they had no interest in selling any part of MCA, the New York Times has quoted a source close to the company in Japan as claiming that Matsushita is open to the idea.

One factor that may influence the outcome of the discussions is that the Matsushita executives who made the deal to buy MCA are no longer in power. Morishita, who is now president, was critical of the deal when it was made.

Tensions are said to be high between Sheinberg and Morishita. Sheinberg can be abrasive; when agent Michael Ovitz brokered the original deal in 1990, he tried to minimize contact between Sheinberg and the Japanese buyers. For yesterday's meeting, each side brought its own interpreters, to ensure that comments were being translated properly.

The choice the MCA moguls are presenting to Matsushita is clear: Face the exodus of Spielberg and Geffen or reap the benefits of their creativity—with the addition of Katzenberg, who has demonstrated the ability to create hugely success-ful animated films by overseeing the production of hits such as "Aladdin" and "The Lion King" at Disney.

To foil the MCA executives, Matsushita could consider another buyer. John C. Malone, president of cable TV giant Tele-Communications Inc., reportedly ap-proached Matsushita a year ago about acquiring a 50 percent share in MCA and has been in contact with the company since. A deal with a third party might tempt Morishita if he feels offended by Sheinberg's and Wasserman's tactics.

The Matsushita-MCA marriage appears to have been difficult from the start. Within months after the acquisition, MCA executives were fretting about their relationship with the new bosses and concerned that Matsushita executives, with their backgrounds in hardware, didn't really grasp the entertainment business and its volatile personalities.

"Everyone gets married thinking it's forever," Sheinberg told the New Yorker in 1991. "And 50 percent of the time, or something like that, it doesn't work."

Bonfire of the Movie Biz?

PAULA SPAN

What's happened to the movie business in New York?

General Camera, suppliers of filmmaking hardware from cranes to klieg lights, has laid off half its 52 employees in the past two years.

The city boasted four major film processing labs as recently as five years ago. Only two remain.

And then there are ancillary businesses such as E & R Production Coordinators. In most cities, when a film crew needs to park its numerous trucks and trailers on a street, the police put up no-parking signs or orange traffic cones, and drivers leave the curb free. In New York, drivers are apt to plow right over the cones. On the theory that even those desperate for parking are unlikely to run over actual human beings, however, E & R supplies "parking coordinators" to hold the spaces until the crews arrive. A couple of years ago, the company employed 75 to 90 such stalwarts; now it needs only six or seven.

Hard times have befallen Hollywood on the Hudson. The number of shooting days devoted to all kinds of production, from music videos to commercials, fell by a quarter between the 1989 high-water mark and 1991. Preliminary stats from the Mayor's Office of Film, Theatre and Broadcasting show that decline continuing this year, with permits granted for feature films down from 106 to 70 in the first 10 months. It didn't help that that very office, charged with enticing production companies to the city and smoothing their way once they arrive, had gone without a permanent director since April.

That problem, at least, was addressed two weeks ago when Richard Brick, an independent producer (of "Hangin' With the Homeboys," among other movies), took over the long-vacant job. At a City Hall press conference announcing his appointment, he talked about the need to market New York. "But I have to be frank; I am not the Messiah," Brick said.

References to resurrection may overstate the problem. But the fear for an industry that a few years ago generated an estimated $3 billion annually in local economic activity, that has employed 75,000 in union locals alone, is palpable.

"My address book is getting smaller and smaller," says locations manager Brett Botula, who recently worked on such major releases as "The Bonfire of the Vanities" and Sidney Lumet's "A Stranger Among Us," then found himself unemployed for a record seven months. "Many of my friends and co-workers have moved to California."

The industry has never really recovered from a devastating seven-month boycott by the major movie studios in 1990. "We were doing 'Godfather III' in October 1990," says Alan Suna, CEO of Silvercup Studios in Queens. "They finished up and moved out and it was fully a year before we had another feature." Silvercup, a converted bakery that opened in 1983, had averaged 6 to 10 feature films a year; in the past 12 months it's housed three.

The studios eventually wrung their desired concessions from the trade unions. And a tentative agreement reached with the Teamsters is expected to provide more. Labor costs, a number of New York film folks say, now amount to no more here than in Los Angeles.

But while filmmakers were scrambling for substitute skylines during the boycott, they found far too many alternatives to both coasts—many of them nonunion alternatives. "It's not L.A.; it's Houston, it's Atlanta, Chicago, Pittsburgh," says Martin Bregman, producer of such New York classics as "Dog Day Afternoon" and "Serpico." "Other cities said, 'Hey guys, we'll give you a free this and a discount on that. We'll close this avenue, we'll give you this hotel.' They found another ballfield."

Thus, "A Rage in Harlem" was not shot in Harlem, but in Cincinnati. "Lost in Yonkers," adapted from Neil Simon's play, was recently shot there too. Nora Ephron's "This Is My Life," an archetypal tale of life on the Upper West Side, was shot in Toronto, with fake graffiti mounted on its unsullied brownstones for authenticity. New York was the first city, 26 years ago, to open a film office; now every state and more than a dozen cities—including San Jose, Jacksonville, Fla., and Spokane, Wash.—have them.

Meanwhile—the second half of a one-two punch—the entire industry took a pounding from the recession. Local cynics observe that Hollywood's resulting passion for fiscal restraint has had relatively little impact on "above-the-line" costs, such as stars' salaries. But elsewhere in budgets the squeeze is on, and New York remains a pricey place.

"Lumberyards in North Carolina can give you a better price than lumberyards in Astoria, Queens," notes Bryan Unger, an official of the International Alliance of Theatrical and Stage Employees. "How much of a difference that makes in a $40 million film is hard to say. But when companies are increasingly bottom-line oriented, those are the things they look at. 'Keep Tom Cruise, get lower lumber bids.' "

This concern about feature films, the category in which New York has suffered the most conspicuous losses, can obscure the many varieties of film and TV produced here and the fact that they aren't all shrinking. One bright spot is the East Coast Council, a labor consortium that negotiates reduced salary scales to help lure small independent moviemakers to the city. In its first two years the council has made deals for about 20 such films that otherwise could not have afforded to shoot here, including the recently wrapped "Romeo Is Bleeding" with Gary Oldman, and the about-to-wrap "The Night We Never Met," starring Matthew Broderick.

New York-based TV series, although an endangered species compared with the heyday of the '50s and '60s, haven't undergone a net loss: The late "Cosby Show's" sound stages at Kaufmann Astoria Studios in Queens have been taken over by Malcolm-Jamal Warner's new show "Here and Now," though whether the series will be renewed past 17 episodes remains to be seen. Meanwhile "Law and Order" is still here, along with six network soap operas.

Less significant TV production—satellite teleconferences, for instance—is increasing. Music videos are up. TV commercials, a category deeply eroded since the mid-'80s, seem to have stabilized. "There's a lot of the film business that is quite alive in New York," says Suna of Silvercup.

But the economic void left by the continuing absence of big-budget movies has yet to be filled. The mayor's film office estimates that major features generate $100,000 per shooting day in related economic activity (and often give tourism a boost too, if they're not about serial killers or drug dealers). No other category is worth that much.

"A feature film [budget] averages about $20 million, for a major production," says Unger. "How many commercials do you need to replace that? With the budget of an average commercial, about 30. Low-budget films in the $4 million to $5 million range, four or five of them. . . . It's a big hole."

Without natives and adopted natives such as Martin Scorsese, Woody Allen, Robert De Niro and Spike Lee, the city's plight would be even worse. All prefer to shoot their films here and have the clout to do so.

Here and there, several groups are mobilizing to try to bring business back. The just-appointed Brick has alluded to the possibility of creating an independent marketing fund that would allow the city to compete more aggressively for productions. Something called the New York Production Initiative, funded by several local unions, has hired a lobbyist. The Directors Guild of America has commissioned a report on the importance of the local film industry. Yet DGA official Alan Gordon says he's "not tremendously optimistic."

When it comes to the troubles afflicting New York's movie business, the optimists see one of those periodic economic downturns that affect many industries on both coasts and that eventually end. The pessimists see the latest installment in a long history, in which pieces of the entertainment industry leave New York and don't return.

Bregman, waiting to see whether the Teamsters agreement will be signed in time for him to shoot his next picture, "Carlito's Way," in New York or whether he'll have to build sets and shoot it in California, is among the pessimists. "We've lost an awful lot of people," he says. "Actors. Good technical people. DGA members. . . . It's very sad."

Breakfast of Blockbusters

PAULA SPAN

O pening shot: the treetops of Sherwood Forest. Cut to: the archer taking an arrow from the quiver. It whizzes, in the same footage used in the movie, toward its target.

The difference is that in this commercial, the arrow turns into a spoon and plops into a waiting bowl. "Now, Prince of Thieves is an exciting cereal," intones a stately voice, half Richard the Lion-Hearted, half Don Pardo. "Crunchy, fruit-flavored arrows that always hits the mark."

It's only a 30-second spot, so perhaps there wasn't time to mention that Prince of Thieves is coated with multicolored sprinkles. Licensed cereals, the industry term for these edible spinoffs aimed at grade-schoolers, use lots of colors. Pinkish marshmallow pizza wedges and green marshmallow amphibians in Teenage Mutant Ninja Turtles cereal. Orange, lilac and yellow marshmallow musical notes in the brand-new Bill and Ted's Excellent Cereal. Patrick Farrell, spokesman for Ralston Purina, which manufactures all of the above, explains that "the vibrance helps a lot with the excitement and fun."

It might be argued, though, that much of the excitement and fun is occurring at Warner Bros. and at Ralston. The former, its licensing division anticipating the millions generated by Prince of Thieves merchandise, has a shot at every potential moviegoer wheeling a cart down the cereal aisle. The latter, building brand awareness every time a consumer sees "Robin Hood: Prince of Thieves" or an ad or poster thereof, is spending perhaps a third the normal cost of launching a new cereal. The life span of a licensed cereal, however vibrant, rarely exceeds 18 months. But that's long enough.

This particular twist in the world of modern, everything-promotes-everything-else marketing is largely a Ralston Purina development. General Mills ventured in early with Strawberry Shortcake (she was an icky-poo character swathed in gingham) and Pac-Man cereals in the early to mid-'80s. It also created what seems to have been the first true movie cereal, E.T., with chocolate-and-peanut-butter-flavored E's and T's (perhaps designing aliens in grain was prohibitively costly). But the No. 2 cereal maker switched strategies and got out of licensed products by 1985.

"It's such a short-lived thing," says Kathryn Newton, General Mills' public relations manager. "Stick with the tried and true." The company had its own characters to help tykes remember which box to point to and shriek for, like the Trix rabbit and the Lucky Charms leprechaun, so why profit-share with Steven Spielberg? (Royalty rates on food products typically range from 3 percent to 5 percent of sales.) The fact is that with roughly a quarter of the branded ready-to-eat cereal market (in tonnage, not dollars), General Mills doesn't need Robin Hood.

Enter Ralston in 1985 with Cabbage Patch Kids cereal. There's been at least one licensed cereal out of Checkerboard Square, sweetened and spun off from film, toy or video game (categories growing increasingly blurry; anything that's one becomes the others), on supermarket shelves ever since. With only a little more than 5 percent of the market—Kellogg's Frosted Flakes alone has about the same share—plus another 4 percent in private-label manufacturing for supermarket chains, Ralston could use a hand from someone who robs the rich.

"It's a survival technique," says John McMillin, a food industry analyst for Prudential Securities. "It doesn't work for everybody, but it works for the little guy."

The $7 billion cold-cereal business has high profit margins, but introducing a new brand when there are already some 220 vying for shelf space and consumer recognition has become a major investment. Advertising and marketing expenditures of $35 million to $40 million in the first year are not uncommon. But using popular movie or TV characters lets cereal makers use what marketers call "borrowed interest," capitalizing on a craze someone else created.

Ralston will not provide budget figures, but Polly Kawalek director of marketing at rival Quaker Oats' ready-to-eat-cereals division, estimates that Ralston spends a mere $10 million to $12 million to launch its licensed products. She adds that Quaker will wind up spending about the same amount introducing its new entry, Tiny Toon Adventures, which piggybacks on the popular cartoon series and hits the shelves in January. Quaker has a considerably greater market share than Ralston—close to 8 percent—but is still dwarfed by the Big Two, Kellogg and General Mills.

"If your name is Kellogg's and you've got Corn Flakes, you don't have to deal with Ninja Turtles," analyst McMillin points out. But smaller companies need "the savings of not having to advertise Batman"—Ralston introduced a bat-wing-shaped cereal on the heels of the 1989 film. "They don't have to pay for these huge media blitzes."

For Prince of Thieves, for instance, one TV spot shown for a month on Saturday mornings and in other heavy kidvid time slots, plus newspaper-insert coupons to soften up parents, is all the introductory razzmatazz Ralston deems necessary. The steeper prices Ralston sets for its licensed cereals also contribute to a tastier bottom line.

Not that the strategy always works. Quaker may owe its caution in entering the licensing fray—Tiny Toons is not seen as the first in a series—to the lingering aftertaste of Mr. T cereal, which failed to reach hoped-for levels of profitability.

Similarly, the Jetsons movie released last year was a fizzle and so was the Ralston cereal, shaped like moons and meteors and driven from supermarkets in just 10 months. Breakfast with Barbie fared little better. In fact, many of Ralston's licensed cereals—Nintendo, Batman, Hot Wheels—have faded after 14 to 16 months.

But all it takes is one smash like Ghostbusters, whose unprecedented five-year run may have less to do with its ghost-shaped marshmallows than with the sales push of two hit movies and a popular Saturday cartoon, to keep the marketers trying. With the Turtles, just entering Year Three of cerealhood, they've found another winner.

(Footnote: Prince of Thieves cereal might have been even more exciting and fun had the front of the package featured Kevin Costner instead of a generic archer. The star had likeness approval, however, and declined to grace cereal boxes, participate in Taco Bell promotions or be pictured on any Prince of Thieves merchandise except Kenner's action figures.)

That much of what a child eats, wears, rides, plays with, sleeps on and trick-or-treats in can be a product promotion comes as no shock to parents. It's such established practice, in fact, that even a dogged campaigner like Action for Children's Television can't rouse itself to much indignation. "There's so much merchandising targeted to children, so many programs that are in effect commercials, so many commercials finding their way into classrooms, that the idea of having children's cereal commercialized is rather benign," says ACT President Peggy Chaffen.

The nutritional issue has also been back-burnered. Children's cereals are sugary, virtually by definition, but the licensed sort don't seem more cavity-inducing than the rest of the lot. Bill and Ted's is on the high side with 13 grams of sugar per serving, Tiny Toons in the mid-range with 10, both a far cry from sensible Cheerios (1 gram) but not quite as repellent as Fruity Marshmallow Krispies (17). Neither Turtles nor Prince of Thieves currently carries a carbohydrate information label, but Ralston says that future shipments will, showing sugar levels of 11 and 12 grams, respectively.

Anyway, Ralston is completely unapologetic on the sugar issue. "The premise that sweet is bad is just wrong; these are products with nutritional value," argues spokesman Farrell, who wants points for Ralston's having added vitamins and eliminating tropical oils.

Besides, cereal licensing could be worse. The summer's apparent blockbuster, both in box office and in licensing lust, isn't "Robin Hood" but "Terminator 2." Official Terminator tank tops, skateboards, endoskeleton hobby kits and boxer shorts are all coming soon to a retailer near you. But no one's introducing Cyborg Sweeties cereal, with frosted Schwarzenuggets and marshmallow biceps in three pastel shades. Yet.

Smash the Ratings System!

HAL HINSON

The Motion Picture Association of America's ratings system doesn't work. It needs to be changed. It has to be changed.

The problem is with the system's X rating. The industry dances around it, either pretending it's not part of a mechanism of censorship or, if it is, comfortably resigned to it. MPAA President Jack Valenti dances around it, claiming that "the screen is free." That "no filmmaker has to cut one millimeter of his film—at any time." That the ratings process is voluntary and if cuts have been made in order to avoid an "X," it's because of "economic considerations, not First Amendment considerations."

"The marketplace censors, we don't," he says.

That point made, he rests soundly in the knowledge that the system runs smoothly, his sleep cushioned by the results of his survey showing that 70 percent to 73 percent of parents find the guidance his system offers either "very useful" or "fairly useful"—an approval rating that he says any politician would be proud of.

And in a way he's right. The system purrs along—smoothly and invisibly. At least, most of the time. But recently, five films have bobbed to the surface, exposing the ways in which the system breaks down. Three of these pictures—Peter Greenaway's "The Cook, the Thief, His Wife & Her Lover," Pedro Almodovar's "Tie Me Up! Tie Me Down!" and John McNaughton's "Henry: Portrait of a Serial Killer"—went before the MPAA's ratings board and were branded with an X. To avoid the stigma, they were sent into the market unrated, restricting the number of theaters in which they can be shown and the newspapers and television stations that can accept their ads.

A fourth film, Zalman King's "Wild Orchid," was also slapped with an X, and rather than face these restrictions, its producers have cut away the material deemed offensive by the board in order to obtain an R. And the fifth, Sandra Bernhard's "Without You I'm Nothing," falls into a murky catchall category of films that were never officially given an X but were told that one was imminent unless cuts were made. An untold number of films fall into this category, accept their cuts and, like "Without You," are sent out into the world without causing a ripple.

This may not be censorship, but if it isn't, why does it feel so much like it?

No one is claiming that these are great films, or even good films. They have had their champions among critics and their detractors. But the quality of the works is—at least in terms of this debate—irrelevant, just as the artistic merit of Robert Mapplethorpe's photographs is irrelevant. The issue here is access, and whether the labels affixed to motion pictures cause them to be ghetto-ized, subjecting them to hardships so severe as to make their commercial lives untenable.

At issue is whether, some 20 years after its creation, the MPAA's ratings system isn't so much the lesser of evils as a force as regressive as the dangers it was established to prevent.

The system, which the industry instituted as a self-regulating board in 1968 (and whose official name is the Classification and Ratings Administration, or CARA), is Valenti's baby, and he protects it with a maternal ferocity, warding off the threat of new letters for new categories, which he claims would create "alpha-betical chaos." He succumbed only once, in 1984, after intense pressure from Paramount Pictures and Steven Spielberg, with the creation of PG-13.

A product of the '60s, the system was a direct reaction to the confrontational social climate of its time and the impulse in many filmmakers to test the limits of what was permissible onscreen. Being a realist, Valenti knew that movies like "Who's Afraid of Virginia Woolf," with its invitations to "hump the hostess," and Michelangelo Antonioni's "Blow-Up," with its adult themes and partial nudity, would strike a nerve, and anticipating a wave of protest, he began urging the industry to conjure up a board of its own.

It was created partly as a guide for parents and partly to ward off interference by local groups with more restrictive intentions. And at the time, Valenti was hailed for his actions. Variety called him "a hero who saved the industry and its artists from a terrible fate."

In the mind of its creator, though, the ratings system has never been more than the lesser of possible evils. In the best of all possible worlds, Valenti says, he would have the thing abolished—without a tear.

The producers and distributors of the five films in question wouldn't go as far as all that. Given the existing circumstances, though, their companies are left to choose from undesirable alternatives. In case of both "The Cook, the Thief" and "Tie Me Up!," neither cutting the films nor releasing them with the board's rating was acceptable. (The rating for "Tie Me Up!" was appealed by the filmmakers and, just this past Tuesday, was upheld.) Going out unrated was the only possible choice.

"It wouldn't make any sense to take these films out into the market with an X," says Russell Schwartz of Miramax Films, the distributor of both the Almodovar and Greenaway films. "If we sent the films out that way, we might not be able to run an ad. Or if we could run an ad, in some areas we could only run the title. Or it couldn't run any larger than an inch or it had to run in the back, next to the mud wrestling in the sports section."

Also, Schwartz says, the number of theaters available to the film would be dramatically reduced if the films were released with an X, either because the chains have a policy of not playing X-rated or unrated pictures or because there are local real-estate laws prohibiting the showing of anything stronger than an R.

The same situation applied to "Henry: Portrait of a Serial Killer," McNaughton's disturbing psychological study based on the actual story of Henry Lee Lucas. The film falls somewhere between art and exploitation. And David Whitten, president of Greycat Films, "Henry's" distributor, agrees with the ratings board (and disagrees with the film's producers) that the film doesn't fit into the normal definition of an R. Nor does he think that cutting would have helped. "Any attempt to bring the film into compliance with an R would destroy what the film is intended to do," he says.

For "Wild Orchid," which was a box-office winner in Europe because of the popularity of its star, Mickey Rourke, going into release without a rating was not an option due to the releasing company's membership in the MPAA. After the changes in the picture were made, it finally opened in about 900 theaters. But according to Mark Damon, the film's producer, an opening that size would have been impossible without a rating or with an X.

Still, both the X-rated and the unrated films are penalized, Schwartz says. "Now what we're doing is wearing the letter on our back, instead of our front."

Central to the debate is what the X rating has come to mean over the years—what it symbolizes, According to Schwartz, the problem is that the X no longer means what it was meant to mean. When the system was created, Schwartz explains, the skull-and-crossbones X rating wasn't copyrighted, which would have limited its use exclusively to the films given that designation by the MPAA. Instead, the rating can be used by anyone, and has been, particularly by the producers of pornographic movies who pile triple-and-quadruple-X ratings on their films as a badge of hard-core distinction. As a result, he argues, an X rating has become synonymous with pornography.

Greycat's Whitten agrees. "That's what an X means. It doesn't mean that it's a serious film for adults, it means that it's contraband. It means it's dirty."

The message this sends out to filmmakers is clear: You can make films with challenging themes that deal frankly with sexuality and other adult concerns, or that examine violent behavior in an intense, realistic and disturbing manner, but they are not going to be allowed into the mainstream. It's telling them their movies can be adventurous, but only at great risk, and on a very low budget. It's telling them that it's better to be safe and innocuous and formulaic than sorry.

Do we wonder, then, why so many of our movies are bad?

With Valenti out spreading the gospel of American movies in Europe and around the world, urging France and other countries not to erect barriers to free trade and keep their expanding markets open to Hollywood, this implied message to play it safe seems nearly ironic. Britain, Spain, Italy and other European nations have standards for rating films that are far more relaxed (at least in the area of sex) than those in this country and that do not penalize artists for venturing into provocative material. The American movies Valenti is selling, in this context, seem oddly out of step. In a sense, we are exporting our prudishness.

According to Jonathan Krane, who in addition to producing the film version of Bernhard's off-Broadway hit also produced "Look Who's Talking," "The Chocolate War" and "Getting It Right," the current controversy cannot be separated from the tenor of the times—the Mapplethorpe controversy, the questions about record labeling, the pickets and continuing boycotts over "The Last Temptation of Christ."

"I think there is some fear today in Hollywood that the standards may be changing," he says. "That's what this controversy is all about. What people are afraid of with these five films coming out all at once is that it represents a trend. The independents are already at risk because we tend to make pictures the studios won't make. And what scares us is that there is a bureaucracy that's reflective of a more conservative time, that might be wielded in a way that censors us."

Two things, in particular, disturb them. "The first problem," he says, "is the arbitrary, almost star-chamber nature of the process. The second is the lack of identifiable, consistently applied standards." Filmmakers complain that they are forced to comply with rules that are made up as the game goes along. In the case of "The Cook, the Thief," Schwartz says a representative of the board told him that its members liked the film very much. "In fact, they said that the film shouldn't be changed. They agreed that the film was great and that not one frame should be cut. But they said it was an X."

The 11-member board had a similar reaction to Almodovar's "Tie Me Up! Tie Me Down!," a much less combustible, though far from conventional, love story about a young man who becomes fixated on a former porn star. According to Schwartz, with "Cook, Thief," the board's response came not to any one scene, but rather to the film's "overall tone." With "Tie Me Up!," the rating seems to have been prompted by a single incident of heterosexual lovemaking, though a bathtub scene in which a toy scuba diver paddles its way up between the heroine's legs may not have helped matters.

"When we start telling people to cut their movies because they're too intense, or something as vague as 'overall tone,' is pretty egregious," Krane says. "They should be made to objectify the process so that everyone knows what's what."

What many filmmakers, producers, distributors and critics would most like to see is a reform of the system. They have made what they think is a reasonable proposal—the addition of a category between the R rating, which denies admission to anyone under 17 without a parent, and the X rating, which denies admission to anyone under 17. An M (for "mature") category has been suggested. Or an A (for "adult"). David Lynch, whose "Blue Velvet" had to be trimmed to obtain an R, has suggested "RR," and to promote his suggestion named a coffee shop in "Twin Peaks" the RR Diner.

Actually, no one much cares what it's called—they just want it.

The debate here isn't over the age requirements. All three unrated films have gone out with self-imposed restrictions stricter than those in the MPAA guidelines. (The ads limit the admission to moviegoers 18 or older.) And none of the filmmakers question that their pictures are adult in nature and should be restricted to adult audiences. "The Cook, the Thief, His Wife & Her Lover," Greenaway's grandiose satire on capitalism and the decline of Western civilization, is overt in its presentation of cannibalism, murder, frontal nudity, profanity, coprophagy and child abuse. It's a smorgasbord of nearly every imaginable form of perversion, but in no way is it exploitative or titillating. But is it proper to place this serious, corrosive work, by a director with an international reputation, in the same category with "Pussycat Ranch" or "Wet Rainbow"?

Valenti says yes. Furthermore, he says that his committee is not equipped to make the aesthetic judgment call needed to distinguish the bondage in "Tie Me Up!" from the bondage in, say, "Femme De Sade." "These people are parents. . . . They aren't rating for the New York Review of Books or the Harvard faculty, they're rating for the parents of America. One of the main reasons for not changing the ratings is that they are not capable of distinguishing between the good bestiality, necrophilia, incest, sadomasochism, and the bad. . . . We let the American public—theater owners, newspapers, moviegoers—make its judgments. Now what's freer than that?"

What could be freer? For starters, creating a category that would protect the producers and directors of nonexploitative, challenging adult films from laws written to restrict "Danish Pastries" and "Coed Dorm." That would allow the films in that category access to theaters with policies against X movies—policies designed to restrict their screens from pictures showing graphic sex or indiscriminate violence. That would allow companies promoting these films to advertise them in newspapers eager to protect their readers from advertisements of lurid sex shows and strip joints.

It's something of a testament to the success of the system Valenti created that these conflicts have surfaced. If his letters had not become such hard-and-fast guidelines, the basis for many of the current legal restrictions wouldn't exist. But Valenti, who likes to claim the ground high above marketplace realities, says these are not his responsibility. An X is an X, he says. It's not intended to brand a film as pornographic; it merely informs parents that the board does not consider the picture's contents suitable for children under 17.

He rates movies to advise parents which to send their children to. Period. "There's been such a stink about this, but you know, I haven't received one letter from a parent who feels that the system should be changed. Not one."

And he's not likely to. Freedom of artistic expression is not a pressing issue for the great majority of the American people. But the image in which Valenti casts himself as a protector of children and family values amounts to a kind of tyranny. As much as Valenti would have us believe it, we are not a society of children only. And the interests of children are not the only ones to consider.

But freedom of expression isn't the real issue here, Valenti suggests. In fact, he questions the motives of the people associated with the films in question, claiming that publicity, and more money, is their goal, not artistic freedom. "These pictures have gotten more goddamn publicity than 'Gone With the Wind,' " he says. "The publicity wizards who handle these pictures have probably all gotten a bonus.

"I'm not saying they're cynical," he continues. "They're businessmen and they're using creative expression as a bludgeon to make more money. I have no quarrel with that, but I refuse to let them taint the rating system."

"So long as we have the enormous parental approval we have for this ratings system, I am not going to go to my partners in exhibition and suggest that we make radical changes."

And the dance goes on.

Radio　7

Clinton Foes Voice Their Hostility

ANN DEVROY

T he caller was so angry she could barely speak. President Clinton, she said, is "not fit to hold office. He's scum. He's worse than scum and you all are protecting him."

And that message, left on a reporter's answering machine, was one of the milder ones.

Across the radio talk show airwaves, in mail and phone calls to the news media, in letters to the White House and in dozens of other anecdotal ways, Bill Clinton's enemies are making their hatred clear, with a burning intensity and in some cases with an organized passion.

Most pollsters suggest that their measurements of strong approval and disapproval for Clinton are not all that different from those for other recent presidents and that polls, really, cannot measure passion. But even Clinton advisers agree there is something about Clinton that reaches into the emotional gut of some Americans and produces a visceral reaction.

"There are some hard, hard, hard-core Clinton haters," said adviser James Carville. "This guy gins up more feelings and pulls them from greater extremes than any politician I know." White House counselor David R. Gergen agrees, saying the closest thing he has seen to it across the four presidencies in which he has served were the early months of Ronald Reagan's, when his ideological swerve to the right created a depth of opposition on the left.

Dee Dee Myers, Clinton's press secretary who traveled with him through the campaign and does now, said, "There are a lot of people in this country who either love him or hate him."

But it is not those who love him who have become so conspicuous of late. At a town meeting in Charlotte, N.C., last month, a woman rose to her feet without a sign of self-consciousness to sharply question Clinton's character and accuse him of being a hypocrite. At a focus group last week conducted by The Washington Post, a group selected two years ago for its antipathy toward Washington showed signs of having turned that antipathy on Clinton; the men and women used phrases like "con man" and "big fake" and "hypocrite" in discussing the president.

A White House volunteer who handles mail speaks of "letters so angry they almost feel hot." The White House says it does not categorize its mail by approval or disapproval. All that it will say of the numbers, officially, is that Clinton continues to draw a virtual avalanche of mail, at least twice what George Bush did. For the first four months of the year, there were 1.1 million pieces of mail.

Clinton ranks as the most criticized personality, with Hillary Rodham Clinton in second place, on talk radio shows since July 1990. They lead Iraq's Saddam Hussein, former vice president Dan Quayle and [former President] Bush.

Michael Harrison, editor of Talkers magazine, the trade magazine for the talk-show industry, said that based on daily monitoring of every talk station in the top 15 markets and monthly assessments of 200 other stations, "there is no question Bill Clinton is the most criticized individual in the history of the medium."

At least three conservative syndicated talk-show hosts—Rush Limbaugh, G. Gordon Liddy and Ron Reagan, the son of the former president—have made Clinton-bashing the basis of their shows, Harrison said, with no comparable liberal or moderate figure on the other side. Harrison said the notion that "talk radio is totally conservative, a tool of the Republicans, is just not right. It goes both ways." But since Clinton announced for the presidency, the way it has gone for him has been highly negative.

Doug Marlette, a syndicated editorial cartoonist for Newsday and other newspapers, told a White House official recently about the "visceral reaction" in mail he gets after doing Clinton cartoons.

In an interview, Marlette said Clinton material sometimes gets "this incredibly irrational reaction," which he attributes in some measure to Clinton's southern roots and his spouse, but mostly to anxiety and ambivalence in Clinton's generation.

"He and she [Hillary Rodham Clinton] represent something about this time we live in. They are lightning rods for our own conflicts, the ambivalences of our generation," he said. "He is like a hologram that we look into and project deep, visceral reactions onto."

It is not Clinton's policy decisions that produce the reaction, many analysts suggest, but other things: that people increasingly view his character as too flawed for an office that is the visible and revered symbol of the nation; that he has made himself such an Everyman that he has wiped away the invisible barrier of awe and respect for the office that distances presidents from the personalization of opposition; that the change he represents, in policies and in generation, is deeply threatening to some Americans; that Americans are transferring to him their discomfort with Hillary Clinton's powerful role.

Conservatives, with their radio talk shows and Christian television program support, have mastered the art of communicating with one another, and have nurtured visible opposition better than the left ever did for Clinton's Republican predecessors. The invisible barriers that kept political commentary within boundaries somehow have been pierced, allowing anyone to say anything about the president.

Presidential historian Stephen Ambrose said in an interview that he has little doubt Clinton has an unusually vocal minority of haters aligned against him. But beyond generational discomfort or unease with Hillary Clinton's role, Ambrose points to the public perception that Clinton has significant character flaws. "A lot of people think he is so totally insincere. That everything he does is for some political motive. That he works like hell to look like a nice guy instead of just being a nice guy."

Clinton is not the first president to evoke intense hostility. Ambrose cited both Franklin D. Roosevelt and Richard M. Nixon, suggesting FDR had in common with Clinton a controversial spouse who may have caused some of the animosity directed at the husband-president. And he recalled the Nixon-haters who were legion for three decades. Of the last five presidents, however, analysts said Clinton seems unsurpassed in the intensity of emotion he draws.

Glen Bolger, a Republican pollster, said polling in selected congressional districts suggests to him, even if national polls do not, that the intensity of disapproval of Clinton is greater than it was with recent presidents. "I think it is the combination of only getting 43 percent of the vote—people are less sure of his legitimate claim to the White House—along with the sense that, look, he preaches in a moralistic tone about community and greed and values, and his own life reflects none of that. I think character is a major factor."

With Paula Corbin Jones's lawsuit accusing Clinton of sexual harassment, the long investigation of the Whitewater affair and the revelation of Hillary Clinton's commodities trading, doubts about the presidential character are on a steep rise.

Polls have shown that the public's perception that Clinton has a character problem has ebbed and flowed, but it's at high tide this month, even at a time when the overall public approval of the president is either edging down only slightly or holding at slightly over 50 percent approval.

The character numbers for Clinton would be daunting for any politician. In a recent NBC-Wall Street Journal poll, pluralities of Americans now rate Bill Clinton as "poor" in terms of his ethical and moral values, with 36 percent rating him poor, 29 percent mixed and 32 percent good. A Washington Post-ABC News poll found that 56 percent said Clinton has the "honesty and integrity" to serve effectively as president, down from 74 percent the week before he took office.

Clinton's political advisers said they believe the president will be judged by his accomplishments, not by ephemeral concerns about character. But other analysts suggest that the issue detracts from his ability to accomplish the change for which he was elected.

Significant questions about presidential character, said Democratic pollster Peter Hart, can and do have an impact on a president's ability to govern. "It detracts from his ability to get things done," he said. Others describe interconnected circles of presidential success: Public support and esteem for a president encourage congressional support for his programs and produce public gratitude for Washington's getting things done.

Trying to determine why some Americans react with such intensity to Clinton has become something of a pastime among political analysts, historians and armchair politicians. Robert M. Teeter, who ran President Bush's losing campaign to Clinton, adopts some of the Everyman theory.

Teeter, who lives and works in Michigan, said he listens to a lot of local radio and television. "Clinton is out there every day, everywhere," he said, serving in effect as his own press secretary. He called that a "major change" in the history of the presidency where the rule has been that familiarity breeds contempt and dissipates the power of the presidential pulpit.

A constant diet of any president is thought to diminish his impact. For Clinton, there is virtually nothing he won't comment on, and a normal day for him brings a gush of speeches, statements, remarks and photo session interviews. Even some of his own aides lament, as one did last week, that he has "cheapened the currency" of the presidency this way.

Clinton also gives no hint that he thinks anything is too undignified. His willingness to answer questions about his underwear is just the latest example. Said Carville: "You know, he eats too much, he loves sports too much, he talks too much. He is not remote in the way presidents have been, so you are more free to love him or hate him the way you would anyone."

But Carville, Hart and many Democrats say ideology and the organized far right of the Republican Party have the most to do with Clinton-hating. Jerry Falwell, the religious broadcaster, has had his political organization produce a virulently anti-Clinton set of videotapes and has been promoting them during his Sunday and other religious broadcasts.

The infomercials promoting the videotapes include thinly veiled suggestions that the president is mysteriously killing off his potential enemies. Another group— or person—called the American Justice Federation is producing a periodic newsletter called "The Clinton Body Count: Coincidence or the Kiss of Death," which suggests all manner of deaths, suicides and accidents are somehow connected with Clinton.

Floyd Brown, the Washington-based conservative activist, has launched a "Clintonwatch" newsletter-faxletter that daily raises a storm of allegations about Whitewater and all known and obscure Clinton character issues. Reed Irvine, of the conservative Accuracy in Media, ginned up a lobbying campaign to get major publications, such as The Washington Post, to investigate and fully air the Jones sexual harassment allegations.

Clinton advocates maintain that such organized Clinton-bashing had no parallel on the Democratic side when Republicans held the White House. It fans the fears and angers of a minority, feeds what is already historically high anti-government fervor and creates the impression that Clinton has less support than he actually does, they say.

More neutral analysts doubt that.

Organized Clinton-bashing, they say, only plays to that third of voters who traditionally oppose a Democrat in office, no matter who. So the organized efforts of the right might stir up a constituency, but it is one that already exists.

The closest to a consensus on a nonpolitical basis for why Clinton evokes such emotion lies in the generational argument, cited by many. It may be, one of Clinton's aides said last week, that some chunk of the nation believes that no member of the self-indulgent baby boom generation has the character and judgment for the role.

Ambrose, the presidential historian speaking as a representative of the middle-aged, noted, only partially in humor, that he may not be ready for anyone under 60 in the Oval Office. "Guys in their 40s are just too young," he said. "I want maturity. I want a world figure whose reputation is unassailable. I want someone who isn't in the White House to make a name for himself. I want someone who had a respected career before he became president. I think people don't like having a squirt for president. I want Ike."

Bad Taste, Good Business

PAUL FARHI

W omen complain that he's sexist. Minority groups say he's racist. The federal government has been after him for seven years.

Howard Stern, it seems, is nothing but trouble.

The bad boy of morning radio has earned his employer, Infinity Broadcasting Corp., $1.67 million in proposed fines for "indecent" programming. His on-air musings have so infuriated some that two organized groups are pressing the Federal Communications Commission to stop Infinity from buying additional radio stations—and the FCC has come close to doing so.

Why would any self-respecting corporation put up with this?

Infinity says it's a matter of principle—Stern's comments are protected by the First Amendment. Critics say it's a matter of profit—Stern generates about $15 million per year in revenue for Infinity, according to people close to the company, making him too valuable to jettison.

History demonstrates that both arguments are oversimplified. Like controversies involving violent and misogynist music lyrics, sexually explicit movies, and violence in TV programs and video games, Stern's case requires Infinity to perform a tricky cost-benefit analysis.

Deciding whether Stern is worth the trouble depends on what might be called the economics of bad taste. The calculation hinges on how much financial loss may result from a threatened action—a consumer boycott, a government fine, the loss of a broadcast license or a damaged public image. First Amendment or not, business people tend to compromise or capitulate once the heat is turned up high enough.

Infinity, a New York-based company that is the largest radio station owner in the nation, has publicly argued that Stern's on-air comments about masturbation, his racial epithets and general raunchiness are constitutionally protected speech. It has paid none of the FCC's proposed fines and appealed them on these grounds.

Behind the scenes, however, Infinity has engaged in a more delicate give-and-take with the FCC. To mollify the agency's concerns, the company subjected Stern's broadcasts to a 70-second delay in late 1992 to enable a radio manager to bleep questionable material. Infinity's management also has counseled Stern to avoid bits that could engender the FCC's wrath.

What's more, Stern's contract specifically prohibits him from using any of the "Seven Dirty Words" made famous by comedian George Carlin and from reading the FCC's definition of "indecency" during his broadcasts, according to people close to the company. It even prohibits Stern from mentioning Infinity's chief executive, Mel Karmazin, sparing Karmazin some of Stern's famed vitriol.

"He's much tamer now than he was a couple of years ago. . . . We think it's a plus to show the extraordinary lengths we've gone to comply" with the FCC's rules, said one of the company's advisers, who did not want to be identified.

Infinity's advisers recognize that they must strike an uneasy balance. On one hand, they acknowledge the need to be in the good graces of the FCC, if only to get the agency's blessing for deals to come, such as Infinity's pending acquisition of WPGC AM-FM in Washington.

But Infinity has powerful reasons for not muzzling Stern further. Stern's sometimes shocking style has an estimated weekly audience of 4 million listeners on the six Infinity-owned stations and nine independent stations that carry "The Howard Stern Show" around the nation.

Stern is at the top or near the top of the overall ratings in each of his markets during morning drive," radio's prime time. He is especially popular among men from age 18 to 34—the demographic group that advertisers find the hardest to reach. According to Arbitron's most recent ratings, Stern draws more young men than even the highest-rated TV station during prime-time hours in New York, the nation's largest market.

In Washington, the average Stern listener is not only young, but surprisingly affluent, which makes Stern's show even more attractive to advertisers. The program ranks third (out of 35 competitors) in its time slot in the number of listeners who are college graduates, and first in the number of managers, executives and professionals, according to Scarborough Research Corp. of New York. The research company estimates that Stern is second in attracting people here with incomes topping $50,000 a year and 31st in attracting those earning less than $10,000.

The $15 million in revenue that Stern generated for Infinity last year came primarily from advertising (Stern commands as much as $2,000 per 30-second spot). Infinity also makes money by syndicating Stern, to the tune of $300,000 per station per year.

Further, Infinity earns an undisclosed cut of "ancillary" Stern projects, such as the sale of Stern video and audio tapes (one is titled "Crucified by the FCC"), and Stern's record-setting pay-per-view TV special on New Year's Eve (about 400,000 households ordered the anything-goes show, generating almost $16 million in orders, according to the program's marketer, Main Events).

The bottom line: Stern is worth the headaches he's caused. Subtract Stern's annual salary of $7 million, plus such costs as legal fees, from Stern's gross revenue and Infinity is still millions ahead. Sources with knowledge of Infinity's finances confirmed the figures.

While Infinity has remained publicly resistant in the face of government pressure, other companies and industries in similar circumstances have found appeasement more profitable.

Television broadcasters, for example, agreed recently to let independent observers monitor the networks' programs for violence after members of Congress repeatedly criticized the content of TV shows. The agreement not only headed off attempts to legislate a potentially troublesome anti-violence standard, according to broadcasters, but more importantly allowed the industry to preserve its good will on Capitol Hill.

The reason, said Martin Franks, CBS's top Washington representative, is that issues are "linked" in Washington, and legislators don't easily forget a nasty fight.

"We are such a heavily regulated business that at any given point we have a number of things going on in Congress," Franks said. "We always have to be cognizant that if we make a misstep in one area of our business, such as violence, [federal officials] have an opportunity to get our attention in another area of our business." Broadcasters, for example, are attempting to enlist congressional support to fight proposed restrictions on alcohol advertising; the TV industry also is lobbying for new goodies as part of "information highway" legislation that is pending in Congress.

Cleaning Up Their Act

Averting government intervention through self-regulation is a time-tested strategy among media companies.

Faced with state and congressional complaints about "licentiousness" in silent movies, for example, the Motion Picture Producers and Distributors of America, headed by Warren Harding's former campaign manager, Will H. Hays, began a self-censorship board in 1922.

In 1968, with a new outcry building over cinematic explicitness, Motion Picture Association of America President Jack Valenti created the current "voluntary" movie-rating system (such as G, PG, PG–13, R) to head off state and local censorship boards.

More recently, Time Warner Inc. came under fire from police organizations for marketing rapper Ice T's "Cop Killer," a recording that allegedly advocated violence against police officers. Despite a stout public defense of Ice T, Time Warner has since subjected new releases to tighter internal review to screen for controversial material, company officials say.

"You can't let petitions and picket signs tell you what products to market," said one Time Warner source. "On the other hand, you'd be foolish not to realize that people pay attention to what you put your name on. If you value your name, you take extra care with something that could become controversial."

In Howard Stern's case, critics contend that Infinity won't take further steps to rein in its star deejay as long as the government seems disinclined to impose tougher penalties.

"The fines mean nothing. It's business as usual," said Terry Rakolta, who heads a Michigan-based organization, Americans for Responsible Television, that has vowed to contest Infinity's government-granted licenses.

James Quello, the lone FCC commissioner to vote against granting Infinity another license in January and the commission's most outspoken Stern critic, said the fines can "merely be written off as a cost of doing business." Quello said in an interview that the FCC's campaign against Infinity may even have backfired because it has brought additional notoriety to Stern.

Karmazin, Infinity's chief executive, would not comment, and people close to the company asked not to be quoted by name. Although these sources said Infinity will continue to defend its action on First Amendment grounds, they also said that Infinity would have taken stronger action against Stern—such as firing him—if the FCC had subjected its latest station deal to lengthy delays.

"The problem is not the fines; Infinity can afford [to fight] the fines," said one Infinity source. "The problem is . . . putting all of our deals on hold indefinitely. That would mean our whole strategy for growth is being threatened."

Indeed, with $234.2 million in revenue and $14.3 million in profit last year, Infinity has grown into the nation's largest radio-station operator via an aggressive acquisition strategy. The company's goal: to acquire more stations in the nation's 10 largest markets. It already has at least one station in each of them.

From Big to Bigger

Infinity's growth plan includes its deal in February to purchase 25 percent of the Westwood One Inc. programming network. Under a complicated arrangement, Infinity will take over operation of Westwood One's NBC and Mutual radio news networks, bringing under one management such personalities as Stern, Larry King, G. Gordon Liddy, Pat Buchanan, Don and Mike, "The Greaseman," and Don Imus.

Infinity has proposed to buy WPGC AM-FM in Greenbelt for $60 million, and has announced an agreement to buy WXYT-AM in Detroit for $23 million. The FCC is expected to rule on the WPGC deal shortly.

Part of Infinity's formula for success is to use nationally known personalities such as Stern on some of its stations. For years, conventional wisdom held that radio deejays had to be "local" to build a following; Stern and other national radio stars, such as Rush Limbaugh, have proved the opposite.

Some observers say that Stern has helped Infinity in ways that don't show up on its bottom line. Phelps Hoyt, an analyst who follows the company for the Duff & Phelps Inc. debt rating firm, said Stern's notorious conduct has raised Infinity's profile on Wall Street, where its stock has been on a hot streak since it was sold to the public in 1992.

The stock, which has split twice since then and shot up 107 percent in value during 1993, has fueled Infinity's ambitious expansion. In December, the company raised $165 million by selling 5.5 million new shares to the public.

A Helping Hand

Ironically, Infinity also can thank the FCC for an assist. The company has been among the most aggressive in the radio industry in taking advantage of FCC rules, passed in 1992, that liberalized government limits on station ownership. The rules raised the maximum number of stations one company can own nationwide from 24 to 36, and permitted a single operator to own as many as four stations in one market, up from one AM and one FM. If its three pending acquisitions are approved, Infinity will own 26 stations, and it will have three stations in Washington; both exceed the old limits.

To be sure, Infinity has paid some price for Stern's outrageousness. Because of the nature of his program, some "prestige" advertisers—from automakers to airlines to consumer products companies—won't touch the program, Infinity sources said.

Stern's advertisers tend to be smaller companies that appreciate Stern's "edge." These advertisers say they haven't felt any ill effects because of the controversy with the FCC; in fact, Infinity's representatives say the company has never lost an advertiser because of something Stern said on the air.

High-Priced Spots

Stern's advertisers pay a stiff price to be on the show. A "flight" of commercials—one spot per day for a week—costs $10,000 if Stern himself does a "live read" of the advertiser's copy. But advertisers say Stern is worth it because of the influence he has with his audience.

"No one brings in customers like Howard Stern," said Bruce Baron, owner of Car Cash of New York, a retail auto buyer and reseller that has advertised on Stern's program for 10 years. Baron estimates that 75 percent of the calls his company gets are generated by Stern. "He speaks the truth," Barron said. "People listen and people believe him."

Ron Tiongson, advertising manager for Dial-A-Mattress, a direct-market bedding company and Stern advertiser, estimated that Stern was responsible for generating about $3.6 million in company sales last year. "People call up and say, 'Howard told me to call,' " he said. "It's amazing."

Snapple Beverage Corp., maker of juices and iced teas, advertises on the Stern show because it is "a relatively economical way to reach a relatively large audience," said Greg Miller, a spokesman for Snapple, another longtime Stern sponsor. "We don't really use Howard because he's famous or has become famous, but because he has great credibility among his market segment. His fans love him."

Christie Ferris, director of advertising for Roy Rogers Restaurants, said her company has received only one complaint about Stern's show in the five years Roy's has been running ads on the program.

"We don't buy advertising based on how we feel about a [deejay], we buy based on ratings and demographics and what drives our business," she said. Stern's core audience of 18- to 34-year-old men, she noted, is also Roy Rogers's key consumer. Added Ferris, "Most people either like Howard or they don't. If you don't, you always have the option to turn him off."

Washington's Rude Awakening

PAULA SPAN

MEMORANDUM TO: Washington sports zealots, unsuspecting radio listeners, politicos and general populace

FROM: New York correspondent Paula Span

RE: Possibly inexorable dissemination of "Imus in the Morning" radio show, staple of New York airwaves for two decades, into other markets including Washington, where otherwise all-sports station WTEM-AM began simulcasting last week.

Your Typical Show

It originates from a cozily dim studio at WFAN in Queens at 5:30 a.m. in New York and 6 in other cities. Don Imus and sidekicks rant and snigger about Bubba's (i.e., President Clinton's) latest doomed appointments, Mrs. Bubba's (that's Hillary's) overpublicized search for life's meaning ("the traditional questions we all used to ask sitting around a dorm at 2 a.m."), the Mets, Imus himself and whatever unfortunate individual (a congressman, some bureaucrat, this correspondent) has managed to enrage him that day. There's news and sports, which Imus interrupts with further musings. Scattered throughout are taped commentaries by "Richard Nixon" or "Roger Clinton" or "Rush Limbaugh"—generally tasteless, insulting and funny—written and recorded by Imus and a cadre of comic impersonators. Plus phone interviews with actual pols and journalists like Sens. Robert Dole and Bill Bradley, NBC's Tim Russert and ABC's Jeff Greenfield, New York Times columnist Anna Quindlen and Bushling-turned-cablecaster Mary Matalin. Imus regularly chats with his brother, Fred Imus, who runs an auto body shop in El Paso. It's all punctuated with bursts of Sam Cooke, the Isley Brothers and Imus's personal musical messiah, Delbert McClinton.

An Excerpt

Earlier this week, somewhere after the 7 a.m. time check, Imus swigged from a large bottle of Poland Spring water and delivered the business report, which consisted of exultation over a front-page Washington Post story on the troubled Haft family enterprises. "We can revel in the agony of a bunch of rich people!" he concluded jubilantly. "A hair-pulling, screaming, horrible mess! The whole empire will collapse and who will be happiest about it?" His merry men chimed in on cue: "We will!"

"And that's my business report," Imus concluded. Sponsored by Shawmut Bank, "some pretty good folks and they probably won't lose your money."

Recent Outbreaks

With the long-held belief that morning drive-time shows must be local being shattered by the syndication success of New York terror Howard Stern ("Of course, Stern grew up listening to me," Imus notes), Unistar Radio Networks began offering Imus for syndication this spring. The first to sign on, in June, was WQYK in Tampa, which like all-sports WFAN is owned by Infinity Broadcasting. A Boston sports station, a Providence classic rock station and a sports-talk station in Scranton, Pa., all came aboard in early July. Then, last week, Imus came to WTEM-AM (570). Its general manager, Bennett Zier ("that nitwit, that pantload," Imus calls him), is a Lawnguylander familiar with the Imus phenomenon, and Imus's on-air obsessions with public affairs and his own "hideous" life are thought to be attractive to upscale Washingtonians. Next up for Imusizing: a station in Albany, one in the South and another in the Midwest.

All have in common lousy ratings, a condition they hope to remedy by importing Imus at prices (less than $100,000 a year in some smaller markets, the low six figures in larger ones) that are often cheaper than hiring home-grown talent. He returns the favor by ending each show with a stentorian announcement: "This concludes the entertainment and revenue-generating portion of your broadcast day. WFAN New York and the Unistar Radio Network now return you to the rest of your local programming schedule, an indecipherable embarrassment of broadcasting incompetence that compelled this station to subscribe to the 'Imus in the Morning' program in the first place . . ." WTEM-AM does not air this. Zier says that's because it mentions WFAN; it may also reflect his preference for calling WTEM ratings "modest" instead of miserable.

Reaction from the newly invaded territories sounds mixed. A Boston Herald sportswriter finds "trash-mouthed" Imus and his penis jokes unnerving. Providence listeners have complained via call-in line about their loss of morning rock-and-roll. (Imus: "Get a Walkman.") In Washington, (where first-week miscues several times resulted in locals' hearing inscrutable traffic reports about the Bruckner and the Battery Tunnel instead of about the Beltway), Zier says, "people aren't quite sure— is he serious? is he kidding? It creates a little anxiety."

Imus professes utter calm about whether syndication flies; a contract that pays him about $3 million annually for five years probably helps allay any apprehension.

Your Host

Just turned 53. Grew up on an Arizona ranch, broke into radio in California, and claims that his late-'60s stunts like calling a McDonald's and ordering 1,200 hamburgers to go helped trigger an FCC rule requiring disc jockeys to identify themselves when making on-air calls. (So what about the current bit where he plays along with people who call the show thinking they've reached a bank with a similar phone number? Where a woman says she can't understand this $6.18 charge on her boss's account and Imus solemnly explains that it represents a call to a phone-sex number, 970-HUMP? "Those are great, aren't they?" But are they legal? "Well, technically. Maybe. There's a question.")

He's ranked eighth in the New York drive-time ratings but second (to rival Stern) in his target demographic of 25- to 54-year-old men. And he's on the far less listened-to AM band, while Stern's on FM. "If I were on FM? No contest." But Imus's "affluent yuppie" audience accounted for the lion's share of WFAN's $31 million in ad sales last year and its projected $35 million this year, which would make the station the New York billings leader. "This show's not about ratings," Imus says. "It's about huge 25-to-54 demographics and making a lot of money for everyone."

Liberal-looking compared with the right-wing disposition of many talk-radio hosts, Imus admits to no political agenda, just endless fascination with the topic. His guest list was heavily weighted toward pols and journalists long before the show hit Washington. "I voted for Eldridge Cleaver and Jerry Rubin in 1968, and then I voted for Reagan twice," Imus says. He won't say whether he went with Dukakis or Bush but is frank about having voted for Clinton, whose hide he probably helped save in the New York primary last year.

He's frank, too, about the struggles with personal demons that left stretches of the '70s and early '80s a murky haze in his mental databank. Might as well be: "Everybody knew I was a drunk and a coke addict. It was all over the papers when I went to rehab" at a Florida clinic. Imus wonders whether he's doing anyone a favor when he talks about this on the air, because "if I were an ordinary person with an ordinary job, I never could have lasted as long as I did. . . . Most people who aren't making a million dollars for some company or some team aren't cut that slack. . . . I'm not sure it helps an ordinary person to say, 'I can do it, so can you.' "

But he's been sober for six years and drug-free for 11, except that he chews nicotine gum to help kick his last bad health habit. He runs at least an hour a day, keeps to strict veggie diet—his body is a temple. A temple showing wear: He's a bit hard of hearing because "I played Led Zeppelin for 20 years, cranked up loud."

Imus reads at least five newspapers daily and many magazines, faithfully watches C-SPAN and "MacNeil/Lehrer," and even tracks Sunday morning gasathons like "Face the Nation" and "Meet the Press." (He has wondered, publicly, what host Russert looks like in the nude.) His taste in fiction (Larry McMurtry, Cormac McCarthy, John Le Carré, Denis Johnson) runs unexpectedly highbrow for someone who also insists on his right to make penis jokes ("when it's important; not gratuitous penis references").

Imus and the Politics of Demeaning

When Bill Bradley was on the show the other day, he feigned distress. "You said I was tacky," the Rhodes scholar complained, defending his attire and his table manners.

"I don't think I said you were tacky, I said you were tedious," was Imus's correction before he and the senator moved on to a discussion of the budget conference.

For years, local politicians have lined up to be interviewed-slash-insulted by the I-Man. But the ritual gained national attention last year when not-yet-Nominee Clinton, worried by Jerry Brown's unexpected victory in Connecticut and reeling from nonstop assaults by the New York media, stepped up to the mike. Clinton was funny and self-deprecating, turned the sneering Imus into a partisan, and began to regain his footing; the interview entered the lore about the influence of nontraditional media on the '92 campaign.

"You can't quantify that sort of thing," cautions Clinton strategist Mandy Grunwald—but she thinks the show helped. "People loved it, loved learning that Clinton had a sense of humor. In New York, having the guts to go one-on-one with Imus tells you something about a person, and that's what New Yorkers tend to like about people: guts." Bubba's been a guest three times since, most recently in May, when the "Today" show simulcast the interview.

Such treatment is thought particularly valuable for pols who sometimes suffer from stuffed-shirt images, like Connecticut Gov. Lowell Weicker and Bradley. "It's not 'Nightline,' it's not 'Meet the Press,' it gives them an opportunity to reveal their humanity," Imus says. Media figures he'd like to book but that won't appear: Mark Shields, Larry King and Rush Limbaugh, for three. Politicos who have turned him down: zero, he says. Though it's safe to assume that Ted Kennedy would decline; Imus keeps accenting his Kennedy jokes with particularly grisly sound effects, a car crash followed by the gurgling sounds of someone drowning.

To date, no measurable political fallout has resulted from the show's giggling about racial issues, sexual orientation and public figures' weight problems or the repeated playing of "They Ain't Makin' Jews Like Jesus Anymore" by Kinky Friedman and the Texas Jewboys.

Dirty Little Secrets

a. Despite an audience that's 60 to 70 percent male and the show's boys-will-be-jerks attitude to match, Imus has a distinct thing for intelligent women. He boasts of booking Cokie Roberts and Nina Totenberg, dotes on Ruth Bader Ginsburg and Mary Matalin, and probably harbors fantasies of running off with Anna Quindlen. He hung up after a phone interview with Quindlen the other day and yelped to his studio buddies (off-mike), "I love her! That's a smart sonuvabitch!"

b. Despite his fearsome image and a tendency to brutalize people at a distance, Imus is reasonably courteous when he actually gets them on the air. He never mentioned his nude fantasies to Russert during their conversation last week. And he called Clinton "sir" during their famous interview, forcing the candidate himself to bring up the "Bubba" label.

He savaged your correspondent on the air every quarter-hour the day after she phoned to ask for an interview, called her a "prissy yuppie" and derided her lack of knowledge about his show and her request to meet with him before she left on vacation. Days later, said correspondent arrives in the studio armed with various retorts, only to find Imus politely offering food and drink, and refraining from insults. He actually apologizes for swearing, and offers to stop if it offends. He's downright gentlemanly.

He probably doesn't want that to get around.

D.C. Media Executive Succeeds by Knowing Hispanic Market

JONATHAN D. GLATER

Antonio Guernica understands the importance of knowing your market.
World Cup soccer may have drawn outside attention to his D.C. Spanish-language television and radio programs, but the English-speaking audience is incidental to the general manager of WMDO-TV (Channel 48) and WMDO-AM 1540. It's Spanish-speakers that Guernica woos.

"They are the ones who determine the focus of our news coverage; they are the ones who determine the focus of our programming," Guernica said. Immigration issues and political events in Latin America—as well as soccer, of course—are some of the topics especially important to the audience he has studied carefully for years.

Guernica, 43, is president and co-founder of privately held Los Cerezos Broadcasting Co., which owns the broadcast licenses for the radio station and WMDO-TV, an affiliate of national Spanish-language broadcaster Univision Network Inc.

Guernica provides access to the metropolitan area's burgeoning Spanish-speaking market, which otherwise advertisers might not know how to reach. The District's Hispanic population nearly doubled from 1980 to 1990, to almost 33,000 from about 18,000, and that growth has not slowed down.

His knowledge of the target market comes into play at every level, from making programming decisions to reaching potential advertisers. "We do some of the things that in other markets would be taken care of by an ad agency," said Guernica, who has written a book about reaching the Hispanic market in the United States.

"We do everything we can to facilitate an advertiser's entry into the Hispanic market in Washington," Guernica said, from providing demographic information to advising a company on the nature of its television or radio advertising.

If a television ad "is full of blond-haired, blue-eyed, very non-Hispanic-looking people, we would do our best to dissuade them from using that advertising," he said. In the future Guernica said he hopes to provide more information to potential advertisers wishing to "test the waters."

The strategy has paid off, said Stuart Livingston, vice president and director of affiliate relations at Univision in New York. "He's running a station in a market that shouldn't be able to support a full-time television operation that does local news,"

Livingston said, adding that "this station stands out" among Univision's 600 affiliates.

Guernica, whose family fled from Cuba to the District in the early 1960s, became involved with Univision, then the Spanish International Network, in 1978. He was contacted by the network while he was working on a magazine put out by the National Council of La Raza in Washington.

Guernica worked on promoting the 1978 World Cup, then moved to New York to do market research. In 1980 he returned to the District to round up shareholders to found Los Cerezos, and the channel went on the air in 1980.

Guernica, who lives with his wife and three children in Herndon, took a management position at Los Cerezos in 1987, two years before the company acquired the radio station.

Providing both television and radio programming lets Los Cerezos reach more of the Hispanic community, Guernica said.

Television/Cable 8

Sale Speculation Shows TV Networks Are Hot

PAUL FARHI

Old conventional wisdom: The TV networks are dinosaurs. New conventional wisdom: The dinosaurs thrived for millions of years.

All summer long, it seems, people have been trying to buy a network. In July, the QVC cable network nearly merged with CBS Inc. This week, networks were once again "in play." Sources at Time Warner Inc. and NBC disclosed that the two companies were discussing the sale of NBC and its cable networks, while Wall Street traders bid up CBS stock on talk of discussions between CBS and Walt Disney Co. In both cases, there was less than met the eye.

Time Warner's conversations with NBC's owner, General Electric Co., were described as very preliminary by sources at GE, NBC and Time Warner. Moreover, if haggles over price and management were not enough, such a merger has a variety of federal laws and regulations standing in its way. As for CBS-Disney, there were flat denials about any talks from both sides.

Nevertheless, this season of speculation about the fate of the networks does signal a fundamental change of perception. Broadcast networks now are spoken of as hot commodities. What's more, they are likely to stay that way, even when—or if—the era of the 500-channel, interactive TV system finally comes.

Signs of the networks' health are easy to spot. During the recently completed "upfront" advertising sales period (in which advertisers buy air time in advance for the new fall shows) ABC, NBC, CBS and Fox collected a record $4.5 billion. The robust spending reflected not only the end of the recession, but the fact that viewers have stopped deserting network programming for cable and other video alternatives.

"We have been saying for years that the networks are the center of the broadcast business," said Arthur Gruen, president of Wilkovsky, Gruen Associates, an economic consulting firm that specializes in media and entertainment businesses. "For a while people thought broadcast was dying. But we seem to be in a new equilibrium."

Gruen, as well as other observers, say the networks' future seems solid because no other video medium has what the networks have: the ability to attract millions of viewers night after night.

The networks' power is, to an extent, self-perpetuating. Advertisers need mass-audience networks because network advertising, while increasingly expensive, is still the most cost-effective way to tell millions of people about a product or service via electronic means. And the networks can keep attracting mass audiences because, armed with those billions of ad dollars, they are the only ones capable of affording a full season of big-budget programs that attract millions of viewers.

This economic equation has become particularly clear to Hollywood's major studios, which for years have produced and sold their programs to the networks. The studios, including Disney and Time Warner, are taking notice because the traditional supplier-distributor relationship is on the verge of a radical change. In the fall of 1995, 24-year-old federal rules that have limited the networks' rights to produce and syndicate their own entertainment programs will expire. The lapsing of the so-called financial interest and syndication rules will permit the networks to produce more of their prime-time shows, potentially leaving the studios without their biggest customers.

Unless, of course, Hollywood's majors start or buy their own networks first. That is why Time Warner is sniffing around NBC, and why Disney's name keeps surfacing in association with CBS and ABC (Fox already is owned by a studio, which got an early exemption to the "fin-syn" rules).

Analysts say the other major studio owners, Sony Corp. and Matsushita Electric Industrial Co., parent of MCA's Universal Pictures, are likely buyers as well. (Both are Japanese companies; federal law prohibits foreign ownership of domestic TV stations but not of networks).

Alternatively, Time Warner, parent of Warner Bros. studios, and Viacom Inc., parent of Paramount Pictures studios, are racing to establish a fifth broadcast network by early next year.

Sources at NBC and in Washington say it is highly unlikely that regulators would permit Time Warner, in particular, to buy NBC or another network. Federal rules prohibit a company from owning both a network and local cable TV systems, and Time Warner is the nation's second-largest cable operator.

The rules also prohibit a company from owning broadcast TV stations and cable systems in the same market; Time Warner's cable systems therefore wouldn't fit with NBC's six highly profitable stations, including WRC-TV, Channel 4, in Washington.

But Time Warner might still swing a deal by selling some cable assets, or by negotiating a "strategic alliance" to supply programming to one of the networks, with no equity changing hands.

Said an NBC executive last week, "There are still huge hassles and huge hurdles to overcome."

The Fox in the Children's Coop

ELLEN EDWARDS

Barney aside, the most startling success story in children's television in the '90s is the Fox Kids Network. And Margaret Loesch is the woman who made it happen.

In less than four years, the network has gone from nonexistence to No. 1 with kids in the ratings categories for ages 2 to 11 and 6 to 17, with such ratings successes as "Mighty Morphin Power Rangers," "X-Men" and "Batman" as well as Steven Spielberg's "Animaniacs" and "Tiny Toons." And in light of Monday's announcement that Fox is trading up for affiliates with stronger signals in 12 major markets, the kids' lineup seems destined to grow even more powerful. With its signature action programming spread through an after-school schedule and a 3 1/2-hour Saturday morning block, it's a good bet your kids are watching Fox at least part of the time.

Kids Network President Loesch, not an unambitious sort, would like to have a Sunday morning block too, but right now she says the affiliates make too much money from paid religious programming to give up that time to the network—and so instead she'll try a syndicated Sunday morning Fox radio show next fall.

Some critics say the kids' programming is the equivalent of Fox's schlocky nighttime hits, such as "Melrose Place" and "Beverly Hills 90210." But that doesn't seem to bother Loesch.

She is sitting in a small bar in a midtown hotel, and the conversation has turned to one of the big influences in her career, a small mouse with a squeaky voice and big ears.

"The Mickey Mouse Club," she says, "made no pretense about being anything other than entertaining. But I learned a lot of things. . . . There were those little cowboy stories where kids learned to get along and how to deal with bullies and stories on what I call self-esteem."

However much she was influenced by the tiny rodent, Loesch, 48, does seem to know what kids will watch. For years she tried to sell "Power Rangers" and "X-Men" but had no takers until she herself became a buyer.

"Power Rangers," which is about a group of teenagers who become superheroes by summoning the power of the dinosaurs, is not only a hit on TV, but the toys it spun off were the big sellers last Christmas. "X-Men," in which a group of "mutant" foster children vie for respectability ("the teen experience," says Loesch), has become a cult hit of the older set too; the network has gotten calls from 30-year-old Wall Street bond traders asking when a new "X-Men" will air.

Both shows have been criticized in the press for their violent content, but Loesch says that neither parents nor teachers have followed suit—and, she adds, she will take her cues from them.

For the fall, Fox will add an educational program for preschoolers. It's doing it at the urging of the affiliates, who have to prove to a skeptical Federal Communications Commission that they are fulfilling the requirements of the Children's Television Act to provide that kind of programming.

The show, "Fox's Cubhouse," will feature a group of characters introducing and watching three different shows: Mondays and Fridays it will be "Jim Henson's Nature Show," a Muppet talk show about nature; Tuesdays and Thursdays will feature "Johnson and Friends," an Australian television production with big stuffed animals that teaches the values of socialization; and on Wednesdays the show is "Rimba's Island," which will use fantasy animals to teach music and movement.

She'll also add "Spiderman" to the Saturday schedule, a show that happens to be produced by New World Communications, in which Fox acquired an interest this week. In addition, next season will see "The Tick," which Loesch describes as "an animated superhero show that pokes fun at superhero shows."

While Loesch says she is enthusiastic about the "Cubhouse" concept, she's not happy about the Children's Television Act, which she describes as a "kind of gun to the head"—and quite unnecessary, she adds. "I think we were on the road to doing exactly what they wanted," she says, "but I resent people saying it's only because of the act" that certain shows are being scheduled.

And besides, she contends, entertainment programs can teach just as much as so-called educational programming—though critics of Fox would hope she's not thinking of "Power Rangers" or "X-Men" when she says that.

Loesch has been involved in children's television throughout her career, both as a programmer at ABC and NBC and as a producer. Still, in all those years, she couldn't get anyone to buy her idea for either "Power Rangers" or "X-Men."

Even her Fox bosses were skeptical about her vision for Fox Kids—despite her admiration for Disney, she was convinced that "the pendulum could swing over to action-adventure." Loesch sent Fox Broadcasting Chairman Lucie Salhany a tape of "Power Rangers" shortly before it was to air and then went on vacation, during which time she received a fax.

It was from Salhany. She wrote that she had watched the tape and was "troubled. I think it's terrible. We have a real problem here. What are you going to do about it?' " recounts Loesch, laughing. "And she also said, 'Maybe I am too old, but I don't think the show is going to work, and I think it's going to be a disaster.' "

Loesch faxed her back. "I wrote in the margin. Where she said 'Maybe I am too old,' I said, 'Yes, you are. This show is going to work with kids and if it doesn't I'll make a change, but please stick with it.' " She never heard another word from Salhany, and the ratings proved Loesch right.

Still, she says, Salhany still doesn't like it. "But she loves its success," says Loesch.

Others are not so thrilled. Peggy Charren, founder of Action for Children's Television and a longtime observer of children's programming, is particularly dismayed by Fox's success. "The worst shows are winning the ratings game," she says. "Fox will run the questionable programming when others say, 'We won't do that anymore.' 'X-Men' has absolutely nothing to recommend it. . . . It equates foster children with alien life. What kind of peculiar idea is that?"

To help the network understand the effects its programming will have on children, Fox has set up a six-member advisory board made up of child-development specialists who deal with children every day. The board reads scripts and makes suggestions for changes. And according to board member Frank Palumbo, a Washington pediatrician, the group has expressed concerns about the violence in both "Power Rangers" and "X-Men." He says he believes the network is serious about responding to that issue.

Loesch says her standard rule is that violence should not be of the sort that could be imitated by a child to his harm. But then she tells you she saw her own 5-year-old son imitate the karate on "Power Rangers" and had to intervene to get him to stop. "The minute he jumped up and started pretending he was a karate expert, I said, 'You can pretend to be playing karate, but you don't go out and chop the cat and you can't hit your friends, that's unacceptable. This is a fantasy and it's only television.' And he understood. . . ."

One thing she has learned from being a parent, she says without a trace of irony, is "how important it was to a child to have the toy or whatever it is of his favorite show or character. . . . I only saw one side of it—a toy company trying to make money. I didn't realize the comfort it provided a child. . . .

"I think I still have a bit of the kid inside of me," she says. "See, I like our shows."

The Whole World Was Watching

TOM SHALES

The medium was television, the message was pain. One watched in disbelief and horror, first at the not-guilty verdicts in the Rodney King beating trial, then at the brutality and destruction wreaked by rioters in south-central Los Angeles reacting to that verdict.

There was a ghastly symmetry to it as experienced through television. For more than a year, viewers had seen excerpts from an amateur videotape showing a gang of mostly white Los Angeles police officers savagely beating the seemingly defenseless King, who is black, as he struggled on the ground after a high-speed chase.

The tape quickly became part of the iconography of our time.

Now on the TV screen one saw members of a mob pulling motorists from their cars, beating and kicking them, and leaving them for dead in the street. The grimly familiar ritual from the videotape was being reenacted.

CNN, which first aired live pictures of violence at 10:18 Wednesday night, was beaming the nightmarish scenes not only all over the country, but all over the world. America was once more exporting images to confirm the worst stereotypes of itself as a violent and racist society.

Hopelessness was the inescapable aura of the day. The King verdict-acquittal for the four white cops on almost all charges—was denounced as "unbelievable," "insane" and "racist" by people on the street. A woman in Germany interviewed on CNN called it "a disgrace for the American justice system."

At the same time, the marauding mobs evoked memories of the Watts riots 27 years ago, with the clear implication that for impoverished minorities in urban ghettos, nothing had really changed. The pictures seemed to say that divisiveness and hostility run as deep as ever.

"We'd like to say 'good morning' on this Thursday, but frankly there is nothing good to be said about this last morning of April, 1992," said a grim Bryant Gumbel at the start of NBC's "Today" show yesterday. Gumbel narrated footage shot from a helicopter by KCOP, an independent station in Los Angeles, showing a man being dragged from a truck and beaten.

Co-anchor Katherine Couric told Gumbel later that she nearly became sick watching what the KCOP reporter had accurately called "terrible, terrible pictures."

Gumbel said late yesterday from his home in New York that he had indeed felt emotional during the broadcast. "I'm not terribly good at restraining my feelings," he said. "What I feel is less anger than sadness. It was a very sad day. It's a matter of realizing the depth of the divisions between us, as if we're so far apart, it isn't even close."

Like many people, Gumbel said he was astonished by the verdict, especially after seeing the incriminating videotape over and over. "I think any logical person would be floored," Gumbel said. On the air, he spoke by phone to an unidentified juror who insisted that evidence and the videotape showed that King had been "in control" of the situation throughout the beating and therefore called it justified.

King "never lost control of the situation" even while being beaten senseless, the juror claimed. "He was in complete control," she said.

"As somebody in the office remarked today, if Rodney King was controlling the situation, he was doing a very bad job of it," Gumbel said.

On the air, however, Gumbel was objective though upset. Couric was upset too. Ron Allen, a black correspondent for CBS who covered the trial from Simi Valley for "The CBS Evening News," also seemed emotional when reporting the verdict on the air. He looked stunned. Can anyone fault him for that?

Allen said late yesterday from Los Angeles that his seeming shock was partly a result of having learned the verdict just 15 minutes before air time. He said race may have been a factor in the story, but that he tried not to let it affect his reporting.

"I don't think of myself as an African American reporter first," Allen said. "It's something that's there, obviously. But I don't approach a story saying, 'How as an African American should I feel about this?' "

"I'm going to try as much as I can to be first and foremost a communicator," Gumbel said. "My job is not to display my views or interpret what others are saying. My job is to let them say it."

One tough question that has to be asked is whether showing so much of the violence on TV contributes to escalating it, especially when the violence is shown live, as it was on CNN Wednesday night (the verdict having been announced just after 6 p.m. Eastern time) and, later, on a special edition of ABC's perpetually outstanding "Nightline."

Ted Koppel, "Nightline" anchor, said yesterday from his office here that the riots in Los Angeles bring up "all the classic old questions" about how much TV affects the stories it covers and said it "could be argued" that showing fires burning on live TV might inspire others to set more fires.

"Sure, there's always problems with it," Koppel said. "You have to keep asking yourself at which point does the presence of a live camera have a different effect than, say, if you're just taping something. Does taking cameras out of the region altogether contribute to calming the situation?

"If you find someone who can answer those questions honestly and with clarity, good for you. I can't answer them for you."

Koppel said another question should be asked: "If television pulled out, would the people involved rise up in righteous indignation that they were being ignored? These are people who feel disenfranchised as it is. The media does provide something of a safety valve, I think."

Jesse Jackson phoned Koppel at 10 p.m. Wednesday to volunteer to appear on "Nightline" partly in the hope of being a calming influence. Rep. Maxine Waters (D-Calif.), who represents the south-central district, also appeared.

None of the jurors had shown up on television as of yesterday's coverage. Their faces were not shown during courtroom coverage of the trial. Koppel said he was working yesterday to persuade one or more jurors to appear on tonight's edition of "Nightline," which he hopes will originate from, or close to, the riot area. One juror appeared on last night's show with her face obscured by shadows.

"The jurors have no legal obligation to appear in public, but I think they have a moral obligation to tell us how they came to their decision," Koppel said.

Whether members of the media should intervene when they see people victimized by violence also was an issue. The KCOP reporter could be heard saying, "Hit the siren, Doug," to the pilot of the helicopter, perhaps hoping the siren would cause the mob to disperse. Then he shouted, "I think we took a round," suggesting the chopper had been shot at from the ground.

A producer and technician in a CNN news truck parked near the riot zone didn't have to go looking for violence. According to Dave Farmer, CNN's Los Angeles bureau chief, two men broke into the truck just after midnight Wednesday and punched the producer, Veronica McGregor, before she and the technician pushed them out again. Neither, Farmer said, was seriously injured.

"We try to be careful and responsible," Farmer said of CNN's coverage, rejecting the notion that the presence of cameras could encourage violence. "I don't think CNN can accept that we are the instigators here. I don't think news media, by reporting an event, can cause another event."

But Reuven Frank, former president of NBC News, is not so sure. From his home in suburban New Jersey, Frank said it is fair to raise the question.

"Technology has made so many things possible that are questionable both in terms of journalistic ethics and public policy considerations," Frank said. "People in the business are going to have to face these things, but they're not facing anything but the competition, as they chase one another down Market Street."

The relatively recent ability to go "live" from almost anywhere, Frank said, encourages networks and local stations to do live broadcasts without considering the propriety or the consequences.

Frank had just become president of the news division when NBC, and the other networks, faced the challenge of covering the anti-war demonstrations outside the 1968 Democratic convention in Chicago. Equipment was not as portable or unobtrusive then, and live telecasts were not as easy.

Besides, then-Mayor Richard J. Daley forbade the networks from covering the demonstrations live and, Frank says, brought about a phony electricians' strike to make the ban stick. So the networks shot the demonstrations on videotape, then couriered the tape back to the convention center where it could be broadcast

The demonstrators gravitated to the cameras and the chant they sent up became a rallying cry in the new age of television: "The whole world is watching!" Now the whole world is watching again, and in shock.

Television is supposed to be a cool medium, but rage is pouring through it now. Rage, and sadness.

This is what reporter Allen said he felt as he drove through the riot zone Wednesday night with a CBS News crew. Yesterday he remembered "this feeling of sadness that just swept over me." It seems fair to say that it swept over the country as well.

When No News Is Bad News

PAUL FARHI

The news on CNN isn't pretty these days.

The cable TV network that pioneered 24-hours-a-day news, that astonished the world with its live telecasts of the Persian Gulf War and the Russian coup attempt, is in a deep slump. Ratings are down—way down. Profits are falling. Management is busy shuffling anchors and programs.

The problem, in part, is that the news just won't cooperate. From Bosnia to South Africa, from Rwanda to North Korea to the health care debate in Washington, none of the big stories of the moment is capturing the viewing public's attention, CNN executives say.

Indeed, one bit of black humor circulating around the network's Atlanta headquarters, according to CNN President Tom Johnson, is that all CNN needs is a good war.

"Nobody is panicking, but we know we need to address this in every way we can," said Johnson, who has run CNN since 1990. "It has been a frustrating period."

It is also all but unprecedented in the 14-year history of Ted Turner's celebrated brainchild.

After struggling in its earliest days, CNN began turning an operating profit after its fifth year, and profits have been chugging upward ever since. Last year, Turner Broadcasting System's news division, which includes CNN, CNN International and Headline News, had record operating income of $212 million on revenue of $599 million.

But CNN's operating income fell 7.5 percent in the first quarter and shows no signs of coming around in the second, despite a general recovery in TV advertising spending.

Thus far in the second quarter, CNN's prime-time ratings are down 26 percent, a shortfall that will force the network to give advertisers free air time to make up for smaller-than-promised audiences. This has been offset partially by a generally strong advertising market. "If this had occurred in a down market, they'd be in a world of trouble," said Kathy Lawson, senior vice president of St. Louis-based Advanswers Media, which buys air time for sponsors.

Despite the gloomy signs, CNN hasn't scrimped on the hard-news coverage that is its trademark. For example, the network sent a team of 70 employees to South

Africa to cover that nation's first all-race elections in April. It has maintained its bureau in Sarajevo longer than any other American television network. And it recently scored a journalistic coup when one of its reporters, Mike Chinoy, broadcast live from North Korea, an apparent first on American television.

None of these efforts, however, produced much of a stir in the Nielsen ratings (at any given moment, CNN's domestic audience averages a mere 375,000 households). Laments Johnson, "It appears there isn't much interest in international news unless there's some major crisis, or unless there's some U.S. involvement."

In part, CNN may be a victim of a TV news glut. Local all-news cable channels, such as Washington's NewsChannel 8, have proliferated around the country, and broadcasters have expanded their local newscasts to as many as three hours in the afternoons and early evenings. And as always, CNN is up against the big networks' news divisions, as well as such syndicated tabloid shows as "Hard Copy" and "Inside Edition."

But Johnson and others at CNN say Washington is partially to blame for CNN's problems. New federal "must-carry" rules that guarantee local broadcast stations a spot on nearby cable systems have forced many cable operators to rearrange their channel line-ups. As a result, CNN estimates that its channel position on more than half of the nation's 11,000 cable systems has been moved in the past year, presumably making it harder for viewers to find the network.

Although many cable networks were bumped around, CNN was hurt most by this change because it often occupied the popular lower band of channels (2-13) before the new regulations began, said Daniel Fischer, vice president of research for Discovery Networks, the Bethesda-based parent of the Discovery and Learning channels.

Turner Broadcasting has challenged the new cable rules before the Supreme Court.

What's more, people at CNN say government-ordered cable price rollbacks will directly affect CNN's bottom line this year; the cutbacks make it difficult for network owners such as Turner to raise the fees they charge cable operators to carry their material.

Johnson maintains that CNN's basic strategy—round-the-clock news from everywhere, live as often as possible—is sound. But Johnson clearly is tinkering with the rest of the schedule. Yesterday, he named two network veterans, Lou Dobbs and Bob Furnad, to head up programming development.

Even before the announcement, changes were underway. Owing to the success of such personality-driven CNN programs as "Crossfire" and "Larry King Live," CNN recently added a late-night sports talk show called "Calling All Sports" and will soon introduce another chatfest, called "TalkBack Live."

CNN also has moved its anchor chairs around to compete more effectively against the Big Three's evening broadcasts. CNN's best-known newscasters, Bernard Shaw and Judy Woodruff, last month were paired at 6 p.m., the most-watched period for TV news. There is talk that a well-known news personality may be CNN's next hire, part of an overall effort, according to one company source, "to make us something more than a video wire service."

Some Broadcast TV Stations Don't Want Their Business

GREGG ZOROYA

A s suburban candidates scrambled to flood Washington airwaves with their last appeals for votes before the primary election Tuesday, they found themselves shut out by some Washington area broadcasters.

Media buyers for Montgomery County Council member Bruce T. Adams, one of three candidates in the Democratic primary for county executive, said WTTG-TV, Channel 5, and WJLA-TV, Channel 7, rejected their requests to buy commercial air time. State Sen. Beatrice P. Tignor, a Democratic candidate in the hotly contested Prince George's County executive race, could not get her commercials around the contemporary music of Howard University's WHUR-FM radio. Both candidates have found air time on other television and radio stations.

"I've never seen anything like it," said Lesley Israel, who operates CEO Politics Inc., of Washington, an ad-purchasing agency for political candidates, including Adams. "We are having trouble spending our clients' money."

The snubbing is troublesome to suburban candidates because the most popular programming on which to buy advertising is based in Washington, not Prince George's or Montgomery counties.

Broadcasters and media buyers say there are a combination of reasons candidates are being shunned by stations, and all have to do with earnings and lost revenue.

"It is all about supply and demand," said Jennifer Tyce, sales manager at WHUR, which she said has chosen not to sell air time to any local candidate.

Under federal law, candidates are guaranteed the lowest possible rate for air time, said Milton Gross, chief of the political branch for the Federal Communications Commission. And if broadcasters sell time to any candidate in a particular race, they have to sell an equal amount of air time to any opponent who demands it, Gross said. With an unusually large number of hotly contested Washington area races at county, state and federal levels, the number of politicians who could buy up precious air time at budget rates was disconcertingly high for local broadcasters, some of them said.

"If you get enough of those [local campaign ads], it can screw up your bottom line," said a general manager for one local radio station who asked not to be named.

To make matters worse, broadcasters said, the rebounding economy has meant an upswing in advertising, and they can readily sell air time to non-political customers for three or four times the money.

"It's the stations that are in the large markets [like Washington] which are sold out most of the time . . . that are the ones who don't have the room for state and local candidates," Gross said.

Broadcasters are required by federal law to provide a reasonable amount of commercial space to candidates for federal offices, and there are plenty of those demanding air time in the Washington area.

Lynn S. Franaroff, public relations director for WTTG, confirmed that the station is not selling ad time to local candidates. Officials for WJLA did not return telephone calls.

An official at another major Washington television station, who asked not to be identified, said he is still selling ad time to surban candidates but will stop if available air time tightens further.

Television is already a costly and troublesome outlet for suburban candidates, even without the current constraints. It costs about $90,000 to buy enough time so that an average viewer will see a candidate's commercial a minimum of five times in one week, said Rob Engel, senior vice-president for Fenn King Murphy Communications, another political advertising company based in Washington. Tignor is one of the company's clients.

But with all of its cost and complications, television commercials on local network affiliates are still viewed as the best forum for persuasion.

Cable television is an alternative. For county candidates, cable stations can tailor the broadcast to a specific county, and air time is cheaper. Popular cable outlets are ESPN and Cable News Network. Adams and one of his opponents, former Rockville mayor Douglas Duncan, can be seen in advertisements on cable television.

"As it gets toward the end, you want to hit a few more people with each dollar, and the way to do that is to go on TV," said Duncan's campaign manager, Jerry Pasternak.

However, cable television doesn't have nearly the viewership of broadcast network stations, and it cannot take the last-minute orders demanded in hotly contested campaigns.

Less expensive ways of getting a candidate's message out are legion: mailers, signs, telephone banks, door-to-door canvassing, shaking hands at Metro stops and waving at drivers from curbs. Candidates from county executive down employ some or all of these techniques.

But "people are accustomed to getting their information on television," Israel said. "While they can walk out on a commercial, they don't usually. They sit there to see what's coming next."

Going Shopping for a Black Audience

MIKE MILLS

B lack Entertainment Television is going shopping.
For two hours every Saturday afternoon beginning in September, the Washington-based cable channel will look a lot like the Home Shopping Network. Viewers will be able to call in to order jewelry, clothing and other merchandise targeted specifically at the network's mostly black audience.

If the idea catches on in a 13-week trial, BET hopes to create an entirely new cable shopping network geared toward African Americans. That would begin a widely predicted trend toward niche marketing in the $3 billion-a-year television home-shopping industry.

"We think this channel will fulfill the needs of the black consumer by getting into neighborhoods where appliance stores and department stores are shutting down, where it's difficult to get a low price and where there may be trouble getting credit," said Robert L. Johnson, BET's chief executive. "In addition, black manufacturers and distributors often can't get access to shelf space in retail stores. This is a unique way to reach the target audience."

The show, which will have its premiere at 4 p.m. on Sept. 17, will be co-produced with Home Shopping Network.

Buyers also will benefit by getting direct access to products that are hard to find in major retail stores, he said. For example, black women spend roughly $1.2 billion on beauty aids annually. But they often have trouble finding products designed for their types of skin or hair.

Black consumers contributed $282 billion in retail spending to the economy in 1993, according to the Chicago-based newsletter Target Market News.

To be called "BET Shop," the show will be co-hosted by Home Shopping Network veterans Tina Berry and Terry Lewis. It will be transmitted from Home Shopping Network studios in Florida but will run on the BET network under BET's name. BET has an estimated 40 million viewers.

The announcement is Johnson's latest attempt to make BET Holdings Inc. more than just the parent company of the first cable network specifically for African Americans.

The company also has been struggling to keep afloat two magazines aimed at young black people, and last June formed a direct marketing venture with Home

Shopping Network to sell music recordings and skin care products for black women. It also plans a jazz music cable channel, which also may be used as a vehicle for selling BET's compilations of jazz recordings.

Financial analysts have been skittish about whether Johnson is diversifying too quickly, but many welcomed the move toward home shopping.

"The problem investors have is that [BET] may be getting into too many things and losing sight of its core subscriber growth," said John Rezai, director of research for the Chapman Company, a Baltimore-based investment firm. "But the home shopping thing is probably a good mix for them. They can use it to leverage all these different operations with each other."

BET partner Home Shopping Network controls slightly more than $1 billion of the $3 billion TV home shopping market.

QVC Inc. controls a like amount, with program-length commercials making up the rest.

Home Shopping Network reaches more than 60 million households, but its potential is limited by the number of channels available on cable systems, said HSN President Gerald F. Hogan.

Hogan said new cable rate regulations mandated by Congress have stalled development of new cable networks. Until the vaunted 500-channel universe arrives, he said, the BET venture will help Home Shopping Network approach more narrower market segments before someone else does.

"I'd rather it be our team fragmenting the audience than somebody else's team," Hogan said. This way, "we can launch a new service at a fraction of the cost of anybody else."

Crime Doesn't Play

HOWARD KURTZ

Jack Cahalan stops the videotape on the final picture of the murder scene.

The news director of Baltimore's NBC affiliate is playing back a report that aired last December, after two women were killed by a relative while baking Christmas cookies at home. Unlike most grisly crime stories, he proudly notes, there was no graphic footage. But in the final seconds, as a policeman walked away in slow motion, viewers could see the white sheet covering one victim's body, with her foot sticking out.

"If we had to do it today, I'm not sure I'd run that last shot," Cahalan says.

Cahalan's station, WMAR-TV, has embraced what is becoming the hottest trend in local television. Six months after the concept was invented at a Minneapolis station, what some have dubbed "family-sensitive news" has spread to at least 15 cities, including Miami, Pittsburgh, Seattle, Denver, Charlotte, N.C., Tucson, Sacramento, Calif., and Albuquerque.

Cahalan, who disdains the term "family sensitive," traces his station's shift to a series of community meetings. "I'm telling you," he says, "no matter what economic area we're in, white, black, Native American, the moral of the story is always the same: 'Why do we have to look at so much blood and guts every night on the news?' After a while you say, well, these are the customers."

Those who are trying to tone down crime coverage are swimming against a tabloid tide that has washed across the television landscape in the last five years. The softer approach has not yet penetrated such big-city, high-crime markets as New York, Los Angeles and Chicago.

One Washington station, WJLA (Channel 7), says it has been de-emphasizing crime for 2 1/2 years but sees no need to tout it with a special label.

"Being sensitive to families is what we're supposed to be doing," says WJLA News Director Gary Wordlaw. "We've been trying to de-emphasize body bags and bloodstained streets and do more coverage of issues. We don't ignore crime, but you sure don't have to fill up your newscast with it."

Like many fads, family-sensitive news has become a catch-all phrase with no clear definition. For some stations, it simply means eliminating explicit crime footage at 5 or 6 p.m., when children are most likely to be watching, but restoring it on late-night newscasts. For others it means less crime news, period. Still others speak of providing context and perspective for stories about violence.

The family-sensitive concept was created by John Lansing, news director of WCCO in Minneapolis, who now says the idea is being diluted. "Some stations are jumping into it too fast and are missing the fundamental point: It's not just about what you eliminate, it's what you add," he says.

For example, Lansing says, while his station didn't use some of the more graphic testimony about knife wounds in the O.J. Simpson case, "we also added a piece on how parents might deal with their kids on the O.J. story, and the blurred line for kids between fiction and reality."

Rival stations are openly skeptical. "It's the latest gimmick in TV news, a marketing ploy," says David Roberts, news director of Baltimore's WBAL. "I don't feel it's necessary to have a consultant come in with a gimmick and help me and the people here determine how we should cover crime. I don't think you can sugarcoat the news.

"Just because you don't show a body bag doesn't make you more sensitive. In many cases it just means you got to a story late."

So far, at least, no family-sensitive station has claimed a boost in ratings. But researchers say the softer format appeals to baby boomers with kids, as well as to women and better-educated viewers.

By contrast, many stations in search of ratings have emulated the sensational style of Miami's Fox affiliate, WSVN, whose newscasts comprise 49 percent crime news, according to a University of Miami study. Since the late '80s, that has often meant relentless crime coverage punctuated by scary headlines, arresting graphics, slow-motion footage and dramatic music.

Some critics say journalists have no business trying to shield viewers from the ugly realities of crime. "I think it would be wrong not to do crime stories in order to be family sensitive," says David Bartlett, president of the Radio-Television News Directors Association. "Then you're sensitive but you're no longer news."

Yet a few television consultants, who advise stations on everything from happy talk to weatherpersons, have become salesmen for the new sensitivity. "Television is an imitative business," said Ed Bewley, chairman of Dallas-based Audience Research & Development, which works with WMAR and eight other stations taking the milder approach to crime. "Our firm let all our clients know this was happening and suggested they do it as well."

For in a fragmented media world that has made channel surfing a national pastime, every local news operation is trying to carve out a niche. "Oprah looks the same on every channel," Bartlett says. "Third reruns of 'Matlock' look the same on every channel. The only thing a station can do to distinguish itself locally is news."

Some television executives now talk about crime coverage with the fervor of reformed sinners. Sue Kawalerski, news director of Miami's newly sensitive WCIX, says a crime "feeding frenzy" had "junked up" her program and rendered it "un-watchable."

Now, WCIX's broadcasts are only 18 percent crime. "We didn't want people to say after watching our newscast, 'Oh my God, is that all that's happening in the world? What an awful place to live!' "

Recalling a recent triple murder, Kawalerski says: "We covered it the first day. The other stations went on and on for days with team reports, speculation, even relating it to O.J. Simpson," because the case involved the former owner of a Buffalo bar frequented by Simpson.

Cahalan, a former Cincinnati news director, went through culture shock two years ago when he arrived here at Baltimore's NewsChannel 2. "I was burned out on crime after three weeks," he says. "You couldn't get out of the first block [of stories] without seeing all the police cars and red lights. . . .

"Covering crime is easy; it's one-stop shopping. You show up, you shoot your stand-up and you're out. In this city, as in D.C., there are shootings that take place every day. But that doesn't accurately reflect what's going on in the community. . . . Compared to six months ago, there is less air time devoted to crime stories."

Still, ambulance-chasing is deeply embedded in a newsroom culture where adrenaline starts flowing when word of a shooting crackles over police radio. "A lot of us in TV news have been trained to run on those stories and maybe make them bigger than they should be," says Aretha Marshall, WMAR's assistant news director. "It really is harder not to get drawn into that. You almost have to re-program people, calm everyone down."

WMAR's new approach evolved over time. The first, seemingly incremental change in behavior came last summer after a shooting in a Reisterstown shopping center. A reporter raced to the scene, but Cahalan vetoed the obligatory live shot.

"Remember, the shooting took place two hours earlier," he says. "I was not going to have a reporter stand in an empty parking lot with no reason to be there."

Another turning point was the station's restrained coverage of the double murder last December. "In some ways we use the bodies and the blood as a crutch," says reporter Jesse Jones, who covered the killings. "I don't think it's censorship as long as you tell the story that two women were brutally murdered."

In June, all the Baltimore stations dispatched crews when a man named John Porter shot a police officer, fled in his Ford Bronco along Interstate 95, shot his girlfriend in the head and then killed himself. Unlike its rivals, WMAR did not show Porter's body on the pavement.

Joe Lewin, the general manager, later got a call from Porter's sister. "She just told me she was very grateful to us and she knew we were the only news organization that didn't use the picture of her brother's body," he says. "She told me what the family went through every time they saw the body."

In recent weeks, Lewin has been advertising the new policy in a promotional spot: "You let us know there was too much violence in the news, and we agreed with you. . . . There's a difference now: Crime stories are covered only when justified, and we always look for a positive angle. And shots of graphic violence have no home on this station."

But one veteran staffer sees no change in WMAR's approach. Pete O'Neal, an African American cameraman who cruises the streets at night, describes himself as "the guy who tries to get the shot of the person on the ground and asks [relatives] the idiotic question, 'How do you feel?' " The crime issue was dramatically brought home to O'Neal last year when his mother was killed during a robbery.

"I don't see anything we've done differently," he says, saying WMAR had never aired much graphic footage. "All that you see are black males doing bad. Even if it doesn't lead the show, it's still the same story. [Blacks] are still portrayed the same way."

What is missing from the routine homicide stories is "why were they killed? Who were they? What kind of person was Jane Doe? What kind of life did she lead?" Answering those questions, O'Neal says, "takes more time."

But Cahalan insists things are changing. After police arrested 36 people in a drug sweep last week, he says, WMAR aired a story on the progress of another East Baltimore neighborhood that was raided in similar fashion last March. "That was a conscious effort to go back into a neighborhood that had been billed as one of the city's worst and look at how people are trying to take back the streets," he says.

The debate seems to be heating up, in part because of a growing recognition of television's role in shaping a community's image. Nine South Florida hotels recently moved to ban WSVN's crime-ridden newscasts because of concern that tourists might be scared away.

"I was in Washington a year ago and I couldn't believe the parade of body bags," Lansing says. "If you're a black male in a large city, the only way you find your way into a newscast is either in a body bag, handcuffs or sports highlights."

At Washington's WJLA, Wordlaw says he occasionally shows violent footage if it is "germane" to a story but does not repeat it day after day.

"I have kids," he says. "When my kids sit down to watch the news, I want them to be able to watch a fair representation of the total market, and the total market is not death and destruction."

The Multimedia Feeding Frenzy

CINDY SKRZYCKI and PAUL FARHI

John Malone has seen the future and he's determined to bring it into your living room, first.

The chief executive of Tele-Communications Inc. (TCI), the world's largest cable television company, Malone is betting billions of dollars that his company can win the race to rewire the nation for the coming revolution in multimedia communications. "We've got the core piece of the system," he said. "Unless someone trips us up, we win because the first guy there wins."

As Malone's comment suggests, the rush is on in the communications business. From Hollywood to Silicon Valley to the canyons of Manhattan, executives are studying market research, courting joint-venture partners and signing deals to exploit the new technology.

Not since the American wilderness was strung together with a national railroad system has there been so much feverish activity and high expectation over an industry that hasn't been born yet. A few companies will make a killing in this new industry, and many more are likely to lose their shirts. But for the moment, it's impossible to tell which are which.

It's been variously called "the information superhighway," "multimedia convergence" or simply The Network. By any name, the technology amounts to a do-it-all electronic pipeline that will pour phone calls, pay-per-view movies, interactive shopping, video games, computer data and a limitless number of TV channels into your living room.

In the first major alliance of the new industry, Time Warner Inc. and US West Inc. last week announced that they would collaborate to jump-start construction of an information superhighway leading into the living rooms of Time Warner's 7 million cable TV subscribers. US West pledged to put $2.5 billion into Time

Warner's cable and video entertainment subsidiaries, a down payment on a job that Time Warner says will take five years and $5 billion to complete.

Conventional wisdom holds that this won't be the last deal of similar magnitude. Hardly a day goes by without a rumor about the next information age merger or investment: TCI and AT&T; Walt Disney Co. and CBS Inc. or NBC; a "Baby Bell" phone company and one of the smaller cable companies, such as Comcast Corp.

"There is a musical chair quality to this, and a couple of chairs just got pulled away," said Rep. Edward J. Markey (D-Mass.), chairman of the House subcommittee on telecommunications and finance.

Telephone companies already have made moves on their own into uncharted territory.

Several months ago, Southwestern Bell Corp., a major regional telephone company, spent $650 million to buy cable systems in Arlington and Montgomery counties that are widely viewed as a platform for offering all sorts of advanced interactive services, as well as local phone service.

Bell Atlantic Corp., hoping to surmount the key limitation of the current telephone network—its inability to carry much more than conversations and computer transmissions—is gambling on a new technology that enables regular phone lines to deliver video-quality pictures. If successful, Bell Atlantic and its phone industry brethren wouldn't have to invest billions of dollars in replacing their existing systems of copper wires with more versatile fiber-optic lines or coaxial cable links.

But Bell Atlantic also is hedging its bets. It is installing millions of miles of fiber optics in its network, challenging federal restrictions that forbid its being a cable TV operator in its own territory and hiring executives from media and entertainment companies to figure out the best ways to get down the highway.

Investments are budding in technologies that will build pieces of the highway. Microsoft Corp., Apple Computer Inc., Sony Corp., AT&T and others are working to develop the brains of these systems that will manage the different kinds of information coming into and out of the house.

In one closely watched alliance, Microsoft (the world's largest independent software company), Intel Corp. (a leading semiconductor manufacturer) and General Instrument Corp. (a huge cable equipment manufacturer) are jointly developing a TV set-top converter box that will be compatible with personal computers. The idea is to create a device capable of ordering a pizza, selecting a movie, carrying a videophone conversation and downloading stock quotes.

Big long-distance companies such as AT&T and MCI Communications Corp. are well positioned because their transcontinental phone networks stand to have even more traffic loaded onto them if information superhighways are a success. AT&T also sells network equipment to the cable industry, which is rushing headlong to expand its capacity, and its Bell Laboratories researchers have been working for the past two years on interactive multimedia systems.

Nascent Dealmaking

Long-distance carriers love the nascent dealmaking because it moves them closer to the day when monopoly phone companies such as Bell Atlantic will have competition in completing local phone calls. AT&T paid $14 billion last year to local phone companies to complete calls traveling from its network into the local loop. The local wiring challenge is known in the industry as "the last mile."

A fully outfitted information highway would bypass that local bottleneck, giving long-distance companies a choice of carriers to complete the last leg of their calls. AT&T had just this rationale in mind when it spent $3.8 billion last fall for 33 percent of McCaw Cellular Communications Inc., the nation's largest cellular network operator.

But the new Information Industrialists don't plan on concentrating on just one business. Instead, they are angling to take a little bite out of everyone else's pocket—a nibble of home shopping, some electronic banking, perhaps a cut of the phone and video-rental businesses.

Gerald Levin, chief executive of Time Warner, believes the potential of the superhighway is so vast that his company can fund its $5 billion construction project just by selling more pay-per-view movies over the network. And that's just for starters.

"People clearly want all of these services and they are already paying for them now. All we need is a fraction of that demand," said Levin in an interview last week.

Hence, being first to build the superhighway means grabbing a chunk of the other guy's market share. Time Warner wants a piece of what it estimates is $400 billion in current spending on phone calls, video rentals and home shopping and other electronic services that its superhighway may provide.

"It's not simply existing video markets or new services. In many cases, it's substitutions for things like catalogue shopping," said Arthur Bushkin, president of information services for Bell Atlantic.

Added Michael Schulhof, chief executive of Sony USA: "A new technology is rarely a replacement. It's a layering process."

Schulhof pointed out in an interview last week that the portable phone has not replaced the office phone, just as television didn't stop people from going to movies, and home videos did not displace movie theaters and TV. Each industry's market share shifted as behavior changed and new technologies were layered on top of older ones.

But no company is sufficiently diversified to do it alone now. To gain control over the highway requires money, access to consumers' homes and the ability to produce programming.

Major cable companies such as TCI, Time Warner and Viacom Inc. own both the conduit (the wire into the home) and parts of the content (TCI and Time Warner are part owners of Turner Broadcasting System Inc., parent of CNN and TNT, and

Viacom owns the cable networks MTV, Nickelodeon and VH-1). But the cable industry is weighted down with debt and faces new federal price regulations; as Time Warner proved last week, its biggest need is for partners with deep pockets.

Some observers, including TCI's Malone, say that foreshadows a contraction in the cable industry, as small, debt-strapped operators are gobbled up by well-heeled media conglomerates hungry for access to more homes. Malone predicts "a feeding frenzy" as independent cable operators sell out to rich telephone companies. He doesn't expect that to happen to TCI, a large diversified company, but "if it came to that, we would take in outside investors—almost any telephone company, a technology company or a venture capitalist," he said.

On the other hand, the industry least likely to suffer is Hollywood. Major studios hold valuable libraries of old movies and TV programs, and have the means to create new ones. To extend the superhighway metaphor, the studios will make many of the cars and trucks that travel over the road.

"Demand for [programming] will increase exponentially. . . . Whether the future holds 150 channels or 500 channels, or everyone has his or her own channel, we are clearly going to witness an explosion in programming demand," said Frank J. Biondi, chief executive of Viacom International, in a speech in Washington last week.

Hard Questions

Before they divide up the future, however, these companies might want to ask a few hard questions: Who wants all this stuff, and how much are they willing to pay for it?

For all the hoopla, very little information exists on how consumers will react to a high-technology network in their homes. Will people who still can't program their VCRs be adept enough to use the sophisticated gizmos now on the drawing boards?

The new highway demands interactivity and an overwhelming amount of selectivity, the exact opposite of the passivity that so many couch potatoes seem to desire.

The network of the future also would compete with some basic human behaviors—simple things like touching a newspaper or pawing through a rack of dresses, or browsing through a book or record store, notes Sony's Schulhof.

GTE Corp., in a four-year experiment in Cerritos, Calif., has tested a variety of interactive networks that may be the precursors of tomorrow's superhighway. Originally, GTE bet that people would be eager to have home shopping in their living rooms. Not so. The big winners have been the system's pay-per-view movies, financial transactions and educational offerings such as a video college aptitude test course.

GTE also had to go back and simplify the system and make it more foolproof by providing more on-screen instructions and redesigning how its remote control worked. The company came to the conclusion that some people may never want a full-blown menu of interactive services, said William D. Wilson, GTE's vice president of business planning.

Apart from marketing questions, people haven't even begun to sort out the public policy issues that a technological revolution kicks up. Promoters of the superhighway sell it not just as a way to watch more TV, but as way to revolutionize education, medical care and working at home as well. But the rules haven't been written about who gets the benefits of these things; concern is already rising that the answer will be only the wealthy, thus separating information "haves" from "have nots."

"They're not linking fiber to satellites in Harlem," said Mark Berniker, senior analyst with the media consulting firm Jupiter Communications. "All of the announcements that have been made to date have been made in pretty lucrative areas where people have money . . . [Companies know] that it makes the most sense to offer these services to a community that has robust demographics."

Yet another problem: As new alliances are formed, even big companies worry about being kept off the superhighway by would-be rivals. If the country is carved up by several huge media-entertainment oligarchies, companies that want access to their networks may find they can't get it.

Think of the airline industry and its computer reservation system: The airlines that own the systems are often accused of shunting competitors' flight information to less favorable positions or dropping rivals' listings altogether.

"The potential for economic abuse becomes so great that the government steps in and says, 'This is too much power in the hands of one company,' " said Schulhof of Sony.

And that could be the ultimate dead end on the superhighway. In the name of providing more choice and competition, those now jockeying for position in the coming information age may have the same thing in mind as the robber barons of an earlier era—the creation of a gigantic monopoly.

Small-Dish TV Offers Wireless Revolution

PAUL FARHI

For more than a decade, it has been a revolution waiting to happen. Imagine a television receiving dish, with a diameter smaller than the length of this newspaper, capable of pulling in 150 or more super-clear channels. The cost: about the same as your monthly cable TV service.

Soon, it will no longer be pie in the sky.

With the successful launch and deployment of a 6,000-pound satellite last night from a remote site in French Guiana, a long-awaited television technology known as direct broadcast satellite TV, or DBS, finally, literally, got off the ground.

By April, the satellite is to begin beaming about 85 channels to 18-inch-wide receivers perched on windowsills and back-yard decks from orbit 22,300 miles above the Earth.

A second satellite will go up in June, adding at least another 80 channels of pay-per-view movies, sports events and other programs.

DBS's backers harbor hopes as high as their satellites, enthusing that the technology will give monopoly cable operators their first major competition, and provide American consumers with their first look at the much-touted "information superhighway"—or, in this case, skyway.

Indeed, DBS will be the first "wireless" pathway into the home to use digital technology, the computer language around which almost all telecommunications services will be based. The dawn of DBS is thus the beginning of a larger race between wireless and "wired" companies to provide the next generation of residential communications services. The wire-based providers—cable and phone companies—are just starting to rebuild their networks to carry hundreds of channels of TV and other enhanced services.

"Someday, we'll look back on this and say DBS brought the digital revolution into American TV homes," said Stanley E. Hubbard, president of United States Satellite Broadcasting, one of two DBS companies that will begin marketing the service next spring. "We'll say DBS revolutionized the ease, flexibility and choice in a multichannel world."

USSB, based in St. Paul, Minn., is an affiliate of Hubbard Broadcasting Inc., a family-owned company that pioneered commercial radio and television in the

177

United States (it now owns seven TV stations). Hubbard has invested $150 million into developing the DBS system.

The big player in DBS, however, is General Motors Corp.'s Hughes Electronics Corp., the giant defense and aerospace company based in southern California. Hughes has sunk some $600 million to build the two DBS satellites and the Earth station in Colorado that will send programming up to the satellite. It will spend another $40 million next year to advertise and market the service through its DBS subsidiary, called DirecTv.

But DBS has plenty of doubters who see the technology as the basis for little more than a "niche" business, if that. The prospects for DBS, they say, are clouded by these factors:

Cable has a huge, and perhaps overwhelming, head start, having wired up 62 percent of all TV households. Many in the cable business say the remaining households either can't afford more TV or simply don't want it.

The cost of the equipment used to receive DBS signals could discourage many consumers, at least initially. Purchase and installation of the system will cost about $900 per TV set, or $1,000 for two sets (Hughes and Hubbard executives say this cost will drop as more people sign up, and DBS equipment could someday be about the same price as a VCR).

DBS doesn't offer local programming; for that, you'll still need a standard TV antenna to pull in local signals.

Further, competitors point out that cable and phone companies will someday be able to offer more channels and two-way "interactivity," which will eventually make their networks more versatile than DBS.

"I think it's got a hard road," said Barry Diller, the former Hollywood mogul who heads QVC Network Inc., the cable home-shopping company.

Yesterday's launch is actually the culmination of an era that officially began in 1982. That was the year that the Federal Communications Commission first reserved space in the broadcast spectrum for TV transmissions from high-powered satellites.

At the time, DBS looked like it could overcome some of the limitations that had kept existing satellite TV services from achieving mass-market success.

Then as now, such lower-powered systems required dishes up to 12 feet across, making them impractical in densely populated areas.

But the high-powered DBS technology of the time also had its own problems. For one thing, the early systems couldn't effectively compete with cable because of limited channel capacity; older DBS systems now operating in Britain and Hong Kong, for example, offer only a dozen channels or less.

What's more, cable companies often refused to sell their popular programs to non-cable TV companies, or they set exorbitantly high prices to discourage competition.

Several DBS ventures collapsed, including one involving Hughes and NBC in 1991.

DBS has now overcome both these barriers, thanks to politics and technology. Last year, in a victory for rivals of the cable industry, Congress passed a law mandating that cable programming be sold on fair terms to all buyers.

Meanwhile, advances in so-called compression technology have made it possible to squeeze many more video signals through a satellite's transmitters, solving the channel limitation problem (cable and phone companies will eventually employ compression over their wire networks to go beyond DBS's capacity).

"The reason we have been on the sidelines is that DBS was a technology that could not fulfill a marketplace demand," said Eddy Hartenstein, president of DirecTv. "Unless we could offer a system that could deliver 100 or 200 channels, DBS didn't make any sense."

Neither Hubbard nor Hartenstein is concerned about the lead now enjoyed by the cable industry.

They say cable customers will have to wait years to see all of the services promised by wire-based companies.

Besides, they add, DBS can be a successful business on a relatively modest scale; both companies project they'll break even by signing up just 3 million subscribers each, charging about $35 per household per month for basic service.

Hartenstein projects that DirecTv could have up to 10 million subscribers by the end of the decade.

The companies expect customers to come from all segments, from cable subscribers disgruntled with service or selection to those in areas that still can't get cable.

DirecTv will target this latter group, about 9 million households in all, through a marketing agreement with the National Rural Tele-Communications Cooperative, a consortium of rural phone and utility companies based in Herndon.

Although they are competitors, DirecTv and USSB are collaborators as well.

The companies will share space on the Hughes-owned satellite, and have cooperated on a common design for the receiving equipment. This was done to permit subscribers to receive either service or both.

"We wanted to avoid at all costs a 'Beta versus VHS' confrontation," said Hubbard, recalling the competition among manufacturers to establish a predominant VCR format. "Now, it's not going to be a question of whether I should get our format or theirs. It's a question of whether you should get" a DBS receiver at all.

Data Highway Can Be Blessing or Curse

BROOKE A. MASTERS

When E. J. Crane, 28, a postdoctoral fellow at Bowman Gray Medical School in North Carolina, wants to know how fast a particular enzyme reaction occurs, he could calculate it on his Macintosh computer. But that would take 24 hours.

Instead, Crane uses the Mac to sign onto the international collection of computer networks known as the Internet and hook up with a more powerful computer at a hospital in Winston-Salem, N.C. On it, he can perform the same calculation in a minute—using a program made available on the Internet by Washington University in St. Louis.

At other times, Crane signs onto the Internet to send messages to his brother in Minnesota, discuss ideas with other biochemists across the country and copy three-dimensional images of protein molecules from a national database in Upton, N.Y.

The Internet—clusters of large computers linked to high-speed long-distance phone lines—is radically changing the way professors and students carry out their missions. By making all kinds of information available to anyone with an Internet account, the network has begun to blur the differences between big universities—with their big computers and big libraries—and smaller institutions. The computer links also encourage long-distance collaboration, allowing isolated scholars and academic newcomers to tap into the collective wisdom in their fields.

Internet users say titles, sex, race and other distinctions fade, because on the Internet, everyone is just an address. "It's a great leveler," said University of Richmond professor Elizabeth Gruner. "Anyone can ask anything . . . and anyone can respond."

But universal, round-the-clock access makes the Internet a mixed blessing. Highly addictive, it encourages users to spend hours communicating via computer with distant friends and colleagues rather than with the person down the hall. Many users, under the guise of participating in academic discussions, spend hours reading and responding to obvious, repetitive inquiries.

The Internet often encourages scholars to ask for help rather than carry out their own research, and some professors are worried that it will devalue individual accomplishment and encourage intellectual laziness.

"My initial optimism in this technology has faded considerably," said Robert Jay, art department chairman at the University of Hawaii. "Green graduate students . . . now seem to believe they can ask the rest of the [people on the network] to do the most basic bibliographic research for them."

Some are concerned that the Internet's capacity for transferring large files at no cost may encourage the proliferation of low-quality electronic journals that publish papers rejected by more established publications.

For better or worse, however, the Internet has embedded itself in academic life. Consider these developments:

- Trotter Hardy, a law professor at the College of William and Mary, has organized two academic conferences entirely on the Internet. For each, he chose a topic—one was the impact of electronic mail on teaching law—and invited as many as 25 people to participate. They exchanged electronic messages for three weeks, and then Hardy compiled and sent out a transcript, entirely on the Internet. For professors without time or travel money, such conferences help compensate for a lack of mobility.
- Harvard University's government department this year created a special Internet file to help its job-hunting graduate students. With a quick Internet query, recruiters at other universities now can get copies of the students' resumes, their published articles and sections of their dissertations. "I know of three cases where recruiters learned of our students from our [Internet] service and invited them to apply before the positions were officially announced," said government professor Gary King, who set up the system.
- When Solveig C. Robinson, a University of Chicago graduate student, stalled in her research into "Shafts," an obscure 19th-century publication, she posted a query on "Victoria," a list of about 600 scholars interested in the period. "Within 48 hours, I had a couple of responses that put me in touch with a woman from Texas who had done some work on 'Shafts' . . . and we pooled our notes," Robinson said. "Since she hadn't yet published anything, there was really no other way for me to know about her."
- Rochester Institute of Technology mathematician Stanislaw P. Radziszowski has spent 3 1/2 years working on complex logic problems with an Australian colleague, one of only a few mathematicians who had the necessary expertise in algorithms and computer programs. The pair, who are on the forefront of programming computers to do formal reasoning, have met in person only three times and talked on the phone perhaps four times, but they communicate via electronic mail three or four times a day.

  Without the Internet, "our joint work would have been rather impossible," Radziszowski said. "Our computers very often work simultaneously on the same problem. . . . They use the same data, and we check each other's results by computers."

- Many universities, including the University of Maryland and Virginia Tech, offer courses to long-distance learners on the Internet. Students carry on class discussions, work on group projects and submit their papers entirely on-line.

In the last two or three years, the Internet has become ubiquitous in the academic community: While nonacademics usually pay for access, most universities offer free accounts to students, faculty and staff members. Many academics now turn first to e-mail and the Internet instead of the telephone when they need to reach someone. No phone tag, no time-zone considerations and, best of all, no long-distance phone bill.

Scholars simply type up a message of any length, address it, push the send button and whoosh, the electronic letter goes out on the information highway. The next time the recipient signs on, the message—and sometimes hundreds more—will be there, waiting to be read.

"It's like going to the common room for a coffee break," said Simon Stevenson, a humanities professor at Griffith University in Australia. "You hope there will be people there to have a chat with. . . . One need never feel isolated in one's profession with the opportunities for 'conversation' which the scholarly e-conference holds out."

Many professors work from home or in laboratories far from the telephone, so they are easier to reach via the Internet. Many academic committees no longer meet in person; instead, they talk on the Internet.

Recent discoveries, such as a newly identified gene or the solution to Fermat's Last Theorem, spread more quickly via the Internet than they did in traditional journals, allowing reserchers to build more quickly on one another's work.

"E-mail can save a mathematician weeks of exploring a blind alley," said Ohio University professor Ward Just. "Often a quick question posed to the right specialist can help us decide whether or not a given approach is worth pursuing. E-mail allows us to pose this kind of question."

Some computer links also can carry pictures and sound, as well as enormous data files too large to share by "snail mail"—the Internet term for the U.S. Postal Service. More than 20 selective academic journals—for which professors on editorial boards choose among submissions for publication—now are published only in electronic form, and dozens of paper journals offer electronic copies as well. Newsletters and journals that accept all relevant submissions are springing up by the hundreds.

The On-Line Journal of Clinical Trials, published by the American Association for the Advancement of Science, not only sends out electronic copies of articles within 48 hours of their acceptance but also includes abstracts of every article cited in the footnotes. The journal's 463 subscribers can invoke a program to send them a fax whenever an article in their specific area of interest is published.

The Internet's influence reaches far beyond academia. Because the Internet has no command center, no overall record keeper and very few rules, no one knows exactly how big it is or exactly what it is being used for. But estimates of the number using it run as high as 20 million people, with new users joining at a rate of 1 million a month.

But the new users should beware, professors and students said, because the Internet can consume hours of time and deliver limited results. Many "newslists"—computer programs that send queries, conversation and informative postings to and among large groups of subscribers interested in the same topic—swamp their subscribers with e-mail that can take hours to sort. And much of that mail is made up of requests for basic information and electronic showing-off.

When a recent posting on the "Victoria" newslist asked for novels that included descriptions of caged birds, literally dozens of scholars responded with citations. Although the request asked for messages to be sent only to the requester, most of the bird descriptions went to all 600 subscribers, clogging up their electronic mailboxes and prompting a University of Michigan student to quit the list in disgust.

"I really think the thrill of exhibitionism drives many responses," said Princeton University graduate student Hyungji Park. "It's exciting to tell 500 people that you know this factoid."

A study of the role of electronic communication during the 1989-92 controversy about cold fusion found that a computer discussion group that sprang up to talk about the issue was basically useless. "Most of the people . . . were repeating vague generalizations and second- and third-hand knowledge," said the study's author, Cornell University professor Bruce Lewenstein.

There also are questions of plagiarism and who owns material on the Internet.

Articles from newspapers and magazines are regularly posted in discussion groups—often with a note saying that the copying is unauthorized. Plagiarism is as simple as downloading someone else's posting and inserting it into one's own work. As a result, most scholars will not talk on the Internet about their best work for fear it will be stolen.

Scientists who are racing to locate and identify specific genes—such as those that cause breast cancer or cystic fibrosis—have begun to deal with this problem. Submissions to a national genetic database are "sealed" until a date set by the contributing scientist. That way, other scientists cannot copy that gene until the scientific article describing it has been published.

Internet enthusiasts play down the plagiarism problem. "When I publish something electronically, I immediately send it to 1,000 people," said University of Maryland computer scientist Ben Shneiderman. "Who would dare tamper with it? If I publish it in some obscure journal with only 50 copies, who would know" if it was plagiarized?

Dreams of a Paperless Society

JOHN BURGESS

As a private in a Tennessee cavalry regiment during the Civil War, Absolom Tims never could have foreseen that he would assist in computer-age efforts to revolutionize the art of managing documents in bulk.

But today, Pvt. Tims—or, more precisely, his hand-notated personnel file, yellowed and brittle after more than 120 years in boxes—has been pressed into service to this end at the National Archives.

In a basement workroom at the Archives' Constitution Avenue headquarters, technicians have fed the files of Tims and 40,000 fellow Confederate soldiers page-by-page into a high-speed scanning machine that creates an electronic image of each sheet. The paper goes back into its acid-free storage boxes; the images, tagged with computer-readable index codes, go onto optical discs to await a curious human's summons.

By typing a few commands into a computer keyboard, a researcher can call up onto a high-resolution screen images of any of the documents, or assemble groups of them—the records of Tims' fellow members of the 2nd Ashby's Cavalry, for instance. The images are sharp, faithfully recreating the elegant longhand of 19th-century army clerks. Moreover, they don't mildew, tear or get dogeared. They arrive on the screen in a few seconds, eliminating the need for lengthy searches through storage rooms for paper or microfilm.

In theory, this experimental system could one day be expanded to the point at which any number of researchers at any number of computers, located anywhere in the world, could pull out any document contained in the archives' multibillion-page collection. Says William L. Hooton, director of the Archives program, which is being overseen by Unisys Corp.'s Mclean-based defense systems division: "The possibilities are whatever your imagination and budget will allow."

This emerging technology, known as digital imaging, promises to bring the first real advances in management of paper in bulk since the invention of microfilm a half century ago. It is coming of age despite false starts and cost overruns. But it is sufficiently alluring that government agencies are rushing headlong toward it, aided by Beltway computer and software contractors eager for a piece of a market that can only grow.

Applications of the technology extend well beyond archiving, however. Many offices are starting to use digital imaging to streamline the processing of incoming paper—credit card application forms, for instance. The documents arrive in the mail, are immediately scanned into the system, and then are worked on not as paper originals but as images on screens, moving from desk to desk as required. If needed, the finished product can be printed back onto paper and mailed out.

Combined with word-processing, facsimile transmission (fax) and data networks, digital imaging technology promises to bring new levels of integration to information management in the office. "It is taking all of the different forms of information and delivering them to the window of a single workstation in the form that the user needs it, at the time that he needs it," said Ted Smith, president of FileNet Corp. of Costa Mesa, Calif., an industry leader in imaging systems.

The list of fledgling digital imaging projects in the Washington area is a long one. The Navy hopes to use it to lighten its ships, which now carry literally tons of paper technical documents; the Air Force is digitizing criminal records; and the Army is beginning to use the technology to store personnel files. The Internal Revenue Service is trying it out for archiving tax returns (at present it takes IRS employees two to six weeks to obtain the original of a return).

The technology is rapidly gaining fans in the private sector as well. American Express Co. is using it to keep credit card receipts (instead of a carbon copy with their bills, card-holders now get printed images of the receipts) and process applications. Accounting firm Arthur Young & Co. is applying it to legal research, believing it can save about $500,000 a year.

Interest such as this has kept worldwide sales of document imaging systems roughly doubling every year, reaching $1.2 billion in 1988, according to Rothchild Consultants Inc., a San Francisco research company that specializes in imaging systems.

So far, the federal government has dominated the market for large customized document imaging systems, which Rothchild estimates accounts for about half of the $2.7 billion worth of systems currently in use around the world.

Digital imaging also is making itself felt in fields as far removed as map-making, amateur photography, satellite reconnaissance and computer graphics.

Almost since paper was invented, people have been seeking ways to handle and store it more efficiently. Microfilm, first used to record canceled checks, was a stunning breakthrough, allowing entire floors of libraries to be stored in a cabinet or two and easily transported. But it could be examined by only one person at a time and was useful mainly for archiving, since once exposed it could not be altered.

When computer technology came along, there was breathless talk of an emerging "paperless society." Everything, it was said, would be directly typed into computers and never enter the paper medium. Though computers have gained enormous sway, Americans have remained steadfastly wed to paper. An estimated 95 percent of all information in this country is still stored on it; offices may turn out a billion pages of it a day.

The computer industry now realizes it must live with this venerable medium and can find ways to complement it.

Electronic publishing systems are making paper documents easier to read. Facsimile machines are using computer communication methods to move documents from place to place.

Now imaging is taking things another step along. It is possible through the confluence of several related technologies that have been falling rapidly in price, as have computer products in general, to obtain software that allows material to be easily passed around and clearly displayed; networks that can handle high-speed transfers; compact, high-resolution computer work stations that offer image clarity and power a step above those of ordinary personal computers; and optical storage discs.

For years, the computer industry had toyed with the idea of storing documents as images as opposed to characters typed at a keyboard. But progress was slowed by the images' staggering consumption of space in memory units, typically 40 to 50 times more than needed for machine-readable characters. Optical discs, emerging from the labs in the 1970s, solved that problem by vastly outstripping in capacity the magnetic storage media on which the industry was then relying.

Optical discs, similar to the compact discs of home audio systems, store information as series of ones and zeros, represented as microscopic pits that are read by low-energy lasers. Their efficiency is such that physical space is hardly a consideration at all. "One 12-inch platter can store the equivalent, on our system, of about three four-drawer filing cabinets," says Audri G. Lanford, chief executive officer of Micro Dynamics Ltd., a Silver Spring company that specializes in imaging systems based on the Apple Macintosh.

At present, Japan leads the world in sheer numbers of imaging systems installed, with about 11,000 of the 13,000 systems in use at the end of 1988, according to Rothchild. But most of Japan's units function merely as electronic file cabinets. Many American users, particularly government agencies, are moving beyond that, using the technology to process, not just store information.

The Department of Veterans Affairs is a case in point. Using FileNet equipment designed by American Management Systems Inc. of Rosslyn, it is now processing in a St. Louis office the applications of about 17,000 people who are seeking benefits under the Montgomery GI bill.

Each veteran sends in paper forms, which are scanned into the system and form the core of a personal electronic file. DVA officials at 31 terminals work on the applications as images, appending comments to them (these appear as footnotes on the image) and passing them from station to station. Supervisors can check the status of particular documents and determine precisely the location of each one at the end of the day. If a person telephones in with questions, answers can be provided almost instantly by calling the relevant form onto the screen.

Installed at a cost of about $3 million, the system is experimental and small. But DVA officials dream of one day automating everything, saving the heavy lifting, delays and long walks through storage centers that now are required to work on files.

"They [the files] can weigh up to 10 pounds," laments Mary Leyland, the agency's deputy director of vocational rehabilitation and education services. "And they can be a foot thick. There are approximately 20 million of them active right now."

Bit by bit, developers are accomplishing the seamless integration of different office information media, so that images and word processed documents, electronic mail, facsimiles, or data retrieved from a mainframe computer can be viewed at one time on a single screen. In many cases, the main challenge is not hardware but software—writing programs so that things are clearly and simply displayed.

"People want to keep information in more than one form," said Robert Whyte, director of product marketing at Wang Laboratories Inc. of Lowell, Mass. In its office imaging lineup, Wang has included a product called Freestyle that allows people to use an electronic stylus to "write" in longhand on a document displayed on a computer screen. Their handwriting, charts, doodles, whatever, are stored by the computer as images and become part of the file.

Union Pacific Railroad in St. Louis, meanwhile, is getting ready to bring up a FileNet system that will be tied into fax machines around the nation. An agent might fax a waybill to St. Louis, but instead of coming out as paper there, it will go directly onto a storage disc and be viewable on screens. Operators wishing to respond to the agent will punch keys that will set documents rolling out of their fax machines.

Like all new technologies, this one has shortcomings. It can be unforgiving of institutions that try to do too much too quickly, many specialists say. Many cite the Patent and Trademark Office, an imaging pioneer among the Washington bureau-cracies, as proof of that.

With a contract awarded in 1984, it moved to automate its expansive files to streamline the job of comparing new applications against previously granted ones. Behind schedule, over cost and failing to perform as promised, the system eventu-ally drew scrutiny from Congress and a blue-ribbon Commerce Department panel. The group later called for tighter management, an "evolutionary" approach and some redesign to lower cost.

The patent office says the recommendations have been implemented and things are now on track, with one of 15 examining groups in the patent division and the entire trademark division using it in a developmental status. The affair has been treated by other federal agencies as a case study in how not to proceed. Better to go slowly and experiment, automating just a tiny portion of their paperwork before deciding what to do next.

Starting out at $150,000 or so, the systems are not for everyone. "If you aren't spending a hundred grand a year or more in just handling paper," said Floyd Jean, vice president at Computer Sciences Corp., "it's probably not economic."

Very large systems linking thousands of users simply don't exist yet, noted Wick Keating, a vice president at American Management Systems. So far, the biggest to date are ones operating on a department level, with several dozen terminals.

Lack of technical standards, a familiar situation in the computer industry, also stands in the way of mass adoption of digital imaging.

Yet another impediment is that computers generally cannot "understand" documents stored as images and therefore cannot locate them based on their content. Documents generally are indexed through words attached to them by human operators when they are scanned in. If indexed incorrectly, they can be very hard to find again.

For text search, the images must first be processed by character recognition systems that attempt to convert them to machine-readable form. These recognition systems are costly and not entirely reliable, even when working on clear, typewritten documents. For handwriting, they are next to useless.

Unresolved legal issues also are a consideration. Lawyers are wondering how an image of a document would hold up in court. How would a witness feel being asked to identify it on a screen? Would a jury accept such an identification? At least two states have passed laws declaring that images are admissible. But many experts say imaging users are hanging onto their paper until this issue is thoroughly hashed out in court.

But these obstacles have not dampened the enthusiasm at the National Archives. It is working on techniques to make the images easier to read than the originals through the electronic excising of water stains and ink blots. Before they decide what to do next, archive officials plan to get about 1.2 million pages of Confederate records onto discs alongside those of Pvt. Tims.

Wire Me Up, Scotty

JOEL ACHENBACH

U bicomp. Just remember that. Ubicomp. As in You-Be-Comp. As in Ubiquitous Computing.

We're talking computers everywhere, in the ceiling, on the walls, behind the fridge, inside the TV, under the john, just all over the place, literally clipped to your lapel with an infrared light beaming information to the aforesaid computers in the ceiling . . . a big, seamless digital tapestry . . . global, intangible, anarchic . . . data zipping and zapping all over creation . . . everyone and everything wired into the Net . . . this is what we're talking about when we talk about the Future.

Ubicomp! That's your buzzword. To the extent that it's even a word. I advise everyone to find a new and scintillating and befuddling term, cling to it for dear life, and fake your way through this whole new-technology mess we're in. Someone says "Information Superhighway," you just say "Ubicomp." You can't get by dropping stale, everyone-knows-'em terms like multimedia, cyberspace, virtual reality, PDAs, fiber optics or CD-ROM. Those terms are ancient. Even "bandwidth" is played out as a metaphor ("Luther has amazing bandwidth")—it just sounds so 1993.

These are difficult times, technologically. The Future is crashing down upon us. The technoids are ecstatic, the corporate CEOs are scared to death and the rest of us are kind of fidgety, like we've got a test coming up and we haven't studied. The press has trumpeted the arrival of the "digital age" and chances are that most of us don't really know what that means—didn't we already have digits? We read all these stories in the paper about the Internet and the Information Superhighway and the merging of telephone and cable, and we have to think that this probably means we will end up simply throwing away the VCR without ever having learned how to tape one show while watching another simultaneously.

Oh yes, eventually we manage to grasp what's going on—but by then our information is probably wrong, it's way out of date, it's like those supernovae in deep space, which we can see only when they've been over for 10 million years.

Mercifully you have me here to guide you through these bewildering times.

My credentials are: I am an Early Adopter. There is a research field known as "technology diffusion," and it says that we all fit into one of five categories: Innovators, who make up about 2.5 percent of the population and are the kind of

people who sent away for their Altair 8000 personal computer kits back in 1975;
Early Adopters, who make up the next 12.5 percent and are the kind of people who
are "on line" and think E-mail is really nifty; Early Majority and Late Majority, who
make up the great bulk of the population and will start using technology only when
it's cheap and non-perplexing; and Laggards, that final 15 percent who think these
new push-button phones don't work nearly as well as the ones with the rotary dial.
(I'm actually by nature either an Early Early Majority or a Late Early Adopter, since
I still don't know the DOS commands on my computer and thus can't alter my
AUTOEXEC.BAT file, but this assignment forced me to go to California and now
I'm so futuristic I practically wear a spacesuit to work.)

What we're going to do here is take a warp-speed sightseeing trip to the Future,
just to get the flavor of the place. Here is the one guiding thought you might want
to take with you: In the Future, the human craving for communication and bond-
ing—that instinctive longing to overcome the sense of isolation that gnaws at our
souls—will converge with something even more fundamental to the universe, elec-
tromagnetism.

And that's big.

With tiny leaps of electrons you can send digital bits of information, as surely
as with a fire you can send smoke signals. It's borderline magic, what the engineers
can do. They can encode "King Lear" into 0's and 1's and laser that code down a
glass fiber or bounce it off a satellite or store it on a tiny piece of silicon and no
matter how they handle it Lear still goes crazy right on cue.

Our first stop is the Enterprise. The Enterprise is in a place called ARPA. ARPA
stands for Advanced Research Projects Agency. It's part of the Pentagon, a kind of
think tank for the Military Industrial Complex (Futuristic Gadgets Division).
ARPA's most famous achievement was helping to invent the Internet.

ARPA is located in a dark-tinted glass tower on North Fairfax Drive in Arlington. You can ask for the Enterprise at Visitor Control. You'll be told to go across
the hall to the black doors. You will not be able to see through the black doors but
anyone inside the Enterprise can see you, because they're one-way glass.

The black doors slide apart. When you go inside you'll realize why the place is
called the Enterprise. It looks precisely like the command center of a starship. The
futuristic folks at ARPA have obviously married a "Star Trek" obsession with a
serious wad of federal money.

The room is about 60 by 60, with a central control platform. All structures are
modular, heavy on octagons. Young people work at computer terminals on the
control platform, and there are unmanned terminals along the periphery. There is
hardly any paper to be seen, no mess or clutter, nothing so gauche as a wastebasket,
no discernible dust.

A dramatic G-shaped conference table faces a rear-projection screen the size of
a swimming pool. One expects a Klingon commander to appear on it at any moment.

Cool air and soothing dim light emanate from octagonal pods suspended from the ceiling. Startlingly, nothing gleams. Light seems to have a nonreactive interface with surfaces. "The photon field here is DC. So you can have a moderate level of light without the light frequency," says the large balding man in the black blazer.

This is Stephen Squires. He is the commander, if you will, of the Enterprise.

Wait, you are thinking: What the heck is this thing?

Good question. The short answer is, this is an office that doubles as a demonstration center. Or maybe it's a demonstration center that doubles as an office. Squires and these other people seem to actually be working in here, the way normal people work in normal offices, but at the same time the theatrical atmosphere is a demonstration of technological innovation.

Also it seems to be a large toy. They even call the conference area with the big screen "the Bridge." Squires is a brilliant man, you can tell just by talking to him for 10 seconds, but you also get the feeling that if you turn your back he might try to give you the Vulcan Death Grip.

"It could have been Old English style," Squires says of the Enterprise. "We happened to pick 'Star Trek' because a lot of people could relate to that."

The Enterprise represents the Future not because of the design, but because of something you can't see: the flow of information. Everything is connected by optical fiber, the digital data carrier of the Future. Information from the Internet is projected on the big screen, accessed not with clunky codes and messages but with a quick click of a button. The Internet, as you may know already, is not an on-line service like CompuServe or Prodigy, but rather is a network of computer systems, a link among universities, government agencies, private companies and individuals. (If you use the word "Internet" you are advertising how uncool you are; say "the Net.") Most of us have to find some way to access the Net, using a phone line and a modem and a set of computer commands, but the Enterprise is wired right onto the Net, it's always there, cruising along through cyberspace at Warp 8.

Most importantly, says Squires, all this information capacity, this terrific bandwidth as they say, isn't the result of a giant mainframe computer somewhere. Instead it's dispersed throughout the room, in dozens of microchips buried in the support stems of terminals and in small devices in the walls and ceilings. The intelligence is invisible and ubiquitous (Ubicomp!). Every machine, every connection, the lights and phones and computers and smoke detectors and emergency sprinkler heads and doorways and you name it, uses the latest high-performance technology of the computer world.

"The room is just a peripheral to the Enterprise computing system," Squires says.

His words have a specific technical meaning, but they echo one of the larger issues in this futuristic technology: Will life itself become peripheral to computing? We always assume that we use machines, but in some ways machines use us.

I ask Squires if this collection of wires and modules and gizmos will actually make life better. He is not quick to say yes.

"It has the potential" to improve life, he says. But society has to get involved. Everybody. Society has to decide "how it wants to play the game." People can't be passive. "You can't just sit on the sidelines and say, well, I don't understand it, and I'm afraid of it."

The starship commander then returns to his incomprehensible adventure. The opaque black doors close behind me. The photon field of the outside world is blinding. But I feel like I have a mission: to boldly go where no Early Adopter has gone before.

They love the Information Superhighway over at the White House, which, when the Clintonites came to town, still had operators pulling cords and plugging them into jacks.

Greg Simon, who works on technology issues for Early Adopter Al Gore, gave me the bullish view of the future: "You will be able in the next five years to wake up in the morning and have your coffee timer go off and your TV timer go off and your TV display for you the news you want to see"—politely he cited The Washington Post as a possible source of this digital news—"and then it will tell you what shopping specials are happening around town and then your schedule will pop up and your phone messages."

Simon sounds a bit techno-gaga at first. He's a man who's just discovering the joy of the Net. Some people use an Internet access program called Gopher, but Simon can go them one better: "I've got TurboGopher!"

But when I ask him if he thinks all this change is for the good, he's not so bubbly.

"I have three computers and a cellphone," he says. "It used to be people had to find me to talk to me, they couldn't just beep me."

This is the nightmare of Ubicomp: We get caught in the Net. Constant beeping, buzzing, informing. President Clinton, for one, doesn't like it. The revolutionary changes in both transportation and communication have made his job all the harder, he thinks. Your guide to the Future knows this because by freak chance I was able to ask him about it recently during a dinner in honor of Thomas Jefferson. "You have to move more and you have to communicate more because everything is faster," Clinton said that night. He pointed out that Samuel Morse didn't find out that his wife died until seven days after the fact. That's one reason Morse felt compelled to invent the telegraph, Clinton said. Today the situation has shifted to the opposite extreme. Clinton can be anywhere in the country in a matter of hours and can get any piece of information in a matter of seconds. What he can't do very easily is sit down and write a long letter the way someone like Thomas Jefferson did. "You can be a Renaissance person today but it requires more discipline," Clinton said.

Already, people are opting out of this game. Some well-known scholars, faced with hundreds of E-mail messages from around the country, are pulling back, George Mason University Professor of Public Affairs Hugh Heclo recently noted. "Even before the modern self-esteem movement, many people had been seized with the invincible conviction that because one has thought something, it must be worth saying," Heclo wrote. "This innate human tendency to produce what is known as 'blab' has historically been held in check by certain material realities. [But] a person now can, at virtually no personal cost, inflict whatever pops into his or her head onto you and everyone else." The well-known paradox of the information revolution is that we don't really want or need more information. We already are swamped. It will get worse.

"Not only is there a danger, I'm convinced it will happen. We will be overwhelmed," says Don Norman, who has written about the design of everyday things and now works for Apple in Silicon Valley. "But we will fight back. We will have to find the way in which these technologies can merge with our lives so that our lives are still livable. And I think the technology will go along with it because companies will realize there's as much a market in controlling the technology as there is in providing it to you."

The information counterrevolution is the next great step. There will be a push to get unwired. A lust for silence.

Vice President Gore recently said in a speech, "I've often spoken about my vision of a schoolchild in my home town of Carthage, Tennessee, being able to come home, turn on her computer and plug into the Library of Congress."

Kids: Library of Congress. For some reason that is not the word association I'd make. Wouldn't kids rather use videocalls to cruise for dates? To drop into "grown-up" places? "Hey, Buzz, whaddaya wanna do tonight?" "Let's check out obscure journal reports from the Library of Congress!" Please.

Every time a new technology comes out, people put a dignified spin on it. They talk about its utility for democracy-building, for starters. We'll use it to write letters to congresspersons! Nothing ever gets used the way the spinners think it will—but nobody remembers this afterward.

The wheel was invented as a device for making pottery, and no doubt the Sumerian potters would have been appalled to learn that anyone would want to use wheels just to cruise around town. When radio first emerged, it had the grand, serious mission of ship-to-shore communication; no one anticipated Howard Stern. The first commercial stations chose to broadcast church services, football games and election results, but then advertisers started sponsoring hour-long programs of dance music, and the radio purists howled. They said radio was being "debased." The polka was just too degenerate.

When Alexander Graham Bell invented the telephone, people projected all kinds of fusty do-gooder uses for it, none of them including yakking for hours with friends. There's an anecdote in circulation that says Bell himself didn't realize the phone would be used for ordinary conversations, but that's not true. He knew exactly what he was doing.

I looked at Bell's papers at the Library of Congress—in person, in my own living flesh, because there's nothing quite like actually being in a library, opening yourself to serendipitous revelations by riffling through the original documents and seeing the lines crossed out by Bell himself and chatting with a historian who happens to be sitting nearby (remind me to tell you about the wonderfully efficient information storage systems known as "books")—and what I found is that the patent application of February 14, 1876 ("Improvement in Telegraphy") focuses on transmitting musical notes, and only in passing refers to "transmitting vocal or other sounds telegraphically." But Bell's writings show that he clearly understood that his phone was a medium for talking: He was a speech therapist for the deaf, and had gotten interested in inventing the phone as a result of studying how the mouth formed sounds (the tongue lightly taps the alveolar ridge, blah blah blah).

Bell went around demonstrating his contraption, and the press picked up on the dignified, businesslike uses of the thing. "Its applications are numberless," the Washington Evening Star wrote on January 20, 1877. "The merchant may converse with his partner in a distant city or give his orders to his factory in the suburbs of his own town, or from his room may speak with the foreman or chief clerk in any room of a large establishment. There is reason to hope that the Secretary of State may be able before long to discuss by mouth and ear questions of national importance with the ministers of foreign affairs at all the great cities of Europe and with the governors of all our American States . . ."

And kids will be able to telephone the Library of Congress!

In Washington I feel like I am stuck in the past, so naturally I light out for the Coast. We all know that California is the Future, despite being three hours behind. It's got two women senators, very few fat people, nobody smokes, there's nothing that looks even vaguely industrial, and the cafes have computer terminals where people can log on to the Net for 25 cents. I once walked into a guy's office and instead of offering coffee he said, "You want a Calistoga?" (I believe that's a form of water.) Another person offered me coffee and then said, "Do you want regular sugar?"

I fly into San Francisco, rent a car and, because of the nature of my assignment, a cellular phone. Culturally I am trained to burn massive amounts of gasoline on highways but I still can't get used to making a phone call by hitting a "Send" button. Though I am on an expense account, the $2-a-minute access charge bugs me beyond distraction: I find myself talking insanely fast. The technology is using me, I'm not using it.

First stop: Wired magazine.

Wired is to the information age as Rolling Stone was, originally, to rock-and-roll. The magazine's office, a few blocks south of downtown San Francisco, has the rehabbed-warehouse look: brick walls, high ceilings, a great open room containing everyone, creative space, none of this corporate cubicle stuff. Music is supplied by a massive stack of CDs. Everyone moves quickly: Here the Future is a breaking story, and you get the feeling Wired's writers and editors realize they are the only people on the planet who can understand it.

"We're about covering the most important story in the late 20th century," says John Battelle, the 28-year-old managing editor, "and that is the transformation of our culture from an industrial one to one based on information and knowledge."

He adds later, "There are no Luddites here. And I certainly am looking forward to the day when I can sit on my couch and pay my bills, and send a letter to my senator, and have a video chat with my best friend to pick a date when we'll take a mountain bike ride."

Technology, he says, is no longer scary. This is a post-nuclear world and we don't have to assume that everything science produces is a threat. "I'm sure fire scared the [solid waste] out of people before they knew how to control it," he says.

Wired's graphics explode off the page in violent fluorescent oranges and reds and yellows, headlines in hyperspace, a technopunk aesthetic. Battelle wrote a story on Sega, the game maker (Sonic the Hedgehog), and the typeface was white on a red background. A bodacious look! Unfortunately you could not actually read the story. "My story on Sega was destroyed by graphics," he says without bitterness.

There is a lesson there for technology in general: Just because something becomes technologically possible doesn't mean you should actually do it.

From San Francisco I drive to Sausalito, a distance all but insuperable prior to the construction of the Golden Gate Bridge. Today the trip takes about 25 minutes and features spectacular views of the bay and the Marin highlands and of course the amazing bridge itself, and you just know there are people who nonetheless complain because the toll is three bucks.

Here in Marin County you find two seemingly opposite visions of the Future overlapping. One vision is New Age, spiritual rather than scientific, slow rather than fast, body-centric rather than data-centric. The other vision is cyberspace, the rapidly expanding on-line universe, created and patrolled by people sitting at their computers all over the world.

The two visions merge (East meets West, if you will) in one place, the office of the Whole Earth Review. It's a one-story building in a marina.

I'm greeted by Howard Rheingold. He's the editor of the Review, and author of books about future technology, including Virtual Communities. He does not look like a techie so much as a dropout from the Electric Kool-Aid Acid Test. He has shoes with fluorescent flowers printed on them. He's fabulous: a '60s hippie exploring the 21st century.

He tells me that soon he and his colleagues will publish the Millennial Whole Earth Catalog, and he shows me galleys. The first page is devoted to the Tao-te-ching, the second to making a back-yard radio telescope for do-it-yourself cosmology. I catch a glimpse of a later chapter called "The Electric Mystic's Guide to the Internet." The Whole Earth concept is about enlightenment, Rheingold says, guided by an ideology based on "a loss of faith in large institutions of all kinds. If you want to solve the world's problems, you give the world's people the tools to solve them. When personal computers came along, that seemed perfectly in line with that."

He says the future is being shaped at the grass-roots level. There were 30,000 computer bulletin boards a year and a half ago, and now there are 60,000. Virtual communities are springing up everywhere. "The Net is now at the point where computers were when they switched over from punch cards," he says.

And life will get better?

It depends, he says. Communications technology is always beneficial and detrimental at the same time. The telephone brought people together and yet alienated them—they no longer were compelled to go see one another, he says. The telephone is also intrusive, interrupting conversations. By habit we stop talking to the person in front of us and go answer the phone. TV brought people together around a common culture, he says, and yet spelled the doom of the family dinner.

Before I leave he takes me to his house and shows me how he accesses the Well. The Well is an on-line service, much celebrated, stocked with intellectuals, futurists, computer designers, thinkers, kibbitzers and Deadheads. In fact, several different electronic conferences seem to be devoted to the Grateful Dead. Jerry Garcia sometimes signs on. A recent addition is novelist Ken Kesey, he of the Merry Pranksters and the Day-Glo bus of the 1960s. "He's new to this, but an interesting member of the mix," says Rheingold.

This is where the hippies went if they didn't OD or sell out. Cyberspace is the bus of the future, and they all want to be on the bus. But maybe we ought to remember that hippie ideals had a way of being devoured and distorted by the time they reached mainstream society. Right now the world of cyberspace is anarchic—no one owns the Net—but all the big corporate players are desperately figuring out how they can get hold of this thing. Everyone has a price. You saw what they did to rock-and-roll.

I drive around for a few days. I go to places with names like the Institute for the Future.

This is what I learn:

The correct way to envision the Future is as a cone. It extends up and outward from the one-dimensional point that we call the present. It is not a skinny cone. It is a big fat cone. Lotsa possibilities. It's silly to predict what will happen because predictions are almost always wrong, they're almost always based on the idea that people will do the same thing they do now, only more of it, that they'll want an even snazzier and whizz-bangier personal computer, that they'll want to watch 600 cable TV channels instead of 60. (No one has yet explained how you get around the fact that there are only about 12 people in the world who can write a decent TV script; it's one of those things that seem to be built into the fabric of the universe, like the cosmological constant.)

So much is up in the air. No one is even certain what a TV will be called in the Future (a teleputer? a PC TV? Sheldon?). The cable TV people have a nightmare scenario about something they call the Death Star, a giant satellite that saturates the planet with 600 TV channels. So far there is no Death Star, but maybe it's only a matter of time. (I personally would invest my entire life's savings in a company called Death Star Inc.)

Congress is completely rewriting the communications laws for the first time since 1934, and all the artificial barriers are coming down. The very notion of things like "the phone company" or "the computer industry" could become obsolete. How can we sustain entire separate industries if they all use the same digital highway?

No one knows how the digital world will get into our homes. Right now almost every house is hooked up to the world by a twisted-pair phone line, and more than half the homes also have a coaxial TV cable. That's two "pipes," as they say. Plus you may have an extra TV and a radio that picks up broadcast signals from the spectrum; that's a third pipe of sorts. What no one can say right now is how many pipes you'll have in five years or 10 years. You might have only one. That's all you'd need, technologically. A single optical fiber will be able to handle all the communications traffic of your house—TV, phone, banking, E-mail messages, shareholder votes, shopping orders, newspaper story downloads, whatever. There will be a mad scramble among different companies to persuade you to hook up to their pipe, and you may decide to use several at once. Neither the phone company nor the cable TV company nor the broadcast networks can afford to be locked out of your home, so they will beg and plead and whine, they will take out your garbage and scrape the grouting between your bathroom tiles, they will do anything to get you to continue their service. It'll make the ongoing AT&T/MCI groveling seem dignified by comparison.

The fact is, you don't have to have an optical fiber to your house to get the fab new high-tech digital signals. New "compression" technology makes it possible to send lots of information down old-fashioned twisted-pair copper phone lines, or down a coaxial cable, or even over the broadcast spectrum.

As analysts try to figure the cable situation out, along comes this plan from deep-pocketed supernerd Bill Gates and Craig McCaw, the cellular phone guy, to launch 840 satellites in polar orbit and offer a completely wireless "pipe." That's where we're at: billionaire monopolists saying they are going to launch hundreds of satellites. It has the flavor of a Master of the Universe fantasy.

Of course, no one knows what's going to be on those optical fibers or copper phone lines, or bouncing toward your personalized Home Entertainment Center from Bill Gates's fleet of MicroSputniks. In olden days, everyone watched three TV networks, read Life or Look or the Saturday Evening Post and for a really wild butt-kickin' time dug into Reader's Digest or National Geographic. Today there are roughly 12,000 magazines in the country targeted at every conceivable niche of society. Broadcasting is giving way to narrowcasting. Forecaster Laurence Wilkinson of the Global Business Network told me that the Holy Grail is the audience of one, a delivery system catered to the individual. A user won't just watch TV anymore: He or she will be a "co-producer and co-creator of the experience," Wilkinson says.

But of all the "we don't knows," the most important is, we don't know how we'll end up using all this techno-wizardry. What we can do is not the same as what we will do. One thing I've heard a lot is that when the Infobahn is finished we won't be slaves anymore to the rigid TV schedule. Supposedly we'll download our favorite shows at our convenience. But in my house I don't think I want that freedom. There's chaos enough in my place. I want "Seinfeld" to be on at 9 o'clock on Thursday night, period, end of discussion.

Beware the confident prediction: Usually it is just a presumption, with not a jot of research to back it up.

If this new technology has a "killer app" (an application that is so popular it sucks in the Early Majority), it will be whatever most easily puts people into contact with one another. When Prodigy started its on-line business a few years ago it figured it could just provide people with information, top-down, a dignified "vertical" information flow, everything going downstream from the Prodigy masters to the dead-end users. Instead, some subscribers decided to use Prodigy to send messages to each other. The E-mail function took off, and the company briefly tried to punish people for sending too many messages. Finally the Prodigy execs emerged from their coma and realized that they were bucking human instinct.

Now that's the main function of on-line services: blabbing. We just can't stop ourselves.

I get a taste of the interactive Future at a cafe in San Francisco called Muddy Waters. I plug a few quarters in a computer terminal so I can sign onto SF Net. There are lots of coffee houses in the Bay Area with these terminals, the idea being to give cyberspace access to people who might otherwise lack it. The messages flash across my screen. The messages are oddly abbreviated, fragmented, rapid-fire, and they seem to focus inordinately on parties, nicknames, silly jokes. The signal-to-noise ratio is annoyingly high. What are they talking about? Why are they chattering and prattling so? It occurs to me finally that what I am seeing are the words of teenagers. Of course, dumdum! This is a medium for kids. That's who is signing on and shaping this new technology. Kids, geniuses, engineers, nerds, hermits, nuns, psychopaths, the chronically unemployed and the compulsively discursive.

Eventually television will also become an "interactive" technology in which information flows both ways, and will be more like a phone. Ask yourself what you would do if you could "video conference" from your living room to another person's living room. Obviously you would call your mom. You'd see her, she'd see you, you'd hold up the baby, Grandma would coo etc. Then when that was done you'd start checking on friends. You'd "go" to a party you heard about. Connect with a group of fellow hobbyists or sci-fi buffs, maybe. Or maybe you'd go looking for love. You can shop from home! The ultimate safe sex . . . face-to-face video encounters . . . Fiber crawls! Video hot tubs! Virtual discos! Limbo lowah now.

The problem with TV is that it's a heavy, stationary device. So the next big leap will be mobility. Calling Dick Tracy: Wristwatch telecommunications are inevitable.

Small, portable communications devices will be the rage in just a few more years. Notebook computers already exist, as do PDAs, personal digital assistants, such as the Apple Newton. These things are cool, but they have one flaw: They don't work. Not yet. They are designed to recognize your handwriting, for example, but they don't. You will almost never meet an actual person who uses a PDA.

I go into a Radio Shack to check out a PDA called the Zoomer. It's in a glass case, like the Hope Diamond. Price: $699 ($499 on sale). I ask the salesman if he would demonstrate it but he seems uncertain how to even remove it from the glass case. Apparently this is a technology so futuristic it has to be quarantined, like the cyborg's hand in "Terminator 2." When we get it out and turn it on it seems to be a confused little device, possibly stoned. I write "technology" on the pad and the computer spells out "tecnl.GY"), and when I try to use the dictionary it repeatedly gives me the definition to the word "secure," like it is trying to tell me something.

These clunky early models deserve cruel jokes, but not cynicism. Technology gets better. Always. PDAs will soon be ubiquitous. Ubicomp!

One of these days someone will invent a cheap, easy-to-use E-mail machine. Right now, to send and receive E-mail you pretty much have to buy a computer. That's upwards of a thousand bucks. Large swaths of society are effectively cut out of the E-mail market, the poor being the most obvious group, but also those people who aren't technical. Apple-pie-baking, duck-whistle-blowing grandparents don't do E-mail. But someday E-mail will be no more complicated than putting a stamp on an envelope. The syntactical horror of the E-mail addresses will vanish and people will simply write a name and type a message and hit a button.

Soon the most mundane gadgets in your house could contain "Intelligent Agents." They'll know you, they'll track your every move and study you and try to give you what you want, which means they'll reinforce bad habits, nag you, pester you. They'll know you like to watch the Orioles and they'll prey on that weakness. "Hey, you know Mussina's pitching tonight," the machine will say. "You don't wanna miss that one."

A lot of people already find the microwave a bit too powerful and high-tech. They don't want it to be clever.

At a Menlo Park think tank called SRI International, I find a guy who seems to be able to peel the reality from the hype: Steve Krause, a 26-year-old systems analyst who in his spare time composes music on computers. Krause first shows me a prototype personal computer, invented back in the 1960s. It sits on a shelf, with little red light-emitting diodes and a hand control that looks like part of a xylophone. The device is so primitive as to be comical. How did people live back then?

Krause says that today there is no technological obstacle to building a system that would knock everyone's socks off. It's just too expensive. "I can do just about anything you want, within reason, for a cost. . . . It costs a huge amount of money to deliver today the kinds of big visions that people are talking about."

The big corporations dreaming of riches in the technological Future seem to think Americans are anxious to find new ways to part with money. The idea that people may already have too many bills to pay seems rarely mentioned in these discussions. (Poor people, of course, simply don't exist.)

The secret of the success of broadcast television in the last several decades was that it was free once you got the TV set. That's one reason the percentage of homes with TV sets is higher than the percentage with telephones. But corporations have every intention of charging premiums for these new services.

Right now the average cable TV bill is 30 bucks a month. Who is willing to start paying, say, $200 a month? The average American simply doesn't have deep enough pockets to finance the Information Superduperthing.

And the government's not going to build it. Private corporations will have to go it on their own. Moreover, the Clinton administration is insisting that whoever builds the Infoway must make it universally accessible. There is concern that otherwise we'll become a society of Information Haves and Information Have-Nots. Arguably that's precisely what we are already. In any case, the construction of the Future will be hugely expensive and it's simply not clear that anyone out there can pay for it at the moment.

The other obstacle is time. "How much room in people's lives is there to accommodate all these wonderful new services?" Krause asks.

As we speak, Krause trolls through some breaking industry news on his computer:

"Oracle Corp. predicts its interactive television technology will change the way people live and double its revenue to $4 billion a year."

Change the way we live!

Dreamin' is what they do in California. I go to see Dave Lockton at a company called Interactive Network, in another clean, unassuming office building just off a freeway in Sunnyvale. I expect Lockton to be just another Bright Young Man thinking grand thoughts in an office with the obligatory Macintosh computer with the 21-inch screen and the deep cache of E-mail, but instead I find a fast-talking middle-aged guy in a windbreaker, blue slacks, sneakers, designer eyewear. I've seen this look before. He solves the mystery when he reveals his pre-Interactive Network profession: sports attorney.

Lockton talks as though he's got the future of interactive technology just about locked up. His company allows subscribers to compete with other subscribers as they watch sporting events or "Jeopardy!" They buy special $199 "interactive control units" with keyboards that receive, via broadcast signals, data about the games (statistics on players, won-loss records, play-by-play information) typed into computers by numerous youthful employees back here at the Interactive Network headquarters. The subscribers then guess what will happen as the game progresses. At the end of the game they send a cellular phone call back to Interactive Network, and the winner of the competition wins a prize.

But who actually does this stuff? Who is sitting at home interacting with these TV games?

Not us Early Adopters and Innovators. We don't watch much TV. This is a conundrum of the BytePike: The people who like to use technology, who feel comfortable with it, don't actually want to buy all the services the digitizers can deliver.

Lockton doesn't seem worried about these things. "We'll play the winning horse continually until this thing gets sorted out." He says he has about 5,000 subscribers now but he's only in a few markets. He's got patents for all this stuff. He sees himself as a winner. "We're going to revolutionize the way people spend a majority of their spare time," he says.

Change the way we live!

Lockton's secret? People watch television seven hours a day, he says.

"What we have is an enabling technology that takes a preexisting behavior pattern," he says, "and basically leverages it."

I Find Ubicomp at a think tank called Xerox PARC, in Palo Alto, nestled in a pasture where horses gallop freely up and down the grassy green hills.

Xerox PARC is revered and infamous: As every Innovator and Early Adopter knows, the Xerox people have a fantastic habit of inventing amazing things and never cashing in on them. They created an early version of the personal computer back in the mid-1970s, but did nothing much with it. Notoriously they also created the "windows" interface for computers, only to see Steve Jobs lift their ideas for his Apple Macintosh (Jobs was later jobbed by Bill Gates at Microsoft, whose brand-name Windows is now the PC standard).

But you see everyone makes mistakes. IBM could have bought the patent for photocopying documents but turned it down. An early consultant predicted Xerox would sell only 5,000 copiers. "They assumed the purpose of the copier was to replace carbon copies," John Seely Brown, the boss of Xerox PARC, is telling me. "Now we know the main purpose of copiers is to make copies of copies."

Brown takes me into a meeting room and begins writing important words on the blackboard.

"We're a document company. We will follow a document wherever it goes. The document is a technology. It is a social technology. It comes from the Latin Docere . . ."

He writes "Docere" on the blackboard.

". . . to educate, communicate and record . . ."

He writes "Texere."

"Text, to weave together . . ."

Then Brown tells me about Ubicomp. In the ceiling above him is a "nanocell," a computerized monitoring device. It registers the temperature of the room, the humidity, the lighting. Employees wear badges that emit an infrared light that is detected by the ceiling monitors. Thus a supervisor can track down anyone in an instant. If someone calls you on the phone and you are in another room, the computer automatically relays the call to the phone nearest you. Ubicomp!

A man named Mark Weiser, in baggy pants and suspenders, leads me away to a laboratory.

"The purpose of Ubicomp is to make computers invisible," Weiser says. He shows me a large electronic blackboard, called a Liveboard, that costs $200,000 and can be used for computer conferencing; someone in Palo Alto writes a message on the board and it appears instantly on any other Liveboard in the world. Alas, it's busted. "DO NOT USE THANKS MARY 4254," says a note posted on it. Weiser isn't sure what's wrong with it but notes that among other problems it's too big. "It couldn't fit through doorways."

He demonstrates the tracking system by unclipping a wallet-sized tablet from his belt, a microcomputer of sorts, and turning it on. No response. "This room seems to be broken," he says.

We go into the next room. This room isn't broken. Weiser asks his Ubicomp tab to locate a colleague named Barry Kerchevel. The tiny screen shows a rendering of Kerchevel's face, and says he was last seen in Room 2111 at 12:05:14, "alone." We go there and he's gone. He has removed or turned off his badge, apparently. (I assume he was later hunted down and thrown into the Xerox PARC dungeon.)

"There's a big potential for privacy invasion as computers become more ubiquitous and networked," Weiser says.

"This is like the atomic bomb situation all over again, only less serious," he says. "We are inventing technology that could be damaging to the world."

Could be.

Will it be?

Might be.

The future is a cone of possibilities.

Before I leave California, I go back to the Golden Gate Bridge one last time, just to look at it rather than drive over it. There's an old fort almost directly under the bridge on the San Francisco side, and you can stand where the Kim Novak character jumped into the bay in Alfred Hitchcock's "Vertigo"—don't forget to download that one from the Net!—and in this spot the bridge reveals its immensity, its heroic nature.

Looking into the Future is a dizzying endeavor. There are exhilarating sights wrapped in a perpetual fog. Looking up at that bridge, I think: This is what the information age needs. You can't see or taste or smell or feel all those 0's and 1's on the Information Superhighway. We need something big and obvious and declarative like this bridge, something that tells the world that as a species we have reached a new level of technology.

And that it will be not just functional, but beautiful.

The News Business 10

Tabloid Sensationalism Is Thriving on TV News

HOWARD KURTZ

Night after night, local newscasts around the country are going tabloid.

In Chicago: "Tonight, an exclusive interview with a man who is accused of stalking and beating his wife."

In San Diego: "Vicious criminals are on the loose in San Diego. A 10 News extra."

In Los Angeles: "Imagine the horror of pulling into your own driveway, only to be confronted by a gun-waving carjacker."

In Miami: "Two different children, two different vicious attacks. First a little boy mauled by a Rottweiler. . . . It's a Night Team exclusive."

Click the remote control in most major cities and chances are you will find at least one station building its newscast around blood, guts and gore. While crime news has always been a staple of local television, a new sensationalism is sweeping the airwaves as once-sedate network affiliates highlight sex and violence in search of big ratings.

The tabloid format features MTV-style quick cuts, brief stories, bold graphics, slow-motion footage, dramatic music, grieving relatives and flamboyant reporters who inject themselves into the news.

A Washington Post review of local newscasts on five big-city stations on five nights last month found that tabloid news is thriving. On the late-night newscasts, the proportion of tabloid stories—defined for this survey as those involving crime, sex, disasters, accidents or public fears—ranged from 74 percent in Miami to 46 percent in Washington, excluding weather and sports.

At the top of their newscasts, all five stations repeatedly featured the Pepsi tampering allegations, with such headlines as "Soda Scare" and "Syringe Scare." Other graphics included "Voyeur Murder," "Tollway Murder," "Wheelchair Murder," "Rap Music Murder," "Serial Rapist," "Serial Killer," "Caught in the Crossfire" and "Alligator Attack." Floods, tornadoes, fires, mudslides, explosions, plane crashes and train accidents also were a staple.

After depleting the supply of death and destruction, several stations turned to such lesser fare as a snakebite victim, a woman bitten by a deadly spider, a public school flasher, a third-grader hit with a BB pellet, "satanic" activities involving cats and dogs and, inevitably, Gennifer Flowers, Joey Buttafuoco, Madonna and the death of Elvis Presley.

John Lippman, fired in May as news director of KCBS in Los Angeles over his controversial approach, says critics of his "Action News" methods tend to be white, upper-middle-class elitists.

"We tried to put a human face on crime, not do the body-count coverage," he said. "The L.A. Times every Monday runs a story saying '19 People Killed in Weekend Violence,' and everyone gets a sentence and a half. We wanted to bring the horror home. The critics savaged us, but we prefer to call it a populist newscast.

"You got to know something about these people who were dying or being victimized," he said. "What frankly got squeezed out was some of the institutional stuff—'they debated, nothing happened.' " The newscast, Lippman said, was aimed at working-class viewers "living with the kind of crime problems that frankly do not touch Beverly Hills."

But critics say a relentless focus on violence paints a distorted picture of a community and exacerbates fear of crime. "People come to think they're in great danger" because the media tend to spotlight middle-class victims, said James Fyfe, professor of criminal justice at Temple University.

"Children of the inner city are learning about themselves through the local news, and all they see is one black man after another dragged from a paddy wagon to a police station," said Walter Jacobson, who recently quit as the longtime anchor of Chicago's WBBM after it switched to a tabloid format.

Unlike such complicated issues as poverty and health care, crime is easy to cover because it is immediate and provides vivid pictures. "You listen on the scanner and someone died so it's sort of news, but what does that really mean in a big city?" said David Smith, a top executive with Frank Magid Associates, which advises 100 stations on improving their news ratings. "Murder, especially black-on-black murder, is a critically important story. But are you really telling that story one body bag at a time?"

Perhaps nowhere has the shift been as dramatic as at WBBM, a CBS-owned station that once fielded one of the country's most respected local news operations. Anchored for years by Bill Kurtis and Jacobson, WBBM hired newspaper reporters, covered politics intensively and won a closetful of journalism awards.

By 1990, however, WBBM was mired in third place in the ratings, and a new general manager, Bill Applegate, radically overhauled its approach to news.

"Now it leads the way in sex and violence and screaming headlines," said Jacobson, who quit his million-dollar job in April after being dropped as co-anchor. Now with the local Fox outlet, Jacobson said WBBM "bears no resemblance whatever" to the station where he worked for 20 years.

"All the people they hired are 22- to 28-year-old performers, and they've all got this same quality about them: Get right in front of the camera and move around and draw in the audience and create mystery and suspense and drama. . . . They're not covering the General Assembly or the Board of Education to the extent they need to be covered. It's all pizazz."

The spectacular headlines sometimes involve a healthy dose of hype. In May, when WBBM led with news of the prison release of a man convicted of beating his ex-wife, the words "FREE," "FEAR" and "EXCLUSIVE" filled the screen. But in an interview, the man promised never to bother her again.

That story was followed by a kidnapping, a school sex scandal, a local fire raging "out of control," arson at local garages, a cat who saved his owner's life during a fire, footage of riots in Copenhagen, surveillance-camera footage of a robbery and shooting in Michigan, a gunman keeping police at bay in Toledo, guns and knives found in a Boston teenager's room, assault charges dismissed against LaToya Jackson's husband, a kidnapped boy reunited with his mother in Seattle and the "incredible story" of a 12-year-old girl who survived being hit by a train.

Then came a teaser: "The real story of love, manipulation and murder. A Channel 2 news extra tomorrow at 10."

"What I object to is the lack of context," one WBBM staff member said. "It all goes hurtling by, and the world is a frightening and inexplicable place. We owe people more than a body shot and weeping and wailing relatives."

Applegate, transferred to KCBS last month, did not return phone calls. He told the Chicago Sun-Times that he gave WBBM "a more interesting and more colorful newscast" that "increased the ratings."

Television executives say the 1990s version of tabloid news was created by Miami's WSVN, a Fox affiliate. The station has greatly boosted its ratings with a rapid-fire recitation of violence and disaster, features such as "Crime Check" and "Most Wanted" and series such as "Hot Sex."

One night last month, the newscast began: "In Pompano Beach, police say an elderly woman was held captive by her own son. In Miami, two men, one of them an ice cream vendor, charged with molesting several children." This was followed by reports on a 6-year-old shot in a gun accident, a young boy charging sexual abuse and the drowning death of a 2-year-old.

"Crime is a reality down here, but there are some crimes that have no impact on people's lives and don't deserve to be splattered all over the place," said Sharon Scott, news director of rival WTVJ.

"There is a public denial of watching that station," Scott said. "It's kind of like the National Enquirer where people say, 'I'd never read that,' and you go to the supermarket and they're looking at it."

Joel Cheatwood, WSVN's news director, did not return several phone calls. Cheatwood told the Miami Herald in 1991 that he does not get caught up in "highbrow ethics" that fail to recognize "television as an entertainment business."

The Miami formula is spreading to other markets. WSVN's owner, Edmund Ansin, recently bought Boston's independent WHDH and is expected to change its format.

In Los Angeles, KCBS's switch to tabloid news sparked a staff revolt. In an open letter posted before Lippman was fired, angry staffers told him: "It is all deception. You have absolutely no regard for the viewers. You mock them continually, and you make us carry out your daily deceptions, such as your silly and phony 'Satellite News Center' . . . the obvious daily gratuitous LIVE shots for the sake of just being LIVE. . . ."

KCBS relies on such techniques as helicopter footage of police car chases and a Satellite News Center that flashes vivid pictures of violence and disasters from around the world. Lippman said he was fired because he became "a lightning rod" for criticism.

KCBS "Action News," co-anchored on one occasion by Geraldo Rivera, seems to specialize in this-could-be-you reporting. One night, anchor Michael Tuck said, "Coming up on Nightcast: Is any place safe these days? A woman is gunned down watching television in her own home." Another story warned that "you could be the next victim" of cellular phone fraud.

"If you watched Lippman's newscast, you'd get the impression that every time you opened your door there would be a sniper ready to pick you off," said Howard Rosenberg, television critic for the Los Angeles Tines. "It feeds a climate of fear."

Some stories quickly evaporate. KCBS reported that "a cold-hearted thief may be responsible" for stealing a dog from a terminally ill boy, but the next day the dog was found in a nearby neighborhood.

Several stations that were surveyed played up crime stories that might merit a few paragraphs in the local paper. On WWOR, an independent station serving the New York area from Secaucus, N.J., anchor Reg Wells said: "We begin with an exclusive report—charges of police brutality in Glen Ridge, New Jersey." It turned out to be about one black teenager who said a white policeman had slapped him with an open hand.

"Crime reporting should have some socially redeeming value," said Will Wright, WWOR'S news director. "The criticism of TV news is that 'if it bleeds, it leads [the newscast].' I don't particularly believe that. I'm putting together a news organization that looks at crime stories as a social issue. It might exacerbate people's fear of crime, but crime exists. We didn't create it."

WRC (Channel 4), the NBC-owned station here, does not use a tabloid format but has been highlighting local crime stories on its top-rated 11 p.m. newscast.

One week last month, the first four to six stories each night involved crime or disaster—the search for missing 10-year-old George "Junior" Burdynski, developments in the death of Laura Houghteling of Bethesda, a police crackdown on prostitution, a drunken man killed by police, a gas-line explosion in Gaithersburg, a murder in Prince George's County, a rapist found guilty in Arlington.

Anchor Jim Vance began one newscast: "Tonight, a crackdown on prostitution in D.C." Reporter Joe Johns, standing at Franklin Square, announced that "the last police cars are pulling off as I speak." The story was that at least eight streetwalkers had been arrested in a sweep.

Dick Reingold, WRC's news director, said the station tries not to overemphasize crime. "We wrestle with it all the time," he said. "One could cover crime news almost endlessly. The answer is good news judgment and putting on a balanced news broadcast.

"We've tried to be more selective. We're conscious that it can present a distorted view of the community. It can also present a realistic one. If anything, we have raised the selectivity bar in covering crime. There are a lot of other stories out there."

A tabloid format can pump up a station's ratings, and while analysts say the increase evaporates over time, rival stations often feel compelled to move in a similar direction.

"News directors constantly feel the pressure to look at the product across the street," said Bob Reichblum, a former news director here and in Miami who now is with "Good Morning America."

Tabloid news "gains a sliver of the audience," said Smith of Frank Magid Associates. "It tends to be a minority audience because that news is happening in their neighborhoods. But it can be very disorienting and alienating to a broader audience."

As if to prove the point, KCBS's late news has slipped to third among three stations in Los Angeles, while WBBM has dropped to third among four Chicago stations. WSVN's late news is third among four Miami stations, according to the Nielsen service, although Arbitron still rates it No. 1.

Some stations are not content with merely covering the news. KMOV in St. Louis came under criminal investigation last month for paying expenses for a male prostitute, who arranged a liaison with a priest in a hotel room where the station had a hidden camera.

A reporter and cameraman for KCCO in Alexandria, Minn., pleaded guilty in February to supplying teenagers with two cases of beer for a story on underage drinking. A reporter for Denver's KCNC was convicted in 1991 of staging an illegal pit-bull fight for a series called "Blood Sport" during a ratings sweeps week.

Each station surveyed by The Post, except WRC, regularly airs brief highlights of crimes and disasters from around the country. The lineup one night on WWOR's "9 Watch": A Florida girl commits suicide by throwing herself in front of a train. A murderer flees a Mississippi prison. A Milwaukee teacher is arrested for taking out a murder contract on his wife's boyfriend. A sinkhole swallows cars in Atlanta. A tornado rips through part of Florida.

"9 Watch is a way to get viewers back in the tent," Wright said.

Fees for Sleaze

HOWARD KURTZ

P aul Erickson, an Arlington media lawyer, was a virgin when it came to tabloid television. Then he started representing John Bobbitt.

"They call and start throwing cash and gifts at you, but they're paranoid about ever revealing that they're doing it," he says. "Some were simply too sleazy to talk to on the phone. I have been offered cash bribes to break contracts we've had with existing shows."

Erickson found himself in a bidding war while setting up paid interviews for the man with the world's most famous reattached organ. "They all hate each other," he says of the programs. "They tell you how everyone else is scum except them."

The Bobbitt case is merely the latest manifestation of cash register journalism, an increasingly competitive environment in which news is sold, optioned and merchandised for sizable sums. The rise of tabloid TV has transformed the culture of reporting into a profit-driven enterprise that sometimes leaves traditional news organizations in the dust. It also turns celebrities into lucrative targets, a complaint leveled Tuesday by Michael Jackson's attorneys.

Bobbitt, while rebuffing most press inquiries, sold two interviews to the show "American Journal." Joey Buttafuoco, whose affair with 16-year-old Amy Fisher spawned three quickie TV movies, was recently paid to appear with his wife on "A Current Affair." David Berkowitz, the "Son of Sam" mass murderer, did "Inside Edition" after the program paid the producer who arranged the interview.

"They're paying big, big money for exclusive interviews," says Iain Calder, editor in chief of the National Enquirer, which bought exclusive rights to photograph the Donald Trump-Marla Maples wedding. "They don't think twice about paying 30 or 40 grand." The Buttafuoco interviews were reported to cost $500,000, although insiders say such figures are wildly exaggerated.

This thriving tabloid culture has erased the old definitions of news: Tawdry stories about celebrities are no longer confined to the supermarket papers.

The initial allegations of child abuse against Jackson drew heavy coverage from the Los Angeles Times and The Washington Post and made the cover of Newsweek. This, in turn, brought forth a number of Jackson aides and hangers-on with palms outstretched. Blanca Francia, Jackson's former maid, sold her story to "Hard Copy" and was denounced by the pop star's camp as a "paid witness."

Jackson's attorneys said in a statement that he "has been subjected to an unprecedented media feeding frenzy. . . . The tabloid press has shown an insatiable thirst for anything negative and has paid huge sums of money to people who have little or no information and who barely knew Michael Jackson."

To be sure, elite news organizations have long sniffed that paying for information is a disreputable practice. But Calder says the conventional wisdom may be shifting. A decade ago, he says, "it was an unpopular thing to do. People would call us and say, 'This is awful journalism.' I think it's become more accepted. The younger journalists have grown up with the idea that television does it. "60 Minutes" has done it on occasion. The mainstream press has moved closer to the Enquirer."

What is derisively called "checkbook journalism" was once rare enough among American news organizations that the payments themselves became news. In 1975, CBS stunned polite journalistic society by paying former Nixon aide H. R. Haldeman $25,000 for a "60 Minutes" interview, and Watergate burglar G. Gordon Liddy $15,000. Two years later, David Frost upped the ante dramatically when he paid Richard Nixon $600,000 for a series of TV interviews.

But since the 1986 debut of "A Current Affair," owned by Rupert Murdoch, spawned a host of imitators, the pay-to-play arena has become far more crowded.

New York Post reporter Bill Hoffmann recalls flying to Bermuda in 1989 to try to interview Janet Culver, who had miraculously survived 14 days at sea in a rubber raft. But when he arrived at the hospital, Hoffmann was told that People magazine had bought exclusive rights to her story for $10,000.

"She wouldn't talk," says Hoffmann, who watched in frustration as People published a cover story under Culver's byline. "If someone paid me 10 grand, I wouldn't talk either."

While most American newspapers and newsmagazines still have firm rules against paying for news, they routinely treat sources to expensive lunches and shell out large sums for book excerpts. Television stations regularly pay ordinary citizens for videotape (such as the famous Rodney King beating footage, which sold for $500). Network entertainment divisions buy up story rights for docudramas. Why, then, should the peddling of a news story raise an ethical red flag?

"Everyone's entitled to exploit their intellectual property," says Everette Dennis, director of the Freedom Forum Media Studies Center at Columbia University. "The only reason they're likely to talk to newspapers free is to get publicity to help them exploit their story. It may be undesirable and unsavory, but if they want to make a buck, they have the right" to ask for money.

The problem is that paying the subjects of news stories—a practice essentially invented by the London tabloids—raises questions about their credibility. When Gennifer Flowers told the world she had been Bill Clinton's mistress, news accounts invariably stressed that she sold her tale to the Star tabloid for an estimated $100,000.

"If someone says they did something with somebody and can prove it, we'll pay," says Star Editor Richard Kaplan. "I'd much prefer not to for ethical reasons and budget reasons, so that the story is not in any way tainted by the fact that you're paying for it. I'm sure if we'd gotten the Gennifer Flowers story without any exchange of money, the whole cash-for-trash line would have been rendered obsolete."

Jim Gaines, now managing editor of Time, regrets one episode of news-buying when he ran People. During the Gary Hart-Donna Rice uproar, People paid Rice's friend Lynn Armandt for her pictures and story.

"It was a mistake," Gaines says. "I came to be filled with suspicion [about Armandt's motives]. I felt I and the magazine had been badly used."

People Managing Editor Landon Jones says he ended the practice of paying for stories when he took over four years ago. "People come to us every single week and say I have a great story about Michael Jackson or whatever and my client wants to be paid," he says. "They're shopping around. The well has been poisoned."

When Lorena Bobbitt went on trial in Manassas this month for cutting off her husband's penis, the event drew 200 reporters from around the world, some of them prowling the courthouse corridors with cash offers.

"My agent won't let me say anything," John Bobbitt told reporters after his wife was acquitted last Friday of malicious wounding. "American Journal" aired its second exclusive interview with him Tuesday, with Bobbitt declaring himself "shocked" by the verdict and "scarred for life."

Guests on such programs are rarely subjected to withering cross-examination. In an earlier interview after he was cleared of marital assault, Bobbitt told "American Journal": "We had sex a lot, I mean a lot. In the four years we were married, probably 900 times."

Erickson says Bobbitt has done interviews with Jenny Jones, Howard Stern, NBC's "Now" and The New Yorker, among others, and that most of these sessions were unpaid (although Bobbitt raised $260,000 from appeals on a Stern cable special). Erickson says his client is about to embark on a 10-city radio tour and is weighing invitations from Australia and Japan, along with book and movie offers.

"John Bobbitt didn't choose the situation he was placed in," he says. "To begrudge him the opportunity to recover some of his medical and legal expenses is just a cheap shot."

Bobbitt has refused all newspaper interviews (except for one with USA Today) because he suffers from "attention deficit disorder" and is not intelligent enough to fence with agressive reporters, Erickson says. While Bobbitt sounds all right on camera, "he can't understand compound questions. He couldn't get through a [print] interview. He'd be ripped apart."

Erickson says he chose "American Journal" after concluding that "they'd do it as a straight news piece—no reenactments, no hokey weird-angle stuff."

John Tomlin, co-executive producer of "American Journal" and "Inside Edition," says his reporters are not running around waving wads of cash.

"You have to have a senior member of the staff make the decision, and you do it on rare occasions," he says. "The important thing to me is I can sleep at night. I don't believe you should pay people who commit crimes for their stories." In the "Son of Sam" interviews, "I believe no money went to Berkowitz or I wouldn't have done it."

The buying and selling of interviews has become almost routine in high-profile criminal cases. At the William Kennedy Smith rape trial, defense lawyers shredded the credibility of a key witness, Anne Mercer, after she acknowledged she had been paid $40,000 to appear on "A Current Affair." In the Rodney King beating, one police officer convicted in the case accepted $10,000 to appear on "A Current Affair," while another took $25,000 to do "Donahue."

"These television shows are so free and loose with their money," says Hoffmann. "They basically hand over fistfuls of cash. I'm not talking about checks; these reporters carry around cash. Is that real journalism? I don't know. I think people tend to sweeten their stories for 10 grand."

Tomlin bristles at the holier-than-thou attitude of his network competitors. "One of the biggest lies in network television is 'we don't pay for stories,' " he says. "They will pay for so-called consultants to give them stories."

Some programs skirt the rules by paying "for weekends in New York, first-class air travel, a new coat," Erickson says. "You get to the hotel and they give you $500 a day for 'food' and they don't care what you do with the money. These are huge inducements to someone from a trailer park who's popping open his second can of Schlitz."

Philip Morris Sues ABC

HOWARD KURTZ

Philip Morris Co. filed a $10 billion libel suit against ABC yesterday, charging that the network falsely accused the tobacco industry of artificially "spiking" its cigarettes with added nicotine.

ABC News said in a statement that it "stands by its reporting on this issue" but declined to comment further.

The nation's largest tobacco company announced the lawsuit the day before a House subcommittee hearing today in which David A. Kessler, commissioner of the Food and Drug Administration, is to testify about his plan to consider regulating tobacco products on grounds that manufacturers may be using nicotine, the addictive substance in cigarettes, as a drug to hook smokers.

The lawsuit, filed in state circuit court in Richmond, stems from ABC's "Day One" broadcasts on cigarette production Feb. 28 and March 7. The suit also names ABC correspondent John Martin and producer Walt Bogdanich as defendants.

Steven Parrish, senior vice president of Philip Morris USA, said the company, whose best-known product is Marlboro, was "outraged" by the ABC broadcasts.

"We gave them two written statements, both pointing out that we do not spike our cigarettes with nicotine," Parrish said. "They did not use the statements, nor did 'Day One' indicate they had asked us for comment."

One ABC official disputed this account, saying: "We asked them repeatedly to appear for on-camera interviews and they declined. We gave them advance questions and they sent us statements which did not answer our questions."

But Philip Morris general counsel Murray Bring said in a statement that "these allegations are not true and ABC knows they are not true."

ABC charged in the first broadcast that the tobacco industry "artificially adds nicotine to keep people smoking and boost profits." The segment focused mainly on R.J. Reynolds, but said a Philip Morris official had written an internal memo decades ago that a cigarette should be considered "a storage container for a day's supply of nicotine."

Parrish acknowledged that Philip Morris removes nicotine while making reconstituted tobacco, used in virtually all cigarettes, and puts it back later in the process. But, he said, "What gets reapplied is less than what came out. . . . We quarrel with the notion that we are adding extraneous nicotine." The company said the reconstituted product contains 20 to 25 percent less nicotine than ordinary tobacco leaf.

Philip Morris is seeking $5 billion each in compensatory and punitive damages, Parrish said, because the "Day One" segments have played a role in the FDA and congressional investigations and prompted a sharp decline in the price of the company's stock. President Clinton has expressed concern about the ABC allegations, and Kessler announced his inquiry after learning that the "Day One" broadcast was imminent.

While the pretrial discovery process would allow ABC to examine internal documents about the Philip Morris manufacturing process, Parrish said the company plans to pursue the case all the way to trial.

Cliff Douglas of the American Cancer Society called the Philip Morris suit "a desperate act. They're seeking to counter in a big public way the public relations nightmare they've been facing in recent weeks, resulting from the disclosure that tobacco companies manipulate the addictive drug in their product."

Washington attorney Bruce Sanford, a First Amendment specialist, said that as a public company Philip Morris must prove actual malice by ABC, "either knowledge of falsity or reckless disregard for the truth. The issue really is what did ABC know and when did they know it."

The suit comes at a time when federal, state and local governments are enacting broad new restrictions on smoking, and a House subcommittee voted this week to increase the cigarette tax by $1.25 per pack. The cover story in Sunday's New York Times Magazine, which focused on Philip Morris, was entitled "How Do Tobacco Executives Live With Themselves?"

Philip Morris joined R.J. Reynolds and other groups last year in a suit to overturn the Environmental Protection Agency's designation of secondhand smoke as a potent carcinogen.

A number of major corporations have sued network news shows in an effort to counter negative publicity. General Motors sued and won a public apology from "Dateline NBC" last year over the program's staging of a fiery crash of a GM pickup truck. Food Lion has sued ABC's "PrimeTime Live" over a report alleging unsanitary practices by the supermarket chain.

How Sources and Reporters Play the Leak Game

HOWARD KURTZ

O N TUESDAY morning, the Wall Street Journal scooped the world with news that Michael Gartner, the embattled NBC News president, was resigning.

Gartner, once the Journal's Page One editor, was clearly in need of a friendly forum. Under siege over the network's dishonest staging of a fiery truck crash, Gartner (or a friend on his behalf) obviously tipped the Journal that he had been ousted.

He was rewarded with a profile that, while it included some criticism, was generally sympathetic: "Mr. Gartner's supporters see all this as a painful and demoralizing irony. He has been blamed for all sorts of things in his tenure as president of NBC News. . . . Mr. Gartner earned widespread respect in his long career as a newspaper editor. . . . He is 'a journalist's journalist,' says NBC News anchorwoman Maria Shriver." And that was just in the first six paragraphs.

Gartner was engaging in the art of the leak, a time-honored effort by newsmakers to orchestrate coverage from behind a curtain of anonymity. Leaking has become a Washington parlor game, a secret code that the inside players use to send messages and warnings to one another. And reporters (including me), unable to resist a juicy story, are all too willing to serve as a conduit.

Why should anyone outside the journalistic fraternity care? Because, simply put, anonymous sources help shape much of the news you read and see every day.

"There's a trend toward a much higher tolerance among editors for the use of anonymous sources, and the abuse of readers by passing on to them rumor or calculated misinformation," said Bill Kovach, curator of the Nieman Foundation at Harvard University.

In trying to break the code, keep in mind that every leak furthers someone's agenda. All those 1991 stories about how John Sununu was in deep trouble as George Bush's chief of staff were fueled by Sununu's legion of enemies. When budget director Richard Darman wanted to distance himself from the fiasco of Bush's economic policy last fall, he made sure his objections were vividly (and anonymously) recorded in a Washington Post series by Bob Woodward. Media insiders quickly guessed that the source was Darman—and wondered how the story was affecting his day-to-day relations with the president he still served. The average reader may have missed the irony.

And don't forget how James Baker led a charmed media life by feeding not-for-attribution tidbits to key reporters. Soon after he took over Bush's reelection effort, stories started suggesting that the campaign was in shambles and a loss would not be Baker's fault.

Leaks often must be shopped around. Many reporters refused to cover the GOP innuendo about Bill Clinton's student trip to Moscow until the Washington Times gave the matter front-page play and it ricocheted onto the talk shows. This demonstrates an immutable law of journalism: Rumors aren't news until someone else trumpets them. To be sure, much serious journalism would be impossible if people had to attach their names to every scrap of information provided to reporters. The Seattle Times, for example, relied on accounts from eight unnamed women last year in alleging sexual harassment by then-senator Brock Adams. Few folks are willing to put their necks on the line simply to uphold some abstract notion of the public's right to know.

Still, it is often hard to discern motives in the shadowy world of unnamed sources. The New York Times reported last month that Gen. Colin Powell wanted to step down early as chairman of the Joint Chiefs of Staff because—according to "several close associates"—he felt he could not support President Clinton. That morning, Powell took the unusual step of going on four network shows to deny the account.

Had the newspaper been misled by people trying to embarrass the president? Or was Powell merely engaged in some political fence-mending?

Woodward, who has been utilizing unnamed sources since Watergate, argues that the cloak of anonymity is essential to unveiling the truth. Woodward believes the Powell story was on target. (He should know; Powell acknowledged at a congressional hearing that he was a source for Woodward's book "The Commanders.")

"If the sources are good and the story is about an important conflict that persons do not want to proclaim publicly, a story will often be denied when it is true or contains an important, essential truth," Woodward said. "The public version and the private version are often different. To uncritically accept the public version is to do a big disservice."

USA Today, by contrast, discourages the use of unnamed sources and almost never allows them to be quoted—a restriction that helps explain why the paper does little investigative reporting.

"When people's names aren't attached to a story, it becomes much easier for them to say things that aren't necessarily true," Editor Peter Prichard said. "They're protected. A lot of savvy people will use that protection to float stories that aren't true or that embarrass someone else." On serious investigative pieces, most news organizations will check and recheck a source's allegations before publishing them.

Lighter items—say, "Word is Joe Jones is in line to become assistant secretary of such-and-such"—are obviously not intended as holy writ.

Somewhere in the middle is a broad range of political stories in which unnamed folks routinely float trial balloons, criticize policies or disparage rivals. Last August, the New York Times reported that the Bush administration had "decided to provoke a confrontation with Iraq" and that "some United States government officials said the timing appeared calculated to give President Bush a boost during the Republican National Convention." There was no hint of who these officials were and why they were making what Bush called an "ugly and uncalled for" charge.

"Ours is a competitive business, and if someone with an authoritative voice says to us a decision has been made to do X, and we check it a couple of other places, we run it," said R.W. Apple Jr., the Times's Washington bureau chief. "So does The Washington Post. So does the Los Angeles Times.

"You're going to be used on occasion. You do your best to get around being used by figuring out motivation and checking the story out from a number of angles."

In some ways the question comes down to trust. Most readers would regard a "sourced" story in the Philadelphia Inquirer as more credible than one in the National Enquirer. But that trust in the mainstream media is not always justified. The New York Times apologized in 1991 after admitting that a reporter had quoted an anonymous caller as an unnamed corporate official, although the reporter did not even know the man's name.

Sometimes a pledge of confidentiality puts a news organization in an awkward bind. After Judge Kimba Wood bowed out as a candidate for attorney general, the New York Times anonymously quoted her husband, Time magazine political reporter Michael Kramer, as challenging the White House account of her nomination. The next day, the Times quoted Wood as denying the source's account—but, bound by its earlier pledge, was unable to tell its readers that the source was Wood's own spouse. (Kramer's role was leaked to me by anonymous Times sources I cannot possibly reveal.)

The Post faced a similar dilemma last June when Woodward, based in part on four-year-old "background" conversations with Ross Perot, reported that Perot had been investigating Bush in 1988. Woodward said the story was carefully worded and did not violate any agreement with Perot.

A Times story that accused Sen. Joseph Biden of plagiarizing speeches during the 1988 presidential campaign was surely newsworthy. But the disclosure that the leak came from John Sasso, an aide to Democratic rival Michael Dukakis, turned out to be equally newsworthy—and it cost Sasso his job.

Journalistic attempts to unmask sources can also backfire. The Supreme Court ruled in 1991 that Dan Cohen, a Republican operative in Minnesota, had the right to sue two newspapers that identified him as a source after he leaked them information about a candidate for lieutenant governor. The story led to Cohen's dismissal from his advertising agency job.

This debate has been kicking around since reporters were quoting Henry Kissinger as the ubiquitous "senior official" aboard the secretary of state's plane. Such a "senior official" mysteriously reappeared aboard Warren Christopher's plane when the new secretary of state visited the Middle East. The Clinton administration, despite objections from the press, frequently briefs reporters "on background," meaning that the information can be used but not attributed to an official by name. After Defense Secretary Les Aspin was hospitalized for heart problems, his spokesman, Vernon Guidry, would discuss Aspin's health at briefings only as a "senior defense official."

"Most of the time," said Nina Totenberg of National Public Radio, "you're operating on deadline and you need the information, and the person who says this has to be on background has the power."

Prosecutors often use well-timed leaks to pressure potential defendants or witnesses. After several news organizations reported on a probe of Rep. Dan Rostenkowski (D-Ill.), a federal judge here ordered U.S. Attorney Jay Stephens to explain the apparent grand jury leaks. (Stephens convinced the judge that his office had not acted improperly.)

White House officials recently dribbled out key details of Clinton's economic plan as a way of test-marketing unpopular proposals. Several of the leaks turned up in the Wall Street Journal, perhaps reflecting an effort by the Clintonites to reassure the markets.

"We probably have been used as much as anybody in this," said Albert Hunt, the Journal's Washington bureau chief. "There are days when I pick up the paper and cringe. But if you say we're not going to participate in this, they float it to someone else and you wind up chasing it the next day."

Politicians sometimes manage both to orchestrate leaks and denounce them. In 1966, President Lyndon Johnson ordered a top aide, Joseph Califano, Jr., to tell reporters on background that U.S. steel companies were "profiteering" on the Vietnam War. When a business executive later complained, according to a book by Califano, Johnson said the statement was reprehensible and that "if I find out some damn fool aide did it, I'll fire the sonuvabitch!"

Some things never change. Last month, after senior White House officials confirmed to reporters that Clinton had selected Judge Wood as attorney general, she withdrew the next day for having hired an undocumented immigrant as a nanny. The president denied that he had chosen Wood and complained about the leak.

"If I knew who did it, they wouldn't be here," Clinton said.

What's Wrong with News You Can Use?

ELEANOR RANDOLPH

At a gathering of Third World visitors here recently, an African stood to ask a question of columnist James J. Kilpatrick.

"Why is it that American journalists don't care about my country?" the African asked.

"What country do you come from, sir?" Kilpatrick responded.

"Uganda," the man answered.

"Why the hell should I care about Uganda?" said Kilpatrick, as diplomats around the room wheezed and struggled to catch their breaths.

This story, retold recently in an essay published by the Gannett Center for Media Studies in New York, is another case of Kilpatrick's having the nerve to say what so many other journalists were thinking. The American news establishment too often looks at foreign news as something alien. Their rule: The farther it is from home, the less important it is to the readers.

As a result, news organizations over the years have shed foreign bureaus and scaled back costly foreign coverage. One survey shows that the amount of the nation's top ten papers devoted to foreign news dropped from 10.2 percent in 1971 to 2.6 percent in 1987.

With recent events in China, Eastern Europe and Central America, the percentage of foreign news in the nation's newspapers is probably up from 1987, when near-war had broken out in the Middle East and Persian Gulf, says one expert on this trend, Michael Emery, chair of the journalism school at California State University, Northridge. But the percentage of foreign news is still down from 20 years ago, Emery laments.

The problem is that publishers are busy giving readers what they think they want instead of what is important. This is the era of "News You Can Use" the catch phrase for journalism that helps you with your taxes, cholesterol and yearning for the latest in car phones. All that is fine, but you cannot use this news to help understand what's going on—not in your neighborhood, not in your country, not in your world.

If that sounds like a boring flashback to Mrs. Morse's ninth-grade civics class, so sorry. As Mrs. Morse would say: "Informed people make good citizens." But the money men who increasingly run newspapers and television networks seem to think that good citizenship is registered most concretely in the profit margins. Their accountants have found that the numbers for foreign coverage—or Washington coverage, for that matter—aren't good.

Foreign coverage costs big bucks, about $250,000 a year for a one-man bureau. Moreover, unless Americans are involved in the story—from a plane wreck in Scotland to an invasion of Panama—level of interest among many readers and most editors ranges from pale to pallid. Their interest perks up a bit if there are pictures of some major calamity, bloody pictures, such as the ones from Tiananmen Square. Any foreign story without blood or Americans or both has a tough time.

The Times-Mirror News Interest Index, which comes out monthly, noted that the big foreign-news event for most Americans was the one we engineered—the invasion of Panama. More than half of those surveyed said that Panama topped their list of important news events for December and January.

By contrast, the overthrow of the Ceausescu government in Romania ranked as top story for five percent of those interviewed. And although 70 percent of those interviewed knew that Romanian President Nicolae Ceausescu and his wife had been tried secretly and executed, 13 percent said they thought that U.S. troops had been involved in the Romanian uprising.

Many serious journalists, both reporters and editors, have been shocked at the lack of interest here in what has happened in Eastern Europe. Surveys of news consumers show that few people can recognize the name of the man who has suddenly became head of Czechoslovakia.

For most of us in the news trade, the crumbling of the Communist threat is the biggest story in the last decade. It will dramatically affect how America does business, maintains its military and reorders domestic priorities. To learn that this news is falling on disinterested ears and even that some news managers are beginning to scale back their commitment to the story in Europe feels like a punch in the stomach.

More than the overactive journalistic ego is being bruised here. We know that when people aren't interested in news beyond their own bank statement and spa schedule, they are ceding the major decisions in their lives to others.

"As knowledge of foreign affairs drops, the chances for clear decisions in Congress drops because there is less public awareness," said Emery. "They can get away with more and more and more."

The most basic instinct of governments both abroad and at home is to keep everything they do a secret, except for those things they want to advertise. If the press limits its coverage of foreign matters, then it's an all-clear for the people in charge. They like it that way. We shouldn't tolerate it.

The National News

ELEANOR RANDOLPH

The national news media has an unspoken rule: If it happens in Texas, it's quaint. If it happens in New York City, it's serious.

For years, journalists stationed around the country for the news magazines, the networks or New York newspapers talked with frustration about a story being "BAMed"—walloped by an editor inflicted with Big Apple Myopia.

Some of the most classic horror stories about Eastern ignorance include a call from the boss in New York who thought Idaho was next to Texas, or a correspondent who found herself steaming down the highway because her editor was convinced that Denver was just a "hop and a skip from" South Dakota.

With cable channels eating into the networks and magazines suffering from lack of national advertising, however, there has been a lot of talk about how New York editors and news directors have "discovered America." That is, they have decided that there are smart people, good people, bad people and interesting people who do not live within a two-hour (day-trip) radius of Rockefeller Center.

Forget it, says David Shaw, media critic for the—ahem—Los Angeles Times. It's nothing but talk.

In a recent series that has yet to get much notice back East, Shaw explains how it works: Newsweek's Detroit bureau chief was in Houston last year and tried to convince her editors to do a story on ocean pollution. A whale had died from swallowing debris along the Gulf coast. Shellfish beds were off limits near Texas. Volunteers in one three-day period picked up more than 200 tons of debris.

Sorry, she was told, not national. Then, New Yorkers found syringes on their beaches this summer. Suddenly Time and Newsweek—simultaneously, of course— trumpeted the warnings in their Aug. 1 editions. "Our Filthy Seas" said Time's cover. "Our Polluted Oceans" echoed Newsweek.

Calls to reporters and editors who work for various publications around the country brought near explosions of frustration at the networks, the news magazines and the Eastern newspapers for their "arrogant" provincialism.

"The New York Times takes a particularly hard policy," said Dan Thomasson, vice president of the Scripps-Howard News Service. "They figure it's not news until they print it."

Thomasson obviously speaking for many of his colleagues, says that even reporters from outlying areas who go to work for The Times or The Washington Post or The Wall Street Journal "suddenly think that they're more worthy. . . . If you work for those papers it doesn't matter who you are. You could call up and say you're Mickey Mouse from The New York Times and, bam, you get the interview."

Mike Magner, Washington correspondent for the Booth Newspapers in Michigan, says that the way news is covered affects the way legislation is enacted. After New Yorkers and their media discovered ocean pollution, miraculously, so did Congress.

"Michigan congressmen complained that Congress tried to ignore the Great Lakes," Magner said. "In this case, medical wastes were washing up on shores in Lake Erie and Lake Michigan, but Congress wanted legislation that dealt only with oceans."

Nick Hoffock, an alumnus of Newsweek and The New York Times who is now running the Washington bureau of The Chicago Tribune, says that he believes the Eastern bias is dissipating. To help it along, he makes certain the Associated Press offices in Chicago or Washington know about a Tribune scoop.

But in other areas, such as foreign policy, it's still tough going. "I've had guys who say they don't care about being in The Chicago Tribune, even if we got there first and ask the most intelligent questions. . . . They just want to be in The Times."

Some relief comes during presidential campaigns when thousands of national reporters and a few editors are forced to follow the candidates out into the real world. Iowa, New Hampshire, Florida, Michigan and Oregon are all places that have three journalistic advantages: They are not Boston, not Washington and not New York City.

But, this is once every four years. And, too many national political journalists can go to Arizona and spend a lot of time hanging out with their friends from New York, Boston and Washington. When they sit in an Albuquerque bar and talk about the Indian problem this year, they meant the Washington Redskins.

A suggestion: National reporters for national publications should be required by their bosses to visit other areas of the country at least once per quarter—a real place where a press advance crew has not arrived a few days in advance and made sure the phones work. Kennebunkport doesn't count. Editors should make a national tour every year to talk about crime in Texas or the state of the arts in Chicago.

Maybe then some would realize that when they moved to the East Coast, all the best people and the worst problems and the most interesting news stories in the country did not automatically move with them. Maybe.

The Gulf between Media and Military

HENRY ALLEN

The Persian Gulf press briefings are making reporters look like fools, nit-pickers and egomaniacs; like dilettantes who have spent exactly none of their lives on the end of a gun or even a shovel; dinner party commandos, slouching inquisitors, collegiate spitball artists; people who have never been in a fistfight much less combat; a whining, self-righteous, upper-middle-class mob jostling for whatever tiny flakes of fame may settle on their shoulders like some sort of Pulitzer Prize dandruff.

They ask the same questions over and over. In their frustration, they ask questions that no one could answer; that anyone could answer; that no one should answer if they could answer. They complain about getting no answers, they complain about the answers they get. They are angry that the military won't let them go anywhere, the way they could in Vietnam. They talk about war as if it were a matter of feelings to be hashed out with a psychotherapist, or a matter of ethics to be discussed in a philosophy seminar. A lot of them seem to care more about Iraqi deaths than American deaths, and after the big oil spill in the gulf, they seemed to care more about animals than people—a greasy cormorant staggered around on CNN until it seemed like a network logo, along the lines of the NBC peacock. They don't always seem to understand that the war is real.

They don't seem to understand the military either. Meanwhile, the military seems to have their number, perfectly. Media and military cultures are clashing, the media are getting hurt and it's all happening on television, live from Riyadh and the Pentagon.

It is a silly spectacle.

It is so silly that 80 percent of Americans say they approve of all the military restrictions on the reporting of the war, and 60 percent think there should be more. When a Washington Post-ABC News poll asked if we should bomb a Baghdad command and control center in a hotel where American reporters are staying, 62 percent said we should give a warning and then bomb even if the reporters are still there, and 5 percent said we should bomb with no warning.

Yesterday the Los Angeles Times quoted John Balzar, one of its correspondents in Saudi Arabia: "I was a sergeant in Vietnam and now I am a journalist here. In both wars, I feel like I'm in the wrong place at the wrong time, and I am going to go home and have people throw rocks at me."

It is so silly that "Saturday Night Live" recently went after the media with the same wise-guy irony it might have used on the military back in the '70s.

An actor playing a briefing officer says: "I am happy to take any questions you might have with the understanding that there are certain sensitive areas that I'm just not going to get into, particularly information that may be useful to the enemy."

A reporter asks: "I understand there are passwords our troops on the front lines use. Could you give us some examples of those?"

And so on, the point being that the reporters are either fools or traitors.

The point could just as well have been media self-righteousness, or their obsession with connections and ironies.

After a Marine reconnaissance team was trapped near Khafji, a reporter asked Air Force Gen. Pat Stevens IV: "You said recently our communications were 'superb,' but the Marine recon team was taken by surprise. How then can you call our communications 'superb'?"

In a briefing after U.S. planes bombed a building where civilians were hiding, one reporter adopted the Mike Wallace autograph-model tone of astonished innocence: "Are you saying then that you're not watching these buildings that you're going to target 24 hours a day?"

One reporter asked if we had put a limit on the number of Iraqi casualties we will inflict. Then there was the young woman with the National Public Radio accent, that elegant confection of crispness and offhandedness that you hear on "All Things Considered." After the big oil spill, she wanted to know if Gen. Norman Schwarzkopf had been aware before the war began of the damage such a spill could do, and if so, had such a possibility entered his moral reasoning when he was deciding whether to start the war.

Why is this happening? Why do the reporters at the briefings seem to be on one side and the briefers on the other? And why do so many people cringe and hoot at the reporters, and admire the briefers? Oil and water, dogs and cats, Hatfields and McCoys.

In "Battle Lines: Report of the Twentieth Century Fund Task Force on the Military and the Media," Peter Braestrup, a former Marine and journalist, cites studies indicating that military values "are closer to those of middle America than to those of the more permissive members of the media . . . Not surprisingly, given the media's focus on conflict, deviance, and melodrama, most senior military men do not see the media as allies of civic peace and virtue. . . . There is no counterpart in journalism to 'duty, honor, country,' or to the military leader's ultimate responsibility for life and death and the nation's security." The military demands team play. Journalists fight not only with the people they cover but with each other.

The military is hierarchical. Reporters have no rank.

The military values loyalty and confidence in superiors. The press values objectivity and skepticism.

At a Senate hearing yesterday, former CBS anchor and war correspondent Walter Cronkite said the military "has the responsibility of giving all the information it possibly can to the press and the press has every right, to the point of insolence, to demand this."

Sen. John Heinz (R-Pa.) went to the point of insolence himself when he cited a long list of media woesayings about the military before the war started, and a long list of successes since, concluding: "Any advice for your colleagues?"

"No," Cronkite said.

The military is average guys who take pride in their anonymity. The big-time press is high-achievers struggling for the brief candle that passes for stardom in the media. (What's the last time you thought about Dorothy Kilgallen? Westbrook Pegler? Chet Huntley?)

When the military makes a mistake in combat, its own people die. When the press makes a mistake, it runs a correction.

For 20 years, they've been getting further apart, each heading in its own direction, proud of becoming an island of virtue, unto itself.

But why do the reporters look so bad? What's hard for viewers to understand is that they are merely doing the poking, nagging, whining, demanding, posturing and hustling that are the standard tricks of the reporting trade—people don't have to tell them anything, after all, so they have to worm it out of them. And there are many reporters there who have never covered the military before. It's an ugly business, and in the Persian Gulf they do it on television, and they do it with the tone of antagonism, paranoia and moral superiority that arose two decades ago in response to the lies and failures of Vietnam and Watergate.

There is a lot of history here.

Back in the '70s, reporters were heroes of sorts—one bumper sticker even said "And Thank God for The Washington Post."

Government officials and military officers were the villains.

In the years since, the press has changed very little, and the military has changed a lot.

Besides polishing its public relations techniques with courses at Fort Benjamin Harrison, the military seems to have studied the master, Ronald Reagan, and the way he buffaloed the press with his nice-guy rope-a-doping—rope-a-dope, you recall, being how Muhammad Ali let George Foreman punch himself into exhaustion.

In the Persian Gulf briefings, the military briefers adopt the Reagan/Ali style, taking punch after punch, looking humble, cocking their heads, being polite and playing the tarbaby. They don't let the reporters get to them. They confess errors—deaths by friendly fire, bombs that missed. Like the Viet Cong, they only fight when they know they'll win. They come on like the silent majority in desert fatigues, while the reporters come on like Ivy League Puritans, pointing bony fingers and working themselves into rages.

Why, the reporters demand, can't they drive north and interview whatever troops they want? Why can't they talk to fighter pilots? Why are they restricted to pools? Why are so few journalists going to be allowed to cover the ground war?

This is not Vietnam, where combat was only a helicopter ride away—although it's interesting to note that one study says in Vietnam no more than about 40 reporters were ever out where the bullets were flying, except during the Tet offensive of 1968 when the number might have gone to 70 or 80. Access to the siege of the Marines at Khe Sanh was limited to 10 or 12 reporters.

In Saudi Arabia, the military is keeping journalists on a short leash, but no shorter, probably, than it would keep them on in peacetime if they were doing stories at Fort Hood or Camp Pendleton. Corporations, professional football teams, police stations and political conventions keep a close eye on journalists too. And no journalist would expect to get very far with businessmen and politicians by being as quarrelsome and ignorant as some of the journalists covering this war.

The parallel between other institutions and the military doesn't go very far, though. The military is a separate culture that is difficult to explain to anyone who hasn't been in it. As Bernard Trainor, a retired Marine lieutenant general, writes: "Whereas businessmen and politicians try to enlist journalists for their own purposes, the military man tries to avoid them, and when he cannot, he faces the prospect defensively with a mixture of fear, dread and contempt."

Trainor covered military affairs for the New York Times after he retired. He has seen the military-media war from both sides. Last December in Parameters, an Army War College magazine, he wrote: "Today's officer corps carries as part of its cultural baggage a loathing for the press. . . . Like racism, anti-Semitism, and all forms of bigotry, it is irrational but nonetheless real. The credo of the military seems to have become 'duty, honor, country, and hate the media.' "

With the end of the draft, Trainor says, the military "settled into the relative isolation of self-contained ghettos and lost touch with a changing America. It focused on warlike things and implicitly rejected the amorality of the outside world it was sworn to defend. In an age of selfishness, the professional soldier took pride in his image of his own selflessness. A sense of moral elitism emerged within the armed forces."

Hate! Scores to settle! As Secretary of Defense Dick Cheney recently told the U.S. Chamber of Commerce, "You might never know from all the stories we saw in recent years about $600 toilet seats that our defense industry was capable of producing effective systems and weapons to support our men and women in uniform." He went on about "doom and gloom reporting" and cited a 10-year-old story in the Boston Globe attacking the Tomahawk missile, even giving the exact date— Nov. 22, 1981.

The media have pulled away from mainstream America too.

Once, reporters were part of whatever team they covered, in a vague and unreliable way. They cut deals, they protected their favorites. But after Vietnam and Watergate, they declared a sort of ethical independence, and came to think of themselves as inhabiting a neutral territory of objectivity and value-free analysis. (It should be pointed out that objectivity is not an attitude that goes down well when there's an enemy shooting at American troops—hence the antagonism directed at Peter Arnett, the CNN reporter covering the war from Baghdad.)

Anyway, things changed in the '70s. Suddenly, the media had prestige. Instead of drawing their staffs from high-school graduates, failed novelists and the occasional aristocrat looking to get his hands smudged, big-time media were getting résumés from people who had grown up in the class segregation of upscale suburbs, day-school products who had never been in places where you don't let your mouth write checks that your butt can't cash, had never even been yelled at with the professional finesse of a drill sergeant, a construction boss or a shop teacher. The most important experience in their life had been college. During the summers, they had internships, not jobs. A lot more of them were women. After the draft ended, virtually none of them even knew anyone who had been in the military, much less served themselves. They were part of what sociologists called the new class, the governing class, the professional class. They were a long way from most Americans.

The military came closer.

An Army infantry battalion commander in Saudi Arabia recently told his troops what kind of people they all are. "Like I told you before, this is not the Izod, Polo-shirt, Weejuns loafers crowd. Not a whole lot of kids here whose dads are anesthesiologists or justices of the Supreme Court. We're the poor, white, middle class and the poor, black kids from the block and the Hispanics from the barrio. We're just as good as the . . . rest, because the honest thing is, that's who I want to go to war with, people like you."

Not people like the media.

But the military can't go to war without the media, either.

And oh, how the military wants to be honored, to have its deeds recorded for history. And how good journalists are at doing it, if their audiences and editors want to hear it. Both sides, in fact, like to sit around telling stories about their adventures, giving it all a mythological glow. Both feel they are underpaid and undervalued. Both feel they are sacrificing for a greater good. And in wars, journalists for once share a little of the risk with the people they are covering—in most peacetime stories, a story about an election or a stock speculator, say, this would be called a conflict of interest. Secretly, you suspect, the military admires the media's soldier-of-fortune independence, and the media admire the orderliness and blood-and-dirt courage of the military.

They're so close, you say. There's no reason they can't work together. And then you turn on the TV and watch the press briefings.

"General," a reporter drawls, "I wonder if you could dwell for a moment on the apparent contradiction between . . ."

Safeguarding Our Freedoms as We Cover Terrorist Acts

KATHARINE GRAHAM

Picture a warm and sunny day, not in Athens or Cairo, but in Washington. The Israeli prime minister is in town and is scheduled to meet the President.

At 11 a.m., the leader of an obscure Muslim sect and several accomplices armed with guns and machetes storm the headquarters of B'nai B'rith. Three other members of the group seize the city's Islamic Center and two more fanatics invade City Hall, killing a radio reporter in the process. Altogether, the terrorists take 134 hostages in three buildings by gunpoint, force them to the floor and threaten to kill them unless their demands are met.

The news media, as one might expect, descend on the scene en masse. Live television pictures carrying the group's warnings and demands soon go forth over the airwaves. One hundred and thirty-four lives hang in the balance, as reporters compete to get exclusive interviews with the terrorists.

This crisis actually happened, on March 9, 1977, when the Hanafi Muslims staged a terrorist attack on the very day Prime Minister Yitzhak Rabin was meeting with President Jimmy Carter. Happily, it ended with the surrender of the terrorists and no further loss of life.

The Hanafi incident illustrated a troubling fact about modern terrorism: It requires an audience. The terrorist has to communicate his own ruthlessness—his "stop-at-nothing" mentality—in order to achieve his goals. Media coverage is essential to his purpose. If terrorism is a form of warfare, as many observers now believe, it is a form in which media exposure is a powerful weapon.

As terrorism increases, we in the news media are being encouraged to restrict our coverage of terrorist actions. British Prime Minister Margaret Thatcher, for example, has proclaimed, "We must try to find ways to starve the terrorist and the hijacker of the oxygen of publicity on which they depend." Many people, including some reporters in the United States, share her view. Most of these observers call for voluntary restraint by the media in covering terrorist actions. But some go so far as to sanction government control—censorship, in fact—should the media fail to respond.

I disagree. I am against any government-imposed restrictions on the free flow of information about terrorist acts. Instead, I am in favor of as full and complete coverage of terrorism by the media as is possible. Here are my reasons:

- Terrorist acts are impossible to ignore. They are simply too big a story to pass unobserved. If the media did not report them, rumor would abound. And rumors can do much to enflame and worsen a crisis.
- There is no compelling evidence that terrorist attacks would cease if the media stopped covering them. On the contrary, terrorism specialists I have consulted believe the terrorists would only increase the number, scope and intensity of their attacks if we tried to ignore them.
- Our citizens have a right to know what the government is doing to resolve crises and curb terrorist attacks. Some of the proposed solutions raise disturbing questions about how and when the United States should use military force.

In covering terrorism, however, we must also recognize that we face very real and exceedingly complex challenges. There are limits to what the media can and should do. Three critical issues, in particular, must be addressed. All touch the central question of how the press can minimize its role as a participant in the crisis and maximize its role as a provider of information.

Responsible Behavior

The first issue involves knowing how to gather and reveal information without making things worse, without endangering the lives of hostages or jeopardizing national security. One television news executive bluntly explained to me: "Errors that threaten loss of life are permanent; others are temporary. If we have to make mistakes, we want to make the temporary kind."

In the early days of covering urban violence and the first terrorist attacks, the media would descend on the scene—lights ablaze and cameras rolling—in hot pursuit of the news. Sometimes we didn't know what could put lives at risk. And we were often less than cooperative with the police attempting to resolve the crisis.

During the Hanafi Muslim attack that I described earlier there were live television reports that the police were storming a building when, in fact, they were merely bringing in food. Some reporters called in on public phone lines to interview the terrorists inside the building. One interview rekindled the rage of the terrorist leader, who had been on the point of surrender.

These potential disasters led to discussions between the police and the media, and to a more professional approach and mutual trust on both sides. For example, most authorities now know that at the beginning of a crisis, it is best to establish a central point where reliable information can be disseminated quickly and efficiently. And the media, knowing that the authorities intend to help them obtain the information they need, are much more willing to cooperate.

I want to emphasize that the media are willing to—and do—withhold information that is likely to endanger human life or jeopardize national security. During the American embassy crisis in Iran, for example, one of our Newsweek reporters became aware that six Americans known to have been in the embassy were not being held by the Iranians. He concluded that these men must have escaped to the Swedish or Canadian embassies. This in fact had occurred. However, we (and some others who also knew) did not report the information because we knew it would put lives in jeopardy. Similarly, when a group of Lebanese Shiites hijacked TWA Flight 847 with 153 hostages aboard last year, the media learned—but did not report—that one hostage was a member of the U.S. National Security Agency.

Tragically, however, we in the media have made mistakes. You may recall that in April 1983, some 60 people were killed in a bomb attack on the U.S. embassy in Beirut. At the time, there was coded radio traffic between Syria, where the operation was being run, and Iran, which was supporting it. Alas, one television network and a newspaper columnist reported that the U.S. government had intercepted the traffic. Shortly thereafter the traffic ceased. This undermined efforts to capture the terrorist leaders and eliminated a source of information about future attacks. Five months later, apparently the same terrorists struck again at the Marine barracks in Beirut; 241 servicemen were killed.

This kind of result, albeit unintentional, points up the necessity for full cooperation wherever possible between the media and the authorities. When the media obtains especially sensitive information, we are willing to tell the authorities what we have learned and what we plan to report. And while reserving the right to make the final decision ourselves, we are anxious to listen to arguments about why information should not be aired.

The Danger of Manipulation

A second challenge facing the media is how to prevent terrorists from using the media as a platform for their views.

I think we have to admit that terrorist groups receive more attention and make their positions better known because of their acts. Few people had even heard of groups like the Hanafi Muslims or Basque Separatists before they carried out terrorist attacks.

The media must make every attempt, however, to minimize the propaganda value of terrorist incidents and put the action of terrorists into perspective. We have an obligation to inform our readers and viewers of their backgrounds, their demands and what they hope to accomplish. But we must not forget that terrorists are criminals. We must make sure we do not glorify them, or give unwarranted exposure to their point of view.

We often think of terrorists as unsophisticated. But many are media savvy. They can and do arrange their activities to maximize media exposure and ensure that the story is presented their way. As one terrorist is supposed to have said to his compatriot: "Don't shoot now. We're not in prime time."

Terrorists have taken the following steps to influence media coverage: arrange for press pools; grant exclusive interviews during which favored reporters are given carefully selected information; hold press conferences in which hostages and others are made available to the press under conditions imposed by the captors, provide videotapes that portray events as the terrorists wish them to be portrayed, and schedule the release of news and other events so that television deadlines can be met.

There is a real danger, in short, that terrorists hijack not only airplanes and hostages, but the media as well.

To guard against this, the television networks in our country rarely—almost never—allow terrorists to appear live. They also resist using videotape provided by terrorists. If there is no alternative, our commentators continually report that the material is "terrorist-supplied" so that viewers can evaluate its veracity and meaning. Likewise, when terrorists make hostages available for interviews, our commentators repeatedly indicate—or they should—that the captives are speaking under duress.

When one network reporter interviewed the hostages in the recent TWA hijacking by telephone, he said: "Walk away from the phone if you're under duress, or if you don't want to talk." One of them did walk away. Even when there is no evident coercion, the networks repeat that terrorists are standing by, although they are not visible on the screen. We also try to identify carefully and repeatedly the backgrounds and biases of the people we interview, including the hostages themselves.

Forbidding terrorists their platform goes beyond using specific techniques. It is more an issue of exercising sound editorial judgment.

Over the years, the media constantly have been confronted with attempts at manipulation. In the days of the Vietnam war, for example, we would get calls from protest groups saying, "We're going to pour chicken blood all over the entrance to Dow Chemical Company. Come cover this event." We didn't. But we did cover a Buddhist monk who wished to be filmed setting fire to himself.

How did we make the distinction? Here it was a question of trivial versus serious intent and result, of low versus high stakes. Clearly, the suicide was of cataclysmic importance to the monk.

The point is that we generally know when we are being manipulated, and we've learned better how and where to draw the line, though the decisions are often difficult.

A few years ago, for example, a Croatian terrorist group in a plane demanded that its statement be printed in several newspapers, including The Washington Post, before it would release 50 hostages. In the end, we printed the statement in agate, the smallest type size we have, in 37 copies of the paper at the end of our press run. Now I'm not so sure we would accede to this demand in any form.

The Heat of Coverage

That brings me to a third issue challenging the media: How can we avoid bringing undue pressure on the government to settle terrorist crises by whatever means, including acceding to the terrorist's demands?

State Department officials tell me that media coverage does indeed bring pressure on the government But not *undue* pressure. However, I believe there are pitfalls of which the media should be exceedingly careful.

One is the amount of coverage devoted to a terrorist incident. During a crisis, we all want to know what is happening. But constant coverage can blow a terrorist incident far out of proportion to its real importance. Overexposure can preoccupy the public and the government to the exclusion of other issues.

During the TWA crisis, our networks constantly interrupted regularly scheduled programming with news flashes of dubious importance. And one network devoted its entire 22-minute evening newscast to the crisis. Many important topics were ignored.

The media have become aware of these dangers. The network coverage of the Achille Lauro incident was much more restrained. Some say it was only because it was difficult to cover and the crisis ended quickly. But the networks got better notices from the critics and the public.

Interviewing the families of hostages is another pitfall. There is a natural curiosity about how those near and dear to the captured are reacting to the life-or-death event. And the hostage families themselves often are anxious to receive media attention and present their views to the public.

But there is a fine line between legitimate inquiry and exploitation of human sentiment. The media can go too far. Tasteless invasion of privacy can result. The ultimate horror is the camera that awaits in ambush to record the family's reaction to the news of some personal tragedy.

There is also a real danger that public opinion can be unjustifiably influenced by exposure to the hostage relatives and their wives. The nationwide television audience becomes, in a sense, an extended family. We get to know these people intimately. Our natural sympathies go out to them. We often come to share their understandable desire to have their loved ones back at any cost.

This can force a government's hand. Last May, Israel released more than 1,000 Arab prisoners in exchange for three Israelis being held in Lebanon. It was an action that ran counter to Israeli policy. But the appearances of the families of the Israeli prisoners on television apparently made the Israeli government think it was a necessity.

I believe the media must be exceedingly careful with the questions they ask the relatives and, of course, the hostages themselves. When we ask if they agree with the government's policy or its handling of the incident, what they would do if they were in charge, or if they have messages for the president, we are setting up a predictable tension: Hostages and their families are, understandably, the most biased of witnesses. The media must exercise the same standards with them as they would with any other news source.

A final pitfall for the media is becoming, even inadvertently, a negotiator during a crisis. But it's tough to avoid. Simply by asking legitimate questions—such as "What are your demands?"—the media can become part of the negotiating process. Questions that ask "What would you do if . . ." are particularly dangerous. The question put to Nabih Berri, the Amal Shiite leader, during the TWA crisis by the host of one of our morning news shows was completely out of line and is so acknowledged. He asked: "Do you have a message for the president?"

As much as we abhor terrorism, the media cannot be diplomats, negotiators or agents for the government. If terrorists or urban rioters believe we are—if they believe, for example, that we will turn over our unused tapes, or pictures, or notes to the police—they will not give us information. They may even attack us.

Technology intensifies our problems. Before the advent of satellites, there was usually a 24-hour delay between the moment news was gathered overseas and the moment it was broadcast. Indeed, what appeared on the nightly news often had been in the morning paper. This meant that television news executives had at least some amount of time in which to reflect, discuss and decide on whether a story should be broadcast and how it should be presented.

Today our networks have the technological capability to present events live—any time, any place. As a result, the decisions about what to cover and how to cover are tougher. And they must be made faster, sometimes on the spot. The risks of making a mistake rise accordingly.

Intense competition in the news business raises the stakes even more. The electronic media in the United States live or die by their ratings, the number of viewers they attract. As a result, each network wants to be the first with the most on any big story. It's hard to stay cool in the face of this pressure.

This has created some unseemly spectacles and poor news decisions. During the TWA crisis, for example, the U.S. networks ran promotion campaigns on the air and in print touting the scoops and exclusives that each had obtained. This commercialized and trivialized a dangerous and important event.

The most dangerous potential result of unbridled competition is what we have come to call the lowest-common-denominator factor. I believe that all of the serious, professional media—print and electronic—are anxious to be as responsible as possible. We want to do nothing that would endanger human life or national security. But, unfortunately, high standards of professionalism do not guide every media organization and reporter. And I regret to say that once one of these less scrupulous or less careful people reports some piece of information, all the media feel compelled to follow. Thus it is true: The least responsible person involved in the process could determine the level of coverage.

These problems of covering terrorism are serious. But in spite of them, I believe the benefits of full disclosure far outweigh any possible adverse consequences. I believe the harm of restricting coverage far surpasses the evils of broadcasting even erroneous or damaging information.

American democracy rests on the belief, which the centuries have proven true, that people can and do make intelligent decisions about great issues if they have the facts.

But to hear some politicians talk, you wouldn't think they believed it. They appear to be afraid that people will believe the terrorists message and agree, not only to his demands, but to his beliefs. And so they seek to muzzle the media or enlist their support in the government's cause.

I think this is a fatal mistake. It is a slippery slope when the media start to act on behalf of any interest, no matter how worthy—when editors decide what to print on the basis of what they believe is good for people to know. It's dangerous if we are asked to become a kind of super-political agency.

I believe that terrorism is ultimately a self-defeating platform from which to present a case. Terrorists, in effect, hang themselves whenever they act. They convey hatred, violence, terror itself. There was no clearer image of what a terrorist really is than the unforgettable picture of that crazed man holding a gun to the head of the pilot aboard the TWA jet. That said it all to me—and, I believe, to the world.

Publicity may be the oxygen of terrorists. But I say this: News is the lifeblood of liberty. If the terrorists succeed in depriving us of freedom, their victory will be far greater than they ever hoped and far worse than we ever feared. Let it never come to pass.

The Image Makers—
Public Relations Today   11

A Lesson in Lobbying

CHARLES BABINGTON

To Del. John A. Hurson and several physicians and parents, it's a matter of hanging a small sign in restaurant windows. To Maryland's liquor interests, it's a threat to their reputation as one of Annapolis's most influential and unified lobbies.

When the two sides clashed in a legislative hearing room on Thursday, it was an illustration of the forces that ordinary citizens confront when they challenge a sophisticated interest group that spends thousands of dollars a year to stay on good terms with lawmakers.

"They are fighting it as a combined team," said Hurson (D-Montgomery) as he surveyed the half-dozen lobbyists waiting to testify against his measure. "It's a full-court press."

His proposal, similar to laws already enacted by the District and by New York, California and several other states, would require restaurants and bars to post a 9-by-11-inch sign warning that drinking alcohol during pregnancy "can cause birth defects," a condition known as fetal alcohol syndrome.

Lobbyists for Maryland's distillers, wine sellers, beer distributors and restaurateurs don't dispute that fetal alcohol syndrome can result in mental retardation or other problems. But they say that posting signs in restaurants won't help, and they are closing ranks against the measure.

They are a formidable group, not only because they hold classy dinners and receptions for lawmakers, but also because they have reputations for providing timely information to legislators facing hundreds of bills. The alcohol-related groups spent more than $100,000 lobbying the General Assembly last year, and this year's efforts appear equally intense.

Their paid representatives are a virtual Who's Who of Annapolis's top lobbyists:

- Joseph A. Schwartz III for the Maryland Licensed Beverage Association, which paid him $23,502 last year and spent $1,714 for legislators' meals and a reception.
- George N. Manis for beer wholesalers, who paid him $18,500 and spent $2,507 for meals and a reception.
- Robin F. Shaivitz for the Distilled Spirits Council, which paid her $13,462 and spent $1,596 for a reception.
- Franklin Goldstein for the state restaurant association, which paid him $19,500 and spent $6,553 for meals and a reception.
- Bruce C. Bereano for the Wine Institute, which paid him $7,500 and spent $618 for meals and drinks.

All five lobbyists, plus some assistants, worked against Hurson's bill at Thursday's hearing. They made no apologies for ganging up against a measure that Gov. William Donald Schaefer's administration calls a cost-effective means of educating pregnant women about the dangers of alcohol.

"You try to stop it in the beginning and not later on," said Bereano, who has dozens of other clients and is one of Maryland's most visible lobbyists. A proposal such as Hurson's, he said, could be "the camel's nose under the tent," tempting legislators to impose other regulations on alcoholic beverages.

Hurson caught the lobbyists off guard by introducing his measure with enough cosponsors to gain an endorsement from the House Economic Matters Committee. The committee had killed similar proposals in past years, and the industry lobbyists now are trying to pry away some of Hurson's cosponsors to keep their record intact.

"They were wining and dining two of them last night," Hurson said Thursday in an interview. When the hearing began, he pointed to the lobbyists in the room and told his fellow committee members, "The liquor lobby all comes together, you see. It's a team."

The lobbyists see the Economic Matters Committee as the best opening for applying pressure in the legislative process. They exerted much less effort to battle the measure in the Senate, where it was approved under the sponsorship of Sen. Beatrice P. Tignor (D-Prince George's).

The liquor lobbyists say schools and doctors' offices, not bars, are the appropriate places to educate women about fetal alcohol syndrome. "I think it's a feel-good type of bill that sounds great but doesn't do anything," Goldstein said.

Shaivitz said the proposal smacks of paternalism and asked why bars shouldn't be made to warn men about alcohol's influence on domestic violence and lowered sperm counts.

Opposing the lobbyists were several doctors and parents who, unlike the liquor industry lobbyists, are unknown to most legislators.

Jim Haas, a Harford County teacher, said his adopted son suffers from fetal alcohol syndrome and "will require support for the rest of his life. . . . If one poster [in a bar] saves one kid from going through this process, it will be worth putting the poster up."

Howard Birenbaum, a pediatrician and activist in the American Academy of Pediatrics, testified that fetal alcohol syndrome "is the only birth defect which is wholly preventable." He said greater education efforts, including signs in bars, are needed because many women believe that consuming three drinks a day is safe during pregnancy. In fact, Birenbaum said, studies have found that consuming one or two drinks a day "was associated with a substantially increased risk of producing a growth-retarded infant."

At the same hearing, Schwartz and Manis testified against legislation that would require buyers of beer kegs to register their names and addresses so police could track them down if they allowed minors to drink the beer. Officials from Montgomery County and elsewhere say the measure would help prevent teenage keg parties.

Virginia and the District have enacted such laws, and they sent officials to Thursday's hearing to urge Maryland to follow suit. Carl Hayden, a liquor control officer for Virginia, said beer distributors have not complained even though keg sales have dropped since the law took effect Jan. 1, 1993.

In marked contrast to their Maryland counterparts, Virginia's beverage lobbyists did not put up a struggle when the General Assembly approved keg registration.

Disney Packs Its Bags

KIRSTIN DOWNEY GRIMSLEY

S ome public officials around the country would like to cast Mickey Mouse as "The Heartbreak Kid."

Walt Disney Co.'s decision to abandon its Haymarket theme park marks the fourth time in six years that Disney has walked away from such projects.

In each case the company entered communities with great fanfare, spent millions of dollars developing extravagant plans for the sites and then abruptly pulled the plug on the process, leaving local residents stunned and dismayed.

In 1988, Disney dropped its ambitious plans for an entertainment and retail project, the Disney-MGM Studio Backlot, after 17 months of negotiations with the city of Burbank, Calif., where it would have been located.

In 1991, Disney scuttled its plans for a waterfront-oriented theme park called Port Disney in Long Beach, Calif., deciding instead to pursue an expanded Disneyland resort in Anaheim, modeled after Epcot Center at Walt Disney World in Orlando, Fla.

And this summer, the company placed the Anaheim project, dubbed Westcot, on hold as well.

For Disney, the stakes are high in building a theme park. The expense is significant—the proposed project in Anaheim was expected to cost about $3 billion—and the business can be risky, as Disney has learned to its chagrin. Euro Disney Resort outside Paris, completed in 1992 and the company's only new venture of its type in the past decade, has been a money loser despite its popularity with European visitors. The company has been weighed down by the heavy debt it incurred in building the project.

But to the communities that have worked closely on Disney projects that were scuttled, the blow has been devastating.

"They promised us the world and then they pulled the rug," said former Burbank mayor Michael Hastings, who had lobbied hard on Disney's behalf for the entertainment and retail complex. "It was a very cold shower for the community and the community government."

Long-time Long Beach civic activists and observers said they too were disheartened by Disney's decision to drop its project there.

"It seems like since the Disney project went bye-bye, Long Beach just hasn't been the same," said George Economides, publisher of the Long Beach Business Journal. "The city entered a long decline. It was like if Long Beach couldn't make it with Disney, it couldn't make it at all."

The company's defection even had political ramifications in Long Beach, with then-mayor Ernie Kell soundly trounced in his next reelection bid, partially because some Long Beach residents blamed him for not doing enough to hold onto the entertainment conglomerate. Some critics noted that while Kell urged a cautious approach to the massive project and a tough negotiating stance, the mayor of nearby Anaheim was effusively supportive of Disney's plans for his city.

"It was like there was a little tug of war between [Disney Chairman] Michael Eisner and Mayor Kell," said Russ Cugno, owner of the Land of Fruits and Nuts, a waterside retail operation near the site of what once was Disney's proposed park at Long Beach. "Instead, the mayor of Anaheim is out there hugging Mickey Mouse and saying, 'I'll give you the world.' "

Although Kell was held to blame, some people involved in the Disney negotiations at Long Beach said the company made some fatal missteps. Because the proposed project was on the waterfront, it faced many regulatory and environmental hurdles, but Disney's tactics were perceived as bullying and insensitive by many observers. The company also sought costly public subsidies, which raised some ire.

"Some people say they're arrogant, and it caused problems generally," former Long Beach councilman Evan Anderson Braude said. "They think they have such a great reputation that they think what they want will get done."

Economides said Disney appeared ill-prepared for the realities—and real difficulties—of developing projects in today's combative real estate arena. "Maybe Disney got spoiled by its success in Orlando," he said. "It was a different era then . . . a different ballgame."

Disney cited varying reasons why it chose not to pursue the projects on which it had spent millions of dollars. The company said that after lengthy examination it concluded the Burbank project was not economically feasible. Disney officials said they preferred to pursue the Anaheim project instead of the Long Beach one.

Anaheim's situation is less clear, although the project definitely has been placed on hold. The project's chief promoter inside Disney, Kerry Hunnewell, has resigned and project staff members have been reassigned to other duties.

At Haymarket, Disney said the dispute over the risk to historic sites threatened its public image and could become a financial drain.

"We're still going through a series of negotiations with Anaheim," Disney spokesman John Dreyer said. "We'll make a decision sometime down the road."

Part of the shock for some community leaders has been Disney's rapid and abrupt changes of heart even as company executives voiced strong support for the projects.

That rapid flip-flop left Burbank's Hastings feeling "very bitter," he said.

"During the negotiation period it was a very euphoric period—all the pictures, drawings and the Disneyesque feelings. It felt like it all fit. Then at the 11th-and-a-half hour, it didn't fit."

Hastings, who had stuck out his neck to work for the project's approval despite strong local slow-growth sentiment, first learned that Disney had dumped the project when a Price Club executive called to inquire about developing the site. Burbank officials didn't get final official word from Disney for almost a week.

Similarly, Disney officials adamantly promoted their commitment to the Haymarket project even as an internal debate was underway to shut it down.

There was mounting industry speculation late last month that the company would drop the project in the face of public criticism and upper management turmoil at Disney. The company had lost two of its top executives and Eisner had quadruple bypass heart surgery. One former Disney employee who had been involved in the project's planning said he believed the odds were only 50-50 that it would proceed.

At the same time other Disney executives at the company's headquarters used cautious and tentative language when pressed to discuss the proposed theme park. "I'm certainly hoping it all happens as Disney wishes it would happen," said Dean Valentine, a Disney executive.

But Disney spokesman Dreyer bristled angrily at a reporter's question about whether Disney's America would be built at Haymarket. "It will go forward," he said, adding that he considered it journalistically unethical to raise the issue.

Peter Rummell, president of Disney Design and Development, which oversees Disney theme park development, said the same week that the company was "as committed as ever."

But Disney Chairman Eisner, the primary decision maker, refused through Dreyer repeated requests for comment on the question, although he was quoted by the entertainment industry press on other matters that week.

Patterns can be seen in the abandoned projects. In each case, Disney arrived with a flurry, unveiled extravagant plans for exciting activities and displays, and set out to woo each city's economic and political leaders. Then, at some point, even as elected officials offered increasingly valuable public subsidies, things started to sour. Disney might raise the stakes by seeking yet more money, and turn up the heat by emphasizing how many other communities were eager to pay even more to lure Disney to their areas.

For example, Burbank initially offered the 40-acre site for the proposed Disney-MGM Studio Backlot project to Disney for about $10 million, although some published reports at the time valued the site at up to $50 million. After Disney balked, Burbank offered the site for $1 million.

Disney also wanted Burbank to pay to build a 3,500-space parking structure for visitors' cars, at an estimated cost of $35 million. When Burbank officials demurred,

Eisner showed them a videotaped pitch from Dallas begging Disney to build a project there. Burbank officials got the point.

Hastings recalled the initial process as a passionate courtship by Disney, what he called a honeymoon, followed by a bruising return to harsh economic realities.

"We were 'the best and the greatest,' " Hastings said ruefully. "Then, now that we're married, God help you."

The theme park proposals have hurt Disney's image in other cities as well as Haymarket. In Anaheim, for example, which is well known for its enthusiastic support of Disney endeavors, a group of opponents has emerged to fight the company's expansion plans there.

Curtis Stricker, a pro-business Republican and retired sales executive, has lobbied hard against what he sees as overly generous public subsidies to Disney, which made almost $300 million in profit last year.

Stricker said he believes the total tally of public money being spent to help build the Westcot in Anaheim could add up to more than $1 billion.

"Disney controls the city and the city does its tap dance on the taxpayers' heads," said Stricker, who is running for mayor of Anaheim. "It's not the nice sweet company that everybody thinks it is."

Disney forays have left behind unintentional victims as well, as in the Washington area, where some people speculated in land or added employees in anticipation of Disney's arrival.

Cugno, the owner of the Land of Fruits and Nuts in Long Beach, owned a family-run seashell business located on part of the proposed Disney redevelopment site, near the Queen Mary ocean liner. But when Disney took over the site to redevelop it, one of the company's first actions was to cancel the leases of the retailers operating there, because Disney prefers to control all retail operations on its theme park grounds.

"They gave us 30 days' notice to vacate," Cugno said. "I was a newlywed on my honeymoon, and I came back to find I was out of business."

Cugno and a half-dozen other retailers were forced to find new places to work, but some of them, including Cugno, ultimately returned to set up shop after Disney left.

Nevertheless, Disney's allure burns bright for many communities, particularly those with financial woes that are seeking new sources of revenue and jobs. Within hours of Disney's announcement that it would drop the Haymarket project, officials in Maryland, West Virginia, North Carolina and elsewhere in Virginia were scrambling to catch Disney's eye.

And even communities buffeted by Disney in the past still hold out hope the company may one day return.

Disney, which is based in Burbank, has since sought and received permission to expand its corporate campus there, and the city also approved a seven-story headquarters building bedecked with 18-foot dwarfs that appear to be holding up the roof.

"People are in the mood of bashing Disney," Burbank's Hastings said. " . . . but Disney has a mystique about it, and it always will."

Long Beach's Braude is wistful about what might have been. "I've never given up hope they might decide to do something here," he said.

Comics Chaos on the Internet

WILLIAM F. POWERS

B efore cyberspace, you could fool all of the people some of the time. Now the ancient art of public manipulation may be on the verge of a revolution.

Item: Marvel Comics just held the comic book industry's "first on-line press conference," to introduce a new series called "Generation X." The comics, which will hit the newsstands in September, depart from the industry tradition of super-heroes, featuring instead "troubled teenage mutants" who care more about surviving bad times than fighting evil.

Marvel has placed the drawings from the first issue on the Internet and commercial computer networks for viewing and downloading.

So reporters were invited to sign on Thursday night to CompuServe, the national on-line service. In theory, journalists sitting in front of computer screens all over the country could discuss the product with its creators and with readers of Marvel's "X-Men" series, of which the new line would be a spinoff.

"Because the Generation X book is devoted to the issues and interests of the next generation—be they futuristic teenage mutants or today's suburban slackers—we decided to launch the comic book in their domain—Cyberspace," Marvel said in a press release.

But cyberspace is still full of surprises, as Marvel learned the hard way. The news conference descended immediately into chaos. In the corner of CompuServe's ether devoted to comic books, 80 people showed up—almost all fans. From their home terminals, they fired off questions at two of the creators of "Generation X"—writer Scott Lobdell and artist Chris Bachalo—and everyone who was signed on watched the queries pile up on the screen, mostly unanswered.

For 45 minutes, moderator Doug Pratt, who runs the CompuServe comic book forum from his home in Herndon, tried to bring order to the event.

He begged participants to type "??" to indicate they had a question, wait to be recognized before asking it, and when finished, type "GA" (for "go ahead").

Nice try, but cyber-nauts abhor discipline, and the crowd that gathered for this event quickly jumped to future developments in the lives of Marvel characters with names like Blink and Belladonna.

It went this way:

Doug P., Moderator: William Powers has the floor. please.

William F. Powers: Who do you think are the Gen X
Doug P., Moderator: One at a time, guys.
William F. Powers: readers, age-wise? GA
Patrick Kane (Kane): I'MM BACK
Doug P., Moderator: ga, Scott
Scott Lobdell: True—but there will be no "leader" in the classical superhero team sense . . .
Patrick Kane (Kane): ???
From there, it went downhill. Twenty-six totally cacophonous messages followed. They were characterized by such bons mots as:
Scott Lobdell: Chris NEVER waits to talk—that's why we LOVE HIM!
Then came the answer to the question. Sort of:
Scott Lobdell: On the question of the reader's age—I wouldn't have a clue. But let us hope they are at least as mature as Chris Bachalo.
Christopher Bachalo:i changed to uppercase/ could you give me a two-minute break—I'm having dinner right now—it's not nice to type with your mouth full—thanks.
Doug P., Moderator: Boys, boys.
At one point Pratt just surrendered, typing "GOOD LUCK AND GOODBYE." But such disorder is typical of on-line discussion, which often feels like a telephone party line with a hundred or more people speaking at once. Some habitues of the on-line services say they embrace the chaos.

Less usual was an exchange that happened a little later, when Marvel writer Lobdell referred in passing to "the cancellation of the X books."

"What??" one Marvel fan immediately typed.

"I think Doug just committed news," Pratt wrote.

A spirited discussion, interrupted by frequent unintelligible and unrelated questions, ensued over this shocking "revelation." The tension rose when a participant from Marvel (operating under the on-line name "Marvel") typed, "I cannot confirm or deny that."

When a reporter identified himself as representing The Washington Post, and asked if this was in fact a news conference for a series of comics about to be discontinued, Lobdell and Bachalo gave coy, unrevealing answers.

Finally, the reporter received a private message from "Marvel": "Hi, I'm Gary Guzzo from Marvel. Just to clear up a point. . . . We are launching a new X-Title and having some fun with our fans. There is a big development in January in our X-Men family of titles, and rumors of the team being discontinued are a tease at the story line. We want them to be surprised, so we're having some fun. Welcome to comic fandom."

Doug Pratt, who runs the comic book forum and other hobby-related forums as a business, yesterday called the event a "fantastic" success. He noted that about 800 people have viewed the new comic book in its first 36 hours on line. He said he had not known beforehand about Marvel's intention to increase word-of-mouth by planting the rumor. He also said that it probably had been a mistake to bill the event as a press conference.

"It was definitely an experiment," he said. "We are searching for what this medium does well."

One thing it does well is reward those who can manipulate the chaos of on-line communication. The press conference may have collapsed, but out among comic book fans, Marvel clearly has succeeded in generating a buzz about its new product.

Which raises the question of who else might seize upon a communications tool that reaches untold millions of homes and businesses around the world, with lines of words that can be artfully arranged to serve any purpose.

Remember that famous observation about how many of the people you can fool, and for how much of the time?

It came from Abraham Lincoln—a politician.

The Selling of Kuwait

GARY LEE

A long with scenes of wartime rubble and victory celebrations, the spotlight shining on postwar Kuwait has revealed less flattering pictures of the newly liberated country, including brutal treatment of suspected Iraqi sympathizers and efforts to suppress political dissent.

To combat these negative images, the Kuwaiti government has hired a public relations firm, the Washington-based Rendon Group, to manage press centers in Riyadh, Cairo and Kuwait City, to accredit journalists who want to write about Kuwait and to arrange interviews with Kuwaiti officials, according to Rendon spokesman Sandy Libby.

Last week, Kuwait's ambassador to the United States, Saud Nasir Sabah—who receives a daily briefing on things written and said about Kuwait in this country—shepherded a group of U.S. notables, including several members of Congress, on a tour of his ravaged capital.

The model for Kuwait's postwar management of public perceptions has been its own public relations campaign waged during the Iraqi occupation and war—one of the most expensive and pervasive such efforts ever launched by a foreign country in the United States. In its bid to sway the American public to its defense, the oil-rich regime spent more than $11 million, employing three American public relations firms, dozens of image makers, a team of lawyers and a squad of Washington lobbyists.

"Now every American knows where Kuwait is," said Frank Manciewicz, a spokesman for Hill and Knowlton, one of the public relations companies that marshaled Kuwait's campaign in the beginning but was removed from the account after a wave of negative news about Kuwait began to set in. "I guess that means that we did our job well."

The most crucial aspect of that effort, however, was not getting Kuwait on the map, but deflecting attention away from the controversial aspects of the country: the lack of a democratic system of government, treatment of women as second-class citizens, the flamboyant lifestyle of some members of the Kuwaiti elite and a predilection for leaving all nuts-and-bolts work to foreign guest workers.

According to the 1990 Amnesty International report, issued a month before the invasion, Kuwait arrested dissidents and tortured them without trial, and jailed members of the political opposition for defaming the emir. If the American public had focused on these things, said John Paluzek, head of Ketchum public relations, it might have been less enthusiastic in its support of Kuwait.

Kuwaiti officials softened criticism of their government monarchy with frequent references to a meeting held between exiled Kuwaiti officials and opposition leaders in October. There Kuwait made a loose pledge to restore the country's democratic constitution, which was adopted in 1961 but never fully enforced. Officials also announced plans to review proposals to give Kuwaiti women the right to vote.

Since the liberation of Kuwait, however, government officials have become much vaguer in their predictions of when democratic principles or universal suffrage will be introduced. Instead, they emphasize that they must first bring about security and stability.

To experts in the field, Kuwait's efforts were a case study in the way that foreign regimes with ample stocks of money and ingenuity can influence American public opinion.

Between the invasion and the end of the war, Kuwait paid an estimated $8 million to Hill and Knowlton, $770,000 to the Rendon Group, and $20,000 to Pintak-Brown International, another Washington-based public relations group. The lobby group of Neill and Co. received $150,000; the law firm of Cleary, Gottlieb, Steen & Hamilton, $1.7 million.

Kuwaiti officials, who had little experience in media relations before the war, also "got a lot better at dealing with the press," Mankiewicz said. At a recent congressional hearing, for instance, when Rep. Stephen J. Solarz (D–N.Y.) asked Hassan Ebraheem, president of Citizens for a Free Kuwait, a group of Kuwaiti exiles, about Kuwait's commitment to democratic principles, Ebraheem deftly shifted the subject to an article Solarz had just published on the Persian Gulf crisis. "Let me commend you on the excellent article," Ebraheem said. "I read it and I passed it to a lot of my colleagues."

In addition to distributing $1 million worth of copies of the "Rape of Kuwait," a quickie book highly critical of Iraq, Kuwait paid Pintak-Brown $20,000 to distribute a similar publication, "Kuwait on the March."

Shortly after reports surfaced in the press of Kuwaitis living it up in Cairo's discos at the height of the war, another wave of articles suddenly appeared about Kuwaitis sending 20,000 personalized Valentines to Americans at the Front. "A lot of newspapers carried that story," said Rendon Group spokesman Libby. "We were behind that"

Hill and Knowlton organized similar media blitzes, as well as newspaper ad campaigns and speaking tours for Kuwaiti officials. The firm spent more than $600,000 to produce pro-Kuwait videotapes that were distributed to American television networks. On Sept. 23, it helped organize a National Prayer Day, in which pastors around the United States were requested to ask their congregations to pray for Kuwait.

Hill and Knowlton also worked with Citizens for a Free Kuwait in proposing and coaching speakers who were to testify before Congress. Several congressional aides said Hill and Knowlton had proposed the names of some of the witnesses called for hearings about Kuwait. And Mankiewicz acknowledged that his firm briefed the witnesses before they appeared.

Not all of Hill and Knowlton's efforts were successful, however. Among those rejected was a request from the firm that a minute of silence be held for Kuwait during the Super Bowl in January.

The Business of Human Rights

LENA H. SUN

Until the first of the year, John Kamm was a senior executive for a large American company. He enjoyed all the perks that came with working as an expatriate in this bustling, cosmopolitan harbor city: a sleek gray Mercedes-Benz (and driver), membership in exclusive clubs, a housing allowance and subsidized tuition for his two young sons.

That has all changed. Now he drives his wife's Honda and pays with cash instead of credit cards. Gone are the memberships in the Aberdeen Marina Club, the Clearwater Bay Golf Club and the Pacific Club.

It wasn't the recession or a bad business environment that changed Kamm's lifestyle. It was his conscience. On Jan. 1, the 40-year-old native of Neptune, N.J., resigned as vice president of Occidental Petroleum Corp., a major U.S. oil and chemical company, to pursue full time what had become an all-consuming sideline: lobbying China on human rights.

Kamm believes American business in general should take a more activist approach to human rights. Just as U.S. business is realizing that being pro-environment is good for the bottom line, so too will executives see that the same is true for human rights.

"Human rights is good for business," he said recently. "There is a moral course. You can effect change and be popular with the American people who are your shareholders."

For nearly two years, Kamm has used his longtime China business ties to call attention to the cases of Chinese jailed for their political or religious beliefs. In between trips to sell industrial caustic soda and polyvinyl chloride, he made telephone calls and sent faxes to Beijing and other Chinese cities about Chinese students and Catholic bishops.

Last spring, he became involved in a case that he says changed his life. He helped win the freedom of two young men, the Li brothers, who had fled to Hong Kong after the Tiananmen Square crackdown in 1989. After they were assured of clemency by Chinese officials, they returned to their native Hunan Province, in southern China, where they were immediately arrested and tortured with electric cattle prods, he said.

"These guys were nobodies. They were in the bowels of the system, and out of the darkness, a cry of help was heard," Kamm said. At the request of a friend from a human rights organization, Kamm agreed to help. His efforts, along with those of human rights groups and former president Jimmy Carter, finally led to the release of the Li brothers last August.

"I felt responsible in some way for saving a couple guys," Kamm said. "The parents wrote me this letter, how I saved their boys' lives. . . . It was written in this beautiful calligraphy, and I sat there with my wife and read it. I didn't cry, but I was pretty choked up. It was very powerful."

After that, Kamm realized he would not be able to balance his more rewarding human rights work with the demands of a multinational corporation. So he gave up the corporate business. (He is still a consultant to several U.S. and Hong Kong companies and has recently started a newsletter about China-related legislation in Congress.)

Using what he calls a nonconfrontational but persistent approach, Kamm figures he has helped win the freedom of 68 individuals since June 1990. His method is low-key. He goes to Beijing in a private capacity. He speaks to officials as "a friend of China."

The Chinese appear to take him seriously. He meets frequently with a wide range of ministerial level officials from the judicial, prosecutory and police organs. In one trip last year, a senior Chinese leader told him bluntly that Beijing does not like to be humiliated and told what to do. But "if friends come and treat us with respect, we will consider releasing people," Kamm recalled the leader as saying.

Kamm does brief U.S. government officials about his discussions, but he does not consult them. Nor does he belong to any other human rights group.

His greatest credibility, he says, comes from being one of the most outspoken advocates for renewing China's most-favored-nation trading status with the United States. As a former president of Hong Kong's powerful American Chamber of Commerce, Kamm has testified before Congress numerous times on the importance of keeping trade and commercial ties with China.

Kamm, son of a whiskey salesman, is an unpretentious man whose rumpled appearance stands in sharp contrast to the elegantly outfitted expatriates living in Hong Kong, and he clearly relishes his new job. He plans to write a book and to someday teach a human rights course at a business school back in the United States.

Kamm is no stranger to the region. After graduating from Princeton University with a degree in anthropology, he arrived in 1972 to be a school teacher in the Portuguese enclave of Macao, just across the Pearl River from Hong Kong. He went on to teach sociology at Chinese University in Hong Kong, and experienced first-hand some of the turmoil on the Chinese mainland of the disastrous Cultural Revolution of 1966–76. He hired a tutor to learn Cantonese.

Except for graduate work at Harvard University in East Asian studies and economics, he has stayed in Hong Kong. He started his own chemical company, doing business with China. The company was eventually bought out by Diamond Shamrock Corp., whose chemical business was in turn acquired by Occidental in 1986.

Many of Kamm's business colleagues praise his efforts but say there are pitfalls in being identified too closely with human rights, especially in China.

"If business is seen as overtly pushing human rights issues, that might undermine the ability to do business here [in China], because everything here is politics," said one Western business observer in Beijing.

Gareth Chang, president of McDonnell Douglas Corp.'s Asia Pacific division and chairman of Hong Kong's American Chamber of Commerce, says the chamber will focus on the human rights issue as part of an overall discussion this year of U.S.-China relations.

"Clearly human rights has an important role in John's own view, but the world doesn't begin or end on human rights," Chang said of Kamm.

Kamm says neither he nor any of his salesman at Occidental ever experienced any repercussions because of his human rights lobbying. In fact, many Chinese have told him that they support Americans who take a strong stand.

"You have to remember that China has changed," he said. "Decisions have been decentralized. Now there are thousands of potential customers. For every customer who might possibly be offended, I can tell you there are five or six who will actually give you business."

The moral underpinnings for his argument are grounded in the philosophy of Abraham Lincoln. He is particularly fond of one passage, which reads: "Free labor has the inspiration of hope; pure slavery has no hope. The power of hope upon human exertion, and happiness, is wonderful."

For Kamm, the business applications are only too clear.

"The more freedom, the more productivity, the more profit," he explained. "It's good for business."

The Image Makers

PETER CARLSON

Part 1: Clint Eastwood as Federal Bureaucrat

Robert Weed is rolling.

He has shifted into oratorical high gear and now he's roaring toward the stirring emotional conclusion of his speech. He stands behind the podium in the unofficial uniform of the Serious Washington Insider—a blue pin-stripe suit and red power tie—while his shoulders bob to the rhythm of his words and his left fist pumps with passion. He has come to launch a crusade to liberate a despised minority group from the yoke of ancient prejudice. It is a minority group mocked by comedians, attacked by demagogic politicians, scorned by its fellow Americans. A hard-working, generous, 3-million-member minority group unfairly maligned as lazy and greedy.

Weed is talking about federal bureaucrats.

He doesn't call them that, though. He prefers the term "public servants." He says his crusade is designed to change "the public image of public servants." It is a crusade that Weed, who is the director of public affairs at the Office of Personnel Management, has been assigned by no less a public servant than the president of the United States. "This is a presidential initiative," Weed tells the crowd. "The first milestone assigned to OPM by the White House is to strengthen the image of public service."

And on this nasty December morning, Weed has braved a blizzard to travel to Rosslyn to tell the annual convention of the National Association of Government Communicators how he plans to give Americans warm, fuzzy feelings about federal employees.

First he unveils the brand new logo of his "Public Service Celebration Team." It's red, white and blue, of course, and it carries the official slogan of the campaign: "Serving America Today for a Better Tomorrow." Then he reveals his plans for an elaborate public relations campaign that will kick off on March 1 with receptions in six cities and then usher in a "year-round cycle of events," including "Public Service Recognition Week," which is the first week of May.

Meanwhile, Weed says, he hopes to persuade the Ad Council—the public service advertising group that gave us Smokey the Bear and McGraff the Crime Dog—to come up with an ad campaign that will "reinforce the image of public service." Weed hopes the ads will star Clint Eastwood. After all, Eastwood did an ad urging Americans not to litter on federal land, which practically makes him a federal bureaucrat himself.

Meanwhile, Weed outlines his "Federal Heroes" program, which is designed to publicize federal employees who have done amazing things, like the air traffic controller who helped save a crippled plane in Iowa and the Social Security Administration worker who delivers checks to the homeless in Boston. Weed plans to pick up the phone and pitch stories on his federal heroes to the producers of TV talk shows and the editors of magazines like People and Parade—"just like any PR guy for anybody would do."

But Bob Weed can't do all this himself. Persuading Americans to love federal employees is too tough a task for Weed and his staff of 18 and his budget, which is only a measly million bucks a year. That's why, he told the crowd, he'd come to this convention of Government Communicators, a group composed entirely of people doing public relations work for government agencies. He desperately needs their help, he says, and he beseeches them to fill out an official Public Service Celebration Team volunteer card. He promises to reward them if they do.

"Let me tell you what you'll get," he says, "First of all, you'll get our OPM newsletter, Image Update, that talks about this campaign. And secondly, you'll get another newsletter that doesn't yet have a name that will be good ideas from different parts of the image campaign. Third, you'll get advance information on specific image-building activities in your area. And finally, you'll get a bumper sticker with our handsome logo and slogan . . ." Wait a minute. Hold it right there. Bumper stickers? Image Update? People magazine? Clint Eastwood?

A public relations campaign to polish the image of federal bureaucrats?

Sure. Why not?

Washington is a city full of government bureaucrats. It's also a city full of professional image-polishers. It was inevitable that they'd find each other.

Part 2: How Big Is a Pound of Fog?

The National Solid Wastes Management Association has a PR team in Washington.

So does the Salt Institute. And the Sugar Association. And the Future Homemakers of America. And the Natural Resources Defense Council. And the House Education and Labor Committee. And the Federal Grain Inspection Service. And the Retired Officers Association. And the Selective Service System. And United Technologies. And the Air Force's Art and Museum Branch. And Saudi Arabia. And Angola. And Rhode Island. And the American Association of Motor Vehicle Administrators. And . . .

. . . And on and on it goes. In Washington, every government agency, trade association, trade union, congressman, foreign government, corporation, public service group, private interest group and ad hoc coalition to save the world—in short, everybody who is anybody in this town, or who wants to be—has a PR person or a PR department or a PR firm plotting out a PR campaign.

In fact, some Washington organizations were created by PR people and exist only as PR entities, as we shall see in this little tour through the world of Washington public relations, an ethereal realm where teddy bears lobby Congress, where dubious guerrillas become freedom fighters, where Army officers teach generals how to stand and how to sit.

"Public relations," says Ray Hiebert, professor of journalism at the University of Maryland and publisher of the Public Relations Review, "is the art and science of informing, influencing. neutralizing or changing public opinion." Edward Bernays, the oft-proclaimed "father of public relations," coined several other definitions. Some are sardonic: "to make large pedestals for small statues." And some are Orwellian: "the engineering of consent."

Any way you define it, public relations is a gargantuan industry in Washington. But nobody knows just how gargantuan. Part of the confusion stems from the fact that it's awful tough to specify exactly what constitutes public relations.

"It's a foggy business," says Jack O'Dwyer, the publisher of numerous PR industry trade publications. "How much does a pound of fog weigh?" he asks, sounding a bit like a Zen monk. "How big is a pound of fog?"

Another source of confusion is an absurd incongruity: The city's largest producer of public relations—the federal government—spends absolutely no money on public relations. Not one nickel. This is because the federal government is forbidden by law from spending money on public relations. Robert Weed's campaign, for instance, would be classified as "public information" or "public affairs" or public-affairs-related activities." How much money do federal agencies spend on those activities? then-Sen. William Proxmire asked the General Accounting Office back in 1986. The GAO had the same problem as O'Dwyer. "Federal agencies do not uniformly define 'public affairs,' " it complained. Still, it managed to cough up some estimates: $337 million for "Public affairs," $100 million for "congressional affairs"—defined as "day-to-day contact with the Congress"—and a whopping $1.9 billion for "public-affairs-related activities."

Which comes to more than $2.3 billion.

And that mammoth figure only includes federal agencies. It doesn't reflect the PR efforts of Congress, which are massive and eternal. Congressional offices are, as anyone who has ever worked in one can attest, giant machines for the greater glorification (and reelection) of the pol. The average congressional staff churns out a steady stream of constituent newsletters, computer-generated letters, daily press releases, weekly newspaper columns, one-minute radio spots called "beepers" and regular "video news releases" filmed in Congress's own TV studios and beamed by satellite to TV stations back in the home district. Which helps explain why the representatives' reelection rate approaches 99 percent.

And then there's the White House PR operation, which does everything the members of Congress do and a whole lot more.

"In the Washington area alone," says Eiebert, "there are at least 10,000 federal employees whose primary duty is what we'd call PR work."

The federal government's gigantic PR apparatus also serves an unofficial function: It's a farm team for Washington's gigantic private-sector PR industry.

PR prospects who prove their stuff in the federal government can generally find a warm place to park their Rolodexes when they head for the private sector. PR firms, like law firms, are the cushy nirvanas on the other side of Washington's legendary revolving door. So Jody Powell, who was Jimmy Carter's press secretary, goes to Ogilvy and Mather Public Affairs. And Elaine Crispen, who was Nancy Reagan's press secretary, goes to Hill and Knowlton. And Maj. Philip Soucy, who was among the Defense Department's 1,000 public affairs officers, becomes manager of military public affairs at British Aerospace. And Barbara Gleason, who was director of public affairs for the President's Commission on Industrial Competitiveness, becomes assistant director for public affairs at the Nonprescription Drug Manufacturers Association. And . . .

Watching the government's $2 billion PR industry intermarry with Washington's immeasurable (but huge) private-sector PR industry, a cynic might be tempted to conclude that virtually everything that happens in Official Washington is part of a PR campaign.

But that would be exaggerating. Slightly.

Part 3: What Do PR People Do, Daddy?

What does your daddy do? Rachel Swanston was asked one day when she was 5 or 6 years old. He's a public relations man, she replied. What does that mean? her friend asked.

He talks on the phone and gives parties, she answered. "And that's pretty accurate," says her father, David Swanston, president of Stackig/Swanston Public Relations.

Indeed it is. The little tyke came a lot closer to describing what PR people do than most PR people do.

If public relations is a "foggy business," as O'Dwyer put it, then it's at its foggiest in Washington, where PR people are generally pushing abstractions—ideas, opinions, images, influence. Which might account for the fogginess of the prose Washington's PR people churn out when trying to describe what they do. The sentences in their promotional brochures sound like this: "The Canzeri Group focuses its efforts on developing and implementing programs that integrate its clients into the national decision-making process." Or like this: "The KSK PR Department is tightly niched into business to business communications for companies with high technology emphasis."

As the jargon flies, the fog deepens: "designs and carries out strategic communications plans" . . . "creates and manages image enhancement campaigns" . . . "issues management" . . . "issues tracking," . . . "communication audits" . . . "strategic communications" . . . "crisis communications" . . . "audience research" . . . "consumer image building" . . . "comprehensive communications program design . . ."

Burn through this fog of words you find that what PR people do is this: They send out press releases and audio press releases and video press releases. They teach their clients how to appear on television without looking foolish and how to appear before congressional committees without looking foolish. They write speeches and brochures and congressional testimony. They ghostwrite editorials and op-ed pieces and then try to persuade newspaper editors to run them. They lobby Congress and they run grass-roots campaigns to persuade constituents to bombard Congress with letters. They stage press conferences and other media events. And they serve as the Washington equivalent of matchmakers, introducing their clients to the movers and shakers of government and the media: "That's really what we do," says Frank Mankiewicz of Hill and Knowlton. "We get clients time in the right forum to present their point of view."

And, yes, Rachel, they do spend a lot of time talking on the phone and giving parties.

They also do some secret stuff that they won't talk about.

Take, for example, the "nationwide grass-roots campaign to combat restrictive laws in 50 states" touted in the Susan Davis Companies's rather voluminous self-promotional brochure.

Susan Davis won't talk about that campaign. Davis—who is the chairman and CEO of the Susan Davis Companies, which includes Susan Davis Communications Group and Susan Davis International and Susan Davis Events Group and Susan Davis Advertising Group—will only say that it "could be tobacco-related." Why the secrecy? Especially about something as noble as a "campaign to combat restrictive laws?" "We really are behind-the-scenes players," she says, "and I'd like to keep it that way."

Very modest. Admirably self-effacing. Particularly coming from a woman who has named five companies after herself.

Part 4: Dueling Visuals on Capital Hill

Pamela Kostmayer is standing in the closet, looking for her jeans.

Kostmayer, a veteran Washington PR woman, uses the closet at Kostmayer Communications as a warehouse for the props—"visuals," she calls them—she uses to attract the attention of politicians and TV cameras.

She pokes around a bit but can't find the jeans, which she'd silk-screened with statistics and used as a visual in her campaign against a bill limiting textile imports a few years back. But she does find a shirt, an Izod shirt that she used as a visual in a PR campaign for a bill to stop the counterfeiting of designer clothes. Still rummaging through the closet, she tells that story: She invited members of Congress to a lunch where her clients touted the bill, and then she invited the pols to take a souvenir shirt. "And on the day of the vote, we sent them a letter saying, 'If you got a white shirt, it was phony. If you got a colored shirt, it was real. You have the benefit of knowing what is counterfeit and what is not. The American consumer does not. Vote yes on HR-blah-blah-blah. ' "

The bill passed too, she says. "And we'd get calls from the members' secretaries, saying,' The shirt doesn't really fit.' And I'd say, 'It's not really meant to fit. It's supposed to be a visual.' "

Kostmayer is the queen of the Capitol Hill visual, which is a major PR art form in this era of photo-op politics. A former TV reporter and Senate staffer, she is also the wife of Rep. Peter Kostmayer (D-Pa.), who is himself a former PR man. But Pam Kostmayer learned the art of the visual at that ancient fountainhead of PR gambits—the circus. Promoting Ringling Bros. and Barnum & Bailey in the early '70s, she'd show up before the circus hit town, arrange a local contest and stick the lucky winner atop an elephant in the circus parade. Inevitably, the TV cameras loved it. "The best visual of all," she says, "is somebody on an elephant."

Back in Washington in the '80s, she quickly realized that the same rules apply in political PR. "National network news is what I'm aiming for," she says. "There are 22 minutes of news; the rest is commercials. Out of that, maybe five or six minutes comes out of Washington. And I've got to compete with everything else that's happening. So what can I give them that will almost guarantee that cameras will show up? A visual. Because that's what they need. Who wants to see another chart?" So Kostmayer gives her clients—and the cameras—visuals. For Mothers Against Drunk Driving, she parked a wrecked car against the backdrop of the Capitol dome. That "made air." For a group of undertakers, she put caskets and funeral urns in a Senate conference room. That made air too. But those were mere warm-ups for her epic textile bill campaign. For that, she had a college kid dressed as a teddy bear pulling a wagon through the halls of Congress, delivering little imported teddy bears with labels informing the pols how much more these cuddly critters would cost the parents of America's toddlers if the textile bill passed.

The "textile bear" got so much publicity that Kostmayer sent it back out every week to deliver other little goodies—like jeans that said, "The textile bill's got America by the seat of the pants" and socks saying, "Don't let the textile bill sock it to America."

Pretty soon, the groups supporting the textile bill responded with visuals of their own—"the world's largest jeans," which were four stories high; a 60-foot red-white-and-blue zipper labeled "Win one for the zipper"; and life-size cardboard photos of workers who would allegedly lose their jobs if the bill was defeated.

It was dueling visuals on Capitol Hill.

Which is not unusual. These days, Capitol Hill frequently plays host to the sort of, goofy visuals and pseudo events that made the 1988 presidential campaign so, well, memorable. A congressman attaches a five-pound bag of sugar to his "dear colleague" letter about a sugar subsidy bill. The American Association of Retired

Persons sends members of Congress baseballs with the slogan, "Don't throw consumers a curve." A band of representatives clusters around a casket to denounce a particular bill as "dead on arrival." Another band of representatives vandalizes Toshiba products to display its displeasure with the Toshiba Corp.'s selling of sensitive technology to the Soviets.

"This is what we feel about Toshiba," said Rep. Helen Bentley (R-Md.) before swinging her sledgehammer into a boom box as the TV cameras churned.

Sometimes, the search for the perfect visual goes a tad too far, as in the now-infamous incident when the Drug Enforcement Administration lured a crack dealer to Lafayette Park—where there had never been a crack arrest—so that George Bush could hold up a bag of dope for the TV cameras and say, "This is crack cocaine, seized a few days ago in a park across the street from the White House . . ."

In fact, these dueling visuals have gotten so out of hand that even Pamela Kostmayer's carefully planned, quasi-official pseudo events can be upstaged by goofy guerrilla pseudo events. Which is what happened last fall, when Kostmayer put on the official groundbreaking ceremony for the National Law Enforcement Officers' Memorial in Judiciary Square. "I had President Bush," she says. "I had gold shovels. I had crying widows. I had the president of the United States and the attorney general and the director of the FBI. I mean, it was a stellar lineup, it was a great visual. I had 28 television crews, I had 54 news organizations, and I didn't make network. What made network? A flag-burning on the steps of the Capitol with about six people."

That's the cruel law of life in Washington's PR jungle: You live by the visual and you die by the visual.

Part 5: When the Media Comes Banging on Your Door . . .

"We tell them how to sit," says Col. Gordon Bratz, "and we tell them how to stand."

Bratz has a bizarre job. He's a special assistant in the Secretary of the Army's Office of Public Affairs, which means that he's the guy who trains America's generals to face their most frightening enemy—the television camera. These are three- and four-star generals, towers of power, guys who fought the ChiComs in Korea and the VC in Nam, guys who can kill you with their bare hands. But when they see a TV camera, fear freezes them into man's most primal defensive pose.

"In that first stand-up interview, most of the generals are going to stand like this," Bratz says. Feigning terror, he stiffens up and cups his hands over his crotch.

His audience howls with laughter. Bratz is at the convention of the National Association of Government Communicators, leading a seminar titled "How to Put Together a Media Training Program for Your Agency."

"So we're going to tell them how to stand," he continues. "Put your feet about a foot apart with one ahead of the other. That typically prevents them from going like this"—Bratz rocks from side to side. "I tell them, if you do want to rock, rock forward because that engages the audience. . . . In sitting, I'll tell them to sit in a straight chair and sit bent away from the camera, not into the camera with the knees, because that elongates the upper thigh."

"Say that again," a woman calls out. She's sitting in the back of the room, furiously scribbling notes.

Of course: This is important stuff. In an era of sound-bite politics, anybody who has power, or covets it, needs to know how to use television.

"How ready are you," Lew Brodsky, director of public affairs for the Selective Service System, asks the government communicators, "for the day when the media come banging on your door wanting an on-camera interview about a controversial situation?"

Pretty ready, they respond: About three-quarters of the assembled communicators reveal that they or their bosses have already hired PR people to teach them how to stand and how to sit and how to speak in sound bites and how to react when Mike Wallace barges in.

They are hardly alone. In 1986, when the Senate decided to televise its proceedings, the Republicans hired media whiz Roger Ailes to teach the senators how to look senatorial on the Senate floor.

Which is not surprising. These days, to paraphrase Chairman Mao, political power grows out of the tube of a television. In the Third World, revolutionaries don't attack the palace anymore, they seize the TV station. In Washington, things are slightly different: People don't seize TV stations, they simply build their own studios.

Official Washington is crammed with TV studios. The U.S. Chamber of Commerce has one. So does the U.S. Department of Commerce. And the House. And the Senate. And the RNC. And the DNC. And the National Education Association. And the AFL-CIO. And . . . And those institutions that don't have studios rent them. Why? So they can create the technological version of the old press release—the video press release. Some of these are full of video razzmatazz, but most are simply interviews. The Head Honcho is fed questions by his PR man and the result is beamed up via satellite to any TV station that might want it. The stations sometimes splice in questions asked by their own reporters so it looks as if they interviewed the Head Honcho themselves. Despite the fraudulence factor, these are known, believe it or not, as "actualities." Members of Congress love actualities because they enable the distinguished statesmen to appear on home district TV stations that can't afford a Washington bureau. But it isn't just members of Congress who use them. The U.S. Army Reserve Office's Individual Ready Reserve Campaign did a great video news release, which featured rumbling tanks and guys in camouflage and lots of shooting. The Nonprescription Drug Manufacturers Association did a less theatrical one. So did the Association of Flight Attendants and the Postal Service and . . .

In fact, these days, you're not a real Washington mover and shaker until you've beamed your image out to a waiting world via satellite.

But first you have to learn how to stand and how to sit and . . .

". . . Thirdly," Col. Bratz tells his seminar, "you have to be interesting. I think this is very difficult for military people. They're very dull. . . ." A woman in the audience raises her hand and says that at her agency, they give TV training to four or five honchos at a time and then let them criticize one another's performance.

"We don't do that," Bratz says, "because a lot of senior officers would just as soon have their training be private. They've told me that. A four-star general doesn't like to fall on his face in front of a one-star. . . ."

Part 6: To Preserve and Protect the Widget

Gary Nordlinger is pretending to hold a phone up to his ear.

"Is this Mrs. Smith?" he asks.

"Yes, it is," he answers. "I'm Gary Nordlinger from the Widget Manufacturers of America," he says. "We have a real problem going on. Congress is going to be voting tomorrow on HR-12, a bill which would ban the sale of widgets. We need to kill this right away. Mr. Smith, may we send a letter to your member of Congress and sign your name to it?"

And that, says Nordlinger, head of Nordlinger Associates, a Washington political PR firm, is the way you do "grass-roots PR."

"Grass roots" is the big buzzword in Washington PR these days. It's also the third stage in the evolution of lobbying. In the beginning there was the lobbyist. He got friendly with pols and tried to persuade them to vote the way his clients wanted. But now everybody has a lobbyist. "Your lobbyist cancels out my lobbyist," Nordlinger says. "So where else do you turn?"

To a PAC, perhaps. You augment your lobbyist with a political action committee that donates money to the pols campaign. "But as PACs rise and more and more people give money," says Jack Bonner, head of Bonner & Associates, another local grass-roots PR firm, "your $5,000 check to him isn't going to buy you a hell of a lot."

So what's a PR guy to do? "You create a situation," says Mankiewicz of Hill and Knowlton, "in which public opinion back home either is or appears to be on your side of the issue."

Which is a pretty good definitions of grass-roots PR.

The prototype of the modern grass-roots effort was the American Bankers Association's 1982 fight against a bill to compel banks to withhold 10 percent of their customers' interest, just as employers withhold taxes on workers' earnings. ABA lobbyists fought the bill, which was backed by President Reagan, but failed to beat it. So the ABA tried a grass-roots effort, sending 15,000 "repeal kits" to member banks. The kits contained pre-packaged letters to members of Congress; prewritten op-ed pieces, which bankers were to re-type and submit to their local paper; and posters to display in their banks. Meanwhile, the banks inserted millions of protest postcards in their customers' monthly statements, along with the suggestion that they send them to Congress.

The result was a deluge of mail that succeeded in killing the bill.

Since then, grass roots has become much more sophisticated. Pre-printed postcards, for instance, are now considered passe: too obviously a mass mailing. The new thing is laser-printed letters complete with ersatz individual letterheads. "What you're able to do now," says Nordlinger, "is come up with 25 or 30 different messages, combine that against 10 different colors and sizes of paper and 10 different typefaces and"—he starts tapping the numbers into his pocket calculator—"and you're already up to 3,000 combinations there. It's not like getting a ton of post-cards with nothing but a signature."

To find those voters most inclined to sign letters on a given issue, grass-roots PR people turn to direct mail experts who can produce lists of voters in virtually any demographic, geographic or special interest group. "They have the country broken-down into little grids—everything from BMW owners who are yuppies to people who own Fords and go fishing on Sunday," says Bonner. "It's mass marketing. It's the same way that they sell Time magazine. Literally." Sometimes, of course, grass-roots PR people are less than completely upfront about who is behind their campaigns. When the Natural Gas Supply Association tried to mobilize public support for ending price controls on natural gas, the trade association didn't use its own name, it invented a group called the Alliance for Energy Security. When a collection of utility and coal companies battled a bill to control acid rain, they invented the Citizens for the Sensible Control of Acid Rain, which sent out a mailing of 800,000 letters.

Perhaps the most infamous dubious grass-roots campaign came in 1985, when the Environmental Protection Agency debated permitting the burning of toxic waste in special incinerator ships off Brownsville, Tex. Rollins Environmental Service, which operates land-based incinerators, thought that proposal might hurt its business, so it hired Robert Beckel, who was Walter Mondale's deputy campaign manager the previous year, to run a grass-roots campaign against it. Beckel created an ersatz environmental group called Alliance to Save the Ocean, which phoned Brownsville residents and urged them to fight the plan. The tactic raised some criticism, but Beckel defended his actions as standard operating procedure in Washington: "Why does Walter Mondale call his committee the Committee for the Future of America as opposed to the Walter Mondale Committee?"

Predictably, the result of all this grass-roots organizing is a huge increase in mail on Capitol Hill. In the early 1970s, Congress received about 15 million letters a year. By last year, the total was more than 300 million. And the vast majority of those letters were inspired by PR campaigns. "Never, other than the mega-issues of our day, is mail truly spontaneous," says Bonner. "All the rest of the mail is prompted by somebody."

Does this avalanche of manufactured emotion bother the politicians who get buried under it? No way. It just gives them additional ammunition for their own postage-free direct mail PR campaigns.

"They love it," says Nordlinger. "When you send me your computer-generated letter, if I'm a member of Congress, I can send you my computer-generated letters. At that point, you're going to start getting two to three targeted letters a year on what Congressman X is doing to preserve and protect the widget." He grins. "Dear Mr. Smith: Bringing you up to date on what I've been doing about widgets. . . ."

There's a term for this on Capitol Hill: Our computers answering their computers.

Part 7: A Nutritionist Named Meryl Streep

"We got rolled," says Frank Mankiewicz. "When you're dealing with a nutritionist named Meryl Streep, you haven't got a chance."

Mankiewicz is talking about how his company, Hill and Knowlton, the largest PR firm in Washington, got clobbered, got creamed, got its proverbial clock cleaned last year by a little environmental group in a big public PR battle over Alar and apples.

"It was a very good example of what the hell can go wrong," he says.

Alar is a chemical used to keep apples on trees longer, thus producing a brighter red color. In 1973, the chemical was first identified as a carcinogen, and in 1985 the EPA began taking slow steps toward banning it. Ralph Nader and the Natural Resources Defense Council, a Washington-based environmental group, lobbied for an immediate ban. But the issue never really caught fire—until the NRDC hired a PR man named David Fenton.

Fenton was hired to publicize an NRDC study called "Intolerable Risk: Pesticides in Our Children's Food." The report alleged that apples sprayed with Alar represented a dangerous cancer risk for children because of the huge amounts of apple products kids consume. Usually, reports like that live for a day in the media and then fade forever into the ether. Not this one. Fenton engineered a PR campaign that was the worst thing to happen to the apple since Eve.

First, he arranged to keep the report secret until the CBS show "60 Minutes" could "break" the story to 40 million viewers on February 26, 1989. Using the show as an ad, the NRDC released the report the next morning at 13 simultaneous news conferences around the country. The result was enormous publicity. But Fenton wasn't finished yet. A week later, just as the first media blitz was fading, he launched his second: Actress Meryl Streep held a Washington press conference to announce the formation of an NRDC spinoff group, Mothers and Others for Pesticide Limits. Streep also testified before a congressional committee and did 16 satellite TV interviews with local news shows across the country. The Hollywood angle fueled another blizzard of publicity: the "Today" show, "Donahue," "Entertainment Tonight," People magazine, USA Today (the newspaper), USA Today (the TV show) and . . .

"Our goal was to create so many repetitions of NRDC's message that average American consumers (not just the policy elite in Washington) could not avoid hearing it," Fenton wrote in a memo about the campaign. "The idea was for the story to achieve a life of its own."

Which it did, much to the dismay of the apple industry and its PR firm, Hill and Knowlton. "I knew as soon as '60 Minutes' was over," says Josephine Cooper, a former EPA official who now heads up H&K's Environment and Energy group, "that we had a problem." Cooper and her cohorts snapped into action. They rounded up scientists and doctors who declared that apples were safe. Then they spread that information via countless press releases, video press releases and audio press releases. They took out full-page ads in newspapers around the country. They held luncheons to brief House and Senate staffers. They also lobbied the federal agencies responsible for food safety—the EPA, the Food and Drug Administration and the Department of Agriculture—begging them to defend the beleaguered apple. Finally, three weeks later, the agencies did, announcing jointly that apples were safe to eat and that Alar was not an "imminent hazard" to children. Immediately, Hill and Knowlton dispatched that statement via mailgrams to state and local officials around the country. They sent similar messages to thousands of grocers and pediatricians.

But none of it did much good. Apple sales plummeted, schools booted the fruit out of their cafeterias, and editorial cartoonists had a field day making apple jokes. Finally, Uniroyal, which manufactures Alar, withdrew it from the market. A few months later, the EPA announced a plan to phase it out entirely.

PR had killed Alar.

"NRDC and their hired PR counsel did a superb job of playing the news media like a Stradivarius," says Jack Bomer. "The industry did not get their message across and they took punches and went down for the count."

Ironically, though, the Alar battle will probably make Hill and Knowlton—and other corporate PR firms—lots of money in the long run. "I think a lot of industries said, 'My God, there but for the grace of God goes us,' " says Cooper. When those industries find themselves in environmental fights of their own—which will happen more often in the '90s, many PR people predict—they'll turn to PR firms for help. Which is why Hill and Knowlton is setting up environmental divisions in its offices around the country.

"It's very good for business," says Cooper, "and I think we're well-positioned to maximize the opportunities."

Part 8: A Guerrilla with a PR Firm

In Angola, government soldiers aided by Cuban troops were killing and being killed by guerrillas aided by South Africa. Meanwhile, in Washington, the battle was fought on a more lucrative—and more ludicrous—level: It was a PR War.

The war began on September 16, 1985, when Paul Manafort, head of Black, Manafort, Stone—the PR firm that gave America Lee Atwater—flew to Angola with Christopher Lehman. Three days earlier, Lehman had left his job as special assistant to the president for national security affairs to join Manafort's firm. Three days later,

Lehman and Manafort persuaded Jonas Savimbi, head of Angola's UNITA guerrillas, to sign a $600,000-a-year contract with Black, Manafort.

A guerrilla with a PR firm?

Why not? Right-wing Guatemalan guerrillas have had PR reps here. So have left-wing Salvadoran guerrillas. And such dubious characters as Ferdinand Marcos, the shah of Iran, Manuel Noriega and the Sandinistas, among many others.

Savimbi wanted to get American weapons for his war against the leftist government of Angola. Unfortunately, he didn't have the greatest reputation. Trained in guerrilla warfare in Red China in the '60s, Savimbi had espoused a strident blend of Maoism and Black Power. After his rivals took over Angola in the '70s, however, Savimbi jettisoned Maoism and Black Power and found a new patron—the apartheid government of South Africa. Now, gunning for American arms, he needed to create a "freedom fighter" image. So he hired Black, Manafort, a firm with close connections to the Reagan White House.

And Black, Manafort engineered a brilliant PR campaign. It opened with an exclusive interview with "60 Minutes"—filmed in the Angolan bush and timed to air when Savimbi came to Washington on a private jet in January 1986. Meticulously coached in the fine arts of TV repartee and Hill lobbying, Savimbi spent the next 10 days doing interviews, meeting with pols—including President Reagan—and being cheered by conservatives at a banquet at the Capital Hilton. By the time he flew off—in a private jet loaned by an anonymous Texas millionaire—Savimbi had won assurances that his guerrillas would get American arms.

Obviously, the other side—the Angolan government—needed some reinforcements on the PR front. So it hired Gray and Co. for a reported $50,000 a month. The firm, which has since merged with Hill and Knowlton, was headed by Robert Keith Gray, a former Eisenhower administration official with close ties to the Reagans. Gray's media whizzes tutored Angolan foreign trade minister Ismael Gaspar-Martins in the art of TV repartee for his debate with Savimbi on the "MacNeil-Lehrer NewsHour," advising him to wear a nice conservative suit so he'd look more respectable than Savimbi, who favors funky Third World Nehru jackets.

But Gray's campaign reached its absurd apogee when Daniel Murphy—a retired admiral and George Bush's former chief of staff, who was handling the Angola account—touted the deep religious convictions of his Marxist clients. "I was very surprised to learn that everybody goes to church on Sunday," Murphy told the Wall Street Journal. "At least one-third of the Politburo members are practicing Presbyterians."

By then, the Young Conservative Foundation had gotten into the act. Irate that a fellow Republican like Gray would undercut the beloved Savimbi, the group launched a PR campaign. of its own. First, it picketed the Powerhouse, as Gray called his office, but that protest fizzled when the activists failed in their efforts to ignite a hammer-and-sickle flag. A few days later, however, they returned, storming the Powerhouse and handcuffing themselves to a banister. Four of them were arrested, which inspired the media coverage they were seeking.

"They didn't want to talk," Mankiewicz, then a Gray vice president, complained to The Washington Post. "They wanted a media event."

A PR man complaining about a media event? It was the sound of defeat. A month later, after reams of bad publicity, Gray dropped the Angola account.

"It was too difficult," Mankiewicz recalls. "We were becoming the issue instead of Angola."

Ironically, Angola's PR efforts are now masterminded by David Fenton, the man who beat Mankiewicz in the Alar battle.

But Mankiewicz still has plenty of foreign clients. This fall, he traveled to Hungary to advise the Hungarian Communist Party—which recently changed its name to the Hungarian Socialist Party for obvious PR reasons. "That wasn't my advice," Mankiewicz says. "But it would have been if they hadn't done it already."

Part 9: 'Sodom and Gomorrah Was an Attention-Getter'

The room was packed with PR people.

A couple of hundred of them gathered in the Capital Hilton last December for the monthly luncheon of the Washington chapter of the Public Relations Society of America. They drank white wine, ate lukewarm chicken, applauded at least 10 past presidents of the chapter and then listened as the current president introduced the guest speaker—Harold Burson, chairman of Burson-Marsteller, one of the largest PR firms on God's green earth.

As Burson stepped up to speak, a protester dashed to the podium and draped it with blood-stained rabbit fur. "Mr. Burson represents the fur industry," she exclaimed, "and on behalf of the millions of animals that have been killed—the foxes, the lynx, the minks, the rabbits, chinchillas, who have been electrocuted, who have been beaten to death—we bestow the Public Relations Hall of Shame award. . . ."

The audience groaned and hissed.

PR people catch a lot of flack. Not just from animal lovers and Savimbi supporters but from skeptics and scoffers in all walks of life who feel, for some reason, that PR people are somewhat less than totally honest.

"Somehow, if you say the words 'public relations,' " says Soucy, who does PR for British Aerospace, "folks want to rush off and take showers because they've just been in the presence of something contaminated."

It's the great irony of PR: The public relations business, which is composed entirely of experts in the art of manufacturing public images, has a terrible public image. On the popularity scale, PR people are no doubt right down there with lawyers and politicians. Maybe almost as low as journalists.

How come?

"Cause we ain't all choirboys," says Louis Priebe, who handles PR for the Salt Institute. "Joseph Goebbels practiced PR for Adolf Hitler."

True enough. But it probably isn't Goebbels' "big lie" that Americans associate with PR. It's all those little half-truths and weasel words and slick image campaigns. It's the sight of New York City disguising gutted buildings with decals that make them look occupied. It's the stories about the PR guys who help elect the pols and then traipse off to do PR work for people who want something from those pols. It's candidates campaigning in flag factories and presidents who won't make a speech until their personal pollster checks the public pulse. It's the negative ads and the spin doctors and the staged events and the symbol-mongering. It all combines to produce the vague feeling that nothing in politics or government is really real anymore.

These days, the fog produced by the "foggy business" is so dense that even the so-called "insiders" have trouble telling image from reality. Ronald Reagan compared the contras to our Founding Fathers so often that he actually seemed to believe it was true. Remember all the pundits who said that Mikhail Gorbachev was just a slick PR man? Gorby turned out to be the real thing. Or did he? Could tearing down the Berlin Wall be just another PR stunt? It's tough to tell these days. And that's the problem: We've seen so many slick visuals that we don't trust our eyes anymore. We've heard so many soothing slogans that we can't believe our ears. Nonstop PR has left Americans sated and jaded.

"PR," says Soucy, "has come to mean 'to take the unpalatable and make it palatable.' "

Of course, PR people don't see it that way. Quite the contrary. They consider themselves members of an honorable profession, descendants of a long line of people who have educated and elevated public opinion for centuries. In the speech that was interrupted by the fur protester, Harold Burson traced that lineage back to Thomas Jefferson and Alexandeir Hamilton. Soucy traces it back even further, to some even bigger names:

"For what did Christ perform miracles?" he asks. "I'm not comparing us to Him. I'm simply saying that when you use the term 'public relations gimmick' or 'attention-getter,' well, I'm sorry: Sodom and Gomorrah was an attention-getter. Man responds to attention-getters."

So why haven't any of America's estimated 150,000 PR people produced an attention-getting PR campaign to improve the wretched public image of the PR business?

Ray Hiebert, publisher of the Public Relations Review, thinks he knows why.

"They don't want to," he says with a sly smile. "They like it the way it is. They want to be seen as the custodians of some kind of sinister magic."

Part 10: Federal Bureaucrats Redux

Robert Weed is still rolling.

When we left him, Weed was exhorting the National Association of Government Communicators, pleading for help in his official campaign to enhance the "public image of public service," promising free copies of Image Update and free bumper stickers.

And now his voice is rising to a crescendo as he launches into his stirring conclusion: "We have truth on our side. We're going out saying to the American people: 'We want you to take a fresh look at your public employees, at the system that puts them into place, and we know that when you look at these people, you'll trust them.' . . . If they take a fresh look at us, they're gonna recognize that we have truth on our side and they'll say, 'Yes, I can understand why you're proud to be a public employee.' And I'm proud to be a public employee. And I'm proud to be with you this morning. Thank you very much."

He gets a polite round of applause. Then he entertains some questions.

The first questioner notes Weed's rousing endorsement of public servants and then inquires why federal employees hadn't gotten a decent raise lately.

The second questioner launches into a diatribe, lambasting government-bashing presidents who appoint political hacks to boss around dedicated, experienced public servants.

Wait a minute. Hold it right there.

Here is a crowd composed entirely of government PR people and they don't seem terribly excited about a government PR campaign in their behalf. They aren't agog about receptions and Image Updates and ad campaigns and bumper stickers. They want something else. They want the one thing that PR just can't provide:

They want substance.

Don't they know what city they're in?

Advertising 12

Madison Ave. Sets the Dial for Youth

PAUL FARHI

During the last TV season, "60 Minutes" finished second in the Nielsen ratings, with a weekly audience nearly twice as large as that of another Sunday night show, "The Simpsons." The irreverent animated sitcom on Fox ranked a mere 49th in the ratings.

Yet as a new TV season dawns, 30 seconds of air time on either show will cost advertisers roughly the same, about $160,000.

The price similarity illustrates one of the axioms of Madison Avenue: It's not how many people watch, but who. "The Simpsons," in the language of the ad trade, "skews young," meaning its primary appeal is to people in the coveted 12-to-34 age segment. "60 Minutes" is broadly popular, but has a very large audience of people more than 50 years of age. Advertisers have their own word for these viewers too: undesirable.

Such is the fate of older people in the peculiar economic structure of television. Prime-time TV advertisers routinely discount aging viewers, paying rock-bottom prices to sponsor programs popular among them. Conversely, they pay a premium to advertise on programming that draws the young.

Network officials and advertisers say the orientation toward youth does not reflect an inherent bias against older people. Rather, they call it a logical outgrowth of a fact that goes against stereotypes: Young people don't watch that much television, and older people do. Thus, when a 30-year-old actually tunes in, his or her attention can be sold at a higher price than if a 60-year-old is watching.

The ad industry's desire for younger viewers, however, has created a kind of self-perpetuating quality to what appears on network TV each night. Because sponsors demand it, the networks have long aired prime-time programs with themes and characters designed to lure an audience between the ages of 18 and 49. It's hardly a coincidence that network programs dealing with the concerns of aging have been rare.

Indeed, an entire network, Fox, was created with the idea of targeting its programming ("Melrose Place," "Beverly Hills 90210," etc.) to those under the age of 35. By contrast, CBS is sometimes derided as the Geritol Network because many of its programs ("Murder, She Wrote," "60 Minutes") skew older—that is, toward the far end of the 25-to-54 group.

"Half of CBS's audience dies each year," jokes Jon Nesvig, president of network advertising sales for Fox.

To critics, this economic underpinning of prime-time television amounts to a sort of age-group redlining—or in this case, "graylining"—in which broadcasters and their advertisers write off viewers who fit a single demographic characteristic.

The advertising industry "is steeped in stereotypic views of older people. It is engaging in ageism at its worst," said Dixie Horning, executive director of the Gray Panthers, an advocacy group for older people.

"It takes the view that once you reach a certain age you are no longer a productive citizen or person."

Horning finds this "mystifying" in view of several well-documented trends— the general aging of the population, the rising wealth of older Americans and the falling or stagnant wages for younger people, particularly those in the twentysomething generation popularly known as Generation X.

A 1991 survey by the U.S. Bureau of the Census found, for example, that households headed by a person aged 54 to 65 are 15 times wealthier (defined as assets minus liabilities) than those headed by people under age 35.

What's more, a raft of studies and surveys, including one funded by CBS, indicates that older Americans are active shoppers, not stay-at-homes hoarding for old age. Asked by the marketing research firm Yankelovich Partners whether a new TV commercial could induce them to try a product, about 27 percent of respondents over the age of 50 said yes; only 24 percent of those between 30 and 49 agreed.

Said Yankelovich partner Ann Clurman, "We've spent a lot of time trying to tell people that this is a vigorous, vital, vibrant, active market."

So why don't TV advertisers seem to be listening?

To a large extent, the answer boils down to this fact: Compared with their elders, young people aren't in front of the set much. Because of this, young people are relatively harder for a TV advertiser to reach. Hence, sponsors bid up the price for air time on those programs that can "deliver" the youngsters.

According to Nielsen Media Research, men over the age of 55 watch an average of 33 hours and 46 minutes of television per week; men aged 18 to 24 watch 21 hours and 50 minutes. There is an even greater disparity when women are compared. Nielsen's figures also show a similar age gap during prime-time hours, the heaviest viewing period of the day.

Younger people tend to have more active lifestyles than older people, thereby limiting their TV-watching time, said Angela Dunlap, president of consumer markets at MCI Communications Corp., the Washington-based long-distance telephone company. "They're on their PCs, they're at the mall or they're out on a date," she said. "They have a different variety of choices."

Younger audiences also tend to be less loyal viewers of a particular program than older viewers, said Paul Schulman, whose self-named company purchases network time for such clients as Ralston-Purina Group, ITT Corp. and others.

Another reason advertisers pay more to reach these viewers, he said, is that quite simply there are more TV advertisers whose products appeal to younger consumers than older ones. That means more demand for ads in youth-oriented shows.

The 10 largest network-advertised products, according to the Television Bureau of Advertising, fall into such categories as fast food, snacks and soft drinks, movies, beer and footwear—all consumed primarily by younger people.

Marketers of these products must lavish big dollars on network TV ads because their target audience tends to read less, making newspaper and magazine ads a less efficient alternative.

It also doesn't hurt an advertiser to influence a young person before he or she reaches the age at which major purchase decisions are made, points out Schulman.

"If you can get people thinking Whirlpool at the age of 15, you hope that that name is with them when they're 25 and are ready to buy a dishwasher or washing machine," he said.

But time, said CBS research chief David Poltrack, is working against the young and the restless. The number of adults aged 18 to 34 will decline 8 percent during the 1990s, he said, while the 35-to-54 category will increase 30 percent. Advertisers' thinking already has begun to change, Poltrack said, which suggests that someday, TV programming too will have to change.

Morph for the Money

JAY MATHEWS

In a few mismatched buildings near the beach here, Scott Ross and his company, Digital Domain, are developing the tools for a new era of marketing—in which the awesome power of the computer is harnessed to the age-old task of manipulating the consumer.

The goal of Ross and his partners—producer-director James Cameron and special-effects wizard Stan Winston—is to create images that are more powerful and enticing than reality. In the process, they are beginning to take the advertising business deeper than ever before into the thicket of human fantasies.

The offices of Digital Domain are stuffed with supercomputing workstations from Silicon Graphics Inc., an IBM Power Visualisation system and enough software tools to fill a galaxy or two in cyberspace. Young computer artists in shorts and T-shirts move about the computers, fashioning moving pictures from electrons that seem as real as a home movie shot out on Venice's Main Street.

And yet the reality they create is often so bizarre that one cannot bear to stop watching. The Rolling Stones, blown up to the size of Godzillas, prance through the streets of New York. A bedraggled terrorist, his clothing caught on a Sidewinder missile, rockets through a devastated skyscraper to his doom. The Statue of Liberty, curious about the time, pulls her left arm away from her side with a great cracking of metal and plaster to check her new illuminated watch.

Americans have seen the beginnings of this creative computing—in films such as "Terminator 2" and "True Lies," and the "Young Indiana Jones" television series—but now it is moving into advertising. In dimly lit rooms scattered throughout Digital Domain's compound here, technicians are tearing apart barriers to imagination and foreshadowing a day when annoyances such as actors and locations may be obsolete.

The cross-fertilization of films and commercials is everywhere. The motion-control rig used for a new Honda commercial once animated the Tyrannosaurus Rex in "Jurassic Park." The company's "Love Is Strong" video for the Rolling Stones used technology developed for "True Lies."

The assumption here is that the new graphic tools will allow an artist-technician at a keyboard to produce, by a complex manipulation of ones and zeros, an exact duplicate of what most amuses, terrifies or moves the viewer. If so, then the industries that earn their money motivating and entertaining people are never going to be the same.

"If you can dream it, you can do it," said Mitch Kanner, director of Digital Domain's commercial division.

The atmosphere at Digital Domain seems reminiscent of Ross's earlier life, when he worked as a saxophone player and spent time in a Portola Valley commune. Conversations are intense and thoughts float as freely as gulls cruising the beach.

Ross said he prefers this easy atmosphere to the more secretive rules of Industrial Light & Magic (ILM), the pioneer in this field and Ross's former employer. But he and ILM's creator, filmmaker George Lucas, are all after the same thing: making movies and advertisements that are so divorced from reality, and yet so real, that they stay in the mind forever.

This is, in a way, a marriage of Hollywood and New York, of the computer, movie and advertising industries. International Business Machines Corp. owns half of Digital Domain. Cameron has used his new company to produce special effects for his summer hit "True Lies." Ross is an experienced video and recording manager who spent part of his time at ILM beefing up its advertising business.

To make the blend work, Ross said, Digital Domain encourages employees to cross traditional specialty lines and toss ideas around. Staffers dress casually, including the muscular, 42-year-old Ross, who wears jeans and a polo shirt. The CEO (Ross) shares a tiny office with a secretary whose desk is no smaller than his. Lunch at the few nearby Venice eateries can easily be had for under $10. Titles are absent from executive doors.

"We want to take the digital creation process from the technicians and locate it within the creative community," welcoming in the technicians in at the same time, Ross explained.

Lady Liberty Lights Up

At Digital Domain, the most recent amusement has been the Statue of Liberty commercial, an appeal for Timex in which Miss Liberty checks out the illuminated dial of her new Indiglo ladies watch during a New York City blackout.

A month before the commercial aired, Fred Raimondi, a bearded visual effects supervisor, sat in his darkened computer room on the second floor of one of Digital Domain's buildings and studied Miss Liberty's eyebrows on his screen. Should he make them go up at this point in the commercial, or a little later on? Or not at all? "It's like having a conversation with yourself," Raimondi said.

Judy Brink, a spokeswoman for the Fallon McElligott agency in Minneapolis that came up with the statue idea, said the Digital Domain people received it like a splendid new toy. "They have amassed the best people in the industry," she said. "You get those people interested in you because you have interesting things to work on."

Computer graphics is a term that appears now in nearly every advertising pitch and college admissions brochure. It sounds good and creates an impression of modernity and high technology.

But in the hands of the young people now pouring out of universities such as Rensselaer Polytechnic Institute, Cornell, USC and UCLA, these computer drawing skills are connecting viewers with their deepest urges and fears, playing on the imagination in ways that were once reserved for fiction writers.

Leaps of Imagination

"If you can think it, we can execute it," said Ed Ulbrich, the 29-year-old executive producer and vice president of the company's commercial division. He helped with such award-winning ads as one for Jeep that premiered during last winter's Olympics, showing a vehicle so rugged it might have been imagined traveling beneath a vast drift of snow.

"This is a technology that frees up the creative process," said Ulbrich. "Someday you'll have a director sit down at the computer and compose the entire commercial, or movie, or anything else."

John Bruno, an Academy Award-winning visual effects supervisor at the company, arranged the most terrifying footage in "True Lies" (and appeared in one scene as a janitor traumatized by a jump-jet crashing into the office he was vacuuming). He worked on "Terminator 2" and "Abyss," and now directs commercials such as the Timex spot that are becoming the growth part of the business.

Digital Domain also provided effects recently for director Neil Jordan's upcoming "Interview With a Vampire," starring Tom Cruise, and is working on "Apollo 13," directed by Ron Howard, and "Strange Days," directed by Kathryn Bigelow and written and produced by Cameron.

On the advertising side of the ledger, the company's Nike tennis "magazine wars" spot won two awards at the International Advertising Festival in Cannes, and the snow-plowing Jeep spot won the Grand Prix award. The company also worked on a Nike commercial starring Dennis Hopper, which premiered at the last Super Bowl, and on MCI Communications Inc.'s much-discussed surrealistic spots starring 10-year-old Academy Award winner Anna Paquin.

Cameron said he wanted a facility "where the only limitation to what can be accomplished is a director's imagination."

That is also the direction that Lucas's Industrial Light & Magic has taken. "We are merging into a seamless form of filmmaking," said Phillip Collins, director of marketing and sales at ILM, combining what he called "real reality and synthetic reality."

Advertisers are drawn to the new technology, Collins said, because they have "a jaded audience that needs to be visually and verbally stimulated, and . . . seeing things they cannot see in the natural world holds their attention."

Socializing Illusionists

The computerized filmmaking companies are tied into the technology companies of Silicon Valley by long-standing relationships and are quick to snap up the best new software and hardware. They also are in regular contact with one another. Bruno said he often trades ideas with friends at ILM. The best in the business view themselves as part of a informal society of illusionists—for whom the joy is not in the competition for business, but in the creation of something that will make their friends' eyes widen.

In a dark, cool computer room, Bruno watched one of the company's young visual effects experts, 30-year-old Chris Hummel, construct a helicopter on his screen. The metal skeleton came first, then the fuselage; the final electronic product looked like it had come off a factory floor.

Hummel and Bruno discussed the problems of creating human beings on the screen. "We can't get the movement right yet," Bruno said. An animal can be animated to look as if it is really alive, but humans know their own movements so well they notice the tiny jerks of computerized animation.

The power of these new computer tools to alter reality also creates some ethical worries—including the danger that they will be used to deceive consumers or sell them things they don't want or need. "There are certain issues that one has to look at and let good judgment decide," said Ross.

"Thankfully, we have rules and laws and regulations in the advertising business," said Collins of ILM. There was a time, he recalled, when soup advertisers made their brew look chunkier with marbles, "but it would be the very foolish advertiser who did that today."

Ad Ventures in Health Care

PAULA SPAN

H arry, an ordinary Joe in a polo shirt, ambles in after shooting hoops with his unnervingly clean-cut son.

His wife, Louise, is curled up on the sofa, barefoot, with her favorite page-turner: a fat paperback edition of the President's Health Security Act. "Health care reform again, huh?" Harry asks fondly.

Louise looks disgusted. "This plan forces us to buy our insurance through these new, mandatory government health alliances," she complains with a don't-make-me-barf expression.

They spend a few seconds—this is only a 30-second TV commercial, after all—clucking about those danged bureaucrats. Finally the Health Insurance Association of America, the industry group that launched the Harry-and-Louise saga last fall to take issue with key provisions of the Clinton health care plan, urges viewers to call an 800 number and then their congresspersons.

The ad, and a companion featuring Louise's equally disgruntled business partner, Libby, hit CNN and local stations in 48 markets (including Washington) this month. Fixtures of a campaign that will cost the HIAA $3.5 million in the first two months of this year (the tab hit $10.5 million in 1993), Harry and Louise are "our answer to the Taster's Choice couple," HIAA spokesman Richard Coorsh deadpans.

They have few fans among supporters of the president's health care plan, who complain that the ads use scare tactics to undermine reform. "They're designed to be inaccurate and misleading," says Jeff Eller, a White House spokesman. House Ways and Means Committee Chairman Dan Rostenkowski minced no words in a recent speech, warning the HIAA that "your messages are becoming the Willie Horton of the health care campaign—they're increasing the heat of the debate without adding any light."

But Harry and Louise, created by the veteran political agency Goddard*Claussen/First Tuesday, have had the TV ad arena largely to themselves—until now.

Enter the Health Care Reform Project, a universal-coverage coalition of labor unions, medical organizations, corporations and the League of Women Voters. It's been airing a TV spot ridiculing those who scoffed at various visionary efforts of the past: In newsreel footage, JFK proposes the moon landing and a skeptic in a skinny tie objects, "What's the rush? Why not go halfway this decade, halfway next decade?" The spot, created by Boston's Heater Easdon, then demands "Health Security for Every American—Nothing Less."

"No question the critics have had a free ride up till now," says Charles Leonard of Chlopak Leonard Schechter, the communications firm representing the project. "But we think we're ready to mount an effective counter-campaign." The project will spend in the neighborhood of $2 million over the next six weeks to run local TV, radio and print ads in Washington and in critical congressional districts, with phone banks and direct mail efforts backing up the call-your-congressman ads. "We're never going to match what they spend on advertising," Leonard says of the HIAA campaign. "They'll never be able to match what we do in direct citizen action."

There's more noise ahead—a barrage of advertising aimed at the hearts and minds of both citizens and "opinion leaders" as Congress takes up health care reform. The State of the Union Address has only intensified what already threatened to become a cacophonous chorus.

There's the unnerving TV spot just unveiled by William Kristol's Project for the Republican Future, though its paltry budget means it won't be widely seen. The ad lifts censorious quotes from newspapers and magazines and warns, "The Clinton health plan. Everything good about your health care is at risk."

There's the slightly less spooky series of print ads from the American Medical Association, a $1.6 million campaign that represents the group's biggest investment in political advertising since it fought Medicare nearly 30 years ago. Each depicts the literal laying-on of hands, a doctor's on a patient, and raises a series of questions about whether the role of physicians will be undercut by bureaucrats (a favorite heavy) and insurance companies under the new regime. The latest ad, to appear in February editions of weekly newsmagazines, is the most pointed: "Would you rather trust your life to an M.D. or an MBA?"

The American Association of Retired Persons has laid out about $1 million on print and television ads that advocate the inclusion of long-term care. The American Hospital Association's print ads, just a handful so far, talk warmly and nonspecifically about reform. The Pharmaceutical Manufacturers Association TV and print ads don't address reform at all; the PMA merely finds it prudent to spend $13 million this year reminding the public of its good works.

It's possible that in the cross-fire, the public will tire of the din and stop paying attention, some advertisers concede. "But pretty soon, Congress will be voting up or down on real health care issues, one at a time," says Leonard. "I think the American public will focus in."

When it does, it will notice that suddenly everybody's a reformer, or claims to be. "There's more we agree upon than disagree upon," says an HIAA spokesman, describing the areas of contention between its position and the administration's as "relatively minor," though apparently worth millions to explicate. "Please don't portray us as old stick-in-the-muds who've been opposed to reform since 1948," pleads an AMA senior vice president. "That was then and this is now. The AMA supports health system reform."

But both organizations have gone after the regional alliances through which health insurance will be sold under the Clinton proposal. Harry and Louise and Libby have also taken on the Clinton plan's cost containment measures.

In an ad last fall, Harry grimly wondered, "What if our health plan runs out of money?" while Louise shook her head and vowed, "There's got to be a better way."

"That's the keep-the-HIAA-in-business ad," Eller says with scorn. "Insurance companies don't like cost containment."

As for the issue of regional alliances—"an arbitrary government effort at limiting the number of carriers in the marketplace," Coorsh charges—Eller accuses the HIAA of "trying to scare people into thinking they'll no longer get insurance from private insurance companies." Not true, he insists. "If you have your insurance from Prudential now, you'll still get insurance from Prudential. What the alliance will do is say that Prudential can no longer cherry-pick," weeding out customers who will prove expensive to insure.

The HIAA, for its part, says it has "scrupulously" documented its ads' claims. Moreover, it complains that the industry has been vilified by the White House and the Health Care Reform Project's ads. One of the reasons Harry and Louise were created, says HIAA Executive Vice President Chip Kahn, was because administration officials were "using the industry as a whipping boy to sell their plan. . . . We were made the black hats."

Hard to assess, in the general hubbub, is what effect such ads have had. The AMA says 65,000 people have called or phoned to receive its four-page brochure. The HIAA's fall ads brought calls from 23,000 viewers (not to mention, in one ad, Louise's bow-tied dad). But Eller says that "if the HIAA ads were working, I don't think the [poll] numbers we're seeing would be as good as they are."

Whether or not they've changed minds, though, Harry and Louise (played by Los Angeles actors Harry Johnson and Louise Clark) have become staples of the airwaves. Viewers have watched them grapple with their bills at the kitchen table, have heard them talk health coverage instead of turkey around the Thanksgiving table, have seen Louise and Libby muttering unhappily in Libby's darkened office about coverage for the employees of their computer consulting firm.

All three characters exhibit a strong libertarian streak, forever grousing about The Government "forcing" them to do one thing or another. But extensive focus group testing has shown that the public responds, says Ben Goddard, president of the agency that invented them.

"People identify with that scenario," Goddard says. "They see the couple discussing the issues and say, 'Yeah, that's what we do.' . . . These are people they feel comfortable with; they might invite them to a Christmas party."

Anti-AIDS Campaign Aimed at Youth

JOHN SCHWARTZ

The federal government yesterday announced an aggressive public awareness campaign to promote the use of condoms and urge sexual abstinence in the face of the AIDS crisis.

"Every new HIV infection is a needless infection," Donna E. Shalala, secretary of the Department of Health and Human Services, said at a news conference called to unveil 13 federally funded public service ads for radio and television.

"We have the knowledge and the technology to prevent the sexual spread of HIV," Shalala said. "What we have lacked until now is the political will, because we have been too timid to talk openly about the prevention tools at our disposal."

The new ads, commissioned by the federal Centers for Disease Control and Prevention and designed to appeal to a young audience, employ a variety of approaches to discourage sexual activity and warn against the dangers of AIDS and sexually transmitted diseases (STDs) such as gonorrhea and syphilis.

Two of the most straightforward TV ads feature Denise Stokes, 24, an Atlanta AIDS education counselor who is HIV-positive. Stokes looks into the screen and says, "My message is simple. If you're going to have sex, a latex condom used consistently and correctly will prevent the spread of AIDS and other STDs."

Less stark is a television spot in which a computer-animated, packaged condom jumps out of a dresser drawer, to make itself available to a lovemaking couple (of unspecified sex) in a nearby bed. It hops across the room, tiptoes past a sleeping cat and slips between the covers.

The ad's narrator states: "It would be nice if latex condoms were automatic. But since they're not, using them should be."

One of the radio ads features an endorsement by Anthony Kiedis of the rock group Red Hot Chili Peppers. "I wear one whenever I have sex," he says. "Not whenever it's convenient, or whenever my partner thinks of it. Every time. Look— they're easy to open. [Sound of a package opening.] And a breeze to put on. And best of all, they stop the spread of HIV."

He closes the ad telling his audience, "Remember: you can be naked without being exposed."

Other less explicit radio ads feature Martin Lawrence of the Fox sitcom "Martin" and Jason Alexander of NBC's "Seinfeld" show.

The ads, which cost $900,000 to produce, include a toll-free hot line (1–800–342–AIDS) to call for a free brochure on correct condom use and other information about AIDS.

Federal officials said that the program is aimed at those aged 18 to 25. Recent surveys show that 72 percent of all high school seniors have had sexual intercourse. But a study of heterosexual men with multiple sex partners found that only 17 percent used condoms all the time. Nearly one-quarter of all young adults have been infected with at least one STD. Shalala called that "a horrible number."

Some AIDS activists applauded the initiative. Daniel T. Bross, executive director of the AIDS Action Council, said that "in the past, the CDC has told people that the way to prevent AIDS is to 'put your socks on.' Euphemisms such as these have limited value."

But Eric Ueland, spokesman for the Senate Republican Policy Committee, said President Clinton "promised this during the campaign. Unfortunately, this is a campaign promise that he kept." Ueland said that "there's no correlation between more and more explicit advertisements and a slowing of the AIDS rate."

Beverly LaHaye, president of the conservative Concerned Women for America, said, "Telling our young people to use a condom is like telling them to get into a sports car, while knowing that the brakes may not work. The risk is far too great for the fleeting moment of pleasure. . . . Condoms can offer only a slight reduction in what is too high a risk for youth."

The Rev. Robert N. Lynch, general secretary of the National Conference of Catholic Bishops, said in a statement, "The administration is promoting a dangerous myth with its newly announced condom advertising campaign. The advertisements promote promiscuity and a false sense of security which put at risk the very lives of those most likely to be influenced by them."

In a statement last year, the Food and Drug Administration said that, "based on its own studies and published literature, FDA believes that latex condoms can be highly effective barriers to the transmission of HIV, and can also afford protection against many other sexually transmitted diseases." Although latex contains microscopic pores that in theory could allow viruses to penetrate, FDA testing showed that the possibility of such infection was vanishingly small.

Administration officials were careful to underscore the importance of abstinence, which Shalala called "the best way to protect yourself and others." Several of the nine TV ads recommended refraining from sexual activity. In one, a young person—apparently addressing a mate—says, "There's a time for us to be lovers—and we'll wait till that time comes."

Shalala said that all four TV networks had pledged to run the ads, although only Fox promised to run all of them without alteration. The other networks demanded changes in the advertisements or restricted times that they would be broadcast. ABC announced that it would begin showing the advertisements immediately.

One health official who witnessed the recent difficulties that the Whitman-Walker Clinic had in getting its condom-depicting public service announcements on the air earlier this year said, "I think they're going to have a hell of a time" getting the networks and local affiliates to run the ads often enough to sink in with the target audience.

Ultimately, Shalala said, brief radio or TV spots are not going to win the war against AIDS: "Ads alone will have very little impact." The television and radio effort is part of a broader public awareness initiative that includes encouraging community groups to sponsor local education.

AIDS educator Stokes said that she hoped the campaign would help teenagers understand enough about AIDS to avoid her fate. "I wanted so much to prove my independence," Stokes said. "I live today imprisoned by HIV."

Hard News or Soft Sell?

PAUL FARHI

B ob Vila, America's foremost Mr. Fixit, is at it again. On his syndicated TV program, "Bob Vila's Home Again," the friendly handyman hammers, sands and makes lap joints like there's no tomorrow. Not incidentally, he and his guest experts use Craftsman brand tools, which periodically hover into view amid all the hammering and sanding.

Only during the closing credits do viewers learn something about Vila's choice of hardware. "Home Again," reads a credit line, is "produced in association with Sears, Roebuck and Ogilvy & Mather." Sears makes Craftsman tools; Ogilvy makes ads for Craftsman. And Bob Vila makes commercials for both, some of which air during "Home Again."

Confused about where the salesmanship ends and the "infotainment" begins? "Sure, the line is a fine one," said Sears spokesman Greg Rossiter. But Sears isn't concerned about stepping over it: "People aren't stupid," Rossiter said. "We give our viewers a lot more credit for knowing the difference between a commercial and the show."

Maybe, but these days they may have to work harder than ever to tell. Thanks to deregulation of the broadcasting industry, hard times and cutthroat competition for shrinking ad dollars, even the most reputable broadcasters and publishers are knocking new holes in the wall that traditionally has separated news and entertainment from their advertising departments.

"There are so many new vehicles around" that fuzz up the distinctions, said Joel Winston, assistant director of advertising practices at the Federal Trade Commission. "Inevitably, that has to raise some serious questions."

In fact, journalists, and even some advertisers, worry that a growing trend toward blurring the distinctions is leading to a kind of editorial "pollution" that compromises the integrity of a publication or broadcaster.

"There is real fear that the line is becoming too blurred," said William Winter, president of the American Press Institute, a Reston-based journalism-education organization. "Advertisers are being more direct and demanding, [saying] 'deliver the message we want to the customers we want.' It's hard for editors not to be aware of the pressure, even if they don't give in to it."

Just as serious, at least from the government's viewpoint, is whether some ads in editorial clothing amount to an illegal consumer deception. Since 1989, the FTC has sued seven producers of TV "infomercials," those late-night, program-length ads than mimic talk shows or investigative consumer reports. The FTC claims some infomercials dupe viewers into thinking they're watching an actual program; in one case, a diet-product company called Nu-Day Enterprises was cited for using an ersatz newscast to promote the "discovery" of the company's weight-loss program.

Advertisers' efforts to crowd into the space reserved for legitimate articles and entertainment programs aren't new, of course. Magazine "advertorials"—ad inserts that look like a publication's news columns—have been around since at least the 1930s, when Life published one for a clothing manufacturer.

Infomercials, which generated $250 million in advertising for TV stations in 1991, began proliferating in 1986, the year the FCC deregulated commercial time limits.

And for decades, the guilty little secret in the newspaper business has been that many papers carry specialty sections travel, real-estate, automotive, bridal, food, and so forth that are produced in close cooperation with their advertisers, if not by the advertisers themselves. (The Washington Post labels all of its advertising supplements as such and maintains a strict division between its editorial sections and advertisers, according to Robert G. Kaiser, The Post's managing editor).

But with many print and broadcast companies facing difficult times, blurring seems to be occurring with greater frequency.

Major corporations, such as AB Volvo and General Motors Corp.'s Saturn division, have begun to air "documercials," full-length, paid programs that look like TV documentaries, but in fact are extended image ads created by their sponsors. Unlike most infomercials, documercials don't ask viewers to take out their credit cards and buy something. Critics say the more subtle, soft-sell approach of the documercial helps disguise their true intent.

"You're not as likely to have your guard up and think, 'this is a commercial,' " said Jeffrey Bartos of the Institute for Public Representation, a public interest group at Georgetown University's law school. Documercials offer "A greater chance for deception."

Video news releases—the electronic equivalent of the press release—regularly incorporated into many legitimate newscasts, often without the source of the footage disclosed. While most video news release material is typically used as innocuous background imagery, it sometimes becomes the story itself. "NBC Nightly News," for example, never told viewers that major portions of an October report on Oliver North's book "Under Fire" were supplied by Time Warner Inc.

Time Warner produced the material—including on-camera interviews, video clips and various script elements—promote an upcoming issue of Time magazine that carried an excerpt of the book. In effect, NBC ran a video news release for Time made to look like NBC's own reporting.

Steve Friedman, executive producer of "Nightly News," concedes NBC made a mistake in not clearly identifying Time Warner's involvement. But he said the network and other TV outlets are justified in using such material when they can't otherwise obtain it through independent means. "Walter Cronkite made a career out of using NASA tape and no one said he sold out," said Friedman.

The Food and Drug Administration isn't so flip. The FDA last summer began requiring pharmaceutical companies to submit their video news releases to the agency's review, much as the companies must submit traditional marketing materials. In essence, the FDA wants to make sure video news releases for prescription drugs aren't skirting the agency's stringent advertising disclosure guidelines by passing themselves off as news.

Self-promotional reports crop up as news on many major-market TV stations, including those in the Washington area. The practice seems to be most in evidence during "sweeps" months, the crucial ratings periods. For example, WRC-TV, Channel 4, has aired "behind-the-scenes" stories on "The Cosby Show" and "L.A. Law"—programs WRC carries during prime time. Said WRC News Director Kris Ostrowski, "Everyone has their own definition of what constitutes news."

Infomercials are spreading to radio. In several cities, according to the FTC, call-in shows that offer counseling from financial advisers are nothing more than ads purchased by the advisers to tout their own products and services. Disclosure is often limited. So far, the federal government has not moved to stop the practice.

NBC in November aired a program called 'Jock Spots,' a show about the making of TV commercials featuring athletes. Viewers got a behind-the-scenes look at Jimmy Conners going through his paces for Nuprin aspirin, and a look at how other spots for Nike Inc., Coca-Cola Co., Hanes Cos. and other advertisers are created. During commercial breaks—viola!—some of the very same spots popped up again.

An NBC spokesman said in an interview that the program did not violate the network's policy against giving favorable editorial treatment to attract sponsors. But a second spokesman later said that a producer of the program "misinterpreted" the policy by discussing advertising with the program's would-be subjects. Either way, the Texas attorney general is looking into the matter to determine whether "Jock Spots" violated the state's Deceptive Trade Practices Act by disguising ads as informational programming.

Whether a quid pro quo exists may be beside the point. Some observers say even the perception that a publication or broadcaster has lowered its standards to sell an ad damages the company's credibility.

Blurring also can amount to a kind of economic censorship, said Hon Collins, a law professor at Catholic University of America, who views the phenomena with alarm. "If we allow the content of more programs to become more functionally commercial," said Collins, "what we are saying to advertisers is that you can buy something that you couldn't buy before. . . . Editorial decisions that once were less dependent on business concerns now are more dependent." Essentially, advertisers are limiting the range of opinions that can be expressed on television, he said.

For example, Collins points to "the takeover' of children's programming by advertisers. CBS in December aired a Christmas special narrated by McDonald's Corp.'s Ronald McDonald character and sponsored by McDonald's. Fox Broadcasting Co. has announced plans to air an animated show built around Chester Cheetah, a cartoon character created by Frito-Lay Inc. to pitch its Cheetos snacks. And Kraft General Foods Inc. reportedly is considering a syndicated program starring the cartoon symbol of its macaroni-and-cheese dinner.

"Children aren't likely to hear a lot about good nutrition on those programs" when the programs are controlled by companies with vested interests, Collins said.

It's certainly true, as advertisers like Sears suggest, that Americans are relatively sophisticated when it comes to distinguishing ads from news or entertainment, especially when marketers spend $130 billion a year on advertising. But both the sophistication of consumers and the overload of competing messages may be reasons in themselves for advertisers to push the boundaries.

Consider Newsweek's recent blur. The magazine (which is owned by The Washington Post Co.) "celebrated" the 20th anniversary of Disney World by publishing a special issue about the theme park. Yet Newsweek's 3.2 million subscribers, and the thousands more who saw it on sale on newsstands or received it inserted in a Sunday edition of The Washington Post, weren't explicitly told that it was a 64-page promotion bought and paid for by Walt Disney Co.

Instead, a cover line above the Newsweek name notes that the issue was "From the Publisher of Newsweek," a non-distinction at best, given that Newsweek itself is also from its publisher. A boxed note on page three indicates that "the editorial staff of Newsweek magazine did not participate" in the magazine's preparation, leaving open the question of who was involved.

Why didn't Newsweek label the Disney magazine a "special advertising supplement" or "advertorial," as the American Society of Magazine Editors specifies in its guidelines concerning such projects? "That wouldn't have been consistent with our objectives and those of the Disney people," said Newsweek Publisher Peter W. Eldredge. "The Disney people didn't want to see that on the cover."

Newsweek turned down a similar 64-page "contract publishing" magazine for Disney back in the palmy pre-recession days of 1988. The magazine later reported that Time Inc. eventually accepted the job, six weeks after Time magazine had run a laudatory cover story on the company. Newsweek ran its own upbeat cover on Disney in May 1989, after which Newsweek permitted Disney to use the cover and story in its promotional efforts.

But all that may be Mickey Mouse compared to what may be coming soon to a broadcast station or cable system near you. From the people who bring you the Home Shopping Network comes Home Shopping Network Entertainment. The concept: a 24-hour-day channel consisting entirely of . . . infomercials.

Benetton Ads: Clashing Colors

JACQUELINE TRESCOTT

W hen a baby is pulled from a woman's womb and held up for inspection, the usual response of the parents is instant love. But what if a sportswear manu-facturer chooses the same special, albeit messy, moment, with the baby still covered with blood and mucus, to advertise its wares?

When parents raise their children to celebrate their own racial identity and to admire the differences in other people, they look for images to reflect that diversity. But what happens when a magazine advertisement uses a smiling white girl with ringlets and a sullen black boy with his hair twisted into horns, and the company sponsoring the ad claims it is a statement of racial harmony?

Benetton, the Italian sportswear company, has again ignited a heated discussion over family, racial, sexual and religious images. Three of the seven ads in its new $3.5 million campaign have drawn boisterous criticism, and, in a number of cases, have been rejected by national magazines. Some critics are crying improper, disgust-ing and—in the case of an ad depicting a nun and priest kissing—sacrilegious. Other critics, examining the black-white advertisement, see an alarming retreat to the time when black images were often symbols of evil, foolishness and servility.

"I think we are a society that is progressive and pluralistic but along strictly defined lines," says Peter Fressola, director of communications for Benetton North America. "Certain images and certain messages are appropriate only in certain contexts, and the context in which they are deemed acceptable is arbitrary and sometimes based on knee-jerk values."

Once again there is debate over the fuzzy line of proprietorship of these images. It's fine for Keenen Ivory Wayans or Richard Pryor to suggest imperfections within black society, the argument usually goes, but does Oliviero Toscani, an Italian photographer, have the right to repeat negative images? "Toscani is looking to dispel the stereotype by showing it," says Fressola. "Perhaps that is a bit over-intellectual. I am not trying to be condescending to the critics, but he took an intellectual approach, which considering the power of an image and the lack of copy accompa-nying, was a risky venture," says Fressola.

Benetton, which calls its campaign "United Colors of Benetton" as a nod to its sportswear's colors as well as its multiethnic models, has been recognized as a promoter of racial diversity. The company seemed to set itself apart by acknowledging the color differences among black, Latino and Asian people and by avoiding the use of models who prompted a guessing game as to whether the blacks were black or not. In addition, Benetton drew approval from consumers because it used the same advertisements worldwide, sending a firm message that diversity of color should be celebrated.

"It is an unfortunate misunderstanding," says Fressola of the current flap. He says he has received a few letters from customers. "It was not our intention to go back on what we stood for." All the creative work is done by Benetton. Earlier campaigns of a black hand and a white hand cuffed together, a blitz of pastel condoms and a white baby suckling at a black breast also evoked strong reactions.

This time the Anti-Defamation League of B'nai B'rith said the company "has lost sight of simple standards of propriety. In what seems to be a campaign underscoring shock and attention-getting devices, Benetton is now trivializing, mocking, profaning and offending religious values—in this case, especially of the Catholic Church."

Some critics of the current campaign feel the trust that was built in the past has been violated. "One of the problems that Benetton has is that people are outraged that a hip company whose styles are built on fashion established by black people and by black designers" would produce an ad of two children that revived old stereotypes, says historian Fath Davis Ruffins, head of the Collection of Advertising History at the Smithsonian Institution.

Lowery Sims, the associate curator of 20th-century art at the Metropolitan Museum of Art, sees the black-white ad as a continuation of "decontextualization" of images—stealing the image and using it incorrectly and disrespectfully. "The over-40 crowd has had a very classical education, and we know what the images mean. Young people of any race or class don't have the same kind of inoculation. Institutions like MTV have done a lot to decontextualize the images and that is problematic," says Sims.

It is not Aunt Jemimna or the Gold Dust Twins, but the black-white ad generates the same alarm. Called the devil-angel ad by Benetton, the white girl has blue eyes, rosy cheeks and the stare of someone kind. The black child has a scared look, with only the whites of his eye bringing light to his face. His hair is combed into tufts that look like horns.

Mary Anne Sommers knew immediately she couldn't accept the black-white ad for Child magazine. "It is Little Black Sambo and Shirley Temple. It smacks of racism," says Sommers. She had buttressed her rejection to Benetton by complimenting the company. "I said to them, 'Let us first commend your themes of ethnic peace and harmony.' It is our concern, however, the current white-black, angel-devil theme will be perceived by our readers as reinforcing negative racial stereotypes."

On a recent trip to Italy, Sommers visited Benetton's advertising department and asked about the philosophy behind the campaign. "I told them about our racial problems. . . . I stressed we have to be really sensitive. They said they want to promote their ethnic harmony. They have a pat party line," she says.

Though he also felt Benetton had an admirable track record of successful provocative ads, Alex Mironovich, the publisher of YM, a magazine for teenage girls, thought the black-white ad was a risk not worth taking. "I thought it was a beautiful shot and two beautiful children. At first I thought the boy's hair was cat ears. But I was afraid people would misinterpret the boy's hair was horns. And there would be no one from Benetton explaining this ad as our readers looked through the magazine," he says.

Carol Smith, publisher of Parenting, thought long and hard about the ad depicting the two children. She even asked the agency that places the ads, J. Walter Thompson, what the purpose was. "I listened and I decided that based on their explanation . . . 'Our campaign is promoting unity throughout the world' . . . it was logical," says Smith. So far the ad, which is in Parenting's August issue, has prompted a few phone calls and two letters, she says. "Not angry and hostile but more, 'I am puzzled by that. What made you accept that?' "

Cosmopolitan is running the ad in its October issue. "It certainly didn't bother me. I didn't think it was evocative or provocative," says publisher Seth Hoyt.

The devil-angel ad, according to Ruffins, evokes the frequent use of the light-and-dark-skin contrast in the late 19th and early 20th centuries: "Up to 30 percent of American advertising before 1930 employed stereotypical ethnic imagery. It was very common in soap and shoe blacking . . . coffee, chocolate." Ruffins feels Benetton misstepped by not realizing "people in the United States are seeing this as part of a long history. . . . I suspect Benetton is aware of the history of negative portrayal. The company has [trod] into an area which is quite likely to lose the goodwill that was generated by its early ads."

Adding to the heat of this debate is a new study of the advertising industry. "Invisible People," by the New York City Department of Consumer Affairs, found that African Americans are only 3 percent of the people shown in national magazine ads and Asian Americans are only 1 percent.

In Benetton's newborn advertisement, a girl is pictured seconds after birth. Her umbilical cord is still attached. She is red, eyes closed tight and kicking back her legs and thrusting her arm in the first reflex outside the womb.

Reaction to this art was personal. Even Gayle Carlisle, the account executive at J. Walter Thompson, admits she was "startled."

Hoyt of Cosmopolitan conducted his own unscientific survey of women in his family and at the office. "The younger the woman, the more negative the response. The older woman who has had kids is used to the look of the newborn baby. But she would say, 'I don't know what they are trying to say,' " says Hoyt. Finally, he decided, "it just didn't seem to be the right thing at that time."

At Self, the ad was flagged by S. I. Newhouse Jr., the chairman of Conde Nast Publications, as questionable. "I thought it was very provocative and had a place in my magazine," says Alexandra Penny, publisher of Self. She thought it would fill in the same lack of memory for her readers that it did for her. "When I had my own baby I didn't remember that moment with clarity. I was delighted to see it," says Penny.

When Parenting's Smith saw the ad, she thought it was perfect for her audience. "I said, 'I never had a baby and my God!' It was very easy for us to accept because that is what we are about. Our magazine was founded on giving birth to babies and then raising them."

"The consensus here is that the American audience feels childbirth is private," says Child's Sommers. Child rejected the ad.

Parenting will run the newborn baby in December. The ad is in the August issue of Vogue and Self. Essence and Elle have rejected the ad, according to published reports.

Benetton's Fressola finds much of this hard to understand. He remembers being ordered to watch a television show on childbirth while a student at a Catholic grammar school on Staten Island. "That was allowed to be projected into our living room. Maybe the magazine sits there and that's problematic. In real life and in a movie, the scene is moving," he says.

As a self-described fallen-away Catholic, Fressola says he knew the nun-priest ad would be criticized. "Conservative Catholics would not be amused. That is regrettable," he says. The intention was to "communicate universal love, and it does transcend convention and taboo. . . . A kiss should always be appropriate." The ad was accepted by Rolling Stone for its November issue.

"Anything that gets people thinking in this day of information overload is good," says Self's Penny. "This is the kind of image in which the image is much more powerful than the explanation," says the Smithsonian's Ruffins.

And of course Benetton is pleased about the discussion. The United States accounts for 10 percent to 15 percent of the company's worldwide business; and in the past year, Fressola says, Benetton has been reorganizing to accommodate the change from selling mostly folded sweaters to hanging clothes. Benetton is not shying away from the current attention.

"If you think that is not what the company had in mind, we would be disingenuous," says Fressola.

Ad Agencies, Doing the Right Thing

PAULA SPAN

N EW YORK—"Let's play some ball," says Spike Lee in a Nike commercial that premieres tonight during the NBA Eastern Conference final.

"I ain't playin' ball with no ball-hoggin', trash-talkin', show-boatin', hip-hop-pin' homeboy from Harlem," comes the response, approximately, from a series of derisive white faces. As epithets go, these are far milder than the ones leveled in the scene from "Do the Right Thing" that inspired the ad, but network TV has its limits.

Blacks fire back. "And I ain't playin' ball with no left-footed . . . no-dribblin', golden-haired, hockey-playin' farmboy from South Dakota."

Lee, who also directed the 30-second spot, intercedes. "If we're gonna live together, we gotta play together," he says, flashing a two-fingered peace sign.

"Black and White" is part of a wavelet of new advertising that promotes racial tolerance. Though several campaigns were under discussion or in production before the violence that followed the Rodney King verdict, news coverage from Los Angeles has certainly helped speed them onto the airwaves. In its first post-L.A. issue, Advertising Age ran a front-page editorial headlined "A call to admen: Help stop riots." A trickle of ad executives are beginning to tackle the long-untouched issue.

Whether such efforts can have much effect on social attitudes and behavior is always a point of debate; it's unpredictable whether a given piece of advertising can sell deodorant, let alone stem bigotry. "Racism has been with this country for 400 years," Lee acknowledges. "You're not going to get rid of it with a 30-second commercial."

But he and others who are doing the right ads think they can at least spark thought and discussion. "It's phase one, just a starting point, to maintain awareness and reinforce people's perceptions that it's up to all of us," says Allan Corwin of the Mingo Group, a black-owned New York agency. Mingo developed the "Stop the Hate" campaign, which the Ad Council and the sponsoring Leadership Conference Education Fund will unveil next week.

The first of this current batch of ads came from Nynex Corp., one of the seven regional phone companies, and was seen April 25 on an ABC children's special about prejudice, hosted by Peter Jennings. In the spot, called "Marbles" and created by Ogilvy & Mather, "a little blue marble is minding its own business and a little yellow marble comes and bumps it," says Laurie Pollock, an O&M senior vice president. "You'd think, at the beginning, it was a game."

The marbles express anger in chirps and squeaks and—through stop-action photography—recruit reinforcements. Pretty soon, whole armies of marbles are facing off. But two bold individuals roll forward to discuss their differences, causing their comrades to cheer and intermingle, until the camera pulls back to show a globe formed by variously colored marbles. "Nynex believes communication can help bring everyone together," says a female voice-over.

Nynex had no plans to re-air the spot until Los Angeles erupted. The corporation hurriedly bought time on local newscasts in Boston and New York that weekend. A week later Sony donated time on its Jumbotron, the giant video monitor overlooking Times Square, and showed "Marbles" four times an hour, around the clock, for seven days.

The week after the L.A. unrest, New Yorkers also saw a striking series of posters blossom on 250 telephone kiosks, a pro bono effort from a small agency called Smith/Greenland. The decision to address tolerance was reached earlier this spring after conflicts between blacks and Hasidic Jews in Brooklyn's Crown Heights and reports that two black children in the Bronx had had their faces whitened with shoe polish by white teenagers. "It seemed the city was ready to explode, there was so much racial tension," says Creative Director Doug Raboy. Producing and placing the ads cost Smith/Greenland an estimated $150,000.

The posters went up as scheduled May 4, by which time they'd acquired significance beyond New York. "The sad thing is, it's a message that's always timely," Raboy says. In stark black-and-white, the posters posit life-threatening situations—emergency surgery, near-drowning—in which the rescuer is of another race. "Is that a problem?" the posters ask. So many people, churches and schools called the agency to ask for extras that the several hundred leftovers are all gone.

Much higher profile is Nike's $4 million campaign (in air time, plus close to $1 million in production costs), which Lee shot on the roof of a Los Angeles parking garage two weeks before the King verdict. "Black and White" is one of three spots hawking Nike's new basketball shoe. The other two feature Golden State Warriors star Tim Hardaway and a Spikelike sense of urban liveliness but also push the $85 Air Raid model. "Black and White," though it shows the footwear maker's logo and mentions its name (and deftly touts one of Lee's movies with the slogan "The More Colors, the Better"), is not overtly a product plug.

After the disturbances in L.A.—which Lee pointedly calls "the uprising" because "it wasn't just bedlam; it was a calculated response to the acquittal of four police officers and the miscarriage of justice"—Nike wondered whether it wanted to proceed with a commercial that took on race. It decided it did, and "Black and White" will constitute 20 percent to 25 percent of Air Raid TV advertising through August, first on the NBA playoffs, then on MTV and ESPN and prime-time network programming.

"This is something we have to deal with if we're going to move forward in this country," Lee says. "Everybody joining hands and saying, 'We are the world' ain't gonna make it."

The longest-term commitment to anti-bigotry advertising, however, will be the "Stop the Hate" public service announcements by the Ad Council, the folks who brought you Smokey Bear, "A Mind Is a Terrible Thing to Waste" and the Peace Corps' "The Toughest Job You'll Ever Love." The first two 30-second TV spots, in English and Spanish, will be shown at a press conference in Washington next week.

The press conference was to be held this week; its last-minute postponement is testament to the haste with which a multimedia campaign that had been talked about for a year, and was planned for late summer or fall, is now being rushed to completion. In the wake of urban violence, "it was speeded up tenfold," says Ad Council spokesman Brad Lynch. Sponsored by the nonprofit Leadership Conference Education Fund, it will diversify into print ads and billboards and will address many varieties of prejudice, including those against ethnicity, religion, disability and sexual orientation.

The Ad Council typically rounds up $24 million or so in donated media time and space annually for each of its campaigns, which run for years (Smokey's been around since 1945). That makes "Stop the Hate" smaller-scale than the anti-drug crusade of the Partnership for a Drug-Free America (to which it has been compared), but more intensive than any of the other new anti-bigotry entries. "TV has the unique capacity to change how people think about society and about each other," says Ralph Neas of the Leadership Conference on Civil Rights, the lobbying group related to but legally distinct from the sponsoring Education Fund. "I do believe a long-term campaign could have a positive and dramatic impact."

But there is likely to be continued debate about advertising's role in this minefield. The industry is already drawing flak—not for the first time—for helping to shape a materialistic culture that contributes to frustration and anger among those unable to buy into it. Nike, whose shoes have become staples of urban wardrobes, will launch a clothing line this summer called "Spike's Urban Jungle Gym." Retail prices will range from about $17 for a T-shirt to $250 to $300 for a wool and leather stadium jacket embroidered with some of the same phrases Lee uses in his anti-prejudice ad.

The advertising industry has also been criticized for its own racial record, both in creative output and in hiring. Only 4.7 percent of the industry's 255,000 employees in 1991 were black, according to the Bureau of Labor Statistics, and 4.1 percent were Hispanic. (Nike itself was the target, two years ago, of a boycott by the Chicago-based civil rights group PUSH, which decried its employment practices. The company, which says the boycott had no measurable effect, says its U.S. work force is now more than 18 percent minority.)

"You'd find that African Americans are embarrassingly nonexistent in the advertising business," says Fred Danzig, editor of Advertising Age and co-author of its front-page editorial. "It's certainly not what it could be."

Last summer, New York's Department of Consumer Affairs surveyed 11,000 ads from 27 magazines and found that while blacks make up 11 percent of magazine readers, only 3 percent of the models in the publications' ads were black, a proportion that had barely budged since the 1960s. (By comparison, 7.5 percent of models in television advertising are African American, probably as a result of union contracts with affirmative action provisions.) Consumer Affairs Commissioner Mark Green asked nearly 50 ad agencies and publications sign a "visual to integration pledge," which carried no legal force but committed them to work to redress the imbalance. "They ignored us as efficiently as they ignore minorities in their advertising," Green says.

Still, the argument persists that a business whose 30-second spots are frequently more provocative and arresting than the programming that surrounds them must have a contribution to make. "Advertising usually lags behind public moods," says Danzig of Ad Age. "It waits to see what's happening and then seizes upon it . . . Social upheaval is something advertising sees now and recognizes that it has to get involved in. We're really talking about the future of the country."

The Rise and Fall of Saatchi & Saatchi

GLENN FRANKEL

Charles and Maurice Saatchi liked to tell their colleagues the story of the blind beggar in Central Park who sat on the sidewalk with a sign that read: "I am blind."

One fine morning in early spring, an advertising copywriter passed by on his way to work, bent down and wrote something on the sign. When he stopped by that evening and asked how the day had gone, the blind man replied, "Fantastic. Never done so well. What did you write on the sign?"

The copywriter replied, "I added a few words to make it read: It is spring and I am blind."

Even a beggar needs an adman, or so the Saatchis believed. During two frenetic decades of hyperactive deal-making, they set about, to make themselves admen to the world—nothing less than the biggest, boldest, most creative and most profitable advertising and marketing agency that ever existed.

Or, as they themselves put it in one annual report: "It's good to be big, it's better to be good, but it's best to be both."

For a brief moment, some would say, Saatchi & Saatchi Co. was both. Starting only 20 years ago, Charles and Maurice Saatchi transformed their six-man agency on a London side street into the largest advertising conglomerate in the world. Just as the Beatles took American popular music, refined it and brought it back across the Atlantic, so too did the Saatchis lead the British conquest of Madison Avenue with a quintessentially American weapon: the ad.

They did it by a combination of British chic and British cheek. They hit London with a series of stylish, hard-edged ad campaigns—a pregnant man to advertise family planning, a pack of lemmings to illustrate the dangers of smoking, a long unemployment line with the slogan "Labor Isn't Working" to promote Britain's Conservative Party—shaking up an industry that despite its worship of innovation had grown stale and self-satisfied.

By 1979 they were the biggest ad agency in Britain. By 1986 after a corporate buying spree, they were the biggest in the world, operating on five continents and servicing more than 50 of the world's 100 largest companies. Among their clients: Toyota, Honda, Procter & Gamble, British Airways, Colgate Palmolive and Live Aid.

"Charles saw the world as a big supermarket—you go in and buy what you want off the shelf," says a former senior officer at the company, one of many who left on less-than-friendly terms, yet speaks of the brothers with a wary affection. "Everything is for sale. The only question is can you afford the price." Things had to get out of hand—and inevitably they did.

Among the corporate refuse of the '80s from Boesky to Milken to Campeau to Trump, the Saatchis stand out for many reasons. Perhaps the Saatchis were victim to their own hype, believed too deeply in their own infallibility. Meanwhile a chastened stock market caught up with the incredible game of buy and buy and buy with borrowed money that was the key to their breathtaking annual growth in sales and profits.

Their tale is in large part the story of Britain in the era of Margaret Thatcher, when entrepreneurs armed with cash and insouciance set out to reassert British influence in a changed world. Their climb was one of the most swift, their fall one of the most sudden.

The Saatchis helped pioneer the concept of globalization. Thanks to computers, satellite television and films, they reasoned, markets were shrinking, national identities slipping. If everyone was buying the same products, then everyone could be sold in the same way. And a few large, fearless corporations could practically run the world.

Neither of the Saatchis would speak for this article, and many of their closest associates and former colleagues insisted upon anonymity. Once the darlings of the press, the Saatchis now believe the press has turned vicious and unfair. Yet like those former associates who parted on bad terms, journalists remain fascinated, even when appalled, by the brothers and the world they built.

"They had a terribly low boredom threshold and a momentum they felt they had to maintain—they didn't want to do this year what they did last year," says financial journalist Ivan Fallon, author of, "The Brothers," the definitive British book on the brothers' rise.

"You say your bottom line is to become the biggest in Britain, and then in Europe and then in the world, and before you've even arrived there, you're asking, 'What do we do after that?' You keep forging a philosophy to fit whatever pleases you. And all the time you're succeeding, you reinforce your own view that you're infallible. They came to utterly believe that there were no ceilings for them."

Advertising may have been an American invention, but the British have always been masters at image making. A few weeks ago they celebrated the 50th anniversary of one of the most humiliating defeats in their history, the evacuation at Dunkirk, as if it were a triumph, a fable of small boats and brave men. Three generations of Britons believed the myth. They also believed that the gruff, steely voice that entreated them to stand tall during the darkest hours of World War II belonged to Winston Churchill, perhaps Britain's greatest image maker, rather than to the actor who read Churchill's lines over the wireless.

In the 1970s, the British had their chance to assert those skills anew. Like Washington after the Cold War, Madison Avenue had grown uncomfortable with its own vast powers, wary of its own instincts. For all of its explosive growth, the advertising business was still something of a cottage industry—a few giants, but lots of small agencies, and not much attention to bottom lines.

Enter Charles and Maurice. "They arrived at a time when rising American domination had been accompanied by a pervasive blandness and repetition in the actual creative work of advertising," wrote Robert Heller, editor of Management Today. "It gave British agencies, mostly new, the chance to become the Greeks to the Romans of Madison Avenue. A rolling tide of brilliant British advertising reset the standard and the style.

"The Saatchis shared in the flood. The difference was that their ambitions were Roman in scope. They wanted an empire."

The Saatchis were born in Baghdad, the sons of an Iraqi Jewish merchant who fled the country with his young family in the late 1940s. Their place of birth was a fact the Saatchis, keen to be seen as insiders, sought to conceal as they made their way up the mountain of British business.

Maurice went to the London School of Economics while Charles, bored, gifted and restless, skipped college and went directly into the ad business as a copywriter. He made few friends, fewer allies, but gathered a small circle of devotees. Eventually he decided that the only way to get where he wanted to go was to open his own shop. And he persuaded his younger brother to join him.

The Saatchis launched themselves with a typically self-engineered attention-getter—a two-page ad in the London Sunday Times titled "Why I Think It's Time for a New Kind of Advertising." It was bold and arrogant and it cost them a quarter of their start-up money.

They soon became London's hottest ad shop, a place for talented, difficult people. And the most talented and difficult, friends say, was Charles Saatchi himself.

William Muirhead, who now is chairman and joint chief executive of the original Saatchi ad agency on London's Charlotte Street, recalls his first glimpse of Charles Saatchi's witheringly high standards. Muirhead had been dispatched to a client with an ad he had never seen before and didn't quite understand. The client loved it, however, and Muirhead came back pleased.

Charles was not. "Charley said, 'It's crap,' and he ripped it into little pieces." says Muirhead. "I had to call back the client and say, 'You know that ad you really loved? Well, we've done something even better.' That's how Charley operated."

Friends say Charles Saatchi bullied everyone—his clients, his employees, but most of all his younger brother. Now 47, Charles remains a harsh, relentless, profane, reclusive, intensely competitive man with a take-no-prisoners approach— the adman as existential hero. Maurice, now 44, is a charming, quieter but no less assertive person, the ego to his brother's id.

To outsiders they were Rambo and The Nerd, a carefully honed brother act. Charles had the restless energy, the impulses and the intuition; Maurice, the know how to translate the raw energy and ideas into a strategy for the '80s.

Charles was the spark, but Maurice handled the cash. He was the one who convinced London's tightfisted financial markets that an ad agency was a good investment, one worth backing with millions in share issues. And while Charles would skulk and hide from clients, Maurice would turn on the charm.

Between the two, friends recall, there was chemistry and there was terror. Sometimes there was blood as well when Charles lit upon Maurice. "They are Cain and Abel," says a former friend. "You have to remember that Cain loved his brother.

"Even in a hysterical rage, Charley could be very funny. I can remember him one day, red in the face, screaming at Maurice: 'I can't believe you came from the same womb as me.' "

Friends say today Charles still brings his pet schnauzer to work each morning, still plays board games like chess and Monopoly as if they were life-and-death struggles, still dominates the psyche of the company with his brooding presence.

But it is at most a spiritual presence—most employees these days say they never see Charles Saatchi, who has long made a point of avoiding direct contact with clients and the press. After Saatchi & Saatchi went public in 1977, Charles never attended a shareholders meeting. There has been only one official photo in the past decade.

Both brothers tend to hover on the edge London's social scene, a world friends say they have never felt part of.

Maurice is married to Josephine Hart, whose career is as a West End theatrical producer. While less reclusive than Charles, friends say, Maurice prefers the privacy of the vast English garden he has designed for the multi-million-dollar country home where he and his family live in Sussex, south of London.

Charles's marriage to Doris Dibley, an American and former ad copywriter, broke up three years ago, but he still maintains houses in London's Mayfair area and in Long Island, still pursues the art collection he and Doris initiated together. It is now considered one of the world's largest collections of contemporary art—worth more than $100 million, by some estimates—and a small portion is displayed in a stark, white-walled former warehouse turned gallery in north London. Most of it, like Charles himself, remains behind closed doors, sealed off from view.

Among the best and brightest hired by the Saatchis in those early days of the agency were Tim Bell, who started as media director and ended up managing the day-to-day operations of the agency for the increasingly remote Charles; and Martin Sorrell, who did the same on the financial end. Sorrell and Maurice Saatchi together created a management system that monitored the company's financial condition daily and imposed rigid budgets on its new acquisitions yet allowed the new purchases wide-ranging autonomy in conducting business. The system impressed financiers in the City, London's version of Wall Street. They provided the cash that fueled the new acquisitions and made Saatchis the City's top glamour stock.

Both Bell and Sorrell left the Saatchis with bitterness, and their departures are considered among the key reasons for the company's subsequent decline. Sorrell bought a small firm, known as WPP, and began acquiring larger companies until last year he surpassed Saatchi as the world's largest advertising group. Bell has opened his own firm to develop corporate strategies and lobbying campaigns. He is also considered one of Margaret Thatcher's most intimate admirers. Yet friends say Bell, despite the rancor, stiff stands in awe of Charles Saatchi.

"Tim was great on a surfboard," says Muirhead, "but Charley made the waves."

The Thatcher account in many ways was the key to the Saatchis' reputation and acceptance. They won it in 1978 in typical fashion, according to Fallon—neither brother showed up for the meeting at the Conservative Party's central office. But Gordon Reece, then the party's communications director and a member of Thatcher's inner circle, was eager to import American-style techniques to help defeat the ruling Labor Party and he believed the Saatchis could help him do it.

The best ads were sharp and bitter—a slick, fast-moving television spot depicting everything in Britain moving in reverse, and the famous poster campaigns. One depicted an unemployment line above the simple message "Labor Isn't Working"; another showed a young black man with the line, "Labor says he's black—Tories say he's British."

The ads were aimed not at specific policies or issues but feelings, what Bell called "the emotional meaning" of voting for Thatcher. Labor was caught off guard—every time its leaders criticized the ads, the result predictably was more publicity, which made the Saatchis and the Conservatives look even more clever, and Labor more clumsy. Thatcher won a substantial electoral victory in 1979 and the Saatchi legend was born.

But by then the Saatchis were already moving on to bigger battles. Clever ad-making was not enough—they also wanted to be known as the top marketing company. And so the Saatchis had started buying. The first big acquisition was Compton in 1975, a blue-chip ad agency that was twice as big as they were. The Saatchis convinced Compton's owners that the two companies should merge. They even added Compton's name to their own. But within a few days, the headline in Campaign, the London ad weekly with a direct pipeline to Charles, read "Saatchi swallows up the Compton Group." Many of Compton's senior managers left quickly.

After that, says a former employee, the pattern was established. "Charley and Maurice would tell the prospective sellers anything they wanted to hear, invent an ideal version of what life would be like after the deal was signed. And afterward we would just do exactly whatever it was we wanted."

It was the biggest acquisitions binge the London stock market has ever seen. By 1985 the Saatchis were buying companies, most of them American, at the rate of one a month. In the spring of 1986 they paid $100 million for the New York ad firm of Backer & Spielvogel, the largest sum ever paid for an ad agency. A month later they smashed that record by paying nearly $500 million for Ted Bates Worldwide, the third largest agency in the United States.

Bates was the deal that made Saatchi the world's biggest agency, yet it also marked the beginning of the end. Analysts said they paid far too much for Bates and bought a company whose conservative approach to the business was the virtual antithesis of their own. The deal also cost them big amounts of business from major clients upset that Saatchi had grown so large its many little arms were servicing rivals. Procter & Gamble, the Saatchis' biggest client, Colgate-Palmolive and Warner Lambert reportedly removed more than $300 million in business after the Bates deal.

There were other problems. Searching for new worlds to conquer, Charles and Maurice decided that the consultancy business was as ripe for acquisition as the advertising business. As usual they formed a theory to justify the instinct—the Saatchis would become a full-service company that could offer clients not only advertising, but public relations, research, even financial services.

Beginning in 1984, they bought a dozen small agencies, only to discover that their expertise in advertising did not extend to the specialized world of consultancies. The new agencies proved a big drain on corporate profits.

The 1987 British general election was also a minor disaster—Saatchi still designed the ad campaign for the Conservatives but played a much reduced role. The brothers resisted Thatcher's plea that Bell, who had just left the firm, be hired on as a consultant to run the campaign. As Thatcher's lead in the polls melted away, she grew more and more panicky and increasingly inclined to blame her predicament on the Saatchi campaign, which looked lack-luster compared with the crisp new Labor Party ads produced by Hugh Hudson, director of the movie "Chariots of Fire." Hudson's ads personalized the campaign and portrayed Labor leader Ned Kinnock in the same heroic terms as the protagonists of the film, and included the inspiring Kinnock lines about his coal-mining ancestors that U.S. presidential candidate Joseph Biden later got caught plagiarizing.

Unbeknown to the Saatchis, Thatcher started quietly consulting with another agency, Young & Rubicam, then secretly called in Bell. When it was over, less than a month later, and the Conservatives had won another landslide, the Saatchis accused Bell of attempting to undermine them. Weeks of recriminations followed—insiders say Charles Saatchi phoned prominent newspaper editors and businessmen to accuse Bell of drug addiction and criminal wrongdoing—before both sides agreed to an uneasy truce. The brothers formally resigned the Conservative account a few months later. Thatcher, Conservative insiders say, was fed up with the Saatchis.

By then Charles and Maurice were adrift in even deeper waters. They tried to buy Midland Bank, one of Britain's largest, then Hill Samuel, a smaller merchant bank. In both instances they were rebuffed by the owners but word got out around the City, whose financial mandarins viewed the bids with awe and anger.

"Here they had just paid a ridiculous sum for Bates, had had difficulties with consulting, and the next thing you know, Maurice wants to buy a bank," says Emma Hill, an analyst with Wertheim & Co. in New York.

The drain on cash flow of the massive acquisitions began to eat into profits. After Sorrell left in 1986, the financial monitoring system fell into disrepair.

There was also a deep sense of alienation among newly acquired employees in the United States, where people never really caught Saatchi fever. Clients too sometimes felt unloved or ignored. Charles and Maurice increasingly removed themselves from day-to-day operations and turned them over to subordinates who were said to lack Sorrell's brilliance and Bell's feel-good style of inspiration.

After the Midland bank fiasco, investors grew wary and the share price of Saatchi stock tumbled. At the same time, corporate spending on advertising was shrinking as British interest rates soared and sales tailed off. Suddenly the dream was over.

It ended officially last October when Maurice announced that the brothers were relinquishing their roles as joint chief executives and appointing French business-man Robert Louis-Dreyfus to sort out the mess. He has been trying to sell off the consultancies, keep investors from bailing out and ward off the takeover art-ists who are hungrily eyeing the bloody remains like birds of prey after a massacre. Last week Saatchi sold, for only $2 million in cash, plus royalty payments, a Chicago legal consultancy called Peterson that it paid $116 million for only three years ago.

Louis-Dreyfus has quickly forced out a number of the brothers' longtime associates and allies and installed his own people. He has also lowered the com-pany's sights. The new Saatchi image, says an insider hired by the new team, is that of "a company run by mature adults rather than a bunch of young creative guys playing with someone else's money."

The brothers each have accepted a 30 percent cut in their salaries. Maurice is still actively involved but appears to outsiders to have been reduced to a front man, accompanying Louis-Dreyfus when he goes to see fund managers to plead for more time and money, and taking senior clients to lunch. "His name is over the door," says an insider, "and he's not going to walk away from the mess."

Charles still plots and dreams, friends say, but is more reclusive than ever and often deeply depressed. They say he attributes the blame for his downfall to others, never to himself. "Charley is never wrong, he is never ever wrong," says a former associate. "It's the investors' fault for getting cold feet. Or it's Maurice's fault for failing to replace Tim or Martin."

Some of the glory remains. Bill Muirhead, the Saatchi loyalist who runs the original Charlotte Street agency, points out that his shop is still the biggest in Britain and last year was voted tops in the business by clients in an independent survey. It won more creative awards than any other firm and was the first agency to place a billboard on the eastern side of the Berlin Wall.

But even as Muirhead recites those achievements, a certain weariness creeps around the edges of his optimism. "It's a very competitive business," he says. "You've got to have an edge all the time and you can't stop competing, because once you stop, you're dead. I don't worry about the big guys. I worry about the guys who are just opening their doors. They're hungry and they want the money and they're ready to take the risks."

Sometimes the nerve endings show. When Paul Cowan, an accounts manager, and seven other staffers left last month and opened their own shop, boasting that they were the true "keepers of the Saatchi creative flame," Saatchis fired back with derogatory comments in the press and threats of lawsuits. It all looked rather heavy-handed and it contributed to another drop in the share price.

What it all comes down to is not just the loss of money, but of something almost as valuable in the ad business—aura and mystique. Without those two characteristics, the Saatchis are just another pair of hustling admen, Supermen who lost their capes.

"The Saatchi magic was a huge plus factor, and now it's gone," says author Fallon. "These were the people who could do no wrong. But just as the gilt has gone off the Thatcher image, it has gone off Saatchi image as well. And they themselves are terribly conscious of it.

"They still have basically a very good advertising business. But is that enough?"

Mass Media Effects 13

The Kids Who Laughed Till It Hurt

CHRISTINE SPOLAR

I t was a split-second whoop on Martin Luther King Day, but it has been echoing for weeks in the schools, the media, and the black and Jewish communities here.

A group of students from Castlemont High, mostly African American and Latino, went to see "Schindler's List" as part of a class trip. About an hour into the matinee at the Grand Lake Theater, a boy shouted as a young Jewish woman was slaughtered on screen.

"Oh," he said, "that was cold."

Laughter followed. A couple of dozen other moviegoers—some whose family members had died in the Holocaust—besieged the theater manager to complain.

Suddenly, the lights came up in the theater. Owner Allen Michaan walked out and asked for all Castlemont students to go to the lobby. Too many other patrons had complained, he said later, that the students talked and laughed throughout the movie and, in particular, laughed at murder.

As the 73 students walked out, some of the patrons, obviously angry, gave a standing ovation.

No teacher or student expected anything more to happen. In the insular world of Castlemont High, the episode was chalked up as a minor disaster, and the rest of the holiday outing, including a trip to an ice rink, was canceled.

Days later, the school and the students found that the whoop had a formidable echo.

The Oakland Tribune published a short account of what had happened as a front-page parable about racial and religious insensitivity. The story, reported two days after the trip, did not quote students but portrayed the "horror of many in the audience" as students "seemed to laugh and applaud at scenes depicting Nazi atrocities."

Radio talk shows used the story to stoke outrage: Were the students antisemites? Were the other moviegoers racists? The kids at Castlemont made the news on CNN and the opinion pages of the San Francisco papers and the New York Times.

What seemed innocent enough to the students—"We always talk out in movies," said one—became a symbol for something wrong with both Castlemont and American race relations.

Castlemont High was barraged with phone calls after the initial news story. Dozens of letters were sent to the school and the theater. Teachers who had chaperoned the students were criticized for allowing them to act up. Others complained that the students had been treated unfairly and bore the brunt of racist reactions.

Those letters, piled up in a stack in the principal's file cabinet, reveal anger from a large cross-section of people who think they know what happened that day at the Grand Lake. In some cases, the letter writers were at the matinee. Many were not.

In one, a man who identified himself as Jewish labeled the theater manager a Nazi and charged he practiced a double standard with teenagers.

In another, a man chastised the "ill-behaved group" for its manners: "What a strange way to commemorate Martin Luther King's birthday, by insulting the memory of Holocaust victims."

Megan Hughes is not Jewish, but she had gone to the movie with a friend who is. She was irritated at first by the talking. When she heard laughter, she bounded for the lobby.

"We didn't know [their] race, their past, why they were there," she said later about the young people making noise. "We knew nothing but that they laughed at cruelty. . . . People watching the movie still felt the pain caused by them laughing. It didn't matter what their intentions were. It was still incredibly painful to sit there and hear it."

One letter writer, an African American, questioned whether the teenagers would have been thrown out if they were white. Another, who also identified himself as an African American, derided black leaders, including the teachers, for not demanding that the students take full responsibility for their actions.

Whatever the students meant by their laughter—and whatever the audience meant by its applause—became distorted by racial suspicions. Perceptions seemed to override what otherwise might have been taken as ordinary teenage behavior and adult response; assumptions shaded the truth.

Mark Rader was the teacher who planned the trip. He suggested the movie to the students, he said, as a way to think about racial injustice and discrimination on Martin Luther King Day. Perhaps he should have known better when his students, age 14 to 18, begged instead to see "House Party III."

If Rader's first mistake was insisting on the documentary-like movie, he admits his second was one of omission. He didn't lecture about the Holocaust before the film. Some students later said they weren't taught about the Holocaust. Others said they had a seminar years ago in sixth grade. Other teachers, when they found out how Rader prepared the students, were outraged at what they called negligence.

From all accounts, Rader stumbled again in planning the trip. He had trouble finding chaperons for the noon showing, but he finally found four. The class arrived late at Grand Lake Theater, which had drawn a near-capacity crowd.

Rader said he arranged payment and seating by phone the previous week. No one in theater management remembered Rader's call. As Rader and theater manager Roger Brown tried to work out their differences, both were agitated. The students—who trooped in before the other patrons waiting in line—had to be split up among the 850 seats, and mostly in the back of the theater.

Rader spent much of the first hour of the movie trying to figure out who was where. He found students in the bathroom. He dragged them out of other movies at the multiplex: "Grumpy Old Men" and "The Pelican Brief." He saw them at the candy counter.

Rader ended up writing an apology to other teachers about how he had prepared for the trip. Within his one-page letter, he called his leadership "a major contributing factor" in what happened inside the theater. But he challenged those who excused the students and those who thought that "there was nothing wrong with our actions as a group."

"This whole thing has pained me," Rader said. "Everybody's trying to make excuses for everything. What I want the kids to know is no matter what, we have to take responsibility for ourselves."

Tanya Dennis, the school's dean and another chaperon, said she doesn't excuse the student's behavior but has a different take on what may have been going on in the theater. These are kids who see violence every day, Dennis said, and who see violence too often as entertainment. They treated "Schindler's List" like any other movie, she said.

"These kids are bombarded with violence. We have fed our kids a culture of violence. What they did had nothing to do with black-and-white issues," Dennis said. "It had everything to do with how they deal with violence. That's the bigger issue."

But was there something racially insensitive about what happened? She, like many at the school, believes the media jumped on a stereotype of tension between Jews and African Americans, and made the situation out to be something that it wasn't.

"I don't think what happened there was a racial thing," said Dennis, who is African American. "I think it was a lot of kids who didn't want to see a movie. And I think there were a lot of people in the movie theater who didn't want to watch a movie with a bunch of teenagers. But the reality is once the kids acted up, I'm sure there were some people in that theater saying: There go those black kids again."

Grand Lake Theater owner Allen Michaan had never stopped a movie in the 20 years he's been running movie houses. But he regularly throws people out of his theater when other patrons complain that they won't stop talking.

"To me, this is nothing more than a debate over proper behavior at a theater. When the media got hold of it, it got all bent out of proportion," said Michaan, who is Jewish.

"One of the things the media read into this is that the kids were antisemitic. I never thought that was true. . . . I think they were bored. . . . On the other hand, I hear some of the students have accused us of being racists for removing them from the theater. I find that an outrageous defense for what essentially I see as a problem of theater etiquette."

Castlemont students later held a news conference to say they were sorry. The school, contacted by both African American and Jewish community leaders, arranged for seminars on the African diaspora caused by racism and then on the Holocaust. Gov. Pete Wilson commended the school for turning the bad publicity into a reason to instruct.

In all, 11 news stories and two editorials were published in the Tribune about the Castlemont moviegoers. Along with radio and newspaper coverage, television stations broadcast news updates on the incident. Essayist Ishmael Reed wrote about the controversy. The New York Times published a column about it. Director Steven Spielberg was quoted as saying he wasn't mad at the students and he found it "fascinating" that "a lot of our kids are so desensitized to violence."

Castlemont students certainly learned a lesson; they're just trying to figure out what it was.

Tracy Wilson, 15, and Danielle Lytle, 14, sat down in a hallway and talked about what they saw happen at the Grand Lake Theater and what everybody said happened. They said no one really reported their side of the story.

They can't believe the incident made the news. It was the kind of thing that happens all the time in violent movies, they said. People who see something bad in the laughter don't know teenagers, they said.

"We were just expressing ourselves—to relieve the tension, to do what we do in movies," Tracy said. "We're used to going to a movie theater and just talking. The media tried to turn this into an antisemitic thing, but it wasn't that."

"Some people said we were too young for the movie, but I knew about the Holocaust in sixth grade," said Danielle. "We could understand. . . . What I didn't like was it was a three-hour movie—in black-and-white—with no credits or anything in the beginning. When a teenager goes to a movie, you want to see something interesting."

But how could they laugh if they knew how people died in Holocaust?

"That's just it," Tracy said, a bit exasperated. "It wasn't like people were laughing because people were dying. The woman who got shot fell funny and people just laughed. I mean we react differently in school than we do outside school."

Both girls allowed that they were just waiting out the movie until they could do what they really hoped for that holiday: ice skating.

"When it started you could just see a candle," Tracy said. "I mean, what is that? That's not interesting. . . . I think the teachers should have told us more. And I don't think they should have taken us there on Martin Luther King Day. No way. None of us is Jewish."

"I felt we could have seen something more on Martin Luther King," Danielle said. "Why not 'Malcolm X'?"

Tracy pointed out that their teachers "thought it would be good because Martin Luther King died for civil rights and these people were in trouble because people discriminated against them too. . . . But I tell you I was disappointed. It was my first time to go ice skating."

"But it's like taking us to see 'Malcolm X' during Hanukah," Danielle said.

Tracy said that when she got to the theater, she thought some of the other people were not happy to see them. "When we got to the theater, I thought some of the people acted as if they were scared of us. I saw people walking away. . . . I guess the stereotype is that black people will steal. . . .

"You know, you hear you can't trust white people. I hear a lot of bad things about white people and I think I can't stand white people. But then I know all white people aren't the same, because my mom's best friend is white and I put her out of that [category] because she isn't like what I think about white people."

So what did they learn this Martin Luther King Day?

"That the media will blow things up," said Tracy.

"That racism is growing more and more every day," said Danielle.

TV Violence Escalates Sharply

ELLEN EDWARDS

Just when the people who run the television industry thought they had finally conquered the issue of violence on the air, a new study saying it was up 41 percent from two years ago delivered a huge whap to their collective heads.

The study done by the Center for Media and Public Affairs, a nonprofit research organization here, and funded by the Harry Frank Guggenheim Foundation came under instantaneous and intense fire, particularly from the broadcast networks.

The center monitored six Washington broadcast stations (the ABC, NBC, CBS, PBS and Fox affiliates and independent Channel 20) and four cable networks (HBO, USA, TBS and MTV) for 18 hours on Thursday, April 7, reviewing not only all entertainment programming but ads, promos and news shows. The researchers counted 2,605 total scenes of violence; of those, scenes the researchers defined as containing "serious violence" totaled 1,411, up 67 percent from 1992.

Scenes of violence in prime-time programming, which has been the focus of so much attention both on Capitol Hill and in Hollywood, were virtually unchanged.

"The point of a day-in-the-life study," said center co-director Robert Lichter, "is to show how much is out there that people ignore. It is entirely plausible that the networks could hold down violence in prime-time fiction and jack it up in other places. . . . The industry tried to cut violence where it was most visible."

"This is an outrage," said Martin D. Franks, senior vice president of CBS. "There is a legitimate debate on television violence, but this report does not deserve to be a part of it." Referring to some of the network fare on the evening of April 7, Franks asked, "What score does 'Christy' get? What score does 'Seinfeld' get?"

Network representatives were particularly upset that news programming, which has always been exempt from the debate, was included and that the results showed more than a 200 percent increase in violence in that category. April 7, by chance, marked the start of the chaos in Rwanda.

"There is an enormous problem mixing in the news programming," said Richard Cotton, executive vice president and general counsel of NBC. "Is he really saying that reports from Bosnia and Rwanda should be assessed as negative if they contain some violence? The implication is that if you get violence, that's bad—there's no distinction.

"If what he is trying to say is that ads are more violent, that syndicated programming is more violent, that programming on local stations is more violent, that local news is more violent, why doesn't he come out and say that with some precision?"

Responded Lichter: "One, violence is up sharply apart from news; and two, people are beginning to worry about violence on the news. TV news coverage of murders tripled last year even though the murder rate didn't change."

ABC spokeswoman Julie Hoover said that "it was a remarkably placid evening" on her network, which aired "The Byrds of Paradise," a "Matlock" mystery and "PrimeTime Live." At the end of that program, Diane Sawyer had a conversation about reaction to the caning of Michael Fay in Singapore, but Hoover said that couldn't have been counted as violent.

Lichter, however, said that segment did count, in large part because the segment included a demonstration of caning. The licks were applied to a gymnast's vaulting horse but still were considered particularly graphic.

"I don't see how there could be any credibility in any study that only looks at one day of television," said Torie Clarke, spokeswoman for the National Cable Television Association.

It was, however, a day in which HBO, a premium cable service, showed "Batman Returns," which was counted as containing 101 violent scenes, the most of any program airing that day, and "Against the Wall," about the Attica prison uprising. Both carried advisories for violent content.

"When you look at the history of the programming we create," said HBO spokesman Richard Plepler, "we have done as much as any network to deglamorize violence."

One category that showed a 69 percent increase in violence was the promos for upcoming programs and movies. Violence in promos for TV programs was up 97 percent, Lichter said, while violence in those for theatrical movies was up more than 43 percent. The study found, and network spokesmen confirmed, that there are often two versions of the same promo—a less violent one for prime time and a more violent one for daytime and late night.

Several network representatives said the more violent promos air during the day because children are in school and the audience contains more adults.

Washington independent station Channel 20 showed more scenes of violence than any of the other stations monitored, following the pattern shown in a study earlier this year by Lichter that syndicated programming is the most violent on television. Channel 20 General Manager Dick Williams said he had not seen the study and did not want to comment.

The broadcast networks were also angry that they were being labeled as the source of much of the violence, when in fact prime-time violence stayed steady and about half of the programming during any day is the responsibility of the local affiliate.

The television industry has good reason to be concerned—the study is a follow-up to one the center made two years ago, which when published in TV Guide was one of the major triggers in the national debate on violence on television. That study was done on the first Thursday in April 1992.

Since then, Congress has become particularly involved in the issue, holding a number of high-profile hearings. Things quieted down at the end of last year when the networks and the cable industry agreed to hire outside independent monitors to review their programming beginning this fall and issue a public report card sometime next year.

Still, some on the Hill have not let go of the issue. Rep. Ed Markey (D-Mass.) continues to push for the "V-chip," technology that would permit viewers to block programs rated as violent from appearing on their sets. The cable industry has said it would support such technology, while the broadcast networks continue to resist it.

How the Study Was Conducted

The Center for Media and Public Affairs conducted the study by taping 18 hours of programming from 6 a.m. to midnight on Thursday, April 7, 1994, repeating a study done the same way on the first Thursday of April 1992.

Center co-director Robert Lichter said a system of definitions was developed and "coders," the people who would review the tapes, were trained on sample programming. The coders needed to be in agreement 80 percent of the time for them to be used for the project.

Ultimately, two college students and the center's director of research were selected to review the tapes. They were instructed to count scenes of violence—so that a fistfight would count as one scene, rather than each blow being counted separately.

Violence was defined as "deliberate acts of physical force by people against people or property," said Lichter. Serious violence was defined as "an action that would be reasonably expected to cause serious injury or death."

Networks Make Crime Top Story

ELLEN EDWARDS

At a time when the nation's overall crime rate remains essentially unchanged, the three network evening newscasts doubled their coverage of crime and violence around the country last year, according to a new survey.

"People's fear of crime doesn't come from looking over their shoulders," said Robert Lichter, co-director of the Center for Media and Public Affairs, which performed the survey. "It comes from looking at their television screens."

The survey also showed that coverage of murder was three times as high in 1993 as in 1992, while the murder rate remained virtually unchanged. By comparison, coverage of the war on drugs, at one time an issue very much on the front burner, has dropped 83 percent in the past five years.

The study did not include the print media, which some television journalists suggested would reflect a similar increase. Nor did it address the issue of local news programming, which has been widely criticized as increasingly tabloidized.

In 1993, the survey said, the three major network newscasts aired 1,632 domestic crime stories, with NBC accounting for 626, CBS for 557 and ABC for 449. In 1992 the three newscasts aired 830 crime stories. Figures for individual networks were not available, but Lichter offered this comparison: In 1993, one out of every eight stories was about crime. In 1992 the figure was one out of every 18.

Several stories accounted for much of last year's coverage—there were 211 spots about the bombing of the World Trade Center, 195 about the Branch Davidian siege at Waco, Tex., and 138 about the Brady Bill.

Lichter said his study shows that there was a major upswing in coverage of crime and violence in August, about the time several foreign tourists were killed in Florida.

"There was a public response to these stories, and the networks realized people were really concerned about crime. I'm not arguing there is no crime problem, but when the media make more of it than they have, the media coverage can really ratchet up public concern," Lichter said.

"When tourists begin to get killed in one of America's most important tourist cities, that's a major story," said ABC News anchor Peter Jennings, who added that "as the economy improved, people's general interest in crime went up." In Lichter's annual survey, the economy remained the No. 2 topic for coverage, as it was in 1992, when the most-covered story was the election. Crime was No. 3 that year.

While Jennings said he generally distrusted "counts without context" by re-searchers on television, he added that he has noticed a surge in news coverage of violence. He said that newspeople at ABC had watched the increased coverage on the subject at NBC in particular and wondered whether it would make a difference in that network's ratings. He said he doesn't believe it has.

He acknowledged that such syndicated programs as "Hard Copy" and "Inside Edition," which devote considerable attention to crime stories, have "made the media universe just that much larger with just that much less discipline. . . .

"The days of the gatekeeper have evaporated," he said, referring to a time in which stories that weren't pursued by the mainstream media failed to reach most of the public. The story that broke that hold, he said, was Gennifer Flowers's assertion of a longtime affair with candidate Bill Clinton, which was driven by the supermar-ket tabloids.

NBC News Vice President Cheryl Gould said, "The fact of the matter is that the public's perception is that crime is a much more important problem on the agenda." She said that in their emphasis on the issue, the news media "more often than not are followers more than leaders." She added that much of NBC's coverage was community- and issue-based, rather than focused on individual crimes.

A CBS spokesman said no one at the network could comment until they had seen the survey.

Lichter's survey was paralleled by one from Children Now, a children's advo-cacy organization based in California. It showed that more than half of 850 children surveyed felt angry or depressed after they listened to the news. The national survey was conducted in January by the independent research firm of Fairbank, Maslin, Maullin & Associates with children aged 11 to 16 and will be presented at a conference in Palo Alto, Calif., this weekend on children and news. NBC anchor Tom Brokaw is scheduled to moderate a panel there called "Children, Violence and the News Media."

The Children Now survey, which also looked at the content of the three evening newscasts during last November, said 48 percent of all stories about children focused on crime and violence. In a review of five major American newspapers during the same month, that number was 40 percent.

"The predominant image kids get from television news is children as either victims or criminals," said James P. Steyer, president of Children Now. "There's just been this incredible focus on crime and violence in the last six to 12 months that's very damaging to kids, and it has furthered a feeding frenzy of politicians who are in a bidding war, rushing to show how tough they can be on crime."

Steyer cited three reasons he believes account for the upswing in the coverage of violence. First, he said, there have been a few very high-profile cases, such as the kidnapping and murder of 12-year-old Polly Klaas in California. Second, there is an increasing sense of the randomness of violence. And third, the ratings success of tabloid TV shows may influence those who produce news programs.

"In California, juvenile crime has declined," he said. "But you would have thought it quadrupled given the continual repetition of those images in the media."

Rep. Kweisi Mfume (D-Md.), head of the Congressional Black Caucus and a critic of the most punitive aspects of the Clinton administration's crime bill, said yesterday that "to continue to suggest over and over again by the amount of time devoted to the subject that [crime] is more important than anything else" causes a "hysterical" public reaction.

Television in the past six months has acted to reduce the violent content of its prime-time entertainment programming as a way of heading off threatened congressional action. News coverage has always been exempted from any threat of legislation to control violence.

One final ironic note in Lichter's survey: For the first time in the five years he has been doing these reviews, entertainment was one of the 10 most-covered stories of the year, beating out both education and the environment.

Violent vs. Vapid?

ELLEN EDWARDS

I t's Development Season in L.A., and there's a definite chill in the air. Writers and producers say the threat of legislation to regulate violence on television has caused them to censor themselves as they make their preliminary pitches to the networks for shows to air next fall. They're angry that their congressional critics admit they don't even watch much network television, and that they lump it together with cable, syndicated programs and movies.

They warn that the consequences of Washington's actions may mean television will be even more bland and more sitcom-filled, with fewer and fewer adult dramas. "There's no functional difference between censorship and the threat of censorship," says Barbara Hall, who was co-executive producer of "I'll Fly Away." And so, not surprisingly, they are speaking out.

"It's paralyzing the creative community," says Leonard Hill, an independent producer with more than 30 made-for-TV movies to his credit.

"You can feel it in town," says Andy Schneider, executive producer of CBS's relentlessly nonviolent "Northern Exposure." "Everybody's afraid."

Rosalyn Weinman, NBC's vice president for broadcast standards and practices, said the programming executives at NBC are "seeing many producers censoring themselves. That's different. That's very new. And depending on your perspective that's either terrific or quite frightening."

She says NBC tells producers to make all their pitches and let the network decide what gets a green light, although she admits violent programs are not exactly in favor.

And the cause of it all, say a number of writers and producers, is Washington. Janet Reno's testimony before the Senate Commerce Committee last week, in which she said she saw no constitutional impediment to three bills under consideration, only ratcheted up the tension.

Says Hill, who has worked in programming at both ABC and NBC: "A bunch of Washington opportunists are jumping on the bandwagon with a bogus campaign that reeks of McCarthyism. It's like saying to a newspaper, 'If you don't cover the gangs, they'll go away.' They're aiming at the wrong target."

Television writers and producers interviewed this week seemed overwhelmingly angry at being Washington's focus, saying time after time that Congress is taking the easy way out in focusing on violence in network television while ignoring cable and syndication, which none of the legislation would affect, as well as larger societal issues such as gun control.

And they say they are flabbergasted that a parody of a barroom brawl on CBS's "Love & War" was held up at a hearing last week as an example of violence.

Diane English, "Love & War's" executive producer, said in a statement that the episode's intent was to satirize violence on television and that it "accomplished exactly what we intended it to. Senator [Conrad] Burns thought the episode was funny. Senator [Ernest] Hollings thought it was offensive. . . . If they can't agree about content, how can anyone expect to legislate it?"

Steven Bochco's "NYPD Blue" on ABC has been the recipient of much of the ruckus lately, more for sexual content than for violence, but audiences have embraced it enthusiastically, making it the first obvious hit of the season.

Bochco, the show's executive producer, says he has not been pressured to make changes, but added: "Beyond my bias or selfish interest, I have a real philosophical concern about the current furor. I can't help feeling a little cynical about the politicians making hay over a very easy issue. For them it's a no-brainer. . . . They appear unlikely to pass [even] a benign crime bill because of a watered-down gun control provision. And instead they want to shake their sabers at us."

Bochco, whose credits include "Hill Street Blues" and "L.A. Law," says he has had no conversations with anyone in Congress.

"Nobody really wants to talk. Everybody is just interested in sound bites. . . . Government has come to accept the unacceptable—homelessness, hunger, a degree of criminal activity we don't even act on. In amongst all that rubble, to point a finger at television seems not to be addressing the primary cause of our worst social issue."

But he is quick to acknowledge that television influences people. "I am not an idiot," he says. "It's a mass medium. Twenty million people a week watch it. It would be naive to say television has no impact."

Bochco says the most violent show he has done is "Hill Street," which ran on NBC from 1981 to 1987, and that he had one rule: "Violence always had a consequence. It was frightening. It made you puke. You had nightmares. It would mess up your life. We might have 10 seconds of mindless violence and four episodes of dealing with the consequences of those 10 seconds."

Paul Schulman, whose Manhattan-based company buys $175 million each year in network time for advertisers, says he's more excited about "NYPD Blue" as a place for advertisers than he has been about any show since "L.A. Law."

"It's a great show," he says. "It just stands alone. . . . If you've got an action-adventure movie opening on Friday and you're not [advertising] there on Tuesday, you've made a huge mistake."

But Schulman acknowledges that the climate has changed. "There are things that got made a few years ago that would not get made now," he says. "Sponsors are very wary of environment. They will just stay away from gratuitous violence. . . . It's the most advertiser-friendly schedule since I started buying in 1961."

In fact, "NYPD Blue" has not yet attracted the major mainstream advertisers, but Bochco says, "I don't think ABC cares who pays the $2 as long as they get the $2." He says Congress should stay out of programming decisions and let the viewers decide. "I've had my brains beat out in the marketplace," he says, "and I've had some success in it. I love it. I really do."

Dick Wolf, executive producer of NBC's "Law & Order," says that in four years the police officers on his show have never fired their weapons, but in the current climate he worries about reaction to certain types of shows rather than the shows themselves.

"The potential exists," he says, "for these shows, the highest level of television, the dramas, to be destroyed by this legislation because ad agencies are sheep. They will avoid warning labels like the plague. . . .

"I would hate to live in a television environment where there was no 'Hill Street,' no 'Picket Fences,' no 'Law and Order,' no 'NYPD Blue.' "

Hill, the independent producer, says he had a conversation recently with an ABC executive who had just seen a movie he did four years ago for the network called "Nitti: The Enforcer," about Frank Nitti's takeover of the mob. "He said, 'It's too bad we couldn't do that today.' "

He says that two years ago, "shows that would have been a buy, now they say, 'That's an advertising problem for us. That's a Washington problem for us.' The campaign is underinformed and nearly hysterical, and people have sponsored it without watching network television. . . . It is the new political correctness of Washington to bash network television as if it were the cause of violence in society."

Barbara Hall of "I'll Fly Away," the critically acclaimed show on NBC that moved in reruns this year to PBS, says she thinks that show wouldn't get made this year because it showed the graphic violence that accompanied the civil rights movement.

"We showed KKK violence, very upsetting violence," she says. "I don't think we'd be able to do that this year."

Robert Nathan, the supervising producer on NBC's "Law and Order," says he is organizing a group of writers and producers to come to Washington to make their side of the story known. "We would like to talk to senators and congressmen who don't make the distinction between pay cable and network television," he said. He said they want to go from office to office to tell them that with legislation, "You are about to make a mistake of enormous proportions."

Audiences, he says, have shown a real appetite for good drama in the past six to seven years, but he is concerned about the networks' reaction to Washington. "Will they, even on a marginal level, say this show has a possibility of violence or worse, a possibility of controversy? . . . You start to crush creativity left and right."

Others make the point that there are fewer and fewer violent shows on network television. Stan Rogow, executive producer of CBS's new "South of Sunset," says his hero, a private investigator in Los Angeles, isn't a gun-toter because "I don't like guns. . . . I grew up in the '60s. My dear, dear friends of 25 years have to watch what I do. And I have to talk with them."

Rogow, who also has "Shannon's Deal" and what he describes as the "emotionally violent" "Middle Ages" in his past credits, says real-life violence has an effect on the production of the show. "It's hard to find a place to shoot that's gang-free," he says. "The cops advise us, and say don't even think of shooting there at night. . . . Everybody knows what the graffiti on the wall means. It means it's gang territory."

Rogow calls Congress's attack on television "a colossal smoke screen . . . because the other issue is just too big to get around—why people get violent."

" '20/20' gets a 34 share for a story about a wife cutting off her husband's penis," says Rogow. "I haven't seen anything that approached that [on network prime-time entertainment shows]. There's a public appetite in a commercial market, and somebody is saying, 'You can't do that.' "

As for the charge that movies are greater offenders than television when it comes to portraying violence, NBC's Weinman says that the network is being considerably more cautious in buying theatrical movies to air, and is editing heavily when they have any violence.

"And in most cases these are movies that have already been seen by millions of people," she said. "We know we could get a really big kid audience if we put on Freddy Krueger movies. But we won't. And nobody will."

David Wolper, whose "Roots" is often cited as depicting the kind of violence that is acceptable, says he agrees that movies are far worse than television, and echoes the widespread concern in Hollywood that their congressional critics don't watch television and tend to lump all television together.

The violence he depicted in "Roots" and other productions, he says, was historical rather than contemporary violence, unlikely to motivate anyone to violent action.

"It's not violence [Washington is] interested in," he says. "It's violence that may influence people."

Canada Gets Tough on TV Violence

CHARLES TRUEHEART

If the Teale-Homolka case is any measure, Canadians are willing to live with restrictions on the media in the interests of the greater social good as they see it. A recent voluntary ban by private broadcasters here on televised depictions of violence suggests another dimension of this same civic sensibility.

Whatever the social implications, U.S. lawmakers debating ways to protect children from violence on television now can look to Canada for a tough new code of standards—and a portent of the difficulties involved in its enforcement.

Prodded by government regulators and popular outcries against video mayhem and bloodshed, Canada's private broadcasters have adopted a voluntary ban on any programming that "sanctions, promotes or glamorizes violence" or contains "gratuitous violence in any form."

The new broadcast standards, which will take effect Jan. 1, restrict adult-oriented scenes of violence to the hours between 9 p.m. and 6 a.m. and lay out specific guidelines covering the way violence is portrayed in children's programming. The code also calls for the development by next fall of a "viewer-friendly classification system" to advise parents about the violence content and intended audience of programs.

Why would a country with one of the lowest levels of violent crime in the industrialized world become one of the first to restrict television's power to glamorize and foment violence? A provocative answer comes from Trina McQueen, one of the architects of the new code.

"Maybe one of the reasons Canada is a more peaceful country is that when Canadians see a problem that affects 'peace, order and good government' "—Canada's constitutional equivalent of "life, liberty and the pursuit of happiness"—"they tend to act on it fairly quickly and fairly strictly," she said. "Gun control, and other limits that Americans would consider astonishing, Canadians seem to be able to tolerate and live with."

McQueen, chairman of the Action Group on Violence in Television, said, "We believe this is a child-protection issue."

The language in the code is notable for its detail—a level of specificity that heartens advocates of tough restrictions on televised violence and chagrins defenders of untrammeled creative expression.

316

In children's programs involving real-life characters, according to the code, "violence shall only be portrayed when it is essential to the development of character and plot." Animated programming for children, the code says, "shall not have violence as its central theme, and shall not invite dangerous imitation." Another section lays out examples of "dangerous imitation"—for example, "the use of plastic bags as toys, use of matches, the use of dangerous household products as playthings, or dangerous physical acts such as climbing apartment balconies or rooftops."

Other sections of the new code restrict televised depictions of violence against animals and women, as well as "violence based on race, national or ethnic origin, colour, religion, gender, sexual orientation, age, or mental or physical disability."

A final section covering sports programming exhorts broadcasters not to "promote or exploit violent action which is outside the sanctioned activity of the sport in question," raising fundamental questions about whether bloody hockey-rink brawls are inside or outside the "sanctioned activity" of Canada's national pastime.

The code was written by the Canadian Association of Broadcasters, a private industry group, and recently accepted by the Canadian Radio-Television and Telecommunications Commission (CRTC), this country's equivalent of the Federal Communications Commission.

The new standards were praised by advocacy groups concerned about the effect of televised violence on the behavior of young people, but most of them noted the code's limitations: Canadian private broadcasters supply only a small portion of the programming available here. Tom Perlmutter, executive director of Canada's Alliance for Children and Television, pointed out that the new code does not cover the hundreds of hours of foreign—mostly American—programming available to Canadian cable television subscribers.

"We're inundated by American signals," Perlmutter said. "Skip one channel and you're into this realm where the code is not applicable." With the advent next year of what Canadians call "Deathstar"—the multichannel universe available from rooftop satellite dishes—"any existing regulatory mechanism on violence or any other matter is blown out the window," Perlmutter said.

Canada's cable broadcasters are busy working on their own violence code, which they will submit to the CRTC in about two weeks. The cable companies' contractual obligations to program providers, including U.S. networks, typically forbid them to alter or curtail any signal, according to Elizabeth McDonald, vice president of the Canadian Cable Television Association. But she said cable companies were committed to providing subscribers with both information and the latest technologies to enhance their "choice and control" over what their children watch.

The real efficacy of the code, even within the limits of private broadcasting within Canada, remains to be seen on television screens in the coming year or two, and the CRTC has vowed to monitor citizen complaints and broadcasters' adherence to the code. While compliance is officially voluntary, the CRTC said it will make "compliance with the code a condition of license for all privately owned television stations and networks when renewing their licenses."

Some critics of the new code have expressed concern about its possible in-fringements on freedom of expression, but objections on those grounds are not as heated here as they are in the United States.

McQueen stressed that all the constituent broadcasting groups were "committed to creative, artistic and journalistic independence" and that "none is advocating the removal of violence from television." Keith Spicer, head of the CRTC, said in a statement that private broadcasters had successfully walked the "tightrope" of "trying to achieve a delicate but indispensable balance between protecting children and protecting free speech."

Perlmutter, whose Alliance for Children and Television orchestrates public education programs, struck a cautionary note about the promise of legislating or regulating violence on television.

"To hope for change in isolation is foolish, because it puts the onus on televi-sion and the broadcasters," he said. "There has to be a partnership with the commu-nity and with parents. We have to give parents tools and information to help them enforce the values they want in their homes."

Mass Media and Society 14

Purging the Scrabble List of Offensive Language

AMY E. SCHWARTZ

It all started, apparently, with a Scrabble game in Baltimore. One of the three players noticed that the official Scrabble dictionary considered it acceptable to play the word "Jew"—not as a noun, since capitalized words are not allowed in Scrabble, but as a verb. She called Hasbro Inc., which makes Scrabble; then she called the Anti-Defamation League of B'nai B'rith. The ADL got interested, Hasbro got interested, and the result was a furor, still continuing, over the company's announcement that the next official Scrabble dictionary will be 75 to 100 slurs shorter. It's one of the oddest recent battles over the scarred ground of censorship vs. offensiveness, proof that no matter how clear and untroubled your views are on this issue—on either side—someone out there will come up with a case to fuddle them.

At first glance, purging the Scrabble list seems the mildest expedient yet in the range of strategies to curb offensive language. Why would anyone insist on the right to use "kike" or "dago" in a game, though these have been listed as legitimate Scrabble words for years under game rules that "Any words in a standard dictionary are permitted except those capitalized, those designated as foreign words, abbreviations and words requiring apostrophes and hyphens"? Besides, the Scrabble dictionary isn't really a dictionary; it just collects all the acceptable words (up to eight letters long) from four other dictionaries the company deems official, making a handy reference for such Scrabble favorites as "xi" and "jo."

On the other hand, aren't bad words still words? "It's a Pandora's box," admits John D. Williams Jr., de facto spokesman on the issue and executive director of the National Scrabble Association. Since the announcement, Williams laments, he has become "the poster boy of American political correctness, interviewed in England

319

and Singapore and Australia, baited by radio talk show hosts from here to Vancouver." The Pandora problem is, unfortunately, a real one. Williams got letters asking if it was true the game planned to eliminate "cripple" (no) and "wetback" (yes). And he recently got a letter from a representative of Romany, or Gypsy, interests in North America demanding equal non-treatment for the verb "to gyp." There's also a subset of complainers who want the nasty words removed not just from the Scrabble dictionary but from other dictionaries as well, a suggestion that Williams, like most Scrabblers a word lover, terms "insane."

Nobody in the Baltimore Scrabble game had actually tried to play the offensive word or otherwise draw attention to it (two of the players were survivors of the Holocaust). But the book gets used for such quasi-official purposes as Scrabble tournaments, so it constituted a nod of sorts. The Anti-Defamation League wrote Hasbro asking that all racial, ethnic and religious slurs be deleted from the dictionary and accusing the company of "literally playing games with hate." Hasbro, Williams says, had been toying with the idea of a purge anyway. So it went ahead.

"They figured this was as good a time as any," explains Williams, whose not-quite-independent association runs the annual tournaments. "Jew" as a verb, he says, has gotten by far the most complaints over the years, but there are others. "People who write in from the Christian right tend to be more concerned over curse words. They'll write and say they were playing with their child, and the child looked a word up in the dictionary and happened to see a word the household professes never to use. Of course, that's also a danger with a real dictionary, or with just being a person living in a society."

Scratch a political correctness fight over a book or an author, and you'll often find a fight that has less to do with abstract principles than with personal histories, emotions, the combatants' particular affections or experience with the books or even the phrases under attack. I suspected this, but you can't fully appreciate it until the critics come after your own game, one whose odd charm, for me at least, is the way it makes words come loose from their meanings and float around in your head without them, reduced to strange amalgams of letters valuable only as high or low scorers. Playing too much Scrabble can make you catalogue mentally, sometimes for months, any word you hear that contains an "x"; after a particularly rousing game it's not unknown for all parties to spend the next few hours scanning one another's conversation for seven-letter words, which, when set down, get you a 50-point bonus. Over Memorial Day weekend, after a particularly bad drubbing at the board followed by a visit to a museum containing Civil War costumes, I became obsessed with the word "zouave" (it contains not only the "z" and the "v" but four of the five vowels). Just for kicks I asked Williams about this word, and he thought at first it was "foreign," hence unacceptable. But the official Scrabble dictionary listed it as okay, with the definition "a French infantryman."

"Being offended is so subjective, it's ludicrous," Williams says, "but we're trying to take an academic approach. Anything that has an offensive primary definition is out." "Gyp" will most likely stay, because "its primary meaning is not designated offensive in the dictionaries we draw from. Groups who are offended should go after them, not us." "Homo," he says, will stay in (its primary meaning is listed as "man," though some purists would consider that Latin, hence a foreignism). "Lezzie" is out—useful though it might be for someone holding a "z" and a blank—as are a number of words not remotely printable in [the Post]. But when a colleague asked Williams about the vaguely off-color-sounding British word "tup," Williams said it passed muster. "It turns out," he explains, "that the primary meaning has to do with what a ram and a sheep do when they're madly in love." It's not clear what we're to make of all this. But somewhere in there is a 50-point bonus for either the forces of linguistic upright-mindedness or the forces of madness.

India's Lewd Awakening

MOLLY MOORE

> I have blue eyes,
> What shall I do?
> I have red lips,
> What shall I do?
> Sexy, sexy . . .
> People call me sexy.
> —*From a Hindi film song*

All of India is in an uproar over sex.
Sex in film songs, that is.

Mothers of young children are angry. Women's organizations are outraged. Moviemakers are up in arms. The prime minister is fuming. The government censor board is wringing its collective hands. And the music shop salesmen are making a killing.

"My sales have doubled because of these vulgar songs," boasted 25-year-old Dharmendra Mehra, who runs Welcome Audio-Video in one of New Delhi's busiest shopping districts. His hottest seller is a cassette of the best of the lewd and crude called "With the Lover."

The culture that brought the world the Kamasutra and the film industry that can't seem to make a movie that doesn't include a rape scene have become obsessed by the wave of gyrating hips, pelvic thrusts, steamy kisses and bawdy lyrics that has swept through its movie and music productions in recent months. The emotional controversy over the surge of vulgarity in the entertainment business is India's latest episode of cultural angst as it struggles to open its economy and its society to greater Western influences while trying to preserve its own traditions and social mores.

"Our society is going through a massive transitional phase," said Ranjana Kumari, director of New Delhi's Center for Social Research. "Things are changing too suddenly, and we're not prepared."

Certainly nothing prepared India for the clash of East meeting West in the revolution that has exploded on India's silver screens and pop radio stations in the last year. In a country where it's taboo for men and women to touch in public, now preschool kids are prancing around their houses singing the shocking (to Indian sensibilities) "Sexy, sexy" song.

It all started with MTV, which one Delhi newspaper columnist recently compared to "termites eating away at our own traditional values." MTV was first beamed to India via the Hong Kong satellite channel STAR-TV more than three years ago. And its arrival changed the face of entertainment here.

MTV put visuals to American music, which had long been popular among India's middle class and younger generation. But its greatest impact was spreading Western music and attitudes beyond the big cities of Bombay and New Delhi to small towns across the country, where savvy television shop owners began buying cheap satellite dishes and stringing cable wires to village huts for a few rupees a month.

Also, for the first time in modern Indian entertainment history, audiences had an alternative to indigenous film productions and the staid government-controlled television network Doordarshan, snidely referred to by one television critic as "the last upholder of middle-class morality" in India. Even in the poorest of the poor slums, neighbors began pooling their rupees to rent televisions and began watching cable movies rather than going to theaters.

If the conservative politicians and pundits viewed MTV as a termite eating away at Indian values, a nervous Bollywood—the world's biggest film industry, which churns out more than 1,000 flicks a year—saw MTV eating away at its market and its profits. So Bollywood, whose show tunes dominate the music industry charts, decided to fight back.

Filmmaker Subhash Ghai's first blow was a knockout punch that transformed the movie industry almost overnight.

Khal Nayak "The Villain," released last year, starred the country's top actor and actress. Like all Hindi movies, it included dance scenes set to music. But one dance scene was unlike anything that had ever made it past the government censor boards and onto the silver screen. *Choli ke peechay*

In a song that scaled the pop charts, the leading lady is asked, "What's beneath the blouse?" The camera skips over her demurely veiled face and focuses suggestively on the choli stretched tight across her ample, heaving bosom as she replies, coyly, "In the choli is my heart, and this heart I will give to my lover."

Those two lines packed the theaters. Those two lines resulted in record music sales. Those two lines changed the Indian movie industry.

"Choli" was still on the charts when the so-called "Sexy, sexy" hit the streets with a disco beat that repeated the word "sexy" more than 100 times. Then came the movie "Raja Babu" and the refrain "Drag your cot next to mine." And "Vijaypath" ("The Road to Victory"), with its double-entendre play on a cricket match and sex: "First ball broke my bangles, slipped my skirt, very strong his ball was, with full speed." Followed by "Andaaz" ("Style"), with the heroine crooning, "I am a goods train, give me a push." All of which were accompanied by never-before-used camera shots of once-private body parts.

India went ballistic. Every cab driver in Bombay was singing "Sexy, sexy." The radios played "Choli" ad nauseam. Conservative politicians and women's organizations were furious. Lawyers sued movie studios in an effort to shut down what they considered vulgar films. About 150 members of the Hindu fundamentalist Bharatiya Janata Party (BJP) stormed a theater in Bombay a few months ago, throwing black ink on the screen, ripping up marquees and chasing patrons out.

In a parliamentary debate on the shocking trends, both ruling and opposition party members joined in raucous chants of "Shame! Shame! Shame!" during a grilling of the senior minister who oversees the government film censor board.

It all may sound pretty tame by Western standards, but the scenes and the songs are lascivious by Indian norms. Previously, sex was portrayed behind veils of verbal and visual illusion, leaving the rest to the imagination. (Even the required rape scene in most Hindi movies didn't show the act. The camera cut from the menacing leer of the villain to the sobbing face of the victim, leaving out the body contact.)

"I had one dirty song, and I never meant to encourage vulgarity," said a now repentant Ghai. "But it became a precedent. It was like a fashion. Anything that's a hit, the rest of the producers try to copy and imitate it."

Across India, the response has been thunderous.

Subhadra Gupta, 34-year-old steel company executive and mother of two children, watched what she considered an appalling transformation in her 4-year-old son, Varun.

"My son has forgotten all the nursery rhymes he learned," said a distraught Gupta. "He used to come home from preschool and sing 'Twinkle, Twinkle, Little Star.' Now you tell him to recite a nursery rhyme and he makes a face, says, 'No, no' . . . and starts singing 'Choli' and 'Sexy, sexy.'

"I am scared that in a year, when he is ready to go to school, during the school interview if they ask him to sing a song he might just start off with these film songs, and they will chuck him out," said Gupta.

Leaders of women's organizations charge that the new trend is even more denigrating to women than the violence and stereotypes to which actresses are normally subjected in Indian films.

"Since the advent of STAR-TV and MTV into India, women have been portrayed more and more as a commodity," said Ranjana Kumari. "It's a symptom of a growing market economy where everything, everybody has become a commodity."

The ire is not limited to mothers and women's organizations. More and more studies are being published indicating that crimes against women and "Eve-teasing," a euphemism for sexual harassment, are increasing significantly throughout India, particularly in urban areas. And many people say much of the blame falls on Bollywood, where not only sex, but violence, is commanding greater chunks of footage. "Mainstream cinema is being shamelessly imbued with innuendo and vulgarity, which is threatening to strike at the very core of our culture," wrote Shashi Ranjan, president of the conservative BJP, in letters of protest to the government censor board and the Indian Motion Picture Producers' Association.

Even Prime Minister P.V. Narasimha Rao has gotten into the act, recently telling a meeting of state information and cinematography ministers, "Self-regulation is the best antidote, but in case it fails to work, we will certainly have to fall back on other measures."

Most moviemakers interpret "other measures" to mean tougher censorship.

Mahesh Bhatt, one of Bollywood's most successful filmmakers, said India's approach to the entire issue is full of contradictions. India says it wants an open market, yet it wants to censor what Michael Jackson does onstage, he lamented. And as for criticizing sexuality on the screen, he harked back to India's far less inhibited cultural past: "Every temple in India has images of the worst imaginable sex postures."

Although Indian films are technically subjected to review by a government censor board, members of the movie industry often sit on the board. Critics also complain that the board's guidelines are subjective and its members less than diligent.

Subhash Ghai, who made "The Villain" and is a member of the board, asked, "We need censors, but who's going to be the censor?

"At the board they say, 'Look, what are the guidelines? What is aesthetic? What's vulgar?' " he said of his colleagues. "One member is an intellectual, the other is a social worker with limited education. They're paid $1 a day. They come watch some movies and sleep for a few hours in the afternoon."

And even if the censor board deletes a scene or a song, local theaters routinely splice the banned footage back into the film. The government is now considering creating a special police force to raid theaters and arrest owners and distributors who are showing censored bites.

But Ghai and others say there are no easy solutions.

"The problem is constantly arising because of confusion in outlook and belief," he said. "In belief, people want Indian. In outlook, they want West."

NAACP Sees the News Media as Its Latest Foe

EDWARD WALSH

A fter taking on lynch mobs, Jim Crow laws, segregated schools and many other forms of racism over the past eight decades, the NAACP has found a different kind of enemy: the news media.

With executive director Benjamin F. Chavis Jr. setting the tone, the proud civil rights organization's 85th national convention that ended here today displayed a strong sense of discontent and mistrust about what speakers described as distorted and unfair news coverage of African Americans in general and the NAACP in particular.

At today's closing session, delegates overwhelmingly approved a resolution of support for Chavis and other leaders, who were described as "under attack by the news media" for their overtures to controversial Nation of Islam leader Louis Farrakhan. When Vernon H. Ricks Jr., a delegate from Potomac, Md., questioned the need for the resolution, several speakers shot back that, in the words of one, "we know the media is against us."

Earlier, Rep. Maxine Waters (D-Calif.) accused "some members of the press, mostly members of the white press," of attempting to provoke divisions among black Americans. Waters then brought her audience to its feet cheering with a reference to the saturation news coverage of the O. J. Simpson murder case and the controversy over Chavis's attempts to reach out to Farrakhan.

"Tell the press we define who we are," Waters thundered. "Give us as much time as you've given O. J. Run behind us with your camera the way you do when Farrakhan shows up."

Introducing recently retired Chicago Sun-Times columnist Vernon Jarrett, who was honored for his work with the NAACP, another speaker assailed black journalists for caring more about their careers than "the truth."

James Williams, editor of the Baltimore Afro American and a former director of communications for the NAACP and the National Urban League, said the amount of media criticism at the convention was unusual. "I've never seen such a crescendo," he said.

Williams said this was in part because of a defensive circling of the wagons by Chavis and his allies. They feel beleaguered over questions about the NAACP's debt, which officials say is $2.7 million, and criticism of his attempts to change the organization's direction by appealing to young people and focusing more on economic and social issues. In particular, Chavis has come under fire for his inclusion of Farrakhan at a summit conference of African American leaders that the NAACP hosted in Baltimore last month.

But as the spontaneous reaction to Waters's remarks about the Simpson case showed, mistrust of the mainstream media is not confined to Chavis and other NAACP leaders.

"The O. J. Simpson overkill has certainly had an effect on African Americans," Williams said. "Most African Americans believe that O. J. is innocent, so therefore the media have to be held responsible for perpetuating that myth about black males."

Cheering, sign-waving delegates greeted Chavis as he was introduced for the convention keynote address earlier this week. "The media reported there was going to be a demonstration, but they didn't plan on this demonstration," he said. "You can control the networks, but you can't control the Godworks."

Chavis went on to attack Time magazine for its cover photograph of Simpson that was darkened, projecting what critics said was a deliberately sinister image. "It did not surprise me," he said. "That is the perspective they bring when they approach our reality."

There is nothing new about media bashing among groups that feel beset by media criticism. It is a staple, for example, at the annual convention of the National Rifle Association.

But the NAACP does not have a history of antagonistic relations with the news media. During the height of the civil rights movement in the 1960s, the most common criticism came from segregationists who accused mainstream news organizations of being overly sympathetic to the movement and its leaders.

In an interview, Chavis said, "From a civil rights perspective, times have really changed. Go back to the '60s, the media was seen as an ally of the civil rights movement. Now the media is seen almost as an enemy of the civil rights movement."

Where once "freedom fighters like in the Mississippi summer [were] the image young people wanted to be, now the pimp and the drug dealer and the hustler become the new role model" in news accounts of the inner city and the entertainment industry's "romanticization of drugs and violence," he said.

Linda Byrd-Harden of Richmond, executive secretary of the Virginia NAACP, contrasted news coverage of the Simpson case with that of Jeffrey L. Dahmer, the convicted Milwaukee serial killer, many of whose victims were young black men.

"How many people of African descent do you have to kill to get that kind of [Simpson-like] coverage?" she said.

Byrd-Harden said the news coverage has given the Simpson case its racial edge and "helps to feed the stereotype that men of color are violent and want to kill white people, when in actuality we are killing ourselves."

Despite such criticism, Chavis proved adept during the convention at projecting a public image of a leader who is firmly in charge. He visited a drug rehabilitation center and the Cook County jail to underscore his emphasis on broadening the appeal of the NAACP.

When a 20-year-old college student from Oklahoma was elected to the NAACP board over an older activist who was backed by an outspoken Chavis critic, Chavis brought the young woman, Chelle Luper, to a news conference. "The direction we're headed in has now been affirmed by the convention," he said triumphantly.

This afternoon there was a reminder of an earlier, simpler time in the civil rights movement. Chavis led several hundred people on a march to a nearby fast food restaurant where, according to NAACP officials, a group of youth delegates to the convention was denied service Wednesday night. They quoted the manager as saying, "There's too many of you. You're making me nervous."

The Primal Screen

DON OLDENBURG

The 8-year-old New York girl was used to getting her way with the TV remote control. But when she persuaded her parents to rent the video "Child's Play 2," an R-rated horror movie about a possessed doll named "Chucky" that maims and kills, for days afterward she pleaded at bedtime that her mother check under the bed and keep the lights on.

Her parents dismissed it, labeling it "normal fears." No different than the willies they used to get watching werewolf and chain saw flicks. That was until they chanced upon their daughter measuring her grip around her little brother's neck. "She wasn't really trying to hurt him," says the mother now, "but it did make me stop and think."

A clean-cut 15-year-old suburban Maryland boy says he watched lots of police shows and "played guns" with the neighbor kids when he was younger. One friend wanted to be a cop some day so he could shoot people like on television. Another was a Hulk Hogan fiend whose nonstop choke holds and full nelsons got old fast.

But, lately, real-life seems to have caught up with the TV fantasies for him. He was attacked by punks from a nearby high school a year ago. Toughs hanging out in school hallways mimicking the macho rhetoric of MTV rap artists intimidate him. Talk of guns stashed in lockers bothers him.

"I guess you could say TV takes its toll on a lot of people," he sighs.

Researchers have been saying as much, with the preponderance of evidence from more than 3,000 studies over two decades finding that violence portrayed on television influences the attitudes and behavior of children who watch it. Justice Department figures showing the youth arrest rate for murder, manslaughter, forcible rape, robbery and aggravated assault increased by 16 percent between 1989 and 1990 have turned up the volume of that message recently.

In late February, the American Psychological Association (APA) released a task force report, five years in the making and heralded as the most comprehensive look ever at the role of television in society. Titled "Big World, Small Screen," it estimated that the average child who watches two to four hours of television daily will have witnessed 8,000 murders and 100,000 other acts of TV violence by the time he leaves elementary school. "Television can cause aggressive behavior and can cultivate values favoring the use of aggression," it concluded. The Task Force called for a federal TV policy "protecting citizens and society from harmful effects."

Last Tuesday, psychologist Leonard Eron, the respected research professor emeritus at the University of Illinois, in Chicago, delivered a harder hitting indictment of America's favorite pastime to the U.S. Senate Committee on Governmental Affairs at a hearing on violence and the media. "There can no longer be any doubt," he said, "that heavy exposure to televised violence is one of the causes of aggressive behavior, crime and violence in society."

Channeled Aggression

Researchers, however, are only now beginning to tune into which populations of youngsters couched obediently before TV Dearest are most "at risk."

Not every child mesmerized by on-screen violence (about five violent acts per hour prime-time; 26.4 violent acts per hour on children's programming, including cartoons) grows into a troubled adolescent or sociopathic criminal. And those headline-grabbers that do (the 12-year-old Florida boy who set himself ablaze imitating his favorite Motley Crue video; the 13-year-old California murderer who confessed his idea to pour salt on his victim's wounds came "from TV") often convince parents that violent programming affects only other people's children. But despite a fuzzy picture of who is most vulnerable, researchers have determined that "bad kids" aren't the only ones.

"It is the crucial question that has never been answered: Are some children more likely to be affected negatively by violence on television than others?" says Diana Zuckerman, a Washington psychologist and a member of the APA Task Force on Television and Society.

Zuckerman says she saw the negative conditioning of TV violence in a 1981 study in which she worked with third, fourth and fifth graders. Without knowing what TV shows their students regularly watched, teachers at the school rated the children on a variety of measures—including aggressiveness and violence. Zuckerman and her colleagues meanwhile documented the kids' TV-viewing habits by hours and content.

"These were upper-middle-class elementary school kids who were functioning very nicely," says Zuckerman, explaining that the study accounted for the children's intelligence, parents' education, and other factors unrelated to television that could have skewed the results. "There was a definite relationship between what they watched and how they behaved."

Among the questions asked of the students: Had they ever imitated the violence they saw on television? "Most of them said they did," says Zuckerman. "Mostly things like, they'd watched some program on the TV and then they'd hit their little sister."

But if all children are potentially at risk, some researchers fear most those whose community and home environment already overdoses them with violence. "Children in the inner city, children who live in the high crime areas, kids who are on their way home from school who have to dodge bullets," says Eron, chairman of APA's Commission on Violence and Youth. "These are the ones who are most affected.

"What watching TV violence does for those kids is it validates that kind of behavior. They see it on television and think it's happening all over and it's normative . . . and the only way to get ahead is by engaging in violent behavior. They don't see any other alternatives. Kids who live in middle-class suburban areas are affected too. But [the violence] is not as central to their lives."

Carol Beck says she sees that influence among her students at Brooklyn's Thomas Jefferson High School. If bitterness rings in Beck's words when talking about the negative impact of television, videos and films on children, there's good reason: In the five years she has served as principal at the school located in a neighborhood where children are jolted from sleep from the sound of gunfire, where sirens and angry voices are the norm, 50 of her students have been killed in street violence.

"The many decisions our young people make regarding behavior, dress, future aspirations, and nourishment for their bodies are shaped by forces outside of the home," she testified at the Senate committee hearing last week. "Our children are the end result of the saying that 'The media is the message' (sic). Our children are being brainwashed by the constant and insidious violence portrayed in the media."

TV Guidance?

Thirty years ago, when Eron began researching how children learn to be aggressive, he was skeptical that television could have such a deleterious effect. He believed it probably had no greater impact on behavior than did the Saturday afternoon westerns of his youth or the traditional though sometimes graphically violent fairy tales of childhood. But a survey he conducted in 1960 of 875 third graders and their parents in a semi-rural New York county changed his mind.

Looking for clues as to how parenting practices related to children's violence at school, Eron uncovered an unexpected finding: There appeared to be a link between the violence on the TV shows the boys were watching and their aggressive behavior at school.

Returning 10 years later to reinterview more than half of the original subjects, Eron discovered a striking connection between the boys who viewed violent TV shows at age 8 and their aggressive behaviors at age 19. Controlling other variables (IQ, social status, church attendance, parental aggressiveness), he also found that boys who had ranked low on aggression 10 years earlier but watched violent television turned out "significantly more aggressive" than boys who originally ranked high on aggression but didn't watch violent shows.

Two years ago, Eron revisited those subjects. Most were about 30 years old. This time he also looked into other data such as criminal records. "There was no relation to what they were watching at age 19 and how aggressive they were at 19, or at age 30," he says. "But there was a strong relation between what they watched at age 8 and their aggressive behavior at age 19 and at age 30.

If the staying power of TV's violent messages is alarming, so is a tangential finding from the study that serves as a major clue as to what kids are most at risk: "The more hours of television the children watched when they were 8 years old," says Eron, "the more serious were the crimes they were convicted of by the time they were age 30, and the more aggressive they were under the influence of alcohol, and the more severely they punished their own children."

What Parents Can Do

What frustrates researchers is that despite alarming findings over two decades, the message that violent TV programming affects children's attitude and behavior is largely ignored and often denied by those in the best position to control the problem—parents.

The solution is not "all or none." Research indicates that while children who spend a lot of time in front of the TV set do poorly in school, those who spend moderate time watching TV actually perform better than those who watch none at all. So, realistically, parents need to learn not how to ban their children from watching TV, not how to censor the violence and sex and glamorous beer ads and bad attitudes portrayed on the screen, but rather how to cut the losses. The key to that, researchers believe, is being there when your child watches television. Pointers from the experts:

"If you start talking about it with your children, they really do start thinking about these issues," says Kansas State University psychologist John P. Murray, author of "Using TV Sensibly," a brochure available free by sending a self-addressed stamped envelope to HDFS—TV, Kansas State University, Justin Hall, Manhattan, Kan. 66506-1403.

"Too often adults think it is impolite to interrupt a TV program, to comment on it," says Murray, "but it's the best way to get your message across in a comfortable environment rather than preaching."

"The whole idea would be to make it a less passive activity," says psychologist Diana Zuckerman, coauthor of "Use TV To Your Child's Advantage" (Acropolis Books, $9.95). "It can be made a shared experience where you learn important lessons. If parents talk to their kids, ask them 'What do you think happened there?' 'What are the alternatives to behaving like that?' You can teach kids how to be skeptical about the TV commercials they watch, how to tell the difference between reality and fantasy, how to think of alternative solutions to the ones they're seeing on TV."

Teach your children that when they're watching TV, says Zuckerman, "They aren't playing 'Candy Land,' or jumping rope, or reading, or learning to share with other kids. Even if they're watching all great TV programs, they would still be missing out on all those other parts of growing up—like playing."

The TV Tallyman

Media Watchdog Robert Lichter

CHARLES TRUEHEART

E very evening now, in a bare windowless room downtown, the VCRs hum to life to record the evening news on ABC, NBC and CBS. And click off when the day's news is done.

The next morning hired students wander in and play back the tapes, watching like hawks. As dispatches from the presidential campaign begin, they mark their clipboards whenever a reporter, or a candidate, or any talking head, says anything that might be deemed positive or negative.

They are coding television coverage of the campaign, phrase by sound bite. "Content analysis" is the highfalutin term employed by social scientists to describe this exercise, the lifeblood of the Center for Media and Public Affairs. But it is a subjective business, where one person's disparaging remark can be another's plain statement of fact. These young people are told to beware of inferences, to register only the most obviously "positive" and "negative" statements.

The center's bulletins on how many minutes and seconds the networks devoted to such and such an issue, or to candidates' characters vs. campaign handicapping vs. policy debates, turn up frequently in media stories, along with sometimes colorful quotes from S. Robert Lichter, the political scientist who founded CMPA in 1984.

These evaluations, and the scrutiny of the networks' every news bite, make many media types squirm. But to judge by the regular citations of the center's work in the press, both the media and their analyst have come to understand one another better.

In his office down the hall from the coding zoom, the 43-year-old Lichter, who is co-director of the center with his far less visible wife, Linda, has the latest fistful of results from the nightly tracking of campaign "press." (They say "press" at the center, even though the main preoccupation is TV.) Numbers from the month of January, with its presidential tummy trouble and Democratic bimbonics, are just in.

Among Democrats, the percentage of "positive" coverage is high, especially for Paul Tsongas (83 percent), Tom Harkin (80) and Bob Kerry (78). Bill Clinton, the evident front-runner, does less well, with a 42 percent positive rating, below even Jerry Brown's 50 percent.

Another way of putting this is that 58 percent of what ABC, NBC and CBS put on the air about Clinton was "negative." It could be a quote from an opponent, a remark from a voter, or a phrase from the reporter or anchor. The content analysis employed here does not discriminate among sources of negative or positive assessments, let alone between allegations and supportable facts.

As the other Democrats have repeatedly complained, Clinton got the bulk of network television's coverage of the Democratic contest in January—a good deal more than all the others combined (45 "mentions" or "features" vs. 29 for the rest). Throw in the reason for most of the attention—Gennifer Flowers—and it's not surprising that Clinton's press looks so negative.

"Lichter's Law," says Lichter, holding an index finger aloft: "The more powerful a politician is perceived by the press, the more negative his press." He adds, "As soon as someone becomes a frontrunner, he attracts criticism from other candidates and from the media generally."

To the media's professional navel-watchers, this is a truism, too obvious to be uttered. Lichter objects brightly to such cynicism. "Just because you can explain something doesn't make it any less striking," he says. He points to interesting numbers behind the numbers: Breaking out Clinton's coverage by network, Clinton got 54 and 58 percent positive coverage, respectively, from CBS and NBC, but only 8 percent from ABC. Is Peter Jennings a Clinton-hater?

No. The more prosaic reason, Lichter explains, is that, unlike NBC and CBS, ABC didn't do a Clinton profile during January. Clinton profiles, focusing on his record and speaking style, tend to be "positive," and to balance the "negative" coverage engendered by Flowers's allegations.

To ABC's Washington bureau chief, George Watson, such close readings can be misleading—just as polls can be. Speaking of which, Watson notes the "paradox" in CMIPA's numbers that "Clinton has been propelled into being the leading candidate on the basis of negative coverage."

The fortunes of George Bush, as coded on television news programs, fascinate Lichter equally. He calls Bush, in social science lingo, a "negative referent." Another way of saying this is that all the challengers, Democratic and Republican, gang up on him. It's no wonder so many campaign sound bites get coded in the Bush-negative column.

"George Bush is getting the worst press of any candidate in the race with the exception of David Duke, and he's running a close second to Duke," says Lichter— about, 70 percent negative coverage, not just during January but for all of 1991. "If I were a Republican I'd be screaming at this," he says. "As a media analyst I can attribute it to the press's tendency to attack the most powerful political figure."

Does this work the same way for Republicans and Democrats? Lichter has refined a theory about that. "There is clearly no general ideological bias in presidential election coverage," he says, noting that the center's exhaustive coding of the

Bush-Dukakis campaign in 1988 yielded "absolutely identical positive press. You could not possibly have more balanced coverage than that."

But, he adds, "certain candidates will be helped by a burst of good press, and they tend not to be conservative candidates."

His frequently cited evidence is Jesse Jackson's extremely positive press during the 1988 presidential campaign, which coincides with what you might call a corollary to Lichter's Law: The less seriously a candidate is taken, the more positive his coverage.

The media's coverage of Jerry Brown's campaign would have to be put down as an exception to the corollary. And should Pat Buchanan do "better than expected" in the New Hampshire primary, the way the media then handle him, Lichter agrees, will be "a test of my hypothesis."

The Reed Irvine Factor

The Center for Media and Public Affairs is into all kinds of content analysis now, running different projects analyzing: the possible bias of PBS documentaries, political humor on late-night TV monologues, the use of courtroom footage on television, coverage of environmental causes of cancer, the visibility of female and minority reporters on TV, and reciprocal media images of the United States and Canada, to name some.

But the Lichters and their frequent coauthor, Smith College professor Stanley Rothman, doubtless will always be remembered in Washington for their 1986 book, "The Media Elite." Surveys completed by news people themselves suggested that the Washington press corps is composed overwhelmingly of Eastern-educated liberals whose values, practices and politics are sharply at odds with, and to the left of, those of the American people as a whole.

The authors also argued, going beyond the surveys, that the messengers couldn't help but color the message of the news.

The messengers didn't take it lying down.

The Washington Post's executive editor at the time, Benjamin Bradlee, publicly challenged the validity of the surveys. Michael Kinsley, in his New Republic column, called the book "a tendentious piece of pseudo-scientific rubbish of just the sort that drives conservatives up the wall when it doesn't serve their purposes." The center's funding—about $600,000 a year in all—draws heavily from corporate philanthropies and conservative purses such as the John M. Olin, Reader's Digest and Smith-Richardson foundations. Of this suspect backing, Lichter says offhandedly, "Conservatives like to keep an eye on the media, just as liberals like to keep an eye on big business."

Asked whether he regards himself as a conservative, Lichter—who's taught at Princeton and George Washington universities and has been a fellow at the center-right American Enterprise Institute—says no. He adds that it's not in a scholar's blood to have an ideology. In another conversation, defending himself against insinuations about his agenda, he blurts out that he's a Democrat.

Lichter's friend, fellow scholar and professional rival, Georgetown University's Michael J. Robinson, describes Lichter's politics as "a little bit like mine, and I like to describe myself as a Jerry Ford Democrat. . . . But by no stretch of the imagination is he a right-winger." Nonetheless, Robinson says that after the publication of the press book, Lichter was virtually persona non grata in Washington and confessed to Robinson that he felt the pain of a pariah.

" 'The Media Elite' has become the most influential book on the media that was never reviewed by the New York Times, The Washington Post, the Los Angeles Times and the Wall Street Journal," says Robinson.

Be that as it may, both Lichter and the media have changed, according to Robinson. "Bob has become a better analyst of press failings, and the press has become more willing to give Bob's data their due," he says. "We're both down now to accepting the notion that the press is driven far more by commercialism than by anything that could be called ideological."

Robinson adds that Lichter's critics "used to perceive him as a Reed Irvine. Now they perceive him as Midge Decter," the neoconservative thinker. (In interviews Lichter himself repeatedly, self-consciously puts space between himself and Irvine, the habitually enraged media watchdog of the right.)

Watson, for one, says he suspects Lichter came to his position "by an ideological route," but still respects the data and calls the center's work "useful and thought-provoking."

Rothman, who was an informal adviser to Robert Lichter's Harvard PhD work, defends their media studies. "We limit ourselves to doing content analyses that other people can replicate," says Rothman. (The raw contents of their work are available to scholars at the Roper Center at the University of Connecticut at Storrs.) "They can see the questions and criticize the analysis. But the data stands on its own."

TV as Hypodermic

Last year the Lichters and Rothman published a sequel to "The Media Elite" called "Watching America." It applies the same techniques, the same deconstruction of contents, to entertainment, the fiction side of network television.

Having sifted the characters and plots of selected prime-time shows from the mid-1950s to the mid-1980s ("a stratified random sample" of video footage, says Lichter), the authors were able to draw a picture of the world according to Hollywood, noting the attitudes of TV characters about everything from capitalism to sexuality to violence to tobacco use.

From this they concluded: "Television started as an agent of social control but became an agent of social change. Once the servant of the status quo, it now fosters populist suspicions of traditional mores and institutions. . . . Far from always following in the wake of public tastes, the fictional world of prime time . . . tries to guide middle-American tastes in the direction of intellectual trends emanating from New York and Los Angeles.

Some say this is bosh. Todd Gitlin, the Berkeley sociologist who serves as a convenient foil in the pages of "Watching America," calls its analysis (like that of "The Media Elite") simplistic—"the old hypodermic model, that TV is this drug shot into people's veins and automatically usurps them."

Taking another tack, Lichter-Rothman critics ask: If prime time can be credited with opening a few minds and breaking down a few bigotries—"All in the Family" is the obvious example—what exactly is the beef? Lichter replies, "If television is going to teach values constantly and systematically, I think they ought to have the same balance as journalism."

The reaction to "Watching America" in Hollywood seemingly has been a shrug. The only hometown press notice to turn up on the Nexis computer database—and there weren't many notices anywhere—was a dismissive column by Los Angeles Times television critic Howard Rosenberg. Ben Stein, who has been writing of (and from) Hollywood for two decades, imagines that any scriptwriter or producer who stumbled on the authors' work would say, "Who cares what these pishers in Washington say?"

Predictions

These days, monitoring campaign coverage, Lichter makes more modest claims for his science than his critics would suggest. But he believes the content analysis of network news in some cases anticipates the turns of public opinion.

"A changing balance of good press and bad press predicts changes in Bush's poll ratings," Lichter observes, referring to the center's separate project monitoring TV coverage of the Bush administration.

Meaning the media do have power to influence the course of events? "Insofar as the media changes perceptions and perceptions in turn change realities, that's true," he says.

Mass Media and Politics 15

Networks Adapt to Changed Campaign Role

HOWARD KURTZ

S ince the dawn of the television age, the pivotal events of presidential politics have usually unfolded on CBS, NBC and ABC.

There was the Roger Mudd interview in which Sen. Edward M. Kennedy could not explain why he wanted to be president. Dan Rather's tense confrontation with George Bush over the Iran-contra scandal. Dan Quayle hustling from one anchor booth to the next after his surprise nomination as Bush's running mate.

All that has changed in 1992, the year the network news boys dropped off the bus. The most compelling scenes—Ross Perot declaring his availability with Larry King, Gennifer Flowers making accusations live on CNN, Bill Clinton playing the sax for Arsenio Hall, joking with radio host Don Imus, rapping with young folks on MTV—have taken place in farflung corners of the media marketplace.

The networks have scrambled to adapt to the new reality, with "Today," "This Morning" and "20/20" now luring the candidates by offering lengthy interviews, call-in formats or town-meeting setups.

"For almost half a century, the networks literally hosted the presidential campaigns," said Jon Katz, a former television producer who now writes for Rolling Stone. "They anchored primaries, they assigned correspondents to each candidate, they did specials. In the last eight years that whole process has collapsed . . . and it's created a vacuum that the new shows have rushed to fill."

The network evening newscasts have changed in ways that critics say makes it harder for candidates' voices to be heard. The average sound bite—a video clip of a presidential contender speaking—dwindled from 42.3 seconds in 1968 to 9.8 seconds in 1988. In the past six months, reports the Center for Media and Public

Affairs, the typical campaign sound bite has been sliced even further, to just 7.3 seconds.

"That's staggering to me," said Robert Lichter, the center's director. "The networks went on and on about how they were going to do better this time around. The news is so heavily produced that the theme of the story overwhelms the message of the candidates."

But network executives argue that their mission has changed. With local stations, CNN and C-SPAN chronicling each thrust and parry of the campaign, they say, their strong suit is interpreting and analyzing the action.

Steve Friedman, executive producer of "NBC Nightly News," put it succinctly: "We take what they say in the morning and show how they lied."

Several network officials said their compression of the candidates' rhetoric is no different than the brief quotes often published by newspapers.

"We're confined to 22 minutes," said Joe Peyronnin, a CBS vice president. "We have other news to report. It's a matter of packaging. . . . We have been much better in '92 than in '88 at covering the issues."

Budget cutbacks have also taken their toll. During the primaries, senior reporters and camera crews traveled with the candidates infrequently, often replaced by young producers. And the networks may limit their coverage of this summer's party conventions to as little as one hour a night.

While the percentage of American households watching the network evening news has dropped from 74 percent to 55 percent over the past decade, the shows still command an audience of more than 22 million homes. Yet when President Bush granted an interview last week, he bypassed the Big Three networks for a midday appearance with CNN's Frank Sesno, which reached fewer than 350,000 homes. Administration officials say Bush and his advisers believe CNN is less confrontational than the network shows.

Clinton and Perot have been working the talk-show circuit, often getting up to two hours of free air time. Such appearances enable them to bypass the establishment news media, which often felt manipulated by the staged events of the 1988 campaign.

"We all got ready to deal with the photo-op problem," said Paul Friedman, executive producer of ABC's "World News Tonight." "We were never going to get sucked into covering flag factories again. Now instead of flag factories they're doing talk shows. It's a different kind of backdrop that we then cover."

But skeptics find the new formats refreshing, saying journalists have grown too absorbed with the campaign process itself. Between the New Hampshire and New York primaries, Lichter's group found, 14 percent of the network news stories dealt primarily with issues and 37 percent with the campaign horse race.

"The talk shows have liberated the country from the narrow, restrictive agenda of the conventional press," Katz said.

But ABC's Friedman maintained that "the candidates weren't saying anything new about the issues. There were more debates than ever before. . . . Do you really think you didn't get a chance to find out where Paul Tsongas stands on the economy, or Bill Clinton on the need for vocational education? It was all there for people to watch, not necessarily all on the evening newscasts."

While call-in formats allow candidates to speak in generalities with little fear of contradiction, network reporters are more adept at probing for inconsistencies. When Perot appeared on a CBS call-in show this month, Rather asked: "Would you consider raising taxes or not?"

"That's like giving more narcotics to an addict," Perot replied.

After another exchange, Rather said: "Is it fair or unfair to say that you're opposed to raising taxes but you don't rule it out . . . ?"

"The thing we have to do is bring our fiscal house in order," Perot said.

"So, no new taxes?"

"I have said it as clearly as I can."

"Well, I want to hear it from you, though, not from me."

"I would only consider raising taxes if all else fails."

The networks have also grown bolder at challenging candidates. "In selling himself, Perot sometimes misrepresents the facts," Lisa Myers said recently on "NBC Nightly News."

Perot said on "Today" that he "never said" he could save $20 billion by asking affluent Americans to give up Social Security and Medicare. "In fact, Perot has said that," Myers declared. She also said Perot was wrong in saying that his employees were never barred from wearing beards.

You Say You Want a Cultural Revolution?

STEVEN MUFSON

> "There is in fact no such thing as art for art's sake. . . .
> Proletarian literature and art are part of the whole
> proletarian revolutionary cause . . ."
> —"The Quotations of Chairman Mao Zedong"

At the height of the Great Proletarian Cultural Revolution in the mid-1960s, a married couple named Xia, both Beijing sculptors trained by Soviet teachers, were deemed politically incorrect and banished to the impoverished province of Anhui. There they cleaned floors, swept streets and pulled wooden carts. Forced to recite the quotations of Chinese Communist Party Chairman Mao every day, Mrs. Xia had a nervous breakdown.

Twenty-five years later—with the Communist Party devoted to promoting economic growth instead of proletarian revolution, and Mao's Little Red Book regarded as more of a curiosity than a key to wisdom—China is once again in the throes of a cultural revolution. But this one is quite different.

Today, Xia Xing, the 36-year-old son of the once-banished sculptors, is an artist too—an oil painter. But, unlike his parents, he paints as he pleases—in his case, mostly portraits of ordinary Chinese in a style reminiscent of 16th-century Dutch masters. His mother, who has returned to Beijing, still recites Chairman Mao's sayings every day. But what was once a required routine is now seen by her son as a sign of madness.

For a recent New York exhibition marking the anniversary of the late Mao's 100th birthday, Xia Xing painted a sardonic portrait of a gray-haired chairman in his drab trademark "Mao suit"—with the yellow edge of an emperor's robe sticking out from underneath the sleeve and collar. "Young artists treat art as art, not as a propaganda tool for the government," Mrs. Xia's son says.

The new cultural revolution contradicts virtually everything the earlier one stood for. Just as the Maoist-era collectivist spirit has been replaced by entrepreneurship, so too has Maoist conformity in art been replaced by a restless search for individual style—albeit with varying levels of success, and within China's ill-defined limits on free expression.

342

At the center of the new cultural revival is contemporary Chinese oil painting, which is being produced by graduates of elite state-controlled institutes and fed by China's economic reforms and the sudden surge of foreign investment. (Relative to China's history, all Chinese oil painting is contemporary. The medium was imported from the West just 100 years ago; before that, artists used mainly ink and water-color.) Several contemporary art galleries have flowered in Beijing, while galleries from Hong Kong to London have been selling and promoting the new Chinese oil painters.

The revolution is as much about money as art. "Art is not only something to express yourself," says Lu Jie, executive assistant at the Schoeni Gallery in Hong Kong. "It is also a way to make money." The success of the commercial galleries has smashed the monopoly the Chinese government once had as sole patron of Chinese artists. "Before the 1980s, art was controlled by the political system, just as in medieval times in Europe art was controlled by the church," says the younger Xia.

The ability to lure rich new patrons has radically reshaped contemporary Chinese oil painting—at once liberating painters from bureaucratic dictates and threatening to enslave them to commercial temptations. Some painters can now earn as much with one painting as they would have made in a lifetime as salaried members of government art institutes. For instance, Yang Yuan Fei, an art professor in Beijing, commands as much as $10,000 for a portrait. The Schoeni has a stable of 10 Chinese artists working under multiyear, six-figure contracts—a setup that may seem more appropriate for professional basketball players than artists.

Today, a typical exhibition of Chinese oil paintings runs the gamut from classical portraits to pop art, from photo-realism to abstraction. And whereas the faces of workers and peasants once gleamed with enthusiasm, recent paintings show the "common people" as they are, with blemishes and splashes of mud and dirt.

Nevertheless, while the social-realist glorifications have faded, the mood in China's art world today does not match the abandon of 1989, when pro-democracy demonstrators took to the streets. At that time, some Chinese painters became postmodern performance artists: One fired gun shots through his own painting, while another ran an art history book through a washing machine and tacked it on a wall to symbolize the cleansing of official history.

But, Xia points out, art was still being used primarily as a political tool, even if it was directed against the government. "That was its weak point as art: It was still educational," he says. "[Painters] still bore the scars from political developments."

Chinese artists, like most of their countrymen, were sobered by the bloody June 4, 1989, crackdown on dissidents in Beijing's Tiananmen Square. Now oil painters generally send their messages in more subtle, ambiguous ways.

Two galleries, one in Beijing and one in Hong Kong, provide windows onto the contemporary Chinese art market. They display the mixture of unfettered commercialism and guarded expression that make up Chinese art, and society, today.

The Century Gallery, Beijing

Opened in December, the Century Gallery is in the middle of Ritan Park, a couple of miles east of Tiananmen Square, in a building where a 16th-century Ming emperor used to change into ceremonial robes. The gallery is trying to edge its way into the market, and joins a growing field of serious galleries here, including the September, the Red Gate, the Beijing Concert Hall and galleries in the Oriental Gate and the Crown Plaza Hotel. Century's offerings are aimed at foreign business people and companies, embassies and the few newly rich Chinese entrepreneurs; asking prices range from $1,000 to $12,000 per painting. Such figures would be considered cheap on 57th Street in Manhattan, but are king's ransoms in a country where the premier, Li Peng, recently told a Chinese newspaper he earns the equivalent of less than $100 a month after taxes.

But 33-year-old Li Jianguang, Century's manager and co-owner (and no relation to the premier), says he wants the gallery to be distinguished not just by its high prices. "I want to create a new model in this field: a Chinese art dealer helping Chinese artists be successful." (One of his partners is Xia Xing.)

In particular, the portraits at Century show how Chinese painting has departed from the glorification of ordinary people. Among the paintings for sale is a nude by Wang Hua Xiang depicting a middle-aged, grim-faced woman with a tired-looking body twisted away from her image in a mirror. Liu Shao Dong has painted himself in "Artist in a Mosquito Net," a bold, lifelike canvas that portrays the bare-chested artist asleep in a drab gray room with paint peeling from the walls. A tiny pool of blood lies at his side. Chao Ge, in "Girl and Morning," flattens and distorts his subject's features; she appears cross-eyed as she gazes up toward a murky green sky.

Most of the paintings are representational, but in "Breaking Up," Wang Huai Qing forays into abstraction with a canvas of brown and black geometric shapes that appear to be coming apart from each other in ways that suggest they cannot fit back together again.

Like the changing content of the paintings, the commercialization of the Chinese art business reflects a sort of retreat and consolidation by many artists and dealers. "Before the economic reforms," says Century's Li, "artists gave their paintings to friends or put them under the beds. Intellectuals traditionally look down on business. But once in the market, everybody realized the price of a person's painting is one of the most important marks of quality."

So far, though, business in the gallery has been slow. And customers aren't Li's only worry.

The pavilion he rents for $20,000 a year belongs to an association for traditional Chinese painting and calligraphy. A former leading member of the association, who was previously a director of public security, vowed that whenever the gallery sold a nude, he would seal the door shut. Though he is technically out of power, a public security officer visited the gallery and recommended taking down one of the nude portraits that, he believed, suggested an unflattering view of Chinese life. Li put the painting behind one of the display walls, but left up another nude of an attractive model being photographed—"a big risk," he says. But, he adds, "I had to consider the whole situation. . . . We don't want to be looked down on by artists or for them to say we are afraid."

The Schoeni Gallery, Hong Kong

Unlike the Century, the Schoeni Gallery is well established, located in the heart of the British protectorate that is the bustling business and trading center for southern China and much of Asia. Its Swiss owner, Manfred Schoeni, is a longtime dealer in antique Chinese art.

In early 1992 Schoeni visited the mainland to learn about the contemporary oil painting scene. There he met Lu Jie, a recent graduate of one of China's leading art institutes, who helped introduce Schoeni to some of the most promising Chinese painters.

When Lu, now 30, was admitted to Hanzhou's prestigious Zhejiang Academy of Fine Arts in 1984, he was one of eight people chosen from about 20,000 applicants. He took six tests, including technique, perspective and anatomy. For the "creative" exercise, applicants were given a topic: "The Passage to Your Future." Some people painted workers or peasants; Lu painted the other students painting in the testing room, and the blackboard with the topic written on it.

The survivors of these tough programs, Lu says, are proficient at the technical aspects of painting, though they are still searching for the best ways to express themselves.

The paintings in a current Schoeni exhibition include a variety of styles. In "Happiness," a large canvas for sale for about $10,000, Yue Min Jun depicts a sea of young men in identical white T-shirts bearing a logo of the Tiananmen gate. The men's smiling faces are identical, suggesting a lack of individual identity and a falseness to their cheer. Red balloons, normally seen during China's national celebrations of the revolution, float overhead. In a pair of canvases called "Consumer Icons II," for sale for about $8,500, Qi Zhi Long has painted a bikini-clad woman, faceless except for her red lips, who is surrounded by flowers—each with a picture of Mao in the center.

"American pop art, like Andy Warhol's Campbell's soup painting, transformed daily consumer images into serious art, thus raising ordinary subjects to new levels," says Lu. "The Chinese idea is just the opposite: It wants to [take] something very high, like Mao, and mix it with ordinary subjects." Thus, in the painting "Happy Citizen and Police," Yang Shao Bin turns the usually stern soldier into a happy, almost cartoonish figure laughing alongside a worker and an intellectual.

Some paintings are more overtly political, and would be unlikely to be shown in galleries on the mainland. One by Liu Wai shows a Last Supper scene, with Christ replaced by Mao, and with other deceased communist leaders, such as Zhou Enlai and Zhu De, as the apostles. Another, titled "Chairman Mao II" by Zeng Fan Zhi, shows an unhappy-looking Mao surrounded by supplicants and sycophants waving copies of the Little Red Book.

Schoeni has become the patron of several of these painters, urging them to retreat from the world of commerce to concentrate on painting. In return, he promotes and supports them. And he urges them to remain in China rather than be lured into exile.

Agrees Lu, "When I'm in Switzerland, I hate it. Everything is too perfect. I am missing the dirt of China. China is the best place for art. True, in the last 40 years artists have suffered. But as an ancient poet said, 'Tragedy for the country is happiness for the poet.' "

Indonesia Cracks Down on Media

WILLIAM BRANIGIN

A fter a brief fling with limited political "openness," the Indonesian government is cracking down on local press coverage of sensitive issues, drawing sharp criticism from the country's growing middle class, human rights groups and the United States.

The closure of three popular, privately owned newsweeklies by Indonesia's Information Ministry in June triggered demonstrations that were broken up by riot police and soldiers. The subsequent arrest of 42 hunger-striking students last month prompted a strong public objection by the U.S. Embassy here.

The protests resumed Thursday when about 100 journalists demonstrated against the ban on the weeklies.

Now the government is threatening to take action against several leading publications for reporting on the crackdown, related demonstrations and recent unrest in the disputed Indonesian-ruled territory of East Timor. Among those warned were the Kompas daily, the English-language Jakarta Post newspaper and a magazine on legal and social issues, Forum Keadilan, according to media sources.

In East Timor, a van belonging to a local newspaper was blown up July 23 in an incident that editors suspect was related to the paper's recent coverage of protests against Indonesian rule. Authorities denied responsibility for the blast.

The closure of the weeklies followed some hard-hitting coverage of controversial stories, including Indonesia's purchase of a fleet of former East German warships, labor strife and a major banking scandal that implicated senior officials. But it also appeared to reflect increasing touchiness about reports of dissension in the government of President Suharto, diplomats and journalists said.

Friction within the government is an especially sensitive subject these days because of the unresolved issue of succession.

Suharto, a 73-year-old former army general who came to power in 1966 and formally assumed the presidency two years later, is in his sixth five-year presidential term—following unopposed elections in a rubber-stamp assembly. He has indicated that he may step down when his current term expires in 1998, and it is unclear who might succeed him.

The question has raised an element of uncertainty about the political stability of an authoritarian system that has presided over heady economic growth and attracted $28 billion in foreign investment since 1992.

The press crackdown began when the Information Ministry announced June 21 that it had revoked the publishing licenses of Tempo, Indonesia's biggest and most prestigious newsmagazine, and two other weeklies: Editor magazine and a popular investigative tabloid newspaper called DeTik. The government charged that the three publications had violated "the Code of Ethics of Indonesian Journalism," which bars publication of anything deemed harmful to the nation, social harmony, religion or common decency.

The government said the three weeklies in recent months had been "generating friction, heating up interracial dissension and may even be endangering the stability of the nation." No specifics were cited, but Indonesian analysts said the main grievance was a series of stories about the purchase and refurbishment of 39 former East German naval ships as part of a projected $1.1 billion upgrading of the Indonesian navy.

The deal has led to a rift between its chief proponent, powerful Research and Technology Minister B. J. Habibie, and a leading cost-cutter, Finance Minister Mar'ie Muhammad. Some senior military officers also were reported to be unhappy with the acquisition.

Suharto told Australia's visiting prime minister that the publications had threatened "national unity at this time of great economic growth and transformation."

The closures effectively ended the government's year-old experiment with "openness," a policy that appealed to Indonesia's growing middle class and was reflected chiefly in a less fettered press.

"It looks as though press freedom in Indonesia is still a matter of personal whim," said Sidney Jones, the director of Human Rights Watch/Asia. "None of these publications threatened national security. They offended the politically powerful."

After the ban took effect, protesters staged three demonstrations without incident. But on June 27, riot police and soldiers used rattan canes to disperse about 150 marching journalists, artists and students. At least 10 protesters were injured, and 21 were arrested and held overnight.

When police hauled away 42 students staging a hunger strike at the private Indonesian Legal Aid Foundation on July 7, the U.S. Embassy here released a statement deploring the arrests and calling on the government to lift the ban on the three publications.

The students were assessed token $1 fines and released. But there was no sign that the government was prepared to allow the three weeklies to resume publishing. Journalists said the government was seeking the removal of several senior editors at the profitable Tempo, which sold about 200,000 copies a week and was the main target of the crackdown.

Journalism, Colombian-Style

ELEANOR RANDOLPH

L uis Gabriel Cano does not look like a hero. He is small and white-haired, the grandfather of 13. His voice is soft. His English is stiff and measured as he talks quietly about his life and his business.

Without the Superman whiz-bang we have come to expect in our champions, it quickly becomes clear to any listener that Luis Cano and his family are brave people. They publish a newspaper in Colombia called El Espectador; their editorials say no to drugs.

Three years ago, Cano's brother, Guillermo, suggested in print that Colombian drug lords should be extradited to the United States for trial. As Guillermo's car pulled away from the newspaper's office in Bogota one evening, three people on two motorcycles suddenly appeared from the line of traffic and opened fire. After Guillermo's death, the three other Cano brothers continued running the paper. They also continued to push for locking up what Luis Cano calls "the mafia."

Thus, the revenge by this mafia continues.

On Sept. 2, a truck laden with 200 kilograms of dynamite exploded next to the Espectador building. One person was killed, and damage to the building was estimated at about $2.5 million. The explosion destroyed the phone system. It wrecked the computer network. One-third of the newsprint was ruined, and the presses were damaged. Insurance doesn't cover terrorism in Colombia. The cost of the explosion came out of the company's hide.

At the same time, drug traffickers began calling Cano's advertisers. They suggested that when they saw ads in El Espectador, they would come around to visit the advertisers. Not to buy the merchandise they explained. Not hardly.

The big businesses shook off the threat. A lot of the smaller advertisers were not so blase. They canceled their ads. Some apologized, and Cano, a man who understands fear, said he understood theirs. But, for a newspaper like this one, whose circulation is about 200,000, dynamite is mightier than the printing press. Cano, president of the newspaper company, came to the United States last week to look for help.

"If we don't receive support, we cannot continue," Cano explained as he asked about journalistic organizations that support newspapers such as his.

That Cano wants to continue is what is so astonishing to most people. There are easier ways to make money. He explains the reason: His family has run El Espectador since 1887 and is proud of its role in Colombian society.

"We have a tradition of being always against any group or any person that violates the law," he told a group of reporters and editors at the Washington Post last week. After Cano talked last week he left us subdued about the "battles," as I often misidentify them, in the American media.

We howl when a government agency denies us information. That's legitimate, of course, but we also howl when the agency gives us information too late for our deadline. The public is not being deprived of the data, at least not eventually, but we scream anyway.

We hunker down when somebody files a lawsuit—about libel, newspaper boxes on the corner or the way newspapers compile circulation figures. Each prompts newspapers and their lawyers to decry the "chilling effect" on the First Amendment right to freedom of the press.

You want to talk about the chilling effect? Like journalists in China and South Africa and too many other places around the world, Luis Cano can talk about the real chilling effect. His newspaper, what's left of it, is crawling with guards and policemen to protect him from the live weapons of the drug lords. Haven't the drug thugs infiltrated those police or even your newsroom? he was asked.

Cano shrugged. "How could you tell?" he replied.

Bodyguards ride in his car with him. "I feel very, very uncomfortable," Cano explained. "The guard sitting next to me has a very long machine gun, an old one, and I said? 'Why don't you ask for a shorter one so that you can (move) it more quickly?' " He knows, like we know, that the guard probably cannot move quickly enough if the drug lords really want to get him. What a way to live.

Speaking to people accustomed to worrying about cholesterol and the cost of braces on kids' teeth Cano admitted: "We are worried. We are afraid. I always worry about the future of my children and my grandchildren." Then, he added: "I think that's why we have to fight the problem of drugs. If not, I don't know which world they are going to live in."

Thank you, Luis Gabriel Cano and El Espectador, for reminding us that the presses are there to fight corruption and to try to tell the truth. We've got it so easy here, we sometimes forget.

Mass Media Ethics 16

High Fliers: Media and White House Travel

HOWARD KURTZ and MICHAEL ISIKOFF

W hen President Clinton flew to Martha's Vineyard this week, some reporters brought their spouses and children on the White House press plane for $100 round trip, or one-sixth the standard air fare from here to Boston.

Aides in the White House travel office routinely book these charter flights, handle the journalists' baggage, make hotel reservations, set up telephone lines and arrange local bus trips for business and pleasure. During Clinton's visit to Hawaii, the travel staff even arranged to transport reporters to an ocean cruise.

This might seem like an unusual degree of first-class service, but news organizations are paying for it. Spouses and children receive discount rates because the White House Correspondents Association, like any other group renting a charter, sets the rules.

Still, new questions have been raised about such media perks in the three months since White House officials asked the FBI to investigate the travel operation. In an apparent note to himself before he committed suicide last month, deputy White House counsel Vincent W. Foster Jr. wrote: "The press is covering up the illegal benefits they received from the travel staff."

But efforts to document such illegal benefits have been unsuccessful. The most frequently alleged abuse—that some White House reporters have evaded customs duties on expensive foreign goods—is not the responsibility of the travel office staff.

On presidential trips overseas, a Customs Service agent flies on the press charter and hands out forms on which travelers are supposed to declare purchases if they have spent more than $400. Unlike ordinary tourists, however, journalists are not subject to having their luggage randomly inspected by agents seeking contraband.

"Reporters are not in the high-risk category" for smuggling, said Bill Anthony, a Customs Service spokesman. "We don't expect Sam Donaldson is going to be carrying $85,000 in laundered money. . . . There is an honor system involved here."

According to a Customs Service review of records last week after Foster's note was disclosed, 3,190 journalists and crew members have flown on White House press planes on 21 overseas trips since 1988. The review found that 43 customs declarations were filed on eight of these trips and none on the rest.

Anthony said the seemingly low number of declarations is not surprising because journalists are working most of the time. "We don't see any massive horde of unscrupulous reporters out there," he said.

But allegations of abuses persist. The Wall Street Journal has quoted one unnamed White House correspondent as saying he once brought two Chinese rugs worth $10,000 on the press plane without paying duties.

"I've heard people talk about going to Japan and buying pearls or going to Southeast Asia and buying gemstones and bringing them back without declaring them," said David Lauter, a White House reporter for the Los Angeles Times. "But it's not the job of the travel office to enforce the customs laws."

Travel office employees do allow journalists to save shipping costs by transporting large objects on the charters.

"If there is cheating, as has been alleged, it's not anything I've ever observed," NBC's Andrea Mitchell said. "Vince Foster must have been misled by the suspicious and antipress bias of those who wrote the initial reports to him."

Suspicions about the travel office and its cozy relationship with the press corps are nothing new. In 1981, John Rogers, then chief of administration for the Reagan White House, ordered an outside audit of the travel office. This prompted loud complaints from veteran correspondents who viewed it as an effort to oust the office's popular chief, Bob Manning.

The audit found sloppy accounting, loose record-keeping and more than $100,000 in a travel office checking account, according to Rogers. These surplus funds, the result of six months of overbillings, were refunded to news organizations.

Manning retired during this period, but Rogers stressed that the auditors found no impropriety by any employee.

In late 1988, an anonymous letter passed to the General Accounting Office and the White House counsel made several specific charges about conflicts of interest, sweetheart contracts and other abuses within the travel office. A brief White House inquiry was unable to substantiate the charges, according to a Clinton White House official.

This May, the White House fired seven travel office employees after complaints of mismanagement from Harry Thomason, a Hollywood producer and friend of Clinton whose consulting firm had been seeking White House travel business. An internal review later faulted White House officials for appearing to put undue pressure on the FBI to investigate the office.

News accounts have helped to fuel the scandal. An investigative report by the Internal Revenue Service includes in its appendix a Wall Street Journal article quoting "White House and FBI officials" as saying investigators were examining whether kickbacks were paid to obtain travel business.

"We got the information from sources we believed to be reliable," said Alan Murray, the Journal's deputy Washington bureau chief. "It's true that so far there's been no subsequent evidence to back it up."

The travel office handles about $11 million a year, but no public funds are involved. After criticism that a single company was receiving most of the business, the White House now seeks competitive bids for each trip. The cost is divided among participating news organizations.

The bills, which include logistical support and ground transportation, can be quite high. Last year, for example, the Bush White House billed The Washington Post $1,600 for a single trip to Nashua, N.H. Other bills covered trips to Fayetteville, Ark., ($1,111), Chicago ($1,156), Kansas City, Mo., ($1,063), Orlando ($990) and Philadelphia ($311). A 12-day trip to Japan, Korea, Australia, Singapore and Hawaii cost the paper $11,141.

Marlin Fitzwater, President George Bush's press secretary, said news organizations "paid more than their fair share. They paid for everything we provided them in terms of space, tables, typewriters, airplanes, food." The news media even paid the air fare of White House staff members whose job was to help them, he said.

White House reporters say baggage service and other extras are less luxurious than they seem in light of the grueling schedule on many trips.

"The bottom line is we don't get perks, we get expensive transportation that we pay for so we can follow the president everywhere in the world," Mitchell said.

Feeding the Mouth That Bites Them

HOWARD KURTZ

S am Donaldson will be in the news again tonight, although not in the way that he or "PrimeTime Live" might prefer.

There was a bit of a flap last spring when the ABC program reported on a congressional junket to Florida sponsored by the Electronic Industries Association—and had to hurriedly add that correspondent Donaldson had accepted a speaking fee from the same group.

Tonight, "PrimeTime" will report on a Key West, Fla., trip this month for 30 congressional staff members, sponsored by the American Insurance Association and other insurance groups. Donaldson accepted a $30,000 fee from an insurance coalition that includes the American Insurance Association for a speech at New York's Waldorf-Astoria last January. He also received first-class air fare and hotel accommodations.

"I was not beholden to them and they were not beholden to me," Donaldson said yesterday. "I of course do not make the laws under which the insurance industry operates. I have not spoken about the laws affecting the insurance industry on the 'Brinkley' show or in any of my pieces."

Donaldson said his fee, which will be invoked by insurance officials on the program, is "just a smoke screen. We're going to continue to investigate people and groups whether I've spoken to them or not. Raising my name is not going to deter 'PrimeTime' from doing this type of investigation." Still, Donaldson admits to "having second thoughts" about whether to continue making paid speeches.

ABC Senior Vice President Richard Wald said the fee did not create an appearance problem because "Sam doesn't normally cover the insurance industry" and "has had nothing to do with this story." Chris Wallace, the reporter on the junket story, said Donaldson's fee will be disclosed but that the issue is "a red herring."

Lecture agents say $30,000 is a top-of-the-line fee for a journalist. "Nightline" anchor Ted Koppel recently told TV Guide that he has stopped giving paid speeches to industry groups because the fees "reached a point where I didn't believe I could explain it to the average viewer."

Sen. John Breaux (D-La.), one of six members of Congress whose expenses-paid visit to Boca Raton also will be featured on tonight's show, said the trip's purpose is to raise money for charity. He said "PrimeTime" has become "the

National Enquirer with a TV camera. They're running around with cameras hidden in tennis bags. They have to try to make it something sinister."

But Wallace said the corporate sponsors, while donating $64,000 to charity, spent $150,000 on the lawmakers, including the hiring of big-name golf and tennis pros. "If that's Senator Breaux's definition of a charity event, he's welcome to it," he said. Wallace says he'll also mention that the National Association of Broadcasters wines and dines members of Congress at its convention.

Breakfast Brouhaha

After a breakfast meeting with reporters, Rep. Dick Armey (R-Tex.) accused Newsday columnist Lars-Erik Nelson of the most "irresponsible piece of journalism" he has seen "in 10 years in Congress."

Nelson wrote last week that Armey had "talked easily about impeaching President Clinton" over the Whitewater scandal and engaged in "offhand, reckless speculation."

In a letter to the Los Angeles Times, which carried the column, Armey said: "The first time I ever heard the word impeachment used in connection with Whitewater was when Nelson raised the prospect of impeachment at that breakfast. . . . He asks me about impeaching the president, I answer his question, then he blasts me for 'talk[ing] easily about impeaching President Clinton.' What a crock."

But after a vociferous complaint from Nelson, Armey backed off in a second letter to the Times. He acknowledged that another reporter had raised the issue, although Nelson asked a follow-up question. Still, Armey insisted that he "repeatedly qualified my comments to make clear that I was not suggesting impeachment."

Nelson says Armey's complaint "is just not true, and now he admits it's not true. He doesn't deny any of the quotes. What he objects to is my description of his attitude as he made these remarks."

Times Watch

"Behind the Times," a new book by Edwin Diamond, serves up some interesting nuggets about life at the New York Times:

Former food critic Bryan Miller, after being barred from a Manhattan restaurant for writing a negative review, dyed his hair, donned sunglasses and wore a "John Travolta" outfit while dining there undercover.

During the Vietnam War protests, then-managing editor Abe Rosenthal said in a memo: "I think that because of our own liberal interests and our reporters' inclination we overdo this." He said the staff should "make an effort to represent other shades of opinion than those held by the new Left, the old Left, the middle aged Left and the antiwar people."

Former publisher Arthur Ochs Sulzberger Sr. once told his editors in a note: "Every once in awhile I get fascinated by the incredible gobbledygook that finds its way into the pages of the New York Times."

After a reader complained about a picture of a model in skimpy lingerie, Sulzberger wrote Rosenthal: "You put this bosom in the paper, so I think you should reply. . . . I don't like it in the Times."

Eric Lax's biography of Woody Allen was excerpted in the Times Magazine, reviewed on the front of the Book Review and recommended by the review editors. Lax, Diamond notes, is Sulzberger's son-in-law.

Resurrection

The Washington Business Journal reported last week that in an effort to keep Navy jobs in Virginia, Sen. John Warner (R-Va.) and Rep. James Moran (D-Va.) had met with Navy Secretary "and former Virginia governor" John Dalton.

Not very likely, since the former Virginia governor died in 1989. Navy Secretary John Dalton hails from Texas.

Oh, That Code of Ethics

JOEL ACHENBACH

N o wonder American journalism has become a gutter profession—we forgot we have a code!

The "Code of Ethics" is an industry secret. Which is to say, hardly anyone in the industry knows it exists. All across America, reporters are shouting questions at public figures and rifling through government documents and taking two-hour expense-account lunches totally unaware that these actions are governed by a code, a code that is three pages long and has a section on Fair Play and a section on Accuracy and Objectivity and concludes with a Pledge.

A copy was obtained by The Washington Post (after efforts to find one inside the building failed) from the office of Sen. Alan Simpson (R-Wyo.), who carries the code with him to any event where a journalist might be lurking. "He's had this for years," spokesman Stan Cannon reports. "He keeps a copy right in the drawer of his desk."

Simpson read aloud from the code on the Senate floor Tuesday prior to the vote on Clarence Thomas's nomination to the Supreme Court: "Let me read you the code of professional journalism. They don't like to hear me read this, because they think I'm a media-basher. I'm not." He gestured toward the press gallery. "I hear them chuckling."

When Simpson got in a much-publicized shrieking match with National Public Radio correspondent Nina Totenberg early last week, he brandished his copy of the code as though it were a crucifix. (He said she had violated Rule 1 under the Fair Play section, Page 3 of the code, by publicizing Anita Hill's allegations against Thomas. She told him he was an evil man and that all his colleagues hate him.)

The copy secured by The Post includes Simpson's own markings. Virtually every other word is boxed, underlined, double-underlined or highlighted by an arrow or an asterisk. The pen strokes are heavy, thick, pressurized.

"... the duty ... serve the truth ... freedom to learn ... report the facts ... public enlightenment ... justice ... seek the truth ... know the truth ..."

Truth is a big theme with the code.

Where did this thing come from? The answer is: It came from the '70s.

At least, Simpson's copy is dated 1973. It was published by the Society of Professional Journalists, which used to be known as Sigma Delta Chi, or SDX. This is one of innumerable journalism societies that many journalists choose to have nothing to do with, except to the extent that the society might give them an award with a large cash prize.

What happens when an entire profession ignores its own code? That should be obvious: anarchy. Horrible explosions of . . . unstandardized journalism.

Imagine, for example, what would happen if reporters routinely ignored Rule 5 of the Accuracy and Objectivity section, which states: "Sound practice makes clear distinction between news reports and expressions of opinion. News reports should be free of opinion or bias and represent all sides of an issue."

Sounds reasonable, right?

I don't think so.

Sorry. The writer has to stick his own stupid opinions in here! You see, this is the anarchy we're talking about, a total breakdown of dispassionate objective third-person omniscient unbiased voice-from-Olympus journalism.

(Soon, at this rate, you'll pick up the front page and the headline will say something like, "White House Jackals Seek Silly War; Dopey Democrats Self-Destruct As Usual.")

The truth is, this Code of Ethics is a load of malarkey. Whatever malarkey is. No self-respecting journalist would be caught near this thing. Sure, most of it's fine—let's hear it for someone pointing out that reporters shouldn't take free plane tickets from the people they cover. But it never gets specific enough—it ought to say things like, "Journalists should never use the scientific name for snot when they can just say 'snot.' " Instead, the tone is so self-righteous, so excruciatingly lofty, it makes the job seem like a favor we're doing on behalf of the Common Man.

Code: "The purpose of distributing news and enlightened opinion is to serve the general welfare. Journalists who use their professional status as representatives of the public for selfish or other unworthy motives violate a high trust."

Does that mean the movie deals are no-go?

Hard to believe, but journalism is not a form of public service, which, to me, brings to mind people who plant trees in highway medians. There is plenty of selfishness in the press, both in terms of individual desires and corporate profit goals. Fortunately, these selfish goals usually overlap nicely with "public welfare"—truth competes very well in the marketplace of ideas.

In that enterprising spirit, let's make an actual phone call to the Society of Professional Journalists, which, it turns out, is holding its annual convention in Cleveland this very moment. The man who comes to the phone is Ira D. Perry, executive director of SPJ, which he says has 18,000 members and chapters in seven countries (which immediately casts doubt on our previous assertion that no one ever joins this thing).

Perry noted that when the Code of Ethics was last revised, in 1989, the Pledge was changed (Al Simpson, take note) to remove a line that had said that journalists should "actively censure and try to prevent" violations of the code. Now the code just says that the society will use educational means to encourage journalists to adhere to the tenets.

"We do not believe that anybody should license journalists," Perry said. "If you are censuring journalists, by nature you are defining who is and who is not a good journalist. And we believe the First Amendment gives anyone the right to write their views."

As for the lofty tone, he said, "Any code is going to come off sounding a bit preachy."

Huh. Suddenly it seems a bit more reasonable.

That's the problem with reporting—it ruins a good polemic.

Questions of Privacy

HOWARD KURTZ

Psst! Have you heard? Madonna has AIDS!

Well, that was the rumor making the rounds, anyway. And that was enough for Entertainment Weekly to run a story in December, quoting Madonna's spokeswoman as calling the gossip "completely unfounded and untrue."

Quick! Turn on NBC! The network is broadcasting the name of Desiree Washington, the 18-year-old woman who says Mike Tyson raped her.

Check out the latest reports from the campaign trail: Bill Clinton didn't inhale. Jerry Brown partied with people who did inhale. And Hillary Clinton says George Bush has something to hide.

More and more with each passing week, it seems, people are wondering what has happened to the mainstream media. In an era in which Donna Rice, Marla Maples, Tai Collins and Gennifer Flowers have each basked in 15 minutes of white-hot publicity, there seem to be no rules, no boundaries, no corner of human behavior into which prying reporters won't poke.

The sense of public discomfort came to a head earlier this month when USA Today asked Arthur Ashe if he had AIDS, an act that some have described as a "medical outing." Although the editors held off on the story when Ashe would not confirm it, the former tennis star blamed the newspaper—and the leaker—for forcing him to go public.

"I didn't commit any crimes and I'm not running for public office," Ashe said. "I should be able to reserve the right to keep things like that private."

The knee-jerk journalistic defense—that Ashe is a "public figure" whose illness is news—doesn't ring true with much of the public. Most people see a retired athlete with a 5-year-old daughter who wanted to cope with his tragedy in private.

Charles Laquidara host of a Boston radio show, has offered a $ 1,000 reward to listeners who can supply "dirt" on top USA Today editors. "I'm pissed off for the same reason about 50 million Americans are pissed off—there was no reason to do the story," he says. "What does it accomplish? This puts a stigma on his whole family."

But what if Ashe had had an inoperable brain tumor? Would that also have been a huge Page 1 story? Or was it the dark specter of AIDS, and the ever-present question of how it was contracted, that boosted the story into the media stratosphere?

USA Today has gotten more than 600 letters, nearly all of them negative. "People are just emotionally devastated by the news that Arthur Ashe has an illness that's going to kill him, and they're angrily striking out," says Gene Policinski, managing editor for sports. He says it would be news if Ashe had any fatal disease because he is "one of the most famous athletes of the 20th century."

But the Ashe backlash is just part of a growing uproar over media invasions of privacy. "There is a 'We're going to get the story regardless' mentality throughout the press," says Terry Eastland, media columnist for the American Spectator.

That, of course, is not the view from the executive suites of most newspapers and networks. Some editors, in fact believe that news organizations have grown too timid in recent years, too wary of alienating this or that faction.

"As rough and untidy and uncomfortable as it is, this is what we're supposed to be doing," says Geneva Overholser, editor of the Des Moines Register. "If you think about the things that are the most difficult for people—rape victims' names or Arthur Ashe's AIDS—this is how society makes change.

"Our role is not to suppress difficult information. We've got to be willing to offend people. We should be in the business of telling people what we know."

But Overholser is the first to admit did she doesn't always follow her own advice. Although she believes that withholding the names of women who are raped adds to the stigma—and her paper won a Pulitzer Prize last year for a series on a victim who agreed to be named—the Register still doesn't identify rape victims without their consent.

And while Overholser believes that newspapers exacerbate the stigma of AIDS by shying away from it, she declined to publish a story about a prominent Iowa politician who was dying of AIDS complications (although the paper did mention the illness in his obituary).

Just what are the rules, anyway?

Most news organizations don't name adolescents in criminal proceedings—although the Wall Street Journal last year identified a 14-year-old boy accused of killing Jermaine Daniel, a friend of then-D.C. Police Chief Maurice Turner. A Journal editor, Thomas Petzinger Jr., said at the time that omitting the suspect's name "would have conferred an anonymity on this story that would have made it less believable and less powerful." Of course, the same could be said for any story where someone's privacy is violated for the sake of a more realistic drama.

Most news organizations resist efforts by activists to "out" closeted homosexuals—although columnist Jack Anderson and several newspapers last year named a Pentagon official that the Advocate, a gay magazine, had identified as gay. The Advocate generally opposes outing, but said the move was justified in this case because of the military's policy of discharging homosexuals.

Most news organizations don't name women in rape cases without their consent—although NBC and the New York Times named Patricia Bowman, who accused William Kennedy Smith of rape, after the Globe, a supermarket tabloid, published her name and high school photo.

Most news organizations don't print rumors—except when the whispering gets really loud and big names are involved. In the case of Madonna, "the rumors had gained so much currency and were the subject of so much speculation that it was unquestionably a valid news story," says James Seymore, managing editor of Entertainment Weekly.

Most news organizations say they don't report on extramarital affairs by politicians unless it affects their public performance. That fuzzy standard began to change in 1987, when the Miami Herald found Donna Rice emerging from Gary Hart's town house. Justification: the all-purpose character issue. Hart had dared reporters to put a tail on him, and anyone reckless enough to have a fling during a presidential campaign was deemed unfit for the White House.

But each attempt to codify a sexual standard has simply spawned a new set of exceptions. Some editors said extramarital high jinx were relevant only if the politician were running for president—but that went out the window when former beauty queen Tai Collins claimed to have had an affair with Virginia Sen. Charles Robb (who denied it). Some editors said there should be a journalistic statute of limitations on old affairs—until Gennifer Flowers peddled her allegations about Clinton to the Star.

The underlying rationale for such stories—that the politician in question can't control himself, doesn't respect women, or (gasp) has lied to his wife—becomes murkier with each new round. After all, the press seemed a lot more concerned about Bill Clinton's alleged bed-hopping than Hillary Clinton did.

The Flowers episode sparked a hue and cry about a celebrity rag setting the agenda for elite news organizations. But this merely reflected the cacophonous nature of an info-saturated society. The story was out, and no amount of editorial tut-tutting could put it back in the bottle.

The media often wrestle with retroactive morality—to wit, should public figures be pilloried in the '90s for having smoked pot in the '60s, when "youthful experimentation" (to use the standard euphemism) was hardly unusual? Overholser's theory, that media exposure helps takes the sting out of taboo activities, seems to have taken hold here.

After the marijuana issue sunk Douglas Ginsburg's Supreme Court nomination in 1987, numerous public figures, such as Tennessee Sen. Al Gore and former Arizona governor Bruce Babbitt, announced they too had once tried the drug. By the time another high court nominee, Clarence Thomas, owned up to past experience with marijuana, it was a one-day story. (Clinton, however, managed to turn his ancient pot-puffing into a long-running saga with his carefully worded denials.)

If there is one media practice that strikes many people as unfair, it is the use of anonymous sources—or, more pejoratively, unnamed accusers—to blacken someone's reputation. ABC has drawn substantial flak for allowing such sources—two of whom were literally kept in the shadows—to charge on television that Jerry Brown tolerated marijuana and cocaine use in his house when he was governor of California. Brown denied the allegation. As USA Today columnist DeWayne Wickham put it "For ABC to air criminal allegations against Brown that are supported only by those who secretly allege his misconduct but publicly refuted by some of his closest friends and harshest foes is to plunge journalism into the swamp where the tabloids dwell."

The Seattle Times ended Sen. Brock Adams's reelection bid last month by reporting charges from eight women that the Washington Democrat sexually harassed them in incidents dating to the early 1970s. Should the paper have allowed these women to make such accusations from behind a curtain of anonymity? Or was it, as Adams's spokeswoman charged, a form of "journalistic terrorism"?

"I don't mean to impugn your profession, but nobody really wants to stay away from a terrific story," says Todd Gitlin, a sociology professor at the University of Calforina, Berkeley. "When push comes to shove, or ratings point comes to ratings point, the presumption is that if you don't do it, someone else will."

The onslaught of sleaze thrives in a tabloid culture in which everyone—corporate chiefs, politicians, pontificators, athletes and their boyfriends or girlfriends—is grist for the celebrity mill. And there is no shortage of famous folks willing to dish their most infinite secrets under the klieg lights. Such voluntary confessions give the press protective cover, even if other people's privacy is trampled in the process.

Donald Trump, for example, milked his affair with Marla Maples to publicize his Taj Mahal casino, although his estranged wife, Ivana, shrank from the media hype and worried about the effect on their children. Roseanne Arnold told the world she had been abused as a child, an announcement that horrified her parents, who denied it.

Others are all too willing to seek media attention after they have violated someone else's rights, such as former American University president Richard Berendzen, who went on "Nightline" to discuss his penchant for making obscene phone calls.

Still others are dragged into the spotlight through an accident of birth or circumstance. Would anyone care that a college student named John Zaccaro Jr. was busted for cocaine if his mother wasn't Geraldine Ferraro?

The public may have a "right to know" when Time Warner's Steve Ross is diagnosed with prostate cancer, because he runs a huge conglomerate. But what if it was a high-ranking police official, or a TV weatherman, or a middle-level editor at the New York Times? Don't they have some right to privacy?

Jack Limpert, editor of the Washingtonian magazine, says illness should be a private matter for those who hold no public or corporate office.

"When someone has a fatal disease, they ought to be able to have some control over their death," he said.

Still, a "Public figure" now seems to be anyone who was ever famous for anything at any time. Ron Nessen, who was President Ford's press secretary, got a taste of this when the Washingtonian published a batch of 25-year-old love letters he wrote to his ex-wife before and during their marriage. The magazine apologized after Nessen filed suit for copyright infringement and invasion of privacy.

"In retrospect, I would not have published as much from the letters." Limpert said. "I would not have published as much in terms of intimate details. I think we did go too far."

Nessen, now a Mutual radio vice president, says that when he was a UPI reporter in the 1950s, "you just didn't delve into people's personal lives unless it had some obvious effect on their public duties. The standards have changed so rapidly we haven't had time to replace them. Look at what our presidential races have come to—good God! Is anybody proud of what this campaign has turned into?"

Yet there is a slight whiff of hypocrisy in the stem public demands that the media get out of the gutter. Somebody, after all, is tuning in "Hard Copy" and "Geraldo" and "A Current Affair" and buying all those copies of the National Enquirer, the Star and the Globe.

"Everyone is both a voyeur and a citizen," Gitlin says. "The voyeur is reading with eyeballs bugging out, while the citizen is saying, 'These abominations are sinking lower once more.' "

In the Arthur Ashe case, it turns out that many journalists, including Newsweek sportswriter Frank Deford and "Today" show anchor Bryant Gumbel, were aware of his illness. "We had people here who knew it for two years," says Jerry Nachman, editor of the New York Post. "I think they were part of the conspiracy. . . . Frank Deford was ripping off his employers over the last three or four years to protect a friend."

But Deford says that "Arthur had told me as a friend, so obviously I wasn't going to release it. You don't sign a contract when you join a paper that you're going to reveal everything. Under the Nachman theory of journalism, that you can't keep secrets, I wouldn't want to be in the business."

No one is immune to the perpetual tug between journalism and friendship. Nachman says that television journalist Linda Ellerbee, a close friend, recently told him of her double mastectomy, and that he respected her wish that nothing be published. Nachman says he was not ripping off his employer because Ellerbee had agreed to make her breast cancer public within a few weeks.

Is it time for a new era of media sensitivity? Or would that simply return journalists to the days when they acted like privileged insiders, keeping secrets from their audience?

"We must be clear about whom we are protecting from what," says Geneva Overholser. "Are you protecting the public from being offended? Are you protecting the public figure? Or are you protecting yourself from being griped at?"

Is It Real or Is It . . .?

KATHY SAWYER

In the young world of computerized image manipulation, the lion lies down with the lamb (a commercial being aired during the Olympics); Marilyn Monroe flirts with Abraham Lincoln (the cover of February's Scientific American); and the U.S. Capitol looms behind a reporter who is miles away inside a studio (Jan. 26 ABC News broadcast).

The computer hardware required to accomplish these illusions is getting cheaper and more widely available, at the same time the software is getting more sophisticated. These days, it seems, if you can imagine it, you can image it.

With taps on a keyboard, or the sweep of a mouse, the new breed of image-maker can take an object in a real photograph and clone it, move it, paint it a different color, rotate it, flip it, or switch it to another photo scene entirely. Or the manipulator can dispense with the original photo and, using another kind of computer program, create synthetic images that mimic real photographs, with angles, textures and shading in gradations that provide distance perspective.

Ethical Concerns Grow

Along with a flurry of creative experimentation and playfulness, this capability has triggered concern that images are becoming as unreliable as words, no longer defensible as records of criminal behavior, political sin and other historical reality. People know that advertising, art and supermarket tabloids are often fanciful. But when used in news reports or otherwise presented as slices of truth, experts caution, manipulated images tell lies about the world.

Phonied photographs are nothing new. The concern is that the latest technology makes deceptions much easier and faster to accomplish and much harder—if not impossible—to detect.

Until a few years ago, it was difficult to alter the original photographic image. Captured on film, the image existed in chemically altered grains of silver salts suspended in a gel. Prints could be changed, but only by mechanical methods (air brushing, cutting and pasting) that are relatively easy to detect.

Digital technology has changed that.

In digital imaging, the elements of a picture are converted into computer language—numbers made up of zeros and ones. The image then produced is a montage of square electronic dots (pixels). By changing the numerical value of each dot—a process that leaves no "footprints"—the software can be used to alter the picture at will: matching tones and colors and blending edges. (A similar, though much more complicated process, is used to manipulate video images, as depicted, for example, in the hit novel and movie, "Rising Sun.")

No Permanent Original

It may be impossible to tell how a digitized image has been manipulated, except by comparing it to the chemical original. With the advent of cameras that take electronic photographs, many images now begin in digital form. There is no permanent original.

Analysts have compared the process of image manipulation to genetic reengineering, or surgery at the molecular level.

"Photography is dead" in the role it has played over its 150-year existence, William J. Mitchell, dean of the school of architecture and planning at the Massachusetts Institute of Technology, said in an interview. "Traditional photography is not going to go away. But [the new technology] changes its meaning."

In an article in the current Scientific American, Mitchell says it is up to the image consumer to beware: "The question of how to distinguish visual fact from fiction is becoming increasingly urgent as we witness the explosive proliferation of digital-imaging technology. We are approaching the point at which most of the images that we see in our daily lives, and that form our understanding of the world, will have been digitally recorded, transmitted and processed."

Scientific American features a striking cover "photograph" of Marilyn Monroe arm in arm with Abraham Lincoln and cozily integrated into his 1863 surroundings.

Brushes and inks have long been used to retouch, improve color, remove warts and so on. American civil war photographers sometimes rigged battlefield scenes. Stalin-era Soviets expunged inconvenient faces from official photos.

In the past decade or so, media executives, photojournalists and others have been swept up in the seductions of the emerging technology—and in controversy over how to use it ethically while preserving credibility. National Geographic magazine moved the pyramids of Egypt closer together on its cover. Ted Turner began to colorize old movies. Humphrey Bogart and other deceased movie stars were reincarnated electronically to party with the living in television ads. TV Guide put talk show host Oprah Winfrey's head on actress Ann-Margret's body. When actress Helen Hayes died, The Washington Post published a picture of her alone on stage, after electronically erasing another actress from the scene.

Last month, correspondent Cokie Roberts of ABC News donned a coat and pretended to broadcast from the Capitol lawn on State of the Union Address night.

She was actually inside a studio, with an image of the Capitol electronically inserted in the background the way computer-generated weather maps are projected behind television weathercasters.

Finding the Boundaries

Each of these events created a stir. Most news organizations (including The Post) have a policy prohibiting alteration of images that are presented as depicting reality. The difficulties arise when people try to define the wavery boundary that distinguishes news photos from those used for other purposes. New York Newsday defended the doctored cover photo it ran Wednesday (a composite that made it appear figure skaters Tonya Harding and Nancy Kerrigan were skating side by side) on grounds it ran a disclaimer in the photo's caption.

For what it's worth, Mitchell noted, the more information (detail, color, light reflections, shadows, etc.) a picture contains, the harder it is to manipulate without introducing internal inconsistencies that signal deception.

But in the near future, analysts predict, the technology will be available for use by anyone with a home computer (with unknown implications for the old family photo album) and electronic images will fly instantaneously back and forth along the information superhighway.

Freedom of image, like freedom of speech, will be complicated.

Media Law and Regulation 17

Supreme Court Connects Cable TV to Free Speech Protections

JOAN BISKUPIC

T he Supreme Court unanimously said for the first time yesterday that cable television is entitled to nearly the same constitutional guarantees of free speech as newspapers and magazines.

The ruling will have no immediate impact on cable television viewers, but it will give cable systems, telephone companies and other "Information Age" communications systems new protection against government interference and an advantage over broadcasters who are subject to more regulation.

The ruling left unresolved the dispute that was at the heart of the case: whether Congress can require cable systems to devote up to one-third of their channels to retransmitting the signals of local television stations.

Bruce Collins, C-SPAN general counsel, said yesterday he was disappointed that the court did not strike down the "must carry" regulations which require the cable systems to carry some local programming instead of other television programs available nationally, for example, C-SPAN.

Even so, Collins said, the case was important for its "defining statement about the First Amendment rights of cable. In the old days, cable was considered ancillary to broadcasters."

Congress adopted "must carry" provisions in a 1992 cable rate law to offset what it saw as a competitive imbalance between the cable industry and over-the-air broadcasters. Sixty percent of all TV viewers subscribe to cable. Members of Congress feared that advertisers would lose interest in locally based commercial and educational channels if the government did not require cable to carry them.

Cable operators attacked the regulations as a violation of their free speech rights. Meanwhile some cable viewers complained that channels that were personal favorites were dropped to make room for local broadcasts.

While there was unanimity for enhanced constitutional protection for cable, a narrow five-justice majority refused to strike down the "must carry" regulations, as the cable industry had sought. The majority said the regulations may be constitutional because they were intended to preserve access to free television rather than control the content of cable programs. With Justice Anthony M. Kennedy writing for the court, the majority said the regulations "are not designed to favor or disadvantage speech of any particular content," rather "to protect broadcast television from . . . unfair competition."

Dissenting justices, led by Sandra Day O'Connor, countered that the regulations were impermissibly aimed at program "content" and should be rejected as a violation of free speech. The Kennedy majority sent the case back to a lower court for additional findings.

Most significantly, the ruling set up new legal ground rules for cable television and wire-based communications systems. The justices said for the first time that such communications should have more protection from governmental interference under the First Amendment than broadcasters, who traditionally have been subject to more regulation because of the scarcity of channels.

"Cable television does not suffer from the inherent limitations that characterize the broadcast medium," Justice Anthony M. Kennedy wrote in a section of the opinion joined by all the justices. "Indeed, given the rapid advances in [technology], soon there may be no practical limitation on the number of speakers who may use the cable medium."

Kennedy, joined by all of the justices, said a cable regulation should be upheld only if it furthers an "important or substantial" government interest. That speech standard is not quite as high as protections traditionally accorded newspapers, but it is greater than protections for broadcasters.

Yet even with a new standard, yesterday's decision will not necessarily allow cable companies to escape from federal regulations that force them to carry local broadcasting.

Kennedy, writing in this portion for five justices, said a D.C. federal court now must determine how financially burdened the broadcast industry would be without the "must carry" requirement. He said it was "significant" that no evidence that local broadcast stations have fallen into bankruptcy had been presented in an earlier hearing. The U.S. District Court here upheld the regulations last year.

O'Connor, writing a partial dissent, said the regulations ensure that cable programmers will be dropped in favor of broadcasters.

They "are an impermissible restraint on the cable operators' editorial discretion as well as on the cable programmers' speech," O'Connor wrote. "For reasons related to the content of speech, the rules restrict the ability of cable operators to put on the programming they prefer, and require them to include programming they would rather avoid."

For television watchers, the ruling suggests that cable companies will continue to be required to offer local commercial and educational broadcast stations such as Washington's Channel 50, or Howard University Television's Channel 32.

The trade-off, according to cable spokesmen, is that in some areas, C-SPAN or the Discovery Channel, for example, will not offered.

Broadcasters, cable companies and the government accentuated the positive yesterday.

Daniel Brenner, of the National Cable Television Association, lauded the new legal standard for cable and contended the industry would be able to show a lower court that the congressional regulations were not justified because "the economic state of broadcasting is robust."

But Reed Hundt, chairman of the Federal Communications Commission, and Jack Goodman, of the National Association of Broadcasters, asserted that the regulations are necessary to keep some local broadcasters in business.

Joining Kennedy were Chief Justice William H. Rehnquist and Justices Harry A. Blackmun and David H. Souter. Justice John Paul Stevens, who said he wanted to uphold the "must carry" rule, agreed to become the crucial fifth vote.

O'Connor was joined in the dissent by Justices Antonin Scalia, Ruth Bader Ginsburg and Clarence Thomas.

The case is Turner Broadcasting Corp. v. Federal Communications Commission.

America Online Draws Fire

ELIZABETH CORCORAN and SANDRA SUGAWARA

The debate over privacy in the computer age escalated yesterday as a major on-line services company drew fire from Congress and privacy advocates for offering to rent names from its list of 1 million subscribers to direct marketing companies.

Rep. Edward J. Markey (D-Mass.), chairman of the House telecommunications subcommittee, raised numerous concerns about the practice in a letter sent yesterday to Stephen Case, chief executive of Vienna-based America Online Inc.

In a prepared statement released late yesterday, Case said that America Online is sensitive to its members' desire for privacy.

"We are committed to pull the list off the market if we are found not to be compliant with the subcommittee's guidelines for consumer privacy," Case said.

America Online offers customers the opportunity to keep their names off circulated lists. That option is located deep in a series of menus that appear on their screens.

No laws prohibit on-line companies from renting information about their customers, which is used to target people for phone or mail sales pitches. But as more and more people begin using computer and interactive television networks to exchange information and shop, there is growing concern that it will become too easy for governments and corporations to track the activities of individuals.

Electronic information services can collect information on what publications and services a customer likes, what type of computers he or she owns and a vast array of other personal data.

"I feel strongly that comprehensive privacy protections must become part of the electronic ethics of companies doing business on the information superhighway," Markey wrote in his letter, "and a fundamental right of all its travelers."

In a Louis Harris and Associates survey, scheduled to be released today, half of the respondents said they would be at least somewhat concerned with on-line services engaging in "subscriber profiling," the practice of matching users' names and addresses with details about their interests.

Noting that telephone companies are forbidden from selling phone records of consumers, Marc Rotenberg, director of the Electronic Privacy Information Center, said the on-line world is "an example of where the laws have not kept up with technology."

A major telecommunications bill that the House of Representatives passed this summer included provisions aimed at safeguarding consumers by giving them the option to refuse to allow their names to be sold. But that legislation was not passed by the Senate.

Markey's letter was prompted by an ad that appeared in the Sept. 19 issue of DM News, a trade publication for people in the direct marketing industry. In the ad, America Online said it was making available the names from its list of 1 million subscribers as well as demographic information and other details on them to advertisers.

The America Online ad boasted that its subscribers are ". . . computer and modem owners who pay up to $200 a month to enjoy hundreds of entertaining and informative services."

Lists of 1,000 names of America Online subscribers cost $100. For additional charges, marketers can also get such information as subscribers' addresses, income, gender, children and their ages, as well as details about what type of computer they use.

America Online is not alone in renting out its subscriber lists. CompuServe Inc., the largest commercial on-line service, has done it for years. CompuServe gives subscribers the chance to keep their name off the list.

Prodigy Services Co. does not rent out its lists, said Brian Ek, director of marketing programs and communications. Prodigy sells reports that describe the overall demographics of its members, but no names.

"You're asking people to trust you with certain information about themselves," Ek said, who said he thought privacy was a major concern of Prodigy users.

Mothers Want Eighth-Grade Text Banned

ROBERT O'HARROW, JR.

Two Fairfax mothers are demanding that county schools remove an eighth-grade textbook of poetry and stories by Edgar Allan Poe, O. Henry, Robert Frost and other authors, saying it promotes violence and undermines family values.

In challenging the anthology used by about 10,000 Fairfax students and millions of others across the nation, the women have joined a growing number of parents who are trying to ban novels, periodicals and other school material on moral or religious grounds.

Raylene Thurman and Louise Erekson said they have asked School Board members to ban the literature book because they worry that stories such as Poe's "The Tell-Tale Heart" and John Steinbeck's "The Pearl, which have some violent scenes, may "plant the seeds" of crime, depression and disobedience in youngsters.

"It's not the kind of thing any parent wants their children reading," said Thurman, of Centreville, a Christian Scientist, who said she plans to teach her 14-year-old daughter, Jacquie, at home this year. "I was appalled. . . . Something has got to be done."

Their push comes as educators in Fairfax and across the country are fending off attacks on classroom reading lists, sex education topics and library material.

In Fairfax, some conservatives and Christian activists have fought for nearly two years to remove a homosexual-oriented newspaper from county libraries. Others intend to step up efforts this fall to suppress sex education books, videos and other materials they consider sympathetic to homosexuals.

The Fairfax School Board has voted twice in the last year to remove or reduce the use of some children's books because of complaints.

One book was "Jump Ship to Freedom," which some African Americans objected to because of a passage in which the hero, a black youngster, questioned the intelligence of blacks. Another was a family life education text called "Families," which some conservatives criticized because a child in the story wishes his parents were divorced so he could travel in a plane to visit his father.

In Montgomery, Prince George's and other counties, there have been efforts in recent years to ban from schools books with themes about ghosts or the supernatural or with characters considered offensive to minority groups. Targets have included

"Huckleberry Finn" by Mark Twain and "I Know Why the Caged Bird Sings" by Maya Angelou.

Education analysts say they expect to see such efforts increase—particularly among conservative Christian activists—during the coming school year.

"It's clearly a part of a national attack on what we read, what we see, what we discuss," said Deanna Duby, director of education policy for People for the American Way, a liberal group that has tracked efforts to ban books for more than a decade. "This is a typical example."

Despite the increase of such efforts in recent years, the move by Thurman and Erekson against the 800-page "Elements of Literature" took Fairfax officials by surprise. The book recently was approved by Virginia officials.

School officials say the book is filled with literary marvels—short stories by writers such as Stephen Vincent Benet, comical pieces by Bill Cosby, poetry by John Updike and Langston Hughes and speeches by Abraham Lincoln, Red Cloud and Martin Luther King Jr.

Nancy Sprague, Fairfax's assistant superintendent for instruction, said she and others rejected an initial request by Thurman and Erekson because the book has a broad appeal that helps stimulate students to write and think about literature.

"We don't choose literature books to push a point of view," Sprague said. "What I have trouble with is when a very small group ties up the system and tries to deny books to the rest of the world."

Superintendent Robert R. Spillane agreed, saying efforts to ban books are "a growing concern."

"It's great American literature, violent or not," Spillane said. "I'm just not about to be censoring things."

Erekson, of Chantilly, said she wants to protect vulnerable teenagers from stories, such as the "Tell-Tale Heart," that could prompt them to commit suicide or fantasize about violence.

In Poe's study of guilt and horror, a man commits murder, buries the body under the floor and then becomes obsessed with what he believes is the sound of a beating heart.

"It's a story of murder and insanity," said Erekson, who said she plans to teach her son, Joshua, 15, at home this year. "This is not a positive book. This does not bring out the best in human nature."

In a letter to the School Board that cited several other examples, the women said that at "a time when our schools are having an increase in suicide, gangs [and] various forms of student violence . . . we feel that the adoption of this textbook is incredibly irresponsible."

Both women said they were Christian Scientists who want books that portray parents in a good light, encourage students to have some religious faith and otherwise support "family friendly" values.

"What I hope to achieve is have the textbook replaced with literature that is uplifting and builds strong character," Thurman said. "Let's face it, any kind of media that you expose your children to is going to have an effect."

Book Buyers Face a Challenge

For Fairfax librarians Michele Leber and Jan Seabock, the decision to add a book titled "Long Road to Freedom: The Advocate History of the Gay and Lesbian Movement" to the county's collection was pretty much a snap.

Leber and Seabock, half the library team whose purchases shape the county's 2 million-volume collection, noticed the title on a wholesaler's new releases list earlier this year.

They saw that the book came from a respected New York publisher and that 50,000 copies would be printed, an indication that there could be a demand for the book. And so, without knowing what specifically is in the book, they ordered nine copies for the Fairfax County library system.

"Long Road to Freedom" wound up on Fairfax library shelves in July.

It wasn't until Christian activist Karen Jo Gounaud objected that the librarians realized the book contains photographs of naked men and women, along with several hundred illustrations that have appeared in a gay magazine.

To Gounaud and others who want to change the way Fairfax libraries treat "adult" material, the fact that the book buyers did not realize "Long Road to Freedom" contains what Gounaud calls pornography is a strong argument for such change.

Gounaud—a mother of two who has pushed for county libraries to stop distributing a gay newspaper and who more recently called for adults-only sections of libraries to house materials she believes are harmful to children—stopped short of saying the county shouldn't have purchased the book.

But she questioned whether it was a good use of county money and noted that there are 10 residents on a waiting list to read "The Book of Virtues," a conservative commentary by William Bennett.

"There is a big disconnect between the community standards and the library collection standards," said Gounaud, of Springfield. "Why is the government buying books that encourage people to do things that the state says are illegal? . . . The public needs to be informed, but it does not need books on how to perform homosexual sex while they are waiting in line for 'The Book of Virtues.' "

For Leber, Seabock and the two other librarians who purchase about 250,000 books a year for Fairfax's 22 branches, the efforts by Gounaud and her supporters are an unprecedented challenge to a buying process that is based primarily on filling a need and on reader demand, rather than the books' perceived morality.

Gounaud's critics have asked who would decide what materials would go in adults-only sections of libraries and whether such a system eventually would discourage the library system from buying titles that deal with homosexuality, the occult, euthanasia and other subjects that some Christian activists have targeted.

Fairfax's book buyers, although declining to discuss their personal beliefs, said they aren't comfortable with the idea of a more subjective purchasing process.

"I am not a censor," librarian Betty Graham said. "I am not a moral arbiter."

"Long Road to Freedom," which a Library Journal reviewer called "a unique resource that is highly recommended for public libraries," provides a detailed history of the gay rights movement.

That it contains photographs of naked people does not bother the librarians, who said they would have bought the book even if they had known beforehand about the pictures.

"I have no doubt we have books in the collection with pictures of naked Holocaust victims," said Leber, 56, of Arlington, a mother of two. "Because we have a book in the library collection does not mean we advocate what it says. There are things in our libraries that offend me."

The book buyers, who work in a quiet office in Chantilly, take pride in what they say is a commitment to a diverse library collection.

"People have a right to look at what we are doing," said Graham, 54, a Texas native who has been buying books for Fairfax since 1967. "But in any job, trust is an underlying factor. When they hired you for a job, they expect you to do it competently and fairly."

Board members voted this month to consider the proposal for adults-only sections of libraries that would be off-limits to unaccompanied minors.

Next month, at the request of one of its conservative members, the Fairfax Library Board will review the county's book-buying policies.

Gounaud and her supporters are pushing for a policy that would require the county to buy as many books that say homosexuality is immoral as it does books that describe it as acceptable.

The Library Board, Gounaud said, also should ask its book buyers to focus their spending on subjects that she said really matter to Fairfax readers—such as history—instead of books on how to commit suicide or how to find a gay partner.

Fairfax's book buyers—as well as several of their counterparts in other area library systems—said it would be difficult to comply with those standards on topics such as homosexuality, because it can be difficult to find high quality books with an anti-gay point of view.

"Balance does not necessarily mean you own exactly the same number of everything," said Kay Ecelbarger, chief of collection development at the Montgomery County Department of Public Libraries. "It means that at any one time, you have books on all points of view in your collection."

The Fairfax buyers will spend $5.89 million this year on library books and other materials, much more than in an average year because they are beginning new collections in Chantilly and Herndon.

Fairfax's four buyers—all of whom have masters' degrees in library science—focus on different areas. Graham buys books for children and young adults; Leber and Seabock purchase adult fiction and nonfiction; and Julie Pringle oversees the operation.

Shelf space and money are limited, so the buyers spend many hours picking through about 45,000 new titles that are published every year. They rely on loads of information from book publishers, wholesalers and book-buying services, which provide on-line copies of thousands of reviews.

To get books on the shelves shortly after they arrive in bookstores, library systems must order months ahead of time, usually before any reviews are available.

Many of the books that are not purchased before publication are bought at the request of branch managers and library users who can't find a book they want.

The book buyers also get a weekly computer-generated list that provides the title and author of any book for which there are more than two people waiting for each copy the system has.

For example, Fairfax recently bought an extra 40 copies of E. Annie Proulx's Pulitzer Prize-winning novel "The Shipping News" after the waiting list for its 18 copies grew to about 100 people.

Gounaud has given the library staff a list of books she wants added to the collection in an effort to provide a more balanced view of homosexuality.

One of the books, "Alfie's Home," has been ordered for the Chantilly regional library, which opens next year. The book tells the story of a boy who thought he was gay but later in life finds a wife after learning that his previous feelings were the result of being approached sexually by an uncle.

The book was panned as "flat and garish" by one reviewer, but Graham decided to buy it because it presents a different point of view on homosexuality.

The Fairfax book buyers said that they do what they can to diversify their collection but that they can buy only what publishers decide to sell, making it difficult sometimes to ensure that the collection is numerically balanced.

They seek out smaller, Christian-oriented publishers, but most mainstream publishers are releasing books that assume homosexuality is an accepted practice, they said.

"Publishing does not work in nice, even, free-flowing ways," said Leber, who has worked in the county's library system since 1978. "If there is a wonderful new book on one subject, we might not be able to add it to the collection unless we can find something on the other side."

"Balance is whatever your political persuasion makes it out to be," said Valerie Eastwood, a founder of a group called Northern Virginia Citizens Against Censorship. "The librarians should stick to standards based on quality and demand."

Ito's Blackout:
A Manifestation of Frustration

JOAN BISKUPIC

Faced with the delicate balancing act of ensuring a fair trial for O. J. Simpson and guaranteeing the public's right to know, Judge Lance A. Ito has made his frustration apparent in recent weeks.

He has threatened to prohibit live broadcasts of the trial, warned he would sanction reporters who publish incorrect information and pleaded with major television programs to delay interviews with the authors of a lurid book on Nicole Brown Simpson.

But yesterday, the Los Angeles Superior Court judge took his most drastic step and barred the news media and public from the individual questioning of potential jurors in the case.

To legal experts, Ito's dilemma is understandable. But they say it is also dangerous.

"He is obviously frustrated, and judges who are frustrated . . . often end up falling off the tightrope" that traverses the constitutional guarantees of an impartial jury and a free press, said Timothy Dyk, a Washington lawyer who specializes in First Amendment concerns.

Lawyers following the case say that while Ito does have control over electronic broadcasts of the proceedings, he has virtually no constitutional support for barring all reporters from the trial or seeking to restrain the publication of news accounts.

Further, they question whether his attempts to deny press access are effective in ensuring that jurors in America's most celebrated case are not prejudiced about Simpson's guilt or innocence.

"What's going on in the courtroom isn't what's causing the problem," said Los Angeles defense lawyer Gerald Chaleff, who has worked on several high-publicity cases. Chaleff noted that Ito has complained most about press leaks and speculation that originated outside the courtroom.

Lawyers in Los Angeles protesting yesterday's blackout pointed to a 1984 Supreme Court ruling that openness in jury selection is the rule, and can be outweighed only by a compelling government interest. The court's decision in Press-Enterprise Co. v. Superior Court of California said a trial judge must make specific findings that closing a trial is necessary.

"The value of openness lies in the fact that people not actually attending trials can have confidence that standards of fairness are being observed," then-Chief Justice Warren E. Burger wrote. "[T]he sure knowledge that anyone is free to attend gives assurance that established procedures are being followed and that deviations will become known."

In that decision, arising from a trial for the rape and murder of a teenage girl, the court said the guarantees of open public proceedings in criminal trials cover the preliminary step of jury selection. Burger said jury selection is important not only to the adversaries in the case but to the entire criminal justice system.

Ito said he was barring the media based on "the compelling interest" in not tainting potential jurors.

Few people dispute that coverage can affect a trial's outcome. Some press advocates have questioned whether media overkill diminishes the integrity of the judicial process.

But as sympathetic as observers are to Ito's dilemma, they say he went too far in yesterday's order. Some speculate he was not averse to having a higher court review his decision, as a check on whether he is moving in the right direction.

"He can't control and he shouldn't control the press," said Erwin Chemerinsky, a University of Southern California law professor. "I think he's really exaggerating the likely effects of publicity on prospective jurors."

On Wednesday Ito had pleaded, to no avail, with television executives to delay interviews with the authors of a new book about Nicole Simpson, which claims O. J. Simpson stalked her and threatened to kill her if she had sexual relations with another man.

Barring the press from jury selection is unlikely to affect the spread of information in the book.

If Ito tries to suppress publication of the book or any other account, Chemerinsky said, he would likely run afoul of constitutional guarantees against prior restraint on publication. In a key 1976 case, the Supreme Court said such gag orders "are the most serious and least tolerable infringement on First Amendment rights."

Ito has threatened to end all live broadcasting of the trial, which he is allowed to do under a California statute. A hearing on that question is scheduled for Nov. 7.

Ito also has the authority to limit what lawyers, who are officers of the court, say outside the courtroom. He already has required that their motions be filed secretly.

Many observers see such options as far from the extreme move of controlling press access and reporting.

Said Chemerinsky, "I think he should turn his attention back to his own domain, his own courtroom, and carefully instruct the jurors to ignore what they've read."

What's Out of Line, When On Line?

SANDRA SUGAWARA

S o you found an interesting article on an on-line computer service. You transferred it by phone line to your home computer, then sent it to another service for others to read. Or you shared it with a friend by electronic mail.

This practice, common among on-line computer users, may also be illegal. A White House committee, chaired by Patent and Trademark Commissioner Bruce A. Lehman, is scheduled to release a report today that warns that these practices could threaten the commercial vibrance of the so-called information superhighway.

The highway is meant to be a high-capacity electronic network delivering movies, books, musical recordings, photos and software to computers, telephones, televisions and fax machines across the country.

But some movie and publishing executives don't like what is happening on the highway's early stretches, the on-line services. They see materials that they sell for a lot of money being duplicated wholesale by on-line users and sent electronically all over the world.

The fear, Lehman said in an interview, is that companies "won't use the information superhighway to deliver their products unless they feel secure."

The White House committee is recommending a series of refinements in the copyright laws that will make it clear what is allowed and what is not and make it easier to prosecute offenders. It also calls for a public awareness campaign.

But its efforts may not be welcomed in the on-line community. The thrill of cheaply and instantaneously sharing information is a key factor behind the phenomenal growth of commercial on-line services and the global computer network known as the Internet, industry experts say. That ability is viewed as a right by many network users.

"There is a big cultural change that needs to be made," said Steve J. Metalitz, general counsel for the Information Industry Association, a trade association that represents many information providers.

On-line services say that copyrighted material is for the personal use only of subscribers. The subscribers may read or view the material, but may not resell it or send free copies to others, the services say, because that would deprive the copyright holder of selling it again.

Knight-Ridder/Tribune News Service recently pulled humorist Dave Barry's columns from one on-line service when it discovered that the material was being copied and sent over e-mail. A company spokeswoman said letters the news service received made it clear that many people were unaware that the material was under copyright protection.

When there is a clear-cut violation, the culprits can often easily evade detection. Playboy magazine discovered photos from its magazine had been posted without its permission on a computer "bulletin board," allowing people to transfer them to home computers and view them on their screens.

Because it could not detect who did the posting, it sued the bulletin board operator.

Music publishers have complained that unknown computer users are placing protected music on bulletin boards, so that other people can retrieve it and play it through their computers' speakers.

The electronic copying battles in some ways repeat past wars fought over photocopying. But the Copyright Act of 1976 never envisioned a world of magazines and movies delivered in "digital," or computerized form, over telephones and bulletin boards viewed by thousands.

Today's technology makes it possible "for one individual, with a few key strokes, to deliver perfect copies of digitized works to scores of other individuals—or to [send] a copy to a bulletin board or other service where thousands of individuals can [retrieve] it or print unlimited 'hard copies' on paper or disk," the Lehman report said.

Technological advancements also make it possible for individuals to alter articles, photos and other items without detection, said Metalitz. Companies that want to do commerce on-line must consider the possibility that someone could insert libelous accusations or bad information (alter a recipe or a financial report, for example). That could hurt the reputation of a publication and expose it to lawsuits.

The Clinton administration study also concludes that voluntary rules spelling out how schools and public libraries can use copyrighted materials should be revised in regard to digital works and on-line services. The administration plans to hold a conference this summer of copyright owners and users to develop new guidelines.

The report also recommends that it be made a crime to import, manufacture or distribute devices designed to defeat anti-copying systems that are being developed to protect information transmitted electronically.

Some companies are exploring the use of "electronic envelopes" that would make it tougher for consumers to copy and distribute information. Other possible innovations are automatic billing systems that would enable companies to run the meter every time a user made and sent a copy.

Murder Story Goes over the Border

CHARLES TRUEHEART

A state of tension is gripping the normally tranquil U.S.-Canada border as American news organizations defy a Canadian publication ban about a sensational murder case. While many Canadians have cheered the ban-busting south of the border, others regard it as the latest example of American hubris.

Details of the murder case, involving a young couple named Karla Homolka and Paul Teale, were put under a strict publication ban five months ago by an Ontario judge. While the Canadian media have obeyed the ban, last week American newspapers and broadcasters began disseminating "banned" information about Homolka's July manslaughter conviction. And by fax transmissions, computer bulletin boards and cross-border newspaper sorties, Canadians have been lapping up the news they've been denied until now.

So it is that Canada's judicial system finds itself embattled by forces beyond its control—new technologies indifferent to national borders, and the appetite of the curious for the forbidden. But the case has also stirred latent feelings each country harbors for the other.

"I feel the Americans are just thumbing their noses at us," declared a caller named Bernice who phoned a Toronto radio talk show. To which an American caller named Michael responded: "Most Americans—we don't even know you're here. This just shows the difference between our two countries. We in the U.S. want to know what's going on. You in Canada just want to kowtow to what the government says."

Virtually nothing except Homolka's surprisingly light 12-year sentence in the murders of two teenage girls may be published in Canada, according to the ban—not even her plea, let alone the gruesome details of the murders she and her estranged husband allegedly committed against youngsters they lured to a private torture chamber. The ban was imposed to ensure a fair trial for Teale, probably late next year.

Last week, The Washington Post became the first North American newspaper to publish details of Homolka's conviction, as well as allegations of murder against Teale, her purported Svengali. A British tabloid paper and the U.S. television program "A Current Affair" had previously aired information about the case.

Until then, news organizations in American cities near the border town of St. Catharines had observed the publication ban.

Publication of the Post story Nov. 23, however, appeared to change the attitude of the Buffalo News and the Detroit News and Free Press, which announced their intention to reprint the Post story Sunday. Canadian authorities promptly warned the newspapers' Canadian distributors against selling the editions with the banned material, and the distributors complied. The Buffalo News, after warnings from Ontario authorities, substituted a story about dolphins for the Post story in editions bound for Canada.

Nevertheless, the publicity surrounding that flap prompted hundreds of Canadians to flock across the border Sunday to purchase copies of the regular edition from newspaper hawkers positioned at border crossings. As they turned around and headed home, they were briefly detained by Canadian customs officers who limited each returning driver to one copy of the Buffalo News. Extra issues were confiscated.

The border controversy generated a fresh round of interest by major U.S. media—and increasingly awkward efforts to stop their coverage from reaching Canadian audiences. Newsweek's and USA Today's Canadian subscribers and newsstand buyers got special editions with the Homolka story missing. Larry King's Monday night CNN discussion of the case was blacked out by most but not all Canadian cable operators, as were segments of ABC's "World News Tonight" and NBC's "Now" on Wednesday.

The screen blackouts heated up the rhetoric on both sides of the border. Champions of defiance hailed the American media for serving as a kind of "Radio Free Canada," beaming the truth to Canadians living under conditions, they charged, that smacked of Eastern Europe in the 1950s.

"Hear ye, hear ye! Let freedom ring out for all our brothers and sisters to the north!" cried Buffalo disc jockey Darren McKee through a loudspeaker pointed across the Peace Bridge to Canada at Niagara Falls, and proceeded to read the most salient elements of the Post account.

Ontario Premier Bob Rae lamented what he saw as Americans' disrespect for their neighbor's court system, a sentiment echoed by many Canadians who called radio and television talk shows. But Ontario's Conservative Party leader, Mike Harris, was resigned to the ban's failure. "The fact of the matter is we're now perhaps acting irrationally to enforce this ban," he told reporters. "It's starting to get pretty silly."

Columnist Alan Fotheringham wrote in the Financial Times today: "The political scene is aflame with all the alleged advantages of wiping out the border for free trade results. In the meantime, the outmoded court system tries to pretend there is an information curtain at the 49th parallel." ABC News anchor Peter Jennings, who remains a Canadian citizen, said he was a "little surprised at the timidity" of Canadian newspapers in not breaking the ban to date.

"But maybe I shouldn't be," he said. "There's a great respect for institutions in Canada that just doesn't exist down here, and Canada is not a litigious society."

Resourceful Canadians had no trouble getting and circulating electronic copies of the Post story by fax and computer. McGill University in Montreal and the University of Toronto attempted to restrict their Internet computer network users from access to information about the Homolka case. But easily accessible alternate channels made a mockery of those efforts, and gave the curious access not just to the full text of the Post article and nearly 100 other news reports, but lurid rumor and wild speculation to spare.

Referring to one university's efforts to block Homolka-case mavens from reading the latest, one user said: "This is a true test of the freedom of speech here. They'd have to shut down the whole net (and tape our mouths shut) to completely stop all the information flow. . . . Electronic communication is either going to free us or enslave us. Make your choice now."